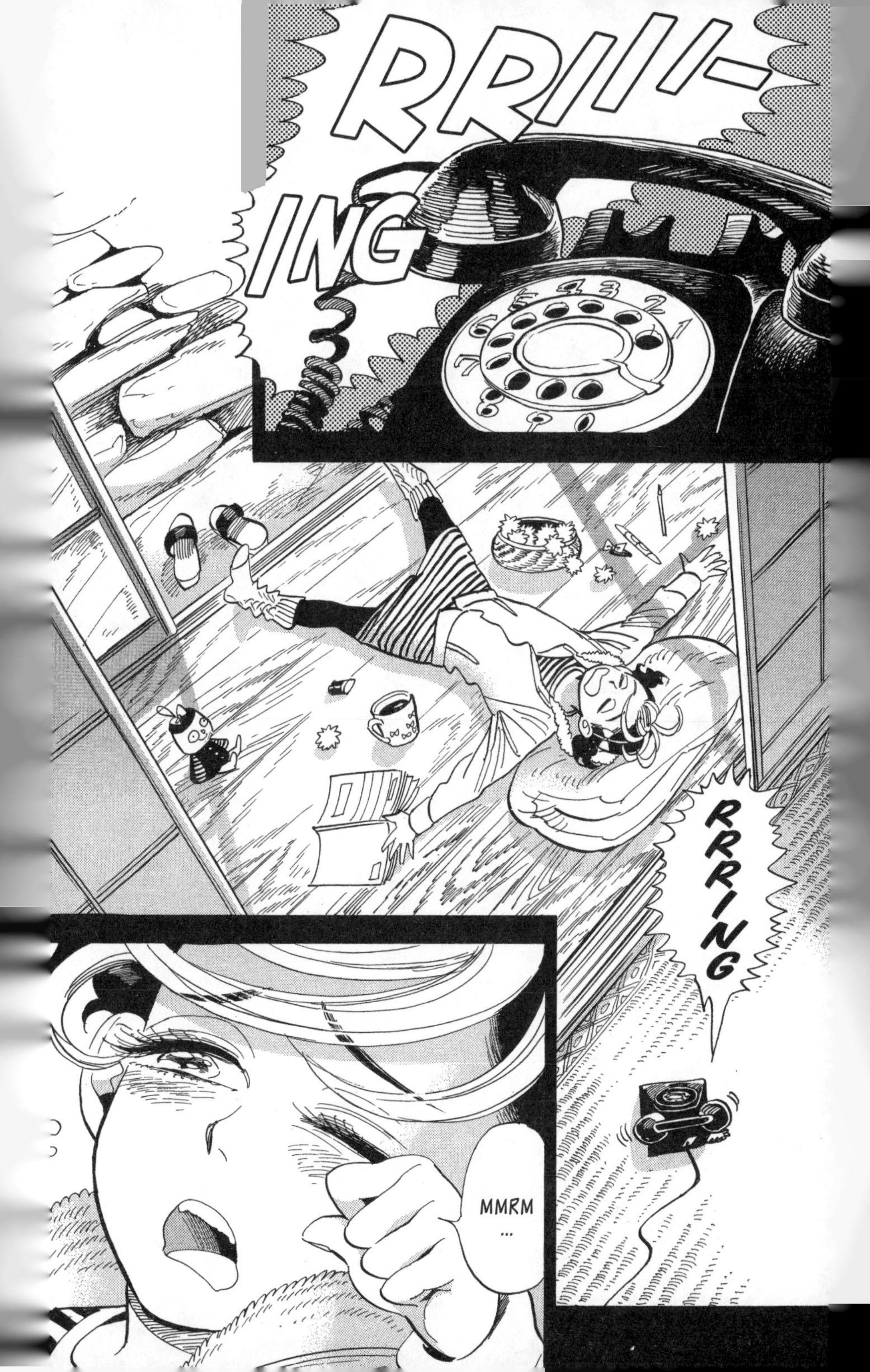
RRIII-
ING
RRRING
MMRM
...

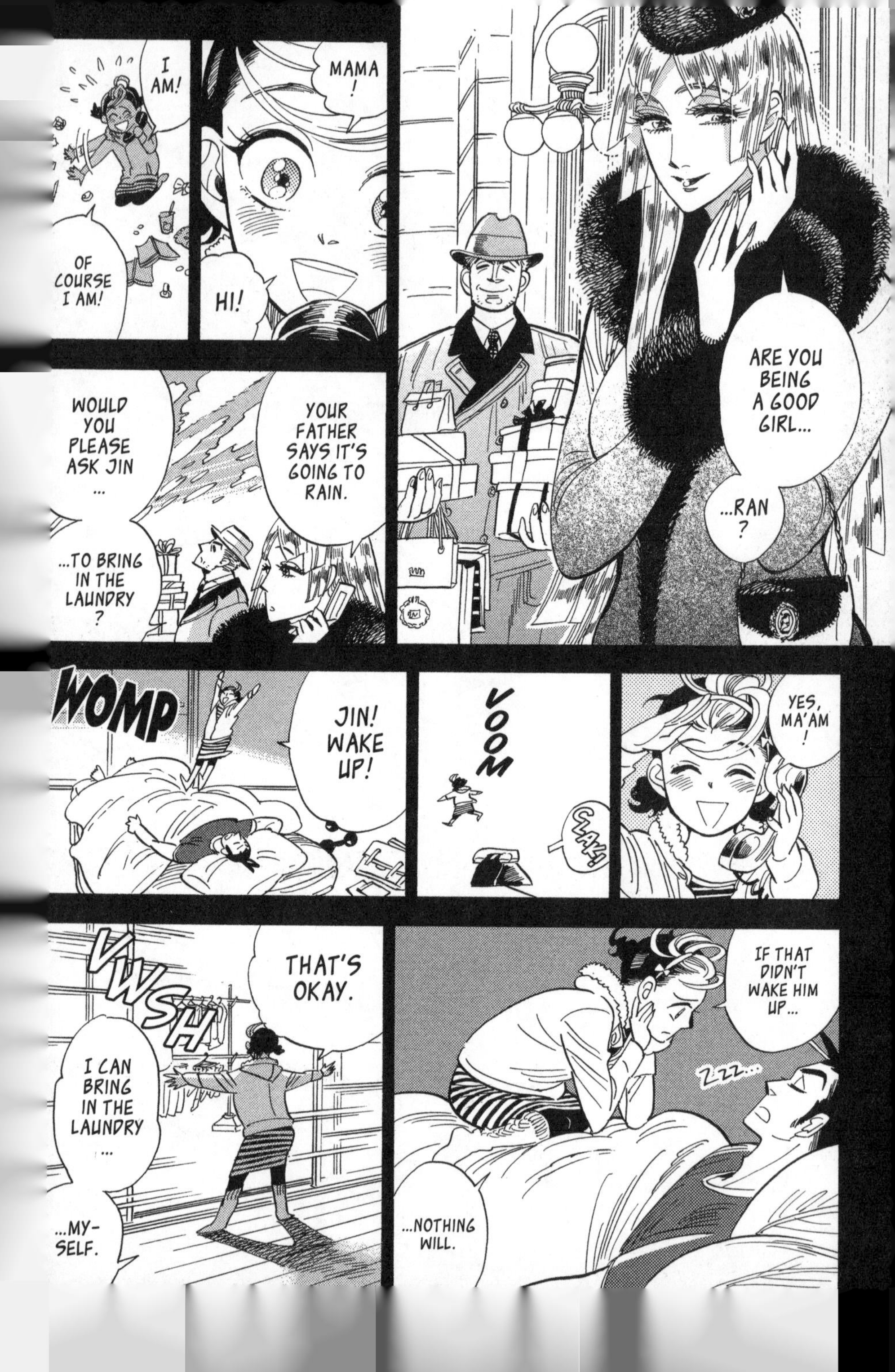
ARE YOU BEING A GOOD GIRL...
...RAN?
MAMA!
HI!
I AM!
OF COURSE I AM!
YOUR FATHER SAYS IT'S GOING TO RAIN.
WOULD YOU PLEASE ASK JIN...
...TO BRING IN THE LAUNDRY?
YES, MA'AM!
CLAK!
VOOM
JIN! WAKE UP!
WOMP
IF THAT DIDN'T WAKE HIM UP...
Z Z Z...
...NOTHING WILL.
THAT'S OKAY.
VWSH
I CAN BRING IN THE LAUNDRY...
...MY-SELF.

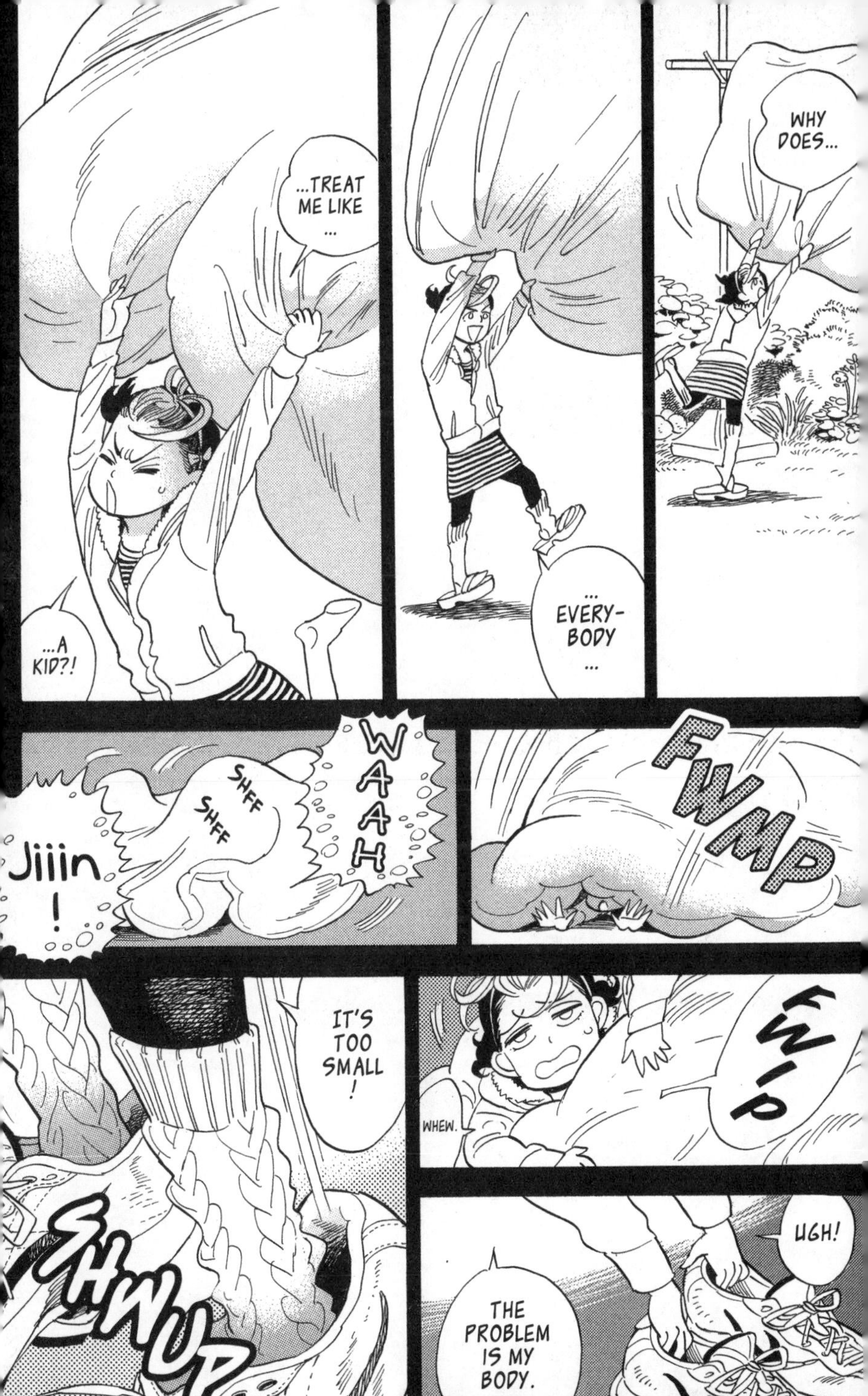
WHY DOES...
...EVERYBODY...
...TREAT ME LIKE...
...A KID?!
FWMP
WAAAH
SHFF SHFF
Jiiin!
FWIP
WHEW.
UGH!
THE PROBLEM IS MY BODY.
IT'S TOO SMALL!
SHWUP

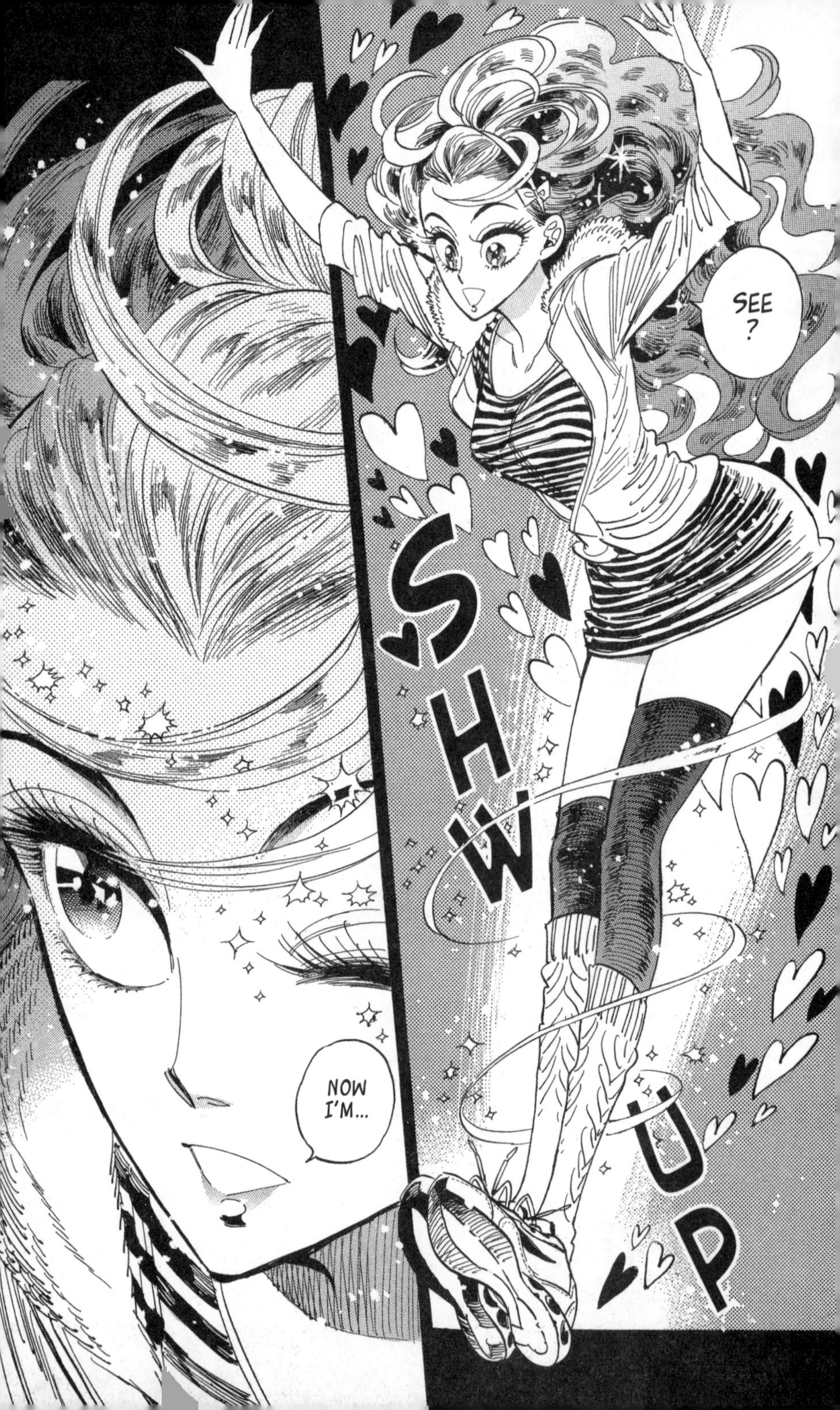
SEE?
SHWUP
NOW I'M...

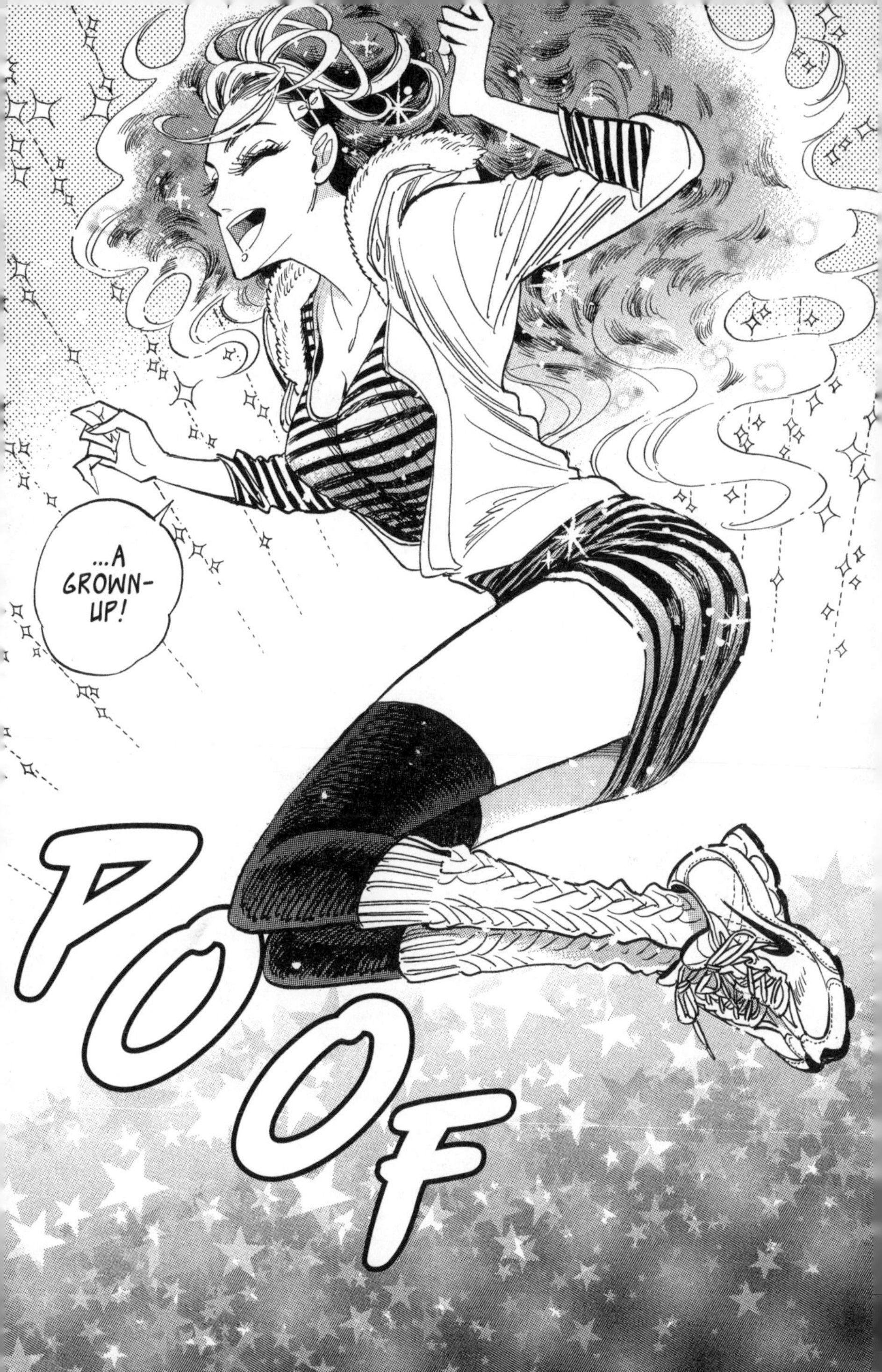
...A GROWN-UP!
POOF

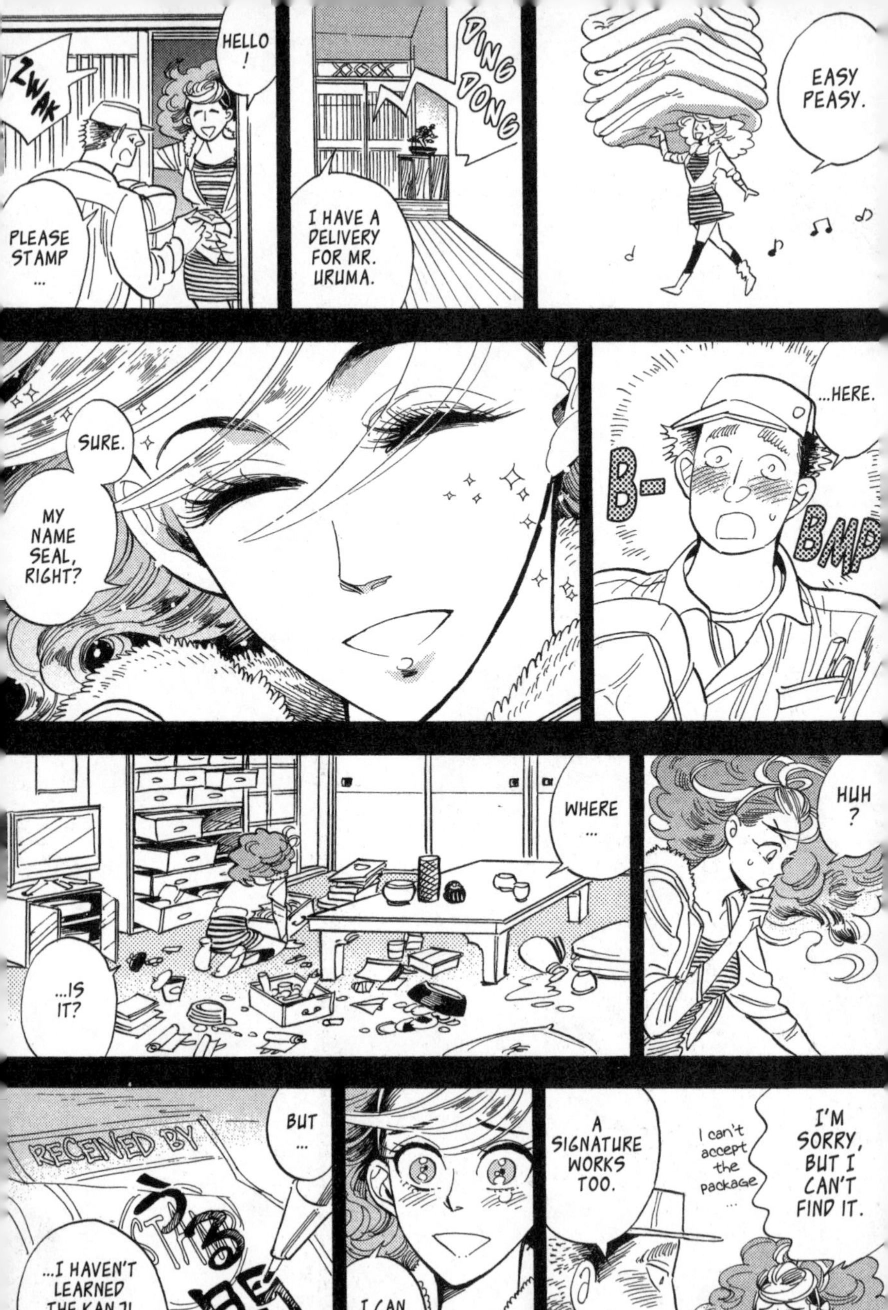
EASY PEASY.
DING DONG
I HAVE A DELIVERY FOR MR. URUMA.
HELLO!
ZWAK
PLEASE STAMP ...
...HERE.
B-BMP
SURE.
MY NAME SEAL, RIGHT?
HUH?
WHERE ...
...IS IT?
I'M SORRY, BUT I CAN'T FIND IT.
I can't accept the package ...
A SIGNATURE WORKS TOO.
I CAN DO THAT!
BUT ...
RECEIVED BY
...I HAVEN'T LEARNED THE KANJI CHARACTER FOR "URU" YET.

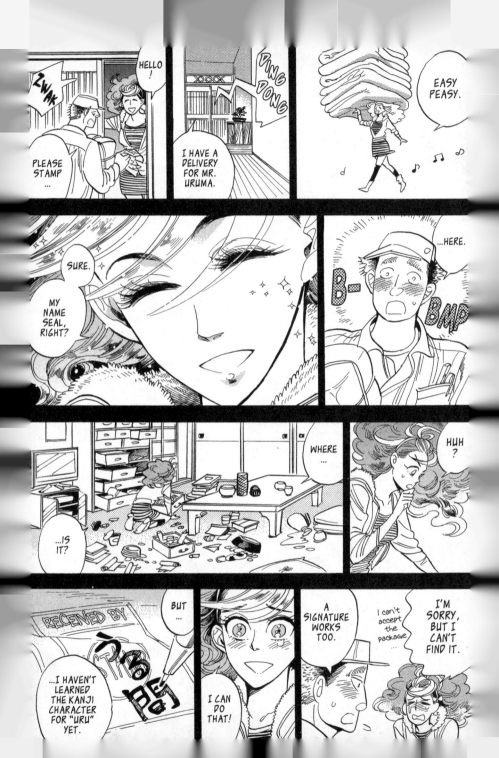

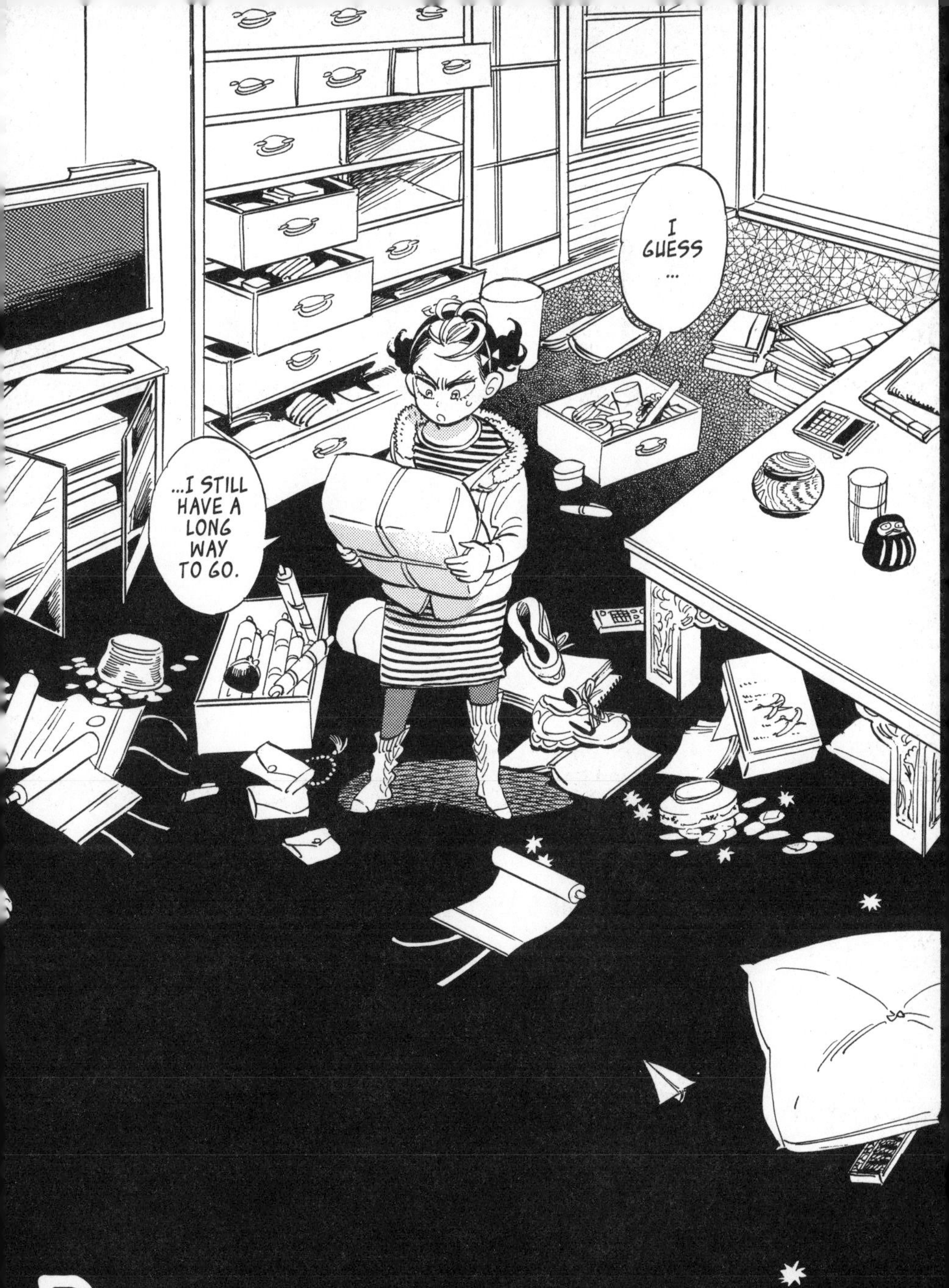
I GUESS ...
...I STILL HAVE A LONG WAY TO GO.

Ran and the Gray World 3

Story and Art by **Aki Irie**

Contents

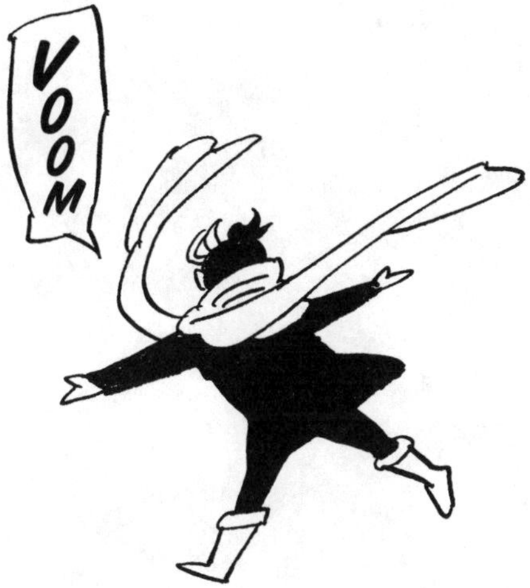
VOOM

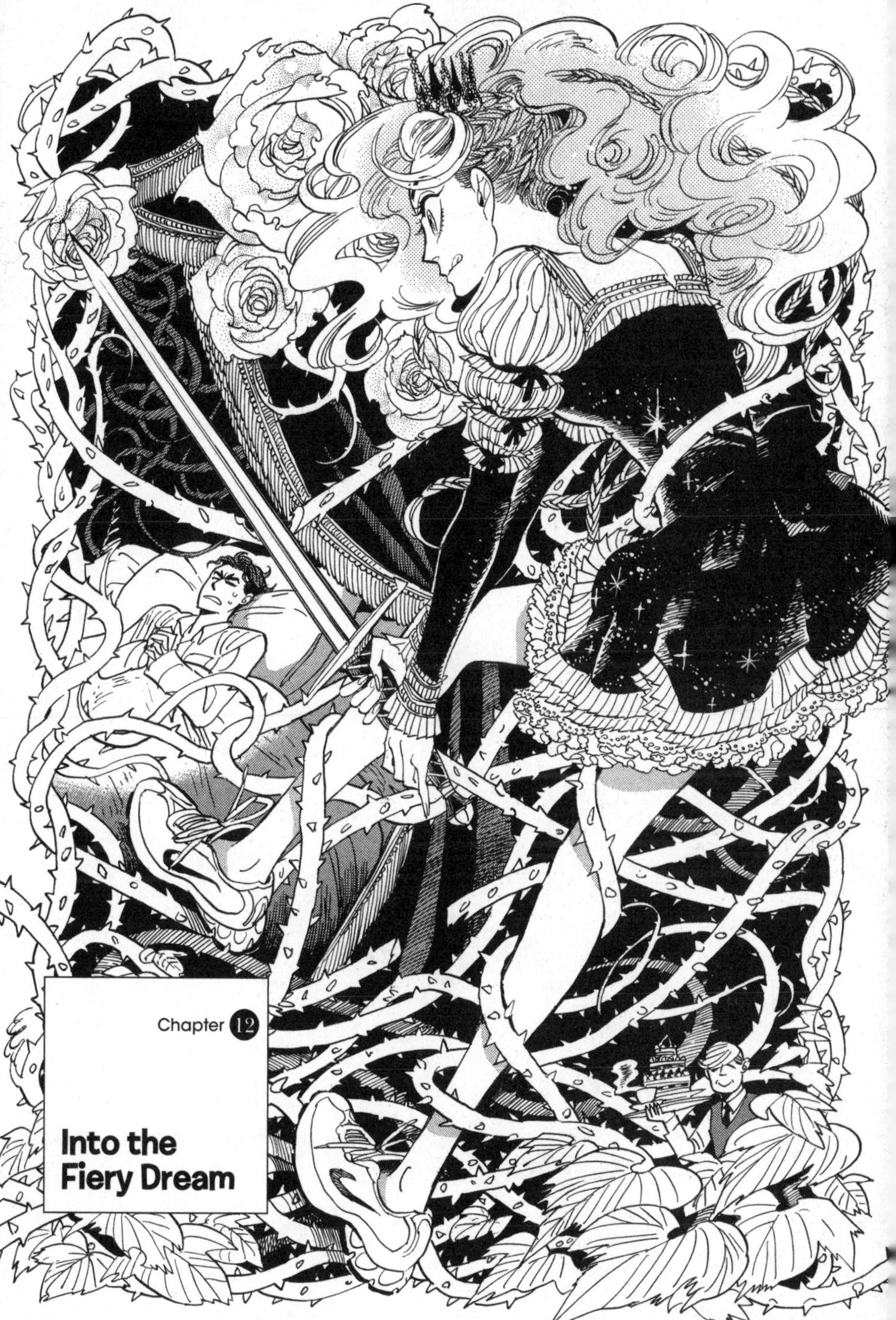

Chapter 12

Into the Fiery Dream

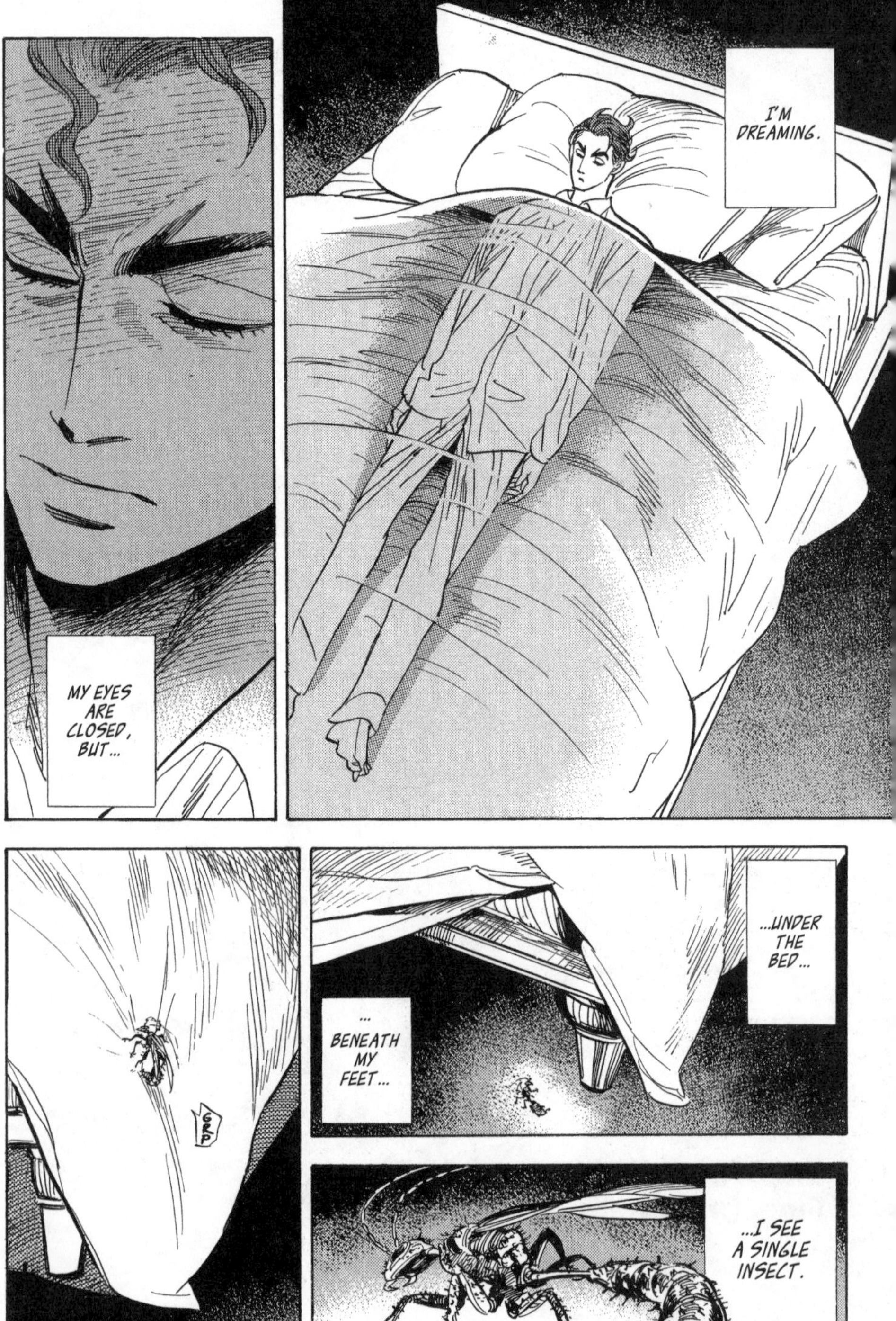
I'M DREAMING.
MY EYES ARE CLOSED, BUT...
...UNDER THE BED...
... BENEATH MY FEET...
...I SEE A SINGLE INSECT.
GRP

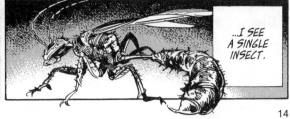

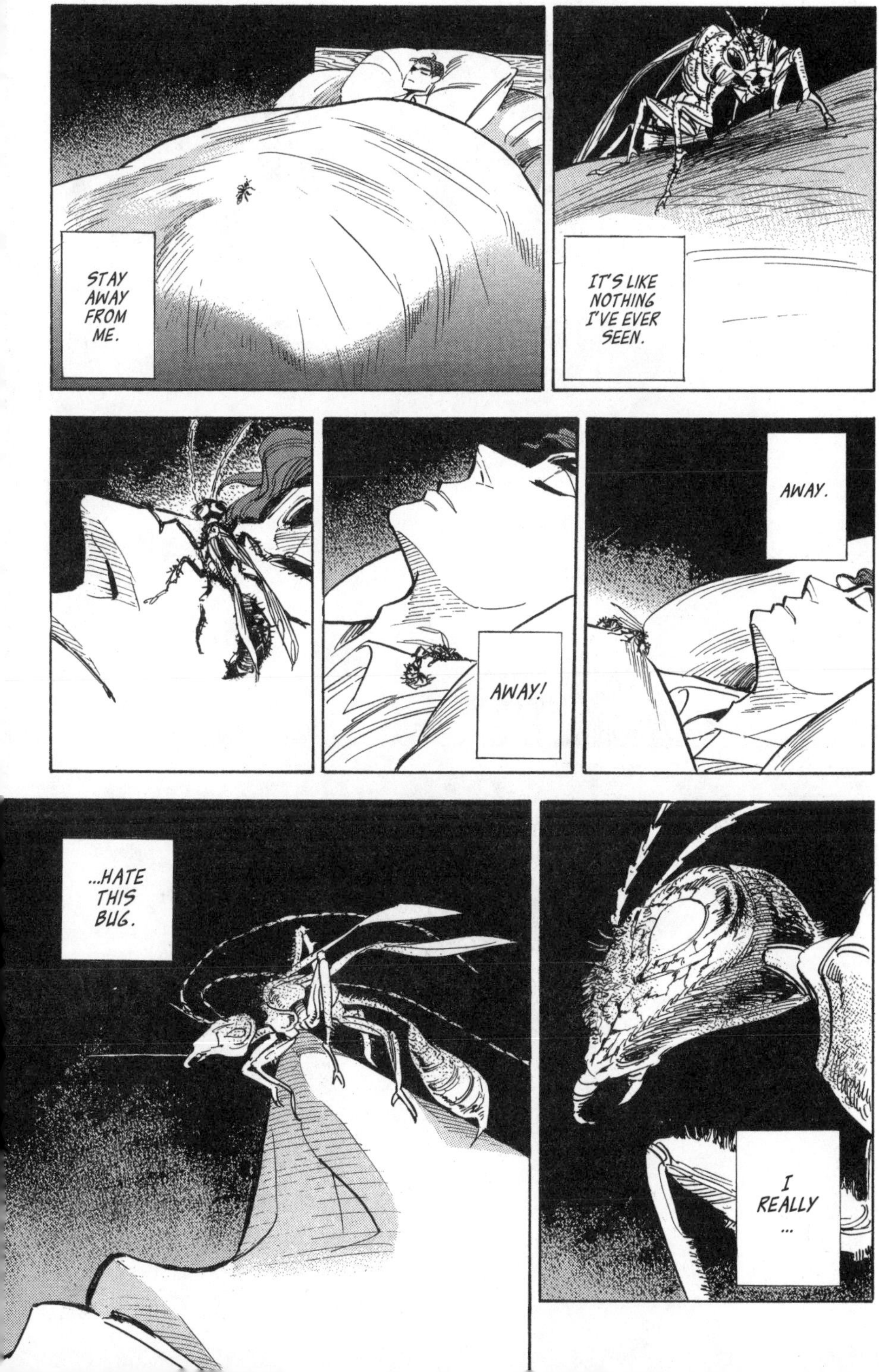
IT'S LIKE NOTHING I'VE EVER SEEN.
STAY AWAY FROM ME.
AWAY.
AWAY!
I REALLY ...
...HATE THIS BUG.

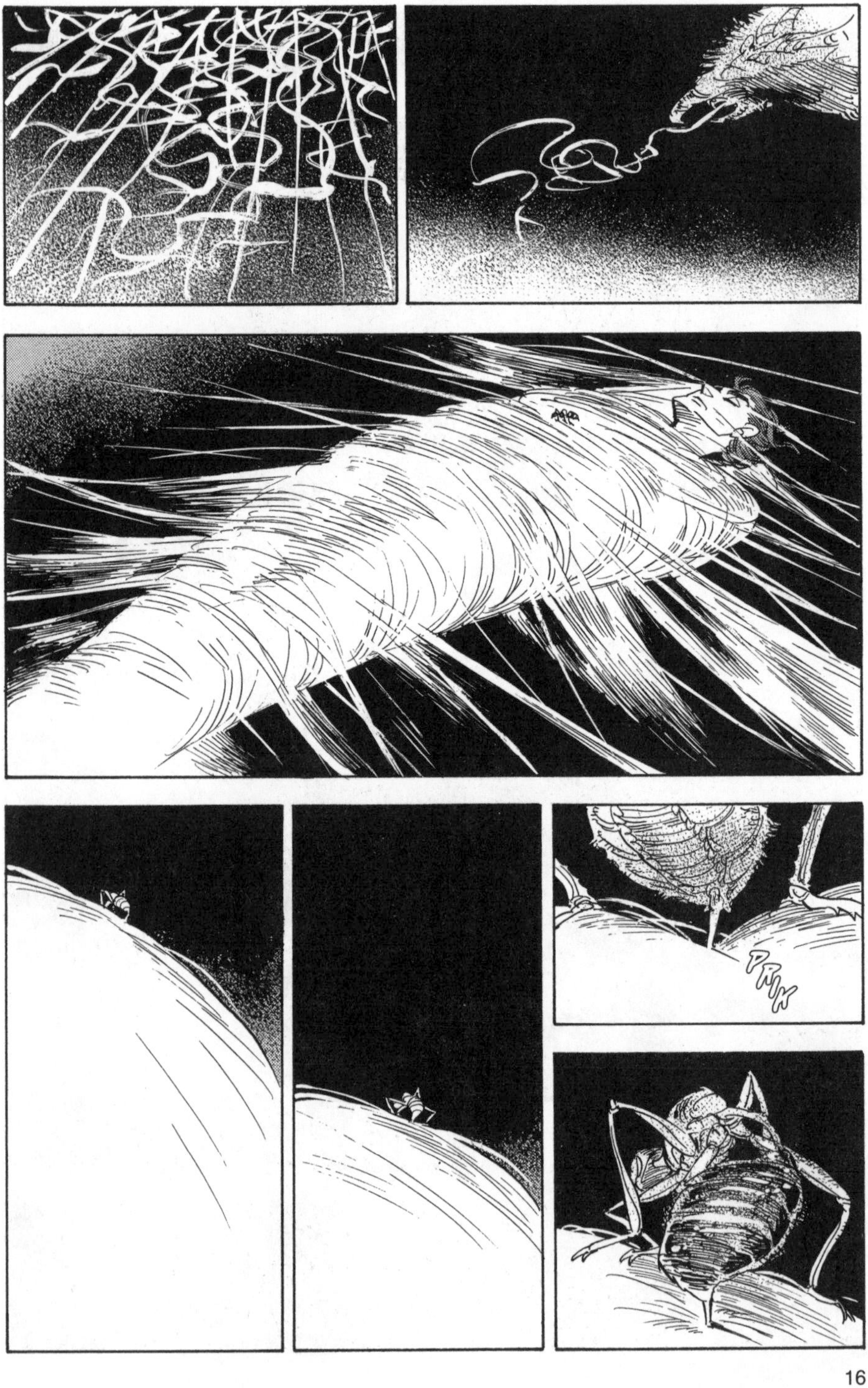
PRIK

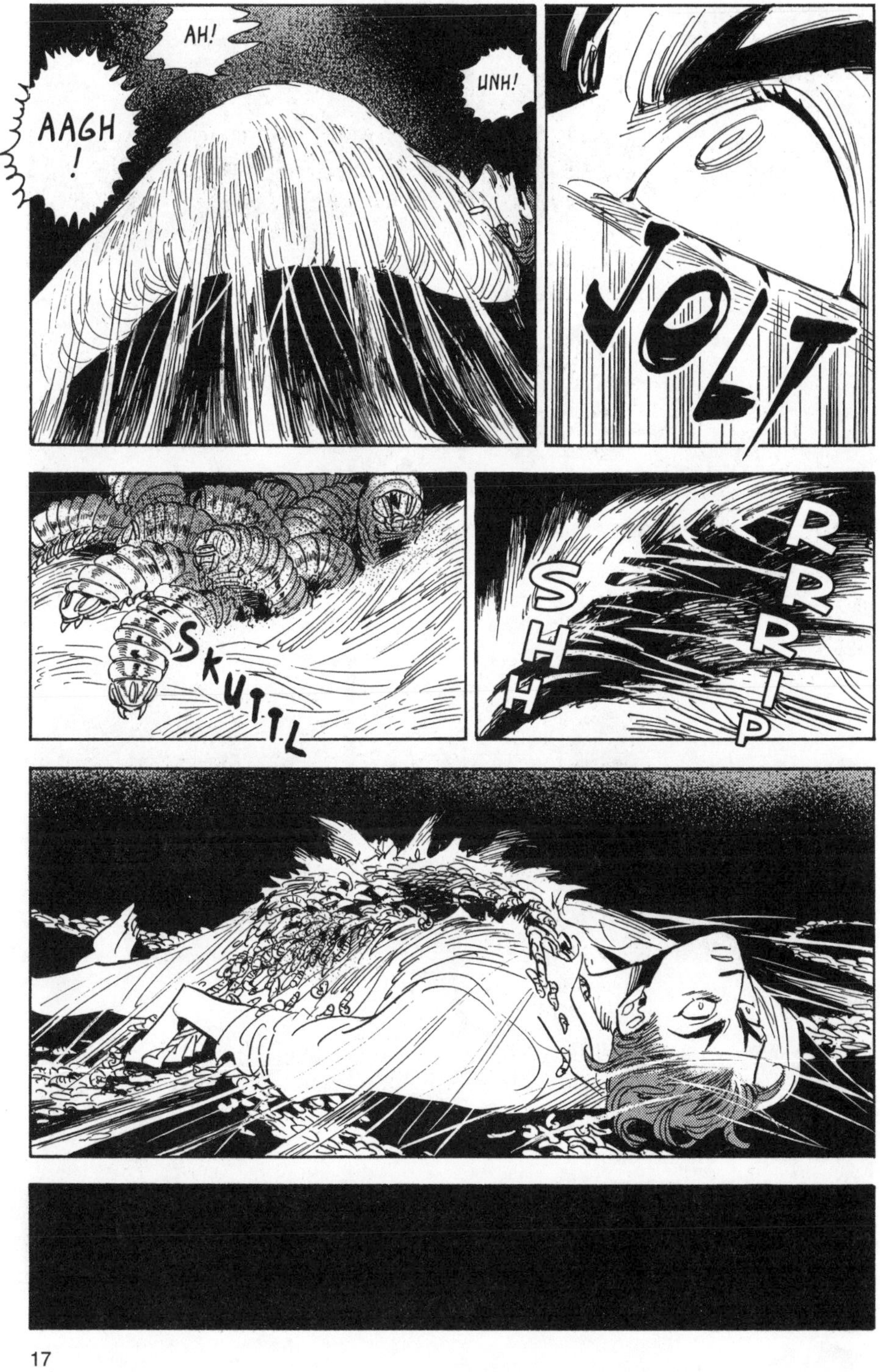
JOLT
UNH!
AH!
AAGH!
RRRIP
SHHH
SKUTTL

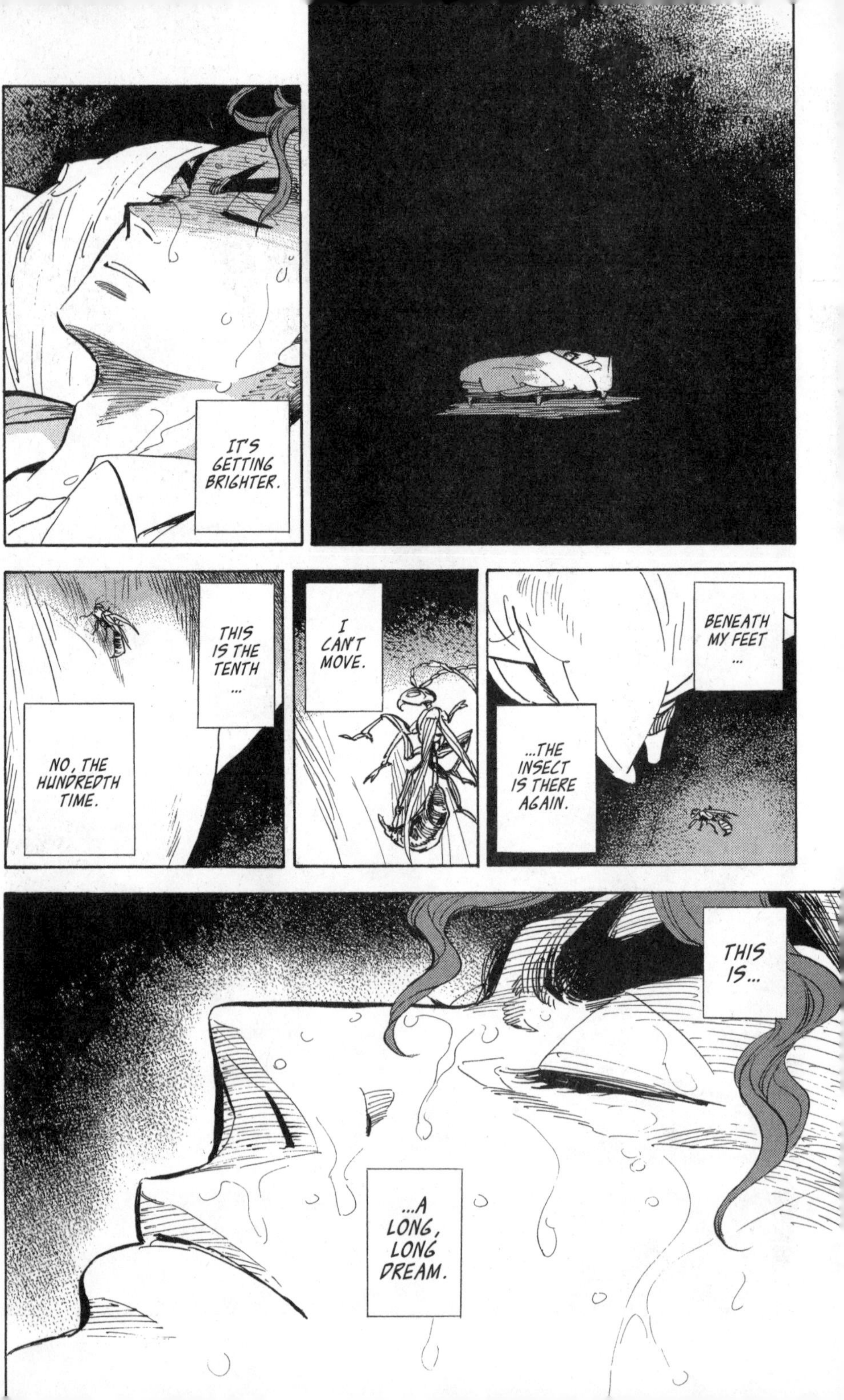
IT'S GETTING BRIGHTER.
BENEATH MY FEET ...
...THE INSECT IS THERE AGAIN.
I CAN'T MOVE.
THIS IS THE TENTH ...
NO, THE HUNDREDTH TIME.
THIS IS...
...A LONG, LONG DREAM.

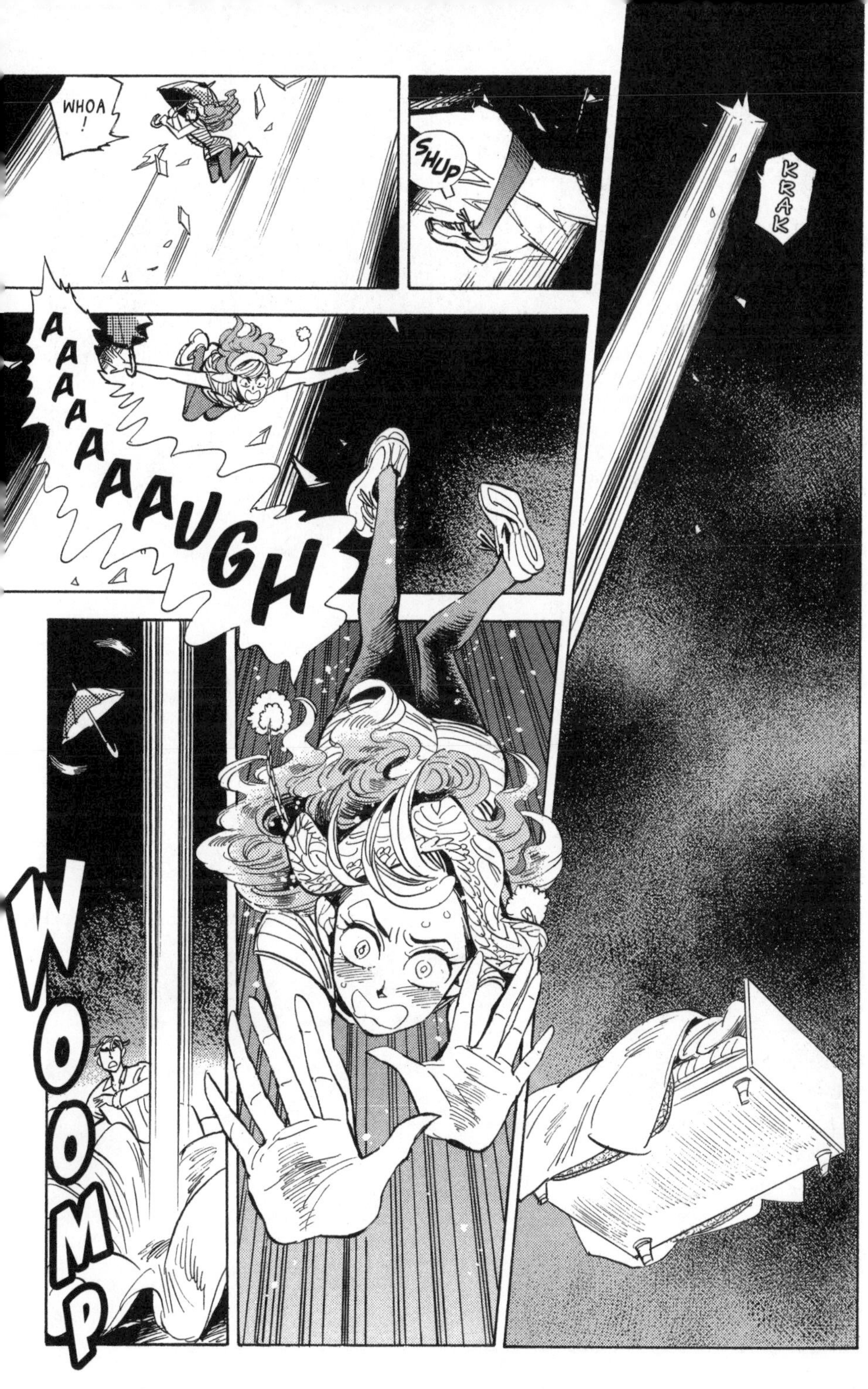
KRAK
SHUP
WHOA!
AAAAAAAUGH
WOOMP

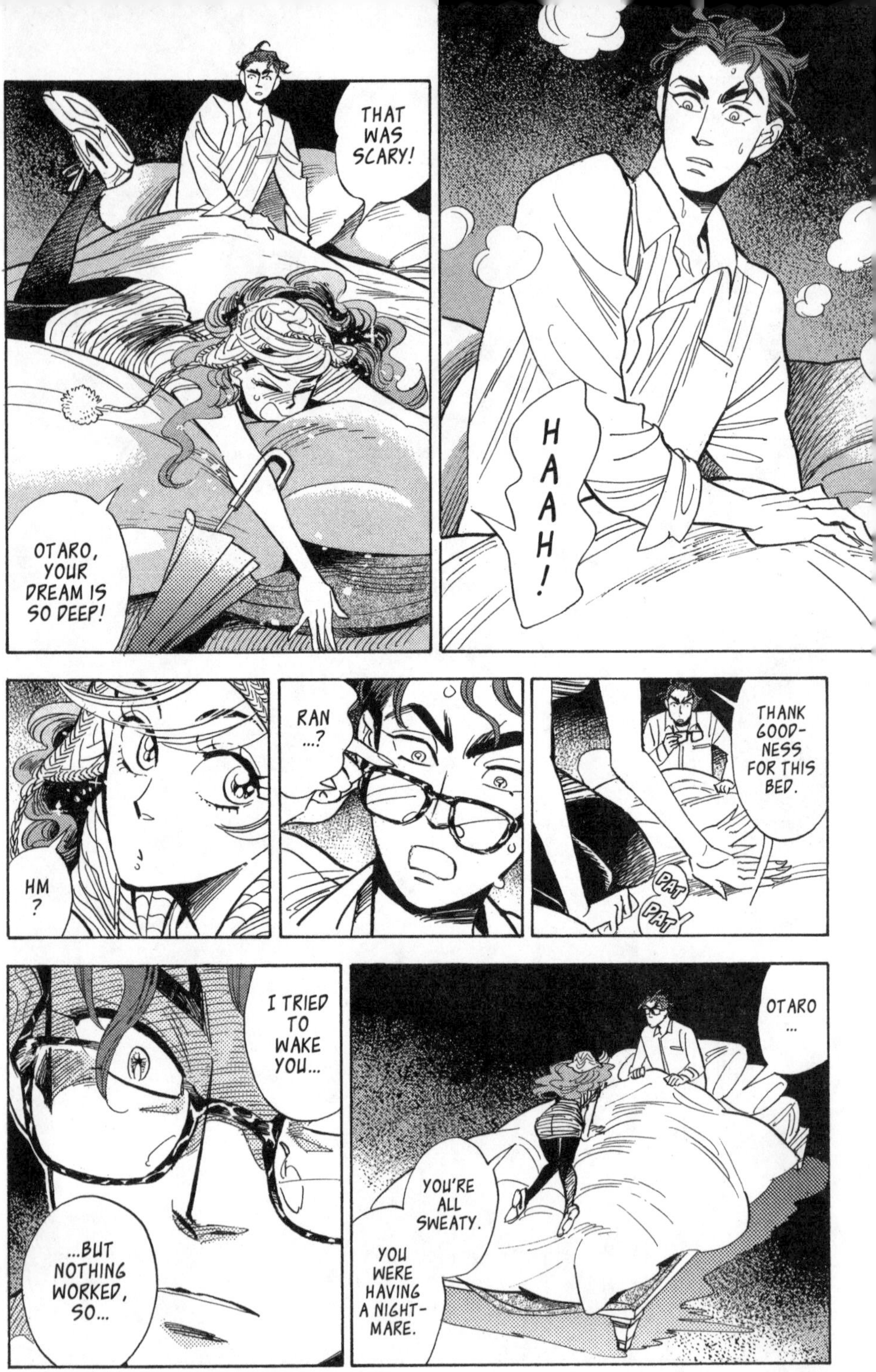
HAAAH!
THAT WAS SCARY!
OTARO, YOUR DREAM IS SO DEEP!
THANK GOODNESS FOR THIS BED.
PAT PAT
RAN ...?
HM ?
OTARO ...
YOU'RE ALL SWEATY.
YOU WERE HAVING A NIGHTMARE.
I TRIED TO WAKE YOU...
...BUT NOTHING WORKED, SO...

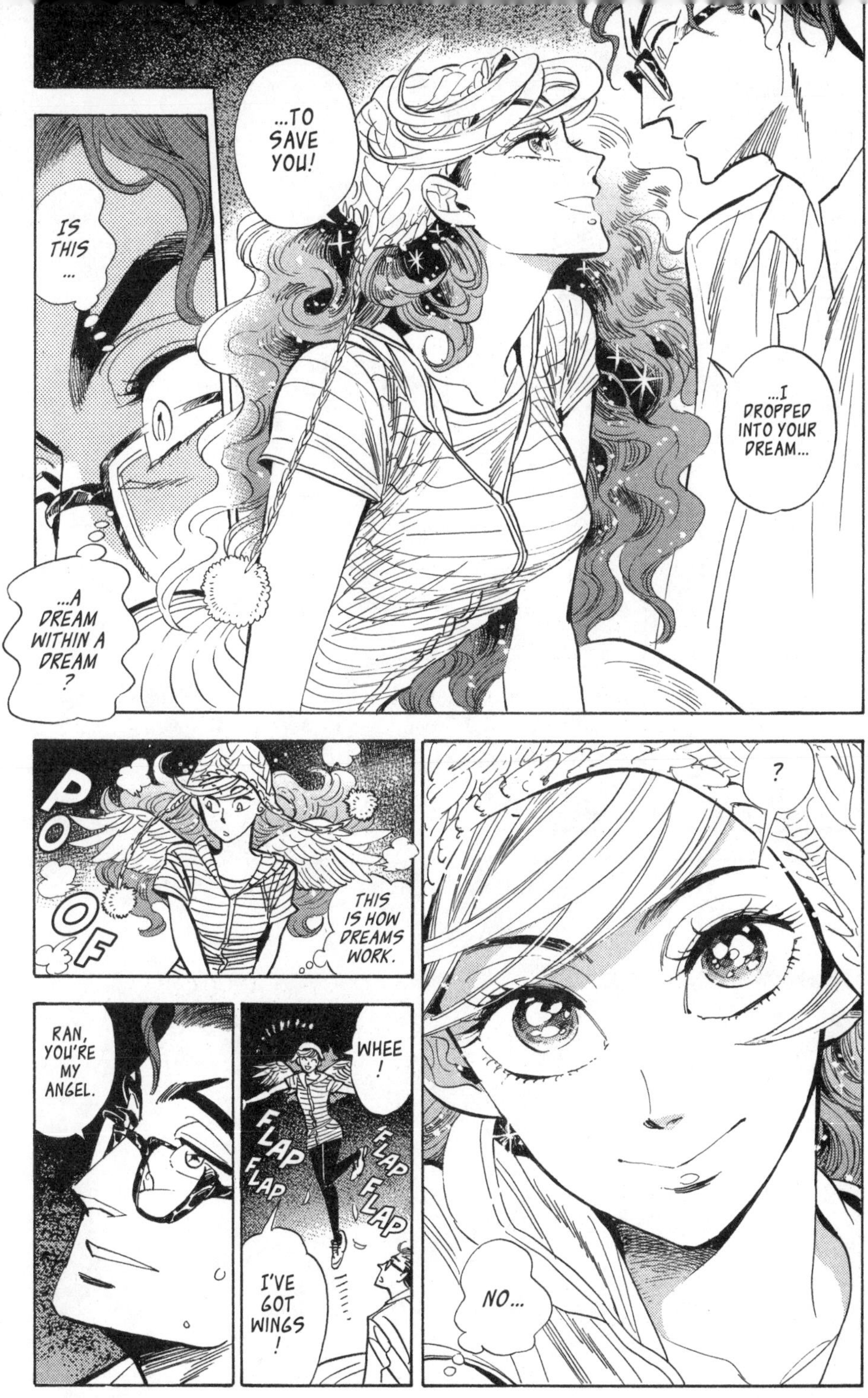
...I DROPPED INTO YOUR DREAM...
...TO SAVE YOU!
IS THIS...
...A DREAM WITHIN A DREAM?
?
NO...
POOF
THIS IS HOW DREAMS WORK.
WHEE!
FLAP FLAP
FLAP FLAP
I'VE GOT WINGS!
RAN, YOU'RE MY ANGEL.

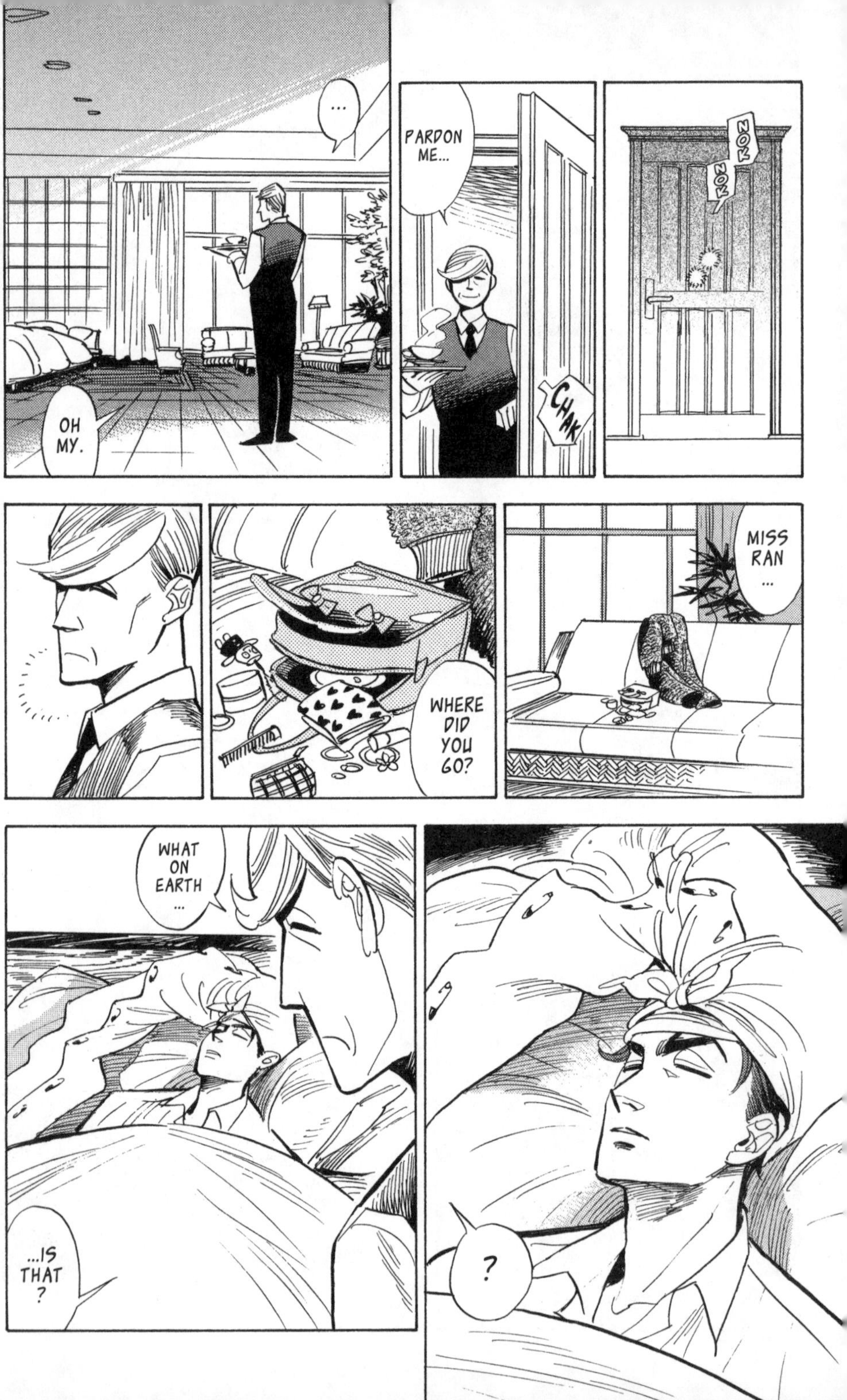

NOK NOK
PARDON ME...
CHAK
...
OH MY.
MISS RAN ...
WHERE DID YOU GO?
?
WHAT ON EARTH ...
...IS THAT ?

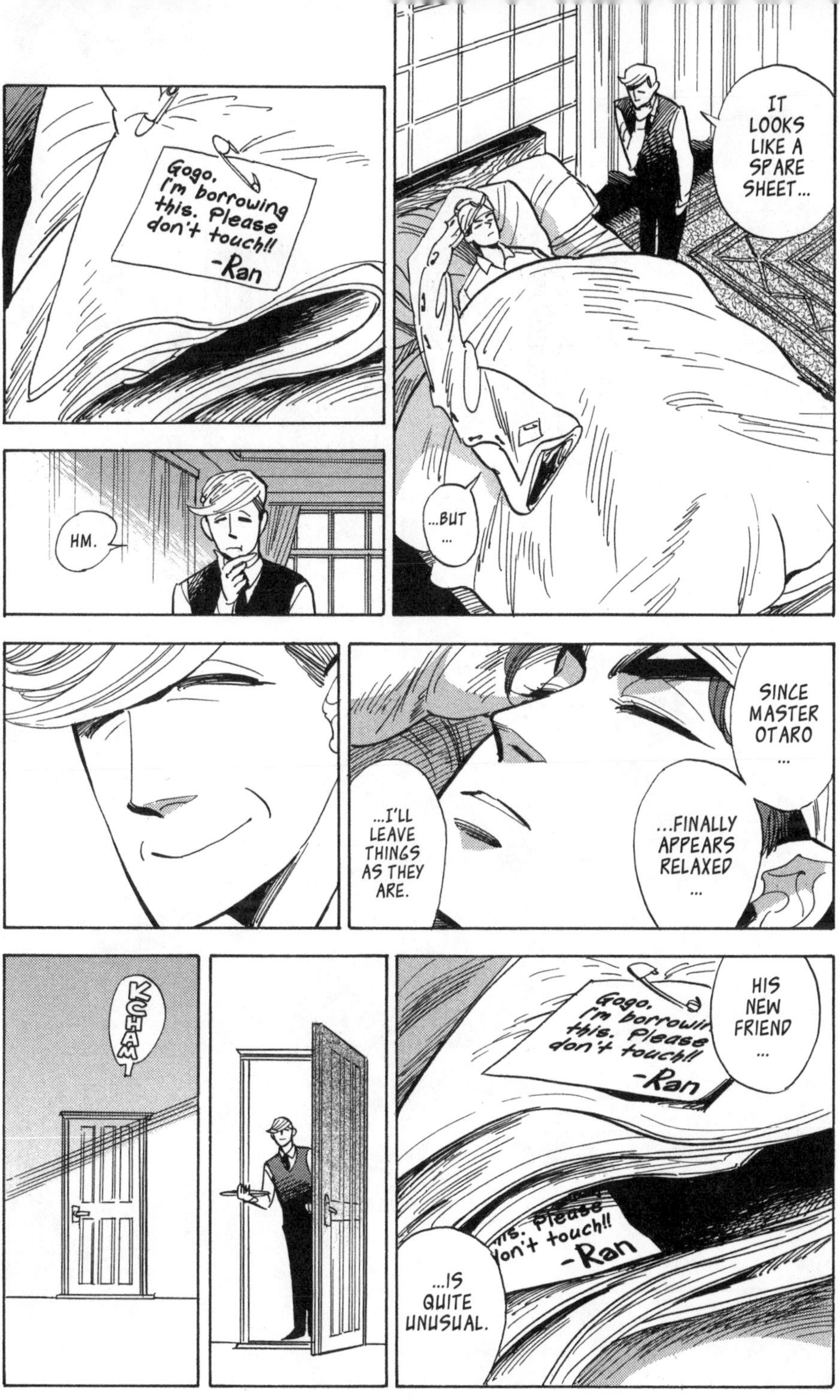
IT LOOKS LIKE A SPARE SHEET...
...BUT ...
Gogo, I'm borrowing this. Please don't touch!! -Ran
HM.
SINCE MASTER OTARO ...
...FINALLY APPEARS RELAXED ...
...I'LL LEAVE THINGS AS THEY ARE.
Gogo, I'm borrowin this. Please don't touch!! -Ran
HIS NEW FRIEND ...
Please don't touch!! -Ran
...IS QUITE UNUSUAL.
KCHAM

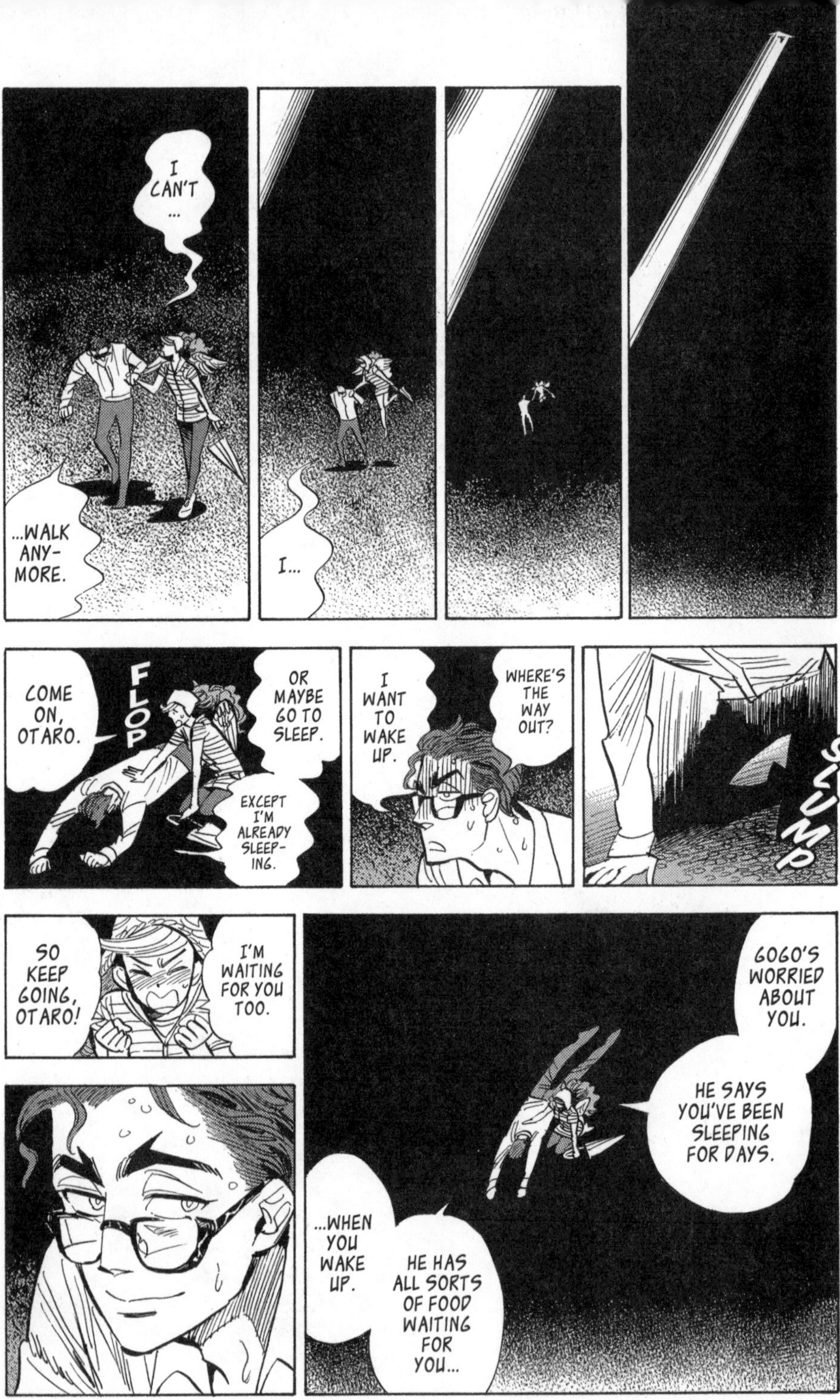
I...
I CAN'T ...
...WALK ANY-MORE.
SLUMP
WHERE'S THE WAY OUT?
I WANT TO WAKE UP.
OR MAYBE GO TO SLEEP.
EXCEPT I'M ALREADY SLEEP-ING.
FLOP
COME ON, OTARO.
GOGO'S WORRIED ABOUT YOU.
HE SAYS YOU'VE BEEN SLEEPING FOR DAYS.
HE HAS ALL SORTS OF FOOD WAITING FOR YOU...
...WHEN YOU WAKE UP.
I'M WAITING FOR YOU TOO.
SO KEEP GOING, OTARO!

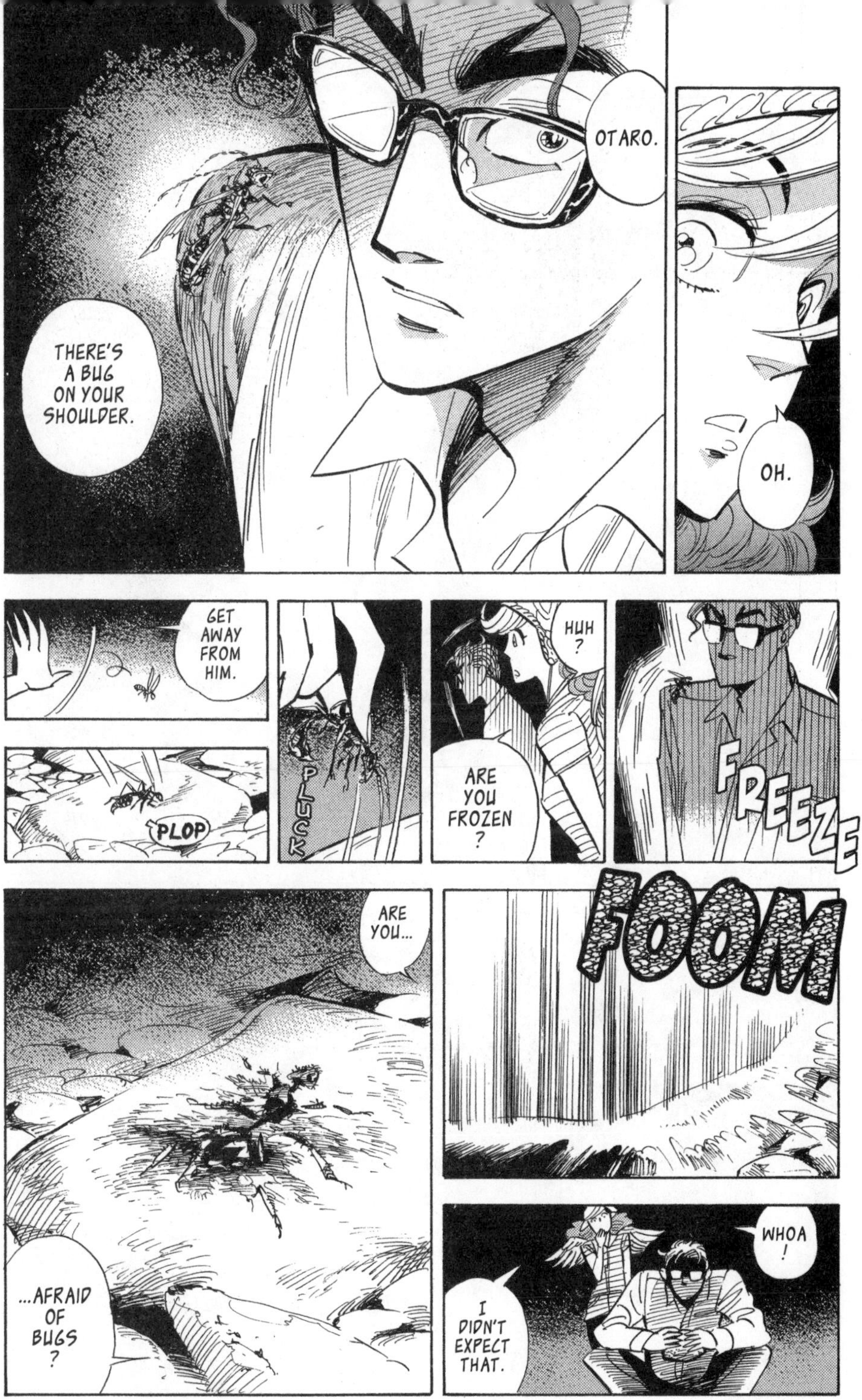
OTARO.
THERE'S A BUG ON YOUR SHOULDER.
OH.
FREEZE
HUH?
ARE YOU FROZEN?
PLUCK
GET AWAY FROM HIM.
PLOP
FOOM
WHOA!
I DIDN'T EXPECT THAT.
ARE YOU...
...AFRAID OF BUGS?

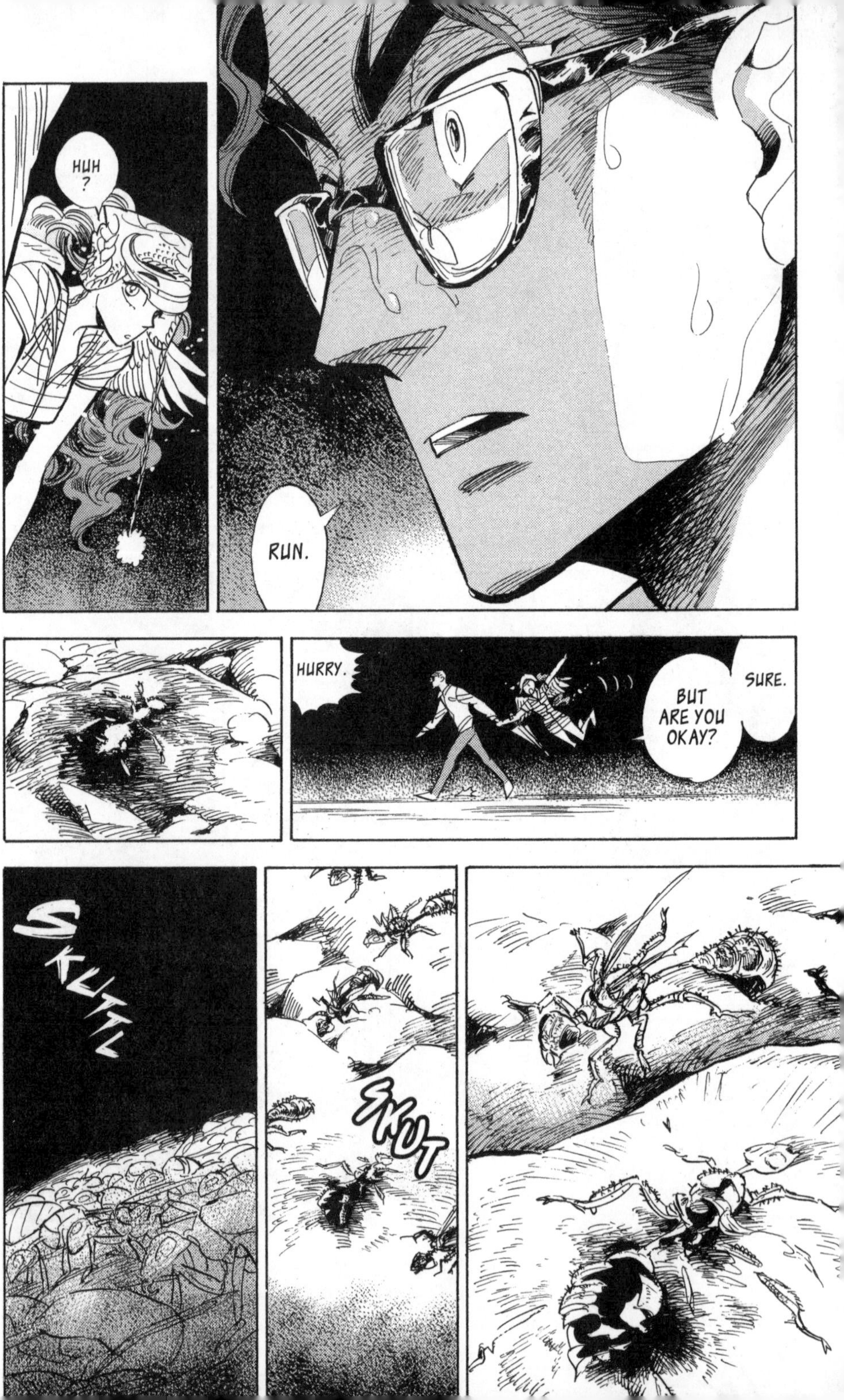
RUN.
HUH ?
HURRY.
SURE.
BUT ARE YOU OKAY?
SKUT
SKUTTL

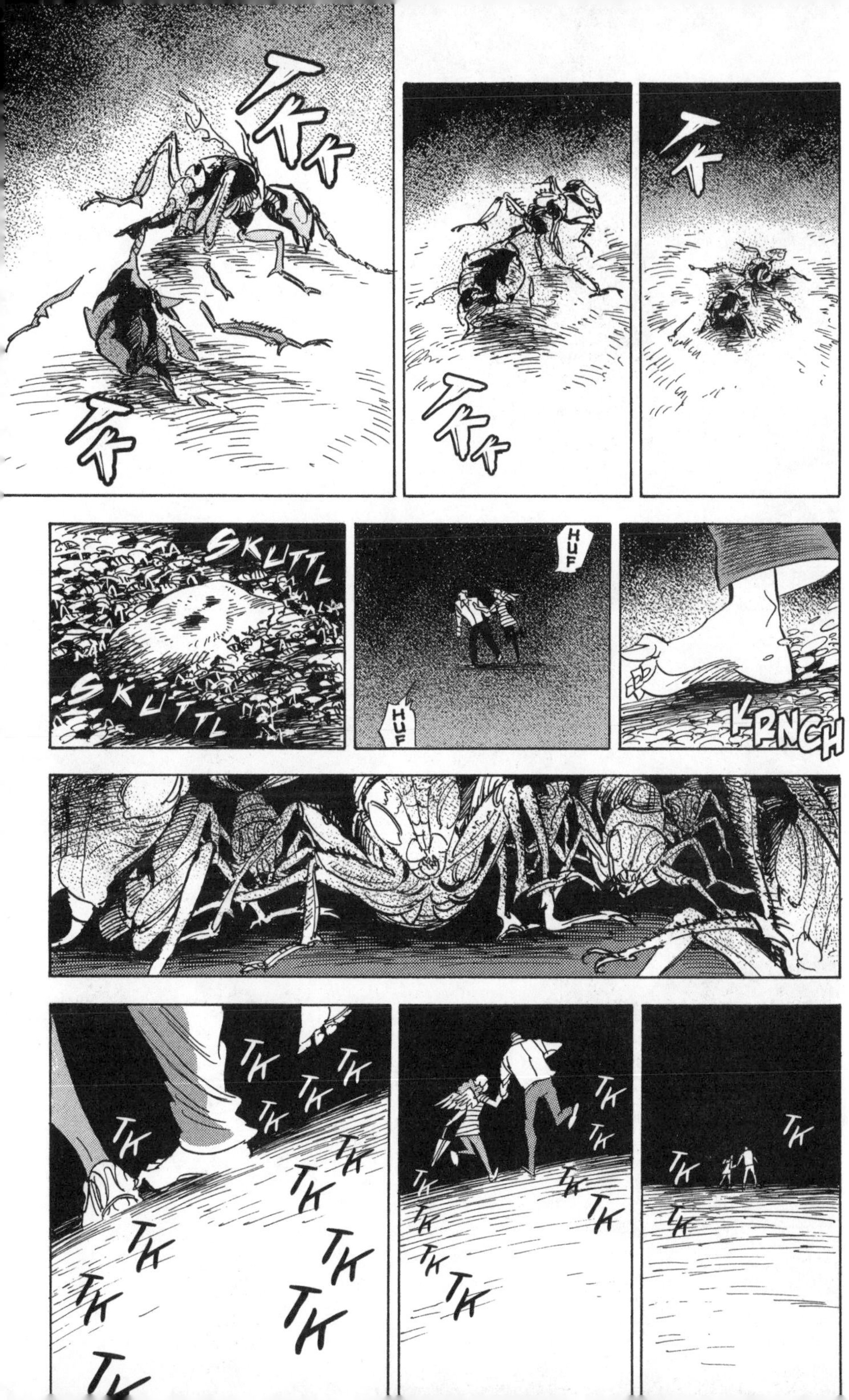

TK
TKK
TKK
TKK
TK
KRNCH
HUF
HUF
SKUTTL
SKUTTL
TK
TK
TK
TK
TK
TK
TK
TK
TK
TK
TK
TK
TK
TK
TK
TK
TK
TK
TK
TK
TK
TK
TK
TK

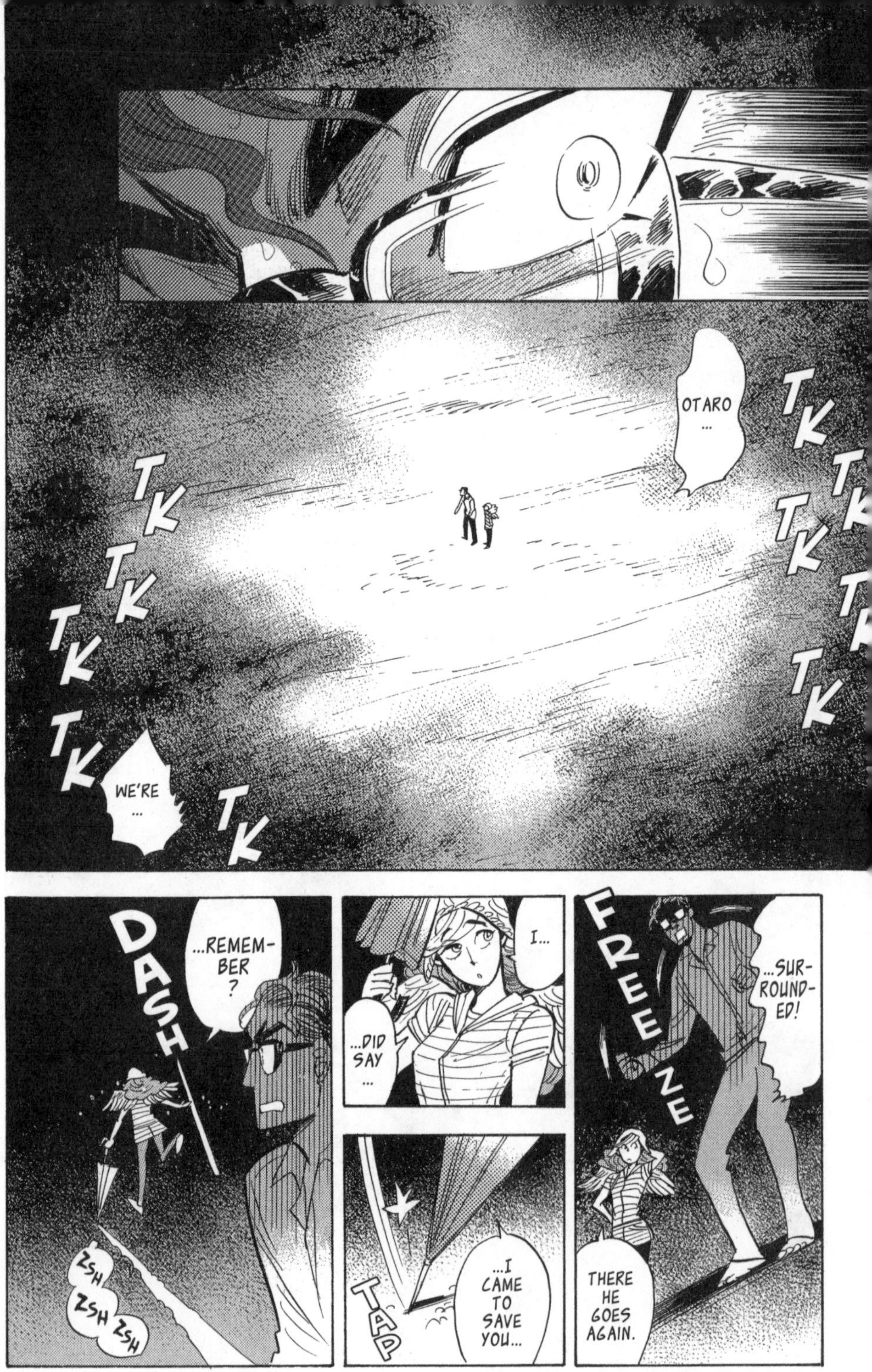
OTARO ...
TK TK TK TK TK TK TK
TK TK TK TK TK TK
WE'RE ...
TK
FREE ZE
...SUR-ROUND-ED!
THERE HE GOES AGAIN.
I...
...DID SAY ...
...I CAME TO SAVE YOU...
TAP
DASH
...REMEM-BER ?
ZSH ZSH ZSH

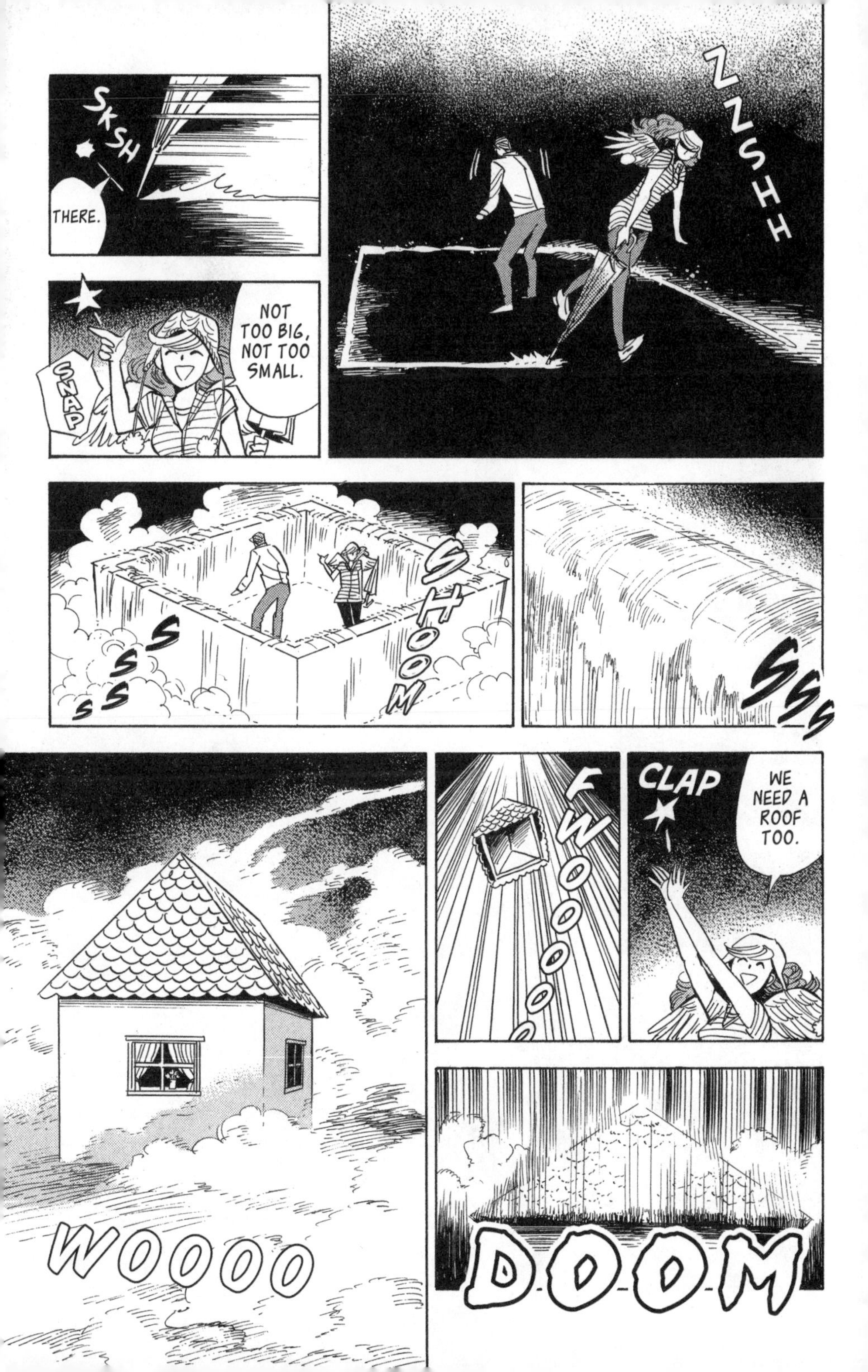

ZZSHHH
SKSH
THERE.
NOT TOO BIG, NOT TOO SMALL.
SNAP
SSS
SHOOOM
SSSS
CLAP
WE NEED A ROOF TOO.
FWOOOOO
DOOM
WOOOO

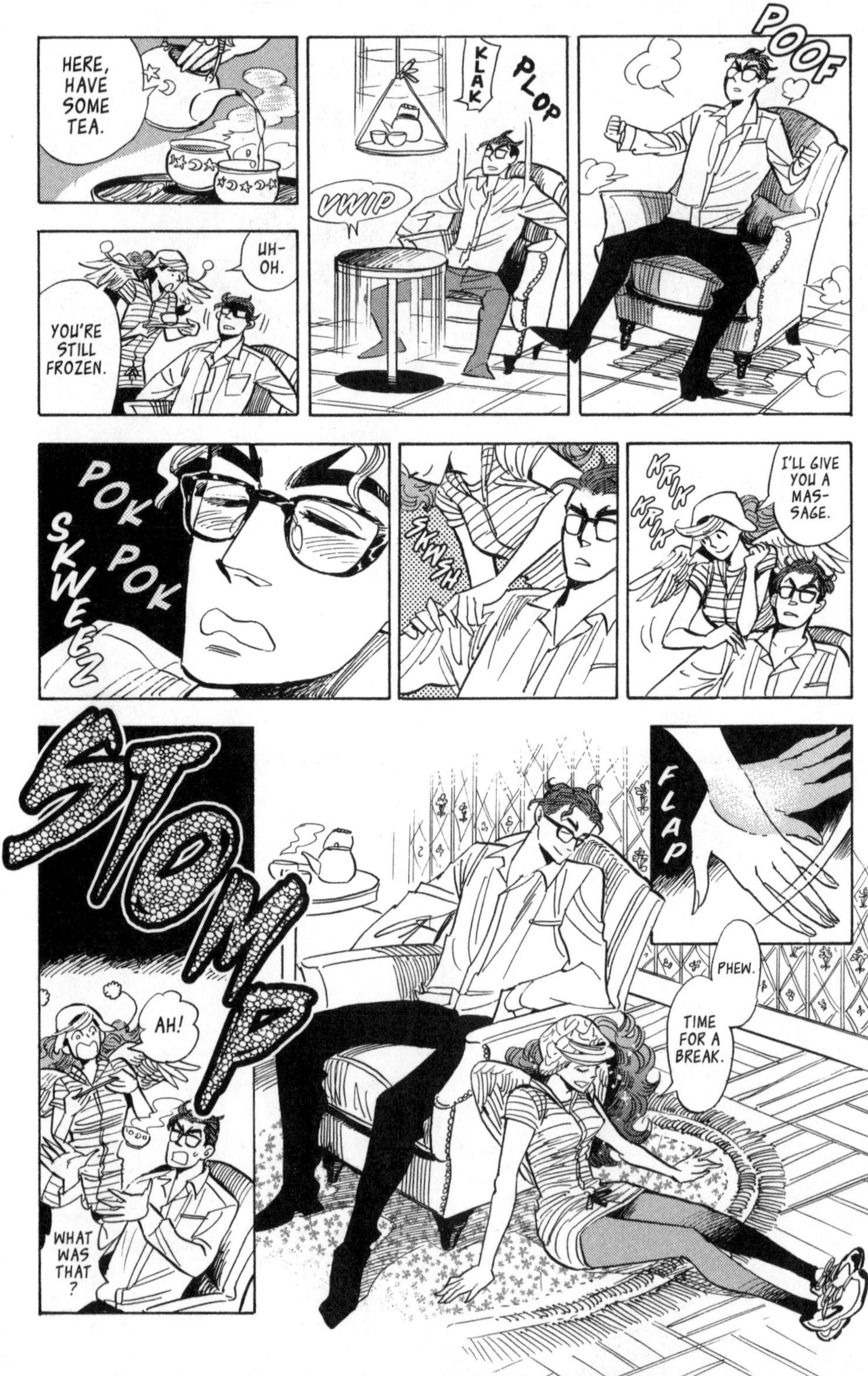
POOF
KLAK
PLOP
VWIP
HERE, HAVE SOME TEA.
UH-OH.
YOU'RE STILL FROZEN.
KRIK KRIK
I'LL GIVE YOU A MAS-SAGE.
SKWSH
POK POK
SKWEEZ
FLAP
PHEW.
TIME FOR A BREAK.
STOMP
AH!
WHAT WAS THAT?

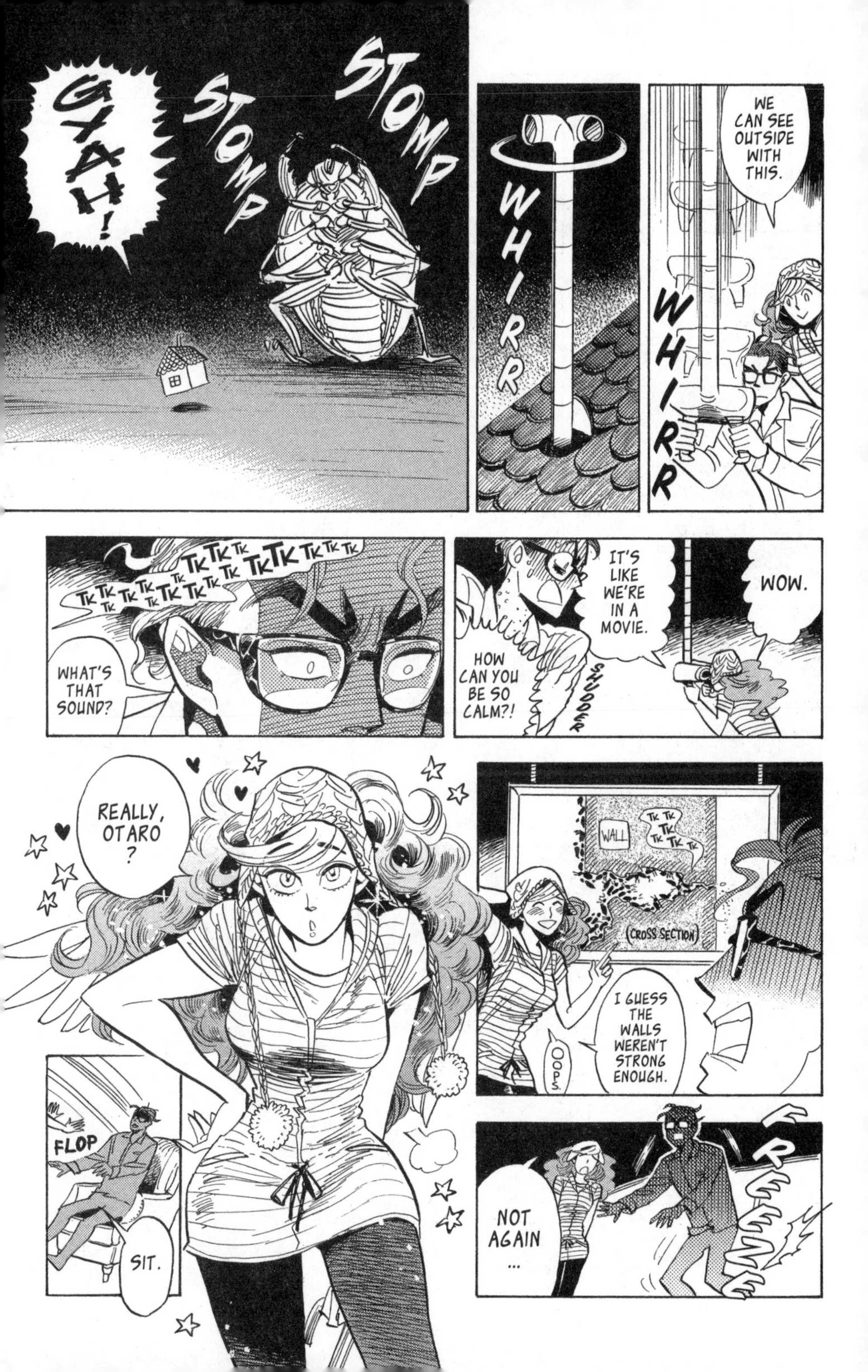
WE CAN SEE OUTSIDE WITH THIS.
WHIRR
WHIRR
STOMP
STOMP
GYAH!
WOW.
IT'S LIKE WE'RE IN A MOVIE.
HOW CAN YOU BE SO CALM?!
SHUDDER
TK TK TK TK TK TK TK TK TK TK TK TK TK TK TK TK TK
WHAT'S THAT SOUND?
WALL
TK TK TK TK TK TK
(CROSS SECTION)
I GUESS THE WALLS WEREN'T STRONG ENOUGH.
OOPS.
FREEZE
NOT AGAIN...
REALLY, OTARO?
FLOP
SIT.

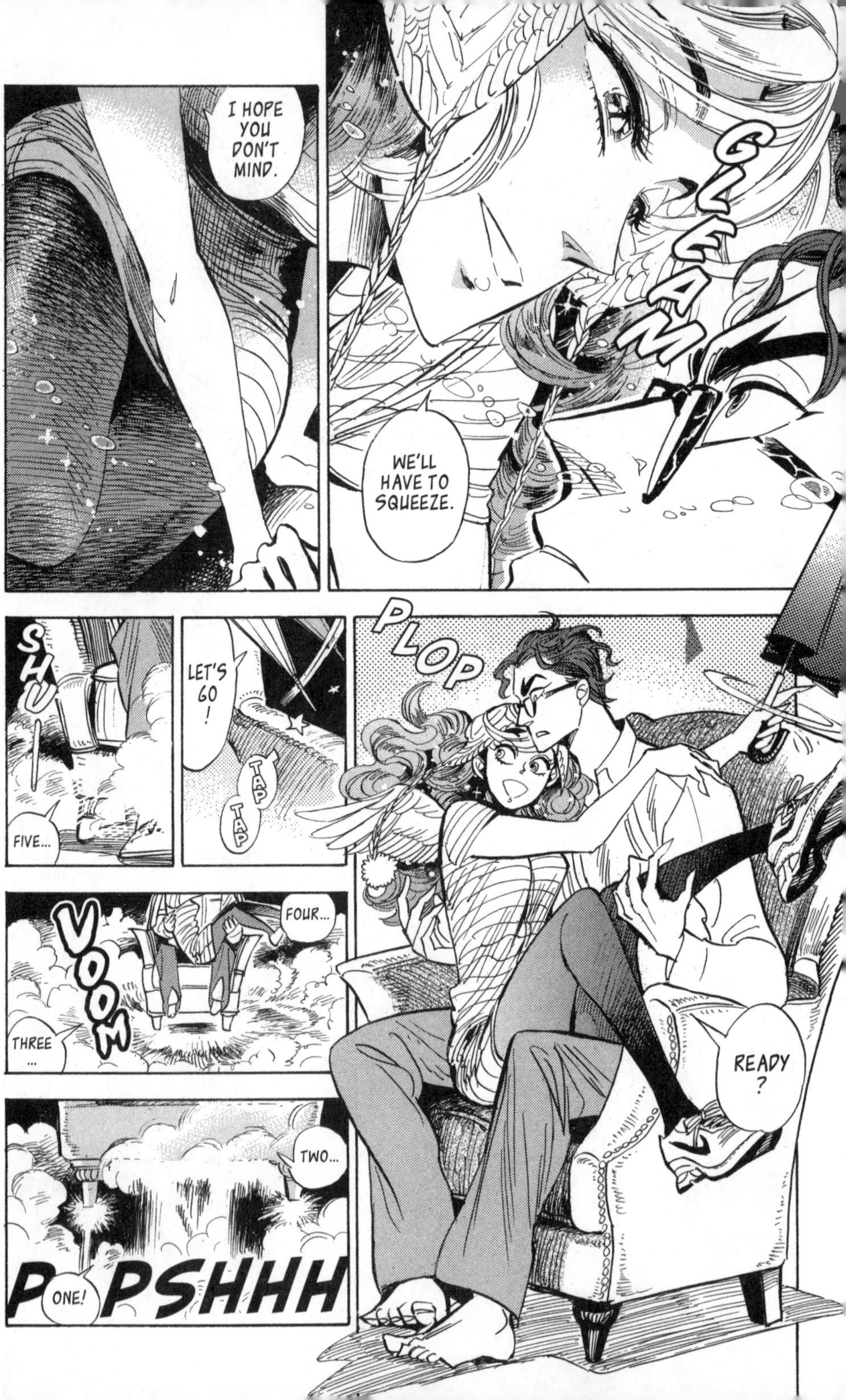
GLEAM
WE'LL HAVE TO SQUEEZE.
I HOPE YOU DON'T MIND.
PLOP
READY?
LET'S GO!
TAP TAP
SHU
FIVE...
FOUR...
VOOM
THREE...
TWO...
PPSHHH
ONE!

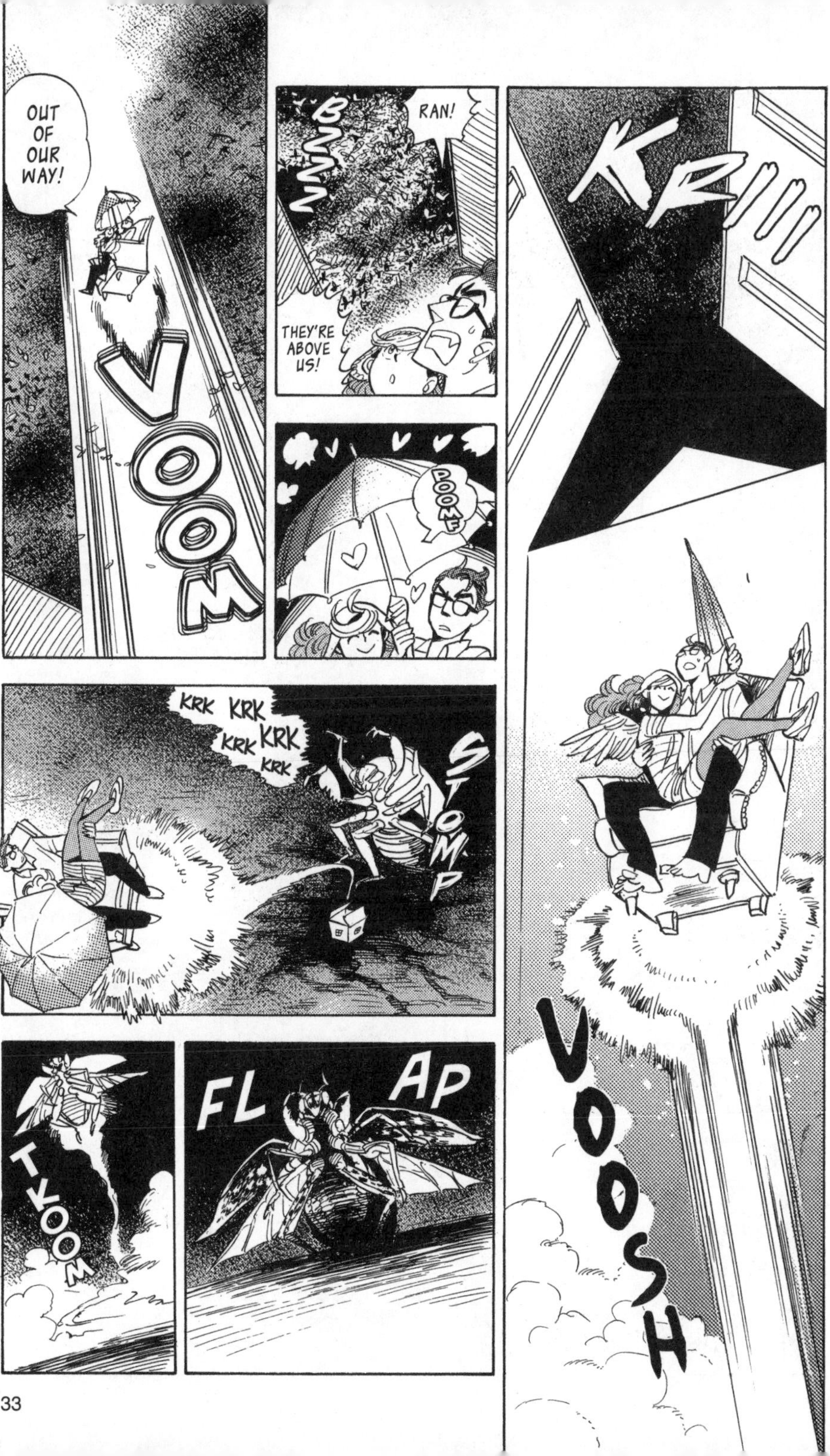
KRIIII
VOOSH
RAN!
BZZZ
THEY'RE ABOVE US!
POOMF
OUT OF OUR WAY!
VOOOM
KRK KRK KRK KRK KRK
STOMP
FLAP
TKOOM

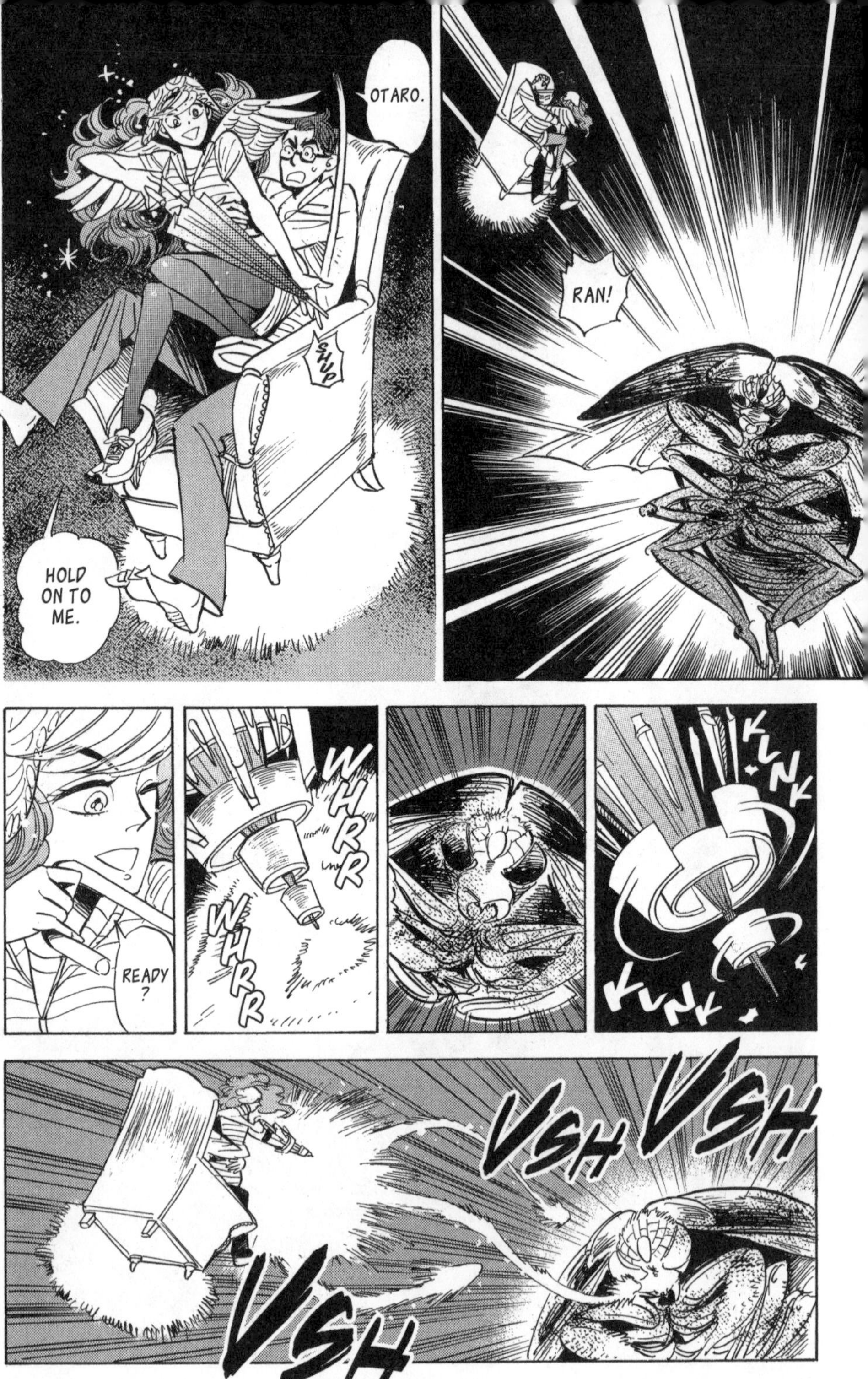
RAN!
OTARO.
SHUP
HOLD ON TO ME.
KLUNK
KLUNK
WHRR
WHRR
READY?
VSH
VSH
VSH

SKRI!!

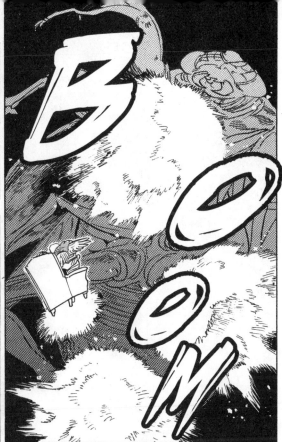

IT'S STILL MOVING.

CHAK

KRKL
KRK

DOOM

KRKL

KRKL

WHOUP

POOF

WHAT WAS THAT?

JUST WATCH.

PIP

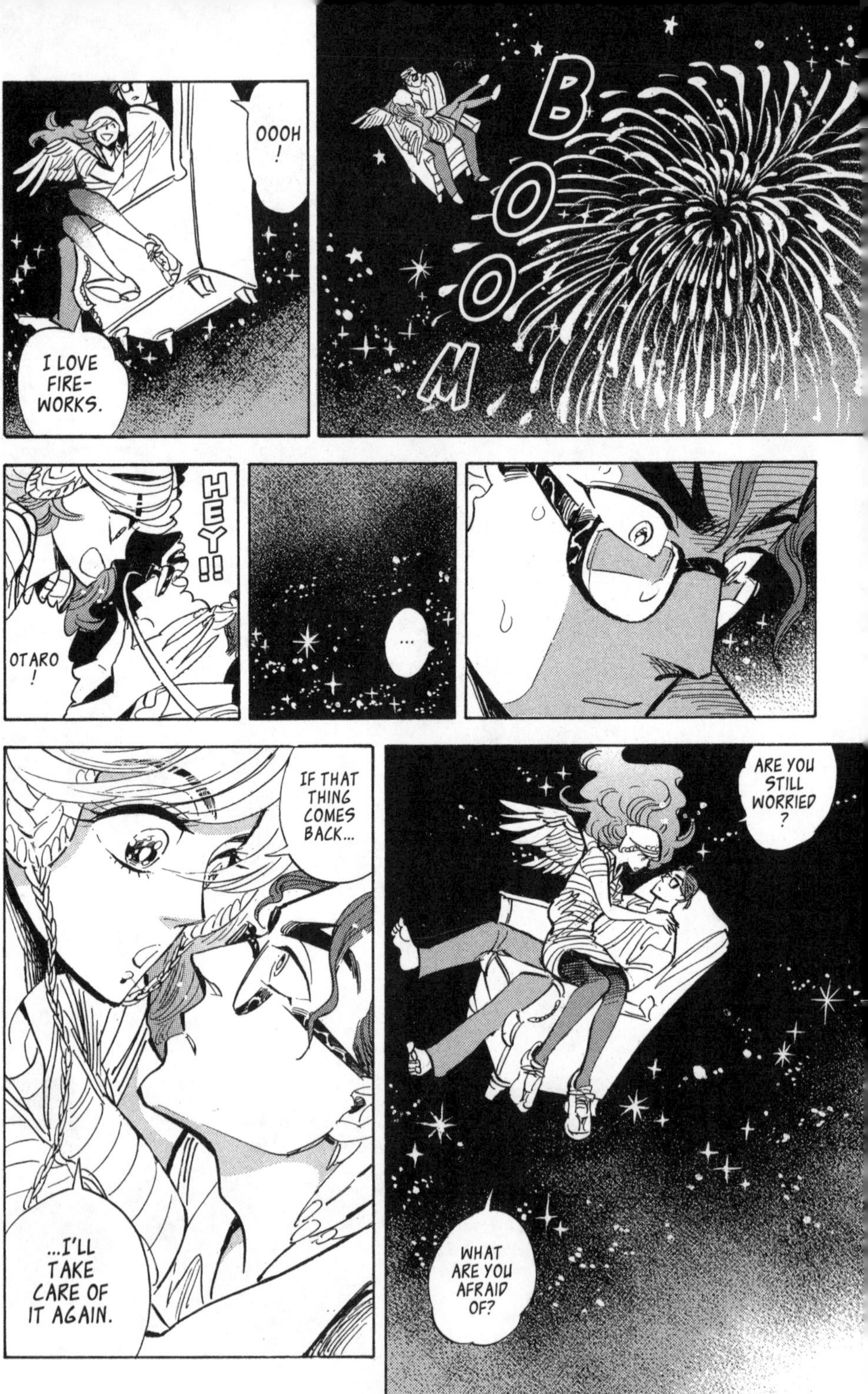
BOOOM
OOOH!
I LOVE FIRE-WORKS.
...
HEY!!
OTARO!
ARE YOU STILL WORRIED?
WHAT ARE YOU AFRAID OF?
IF THAT THING COMES BACK...
...I'LL TAKE CARE OF IT AGAIN.

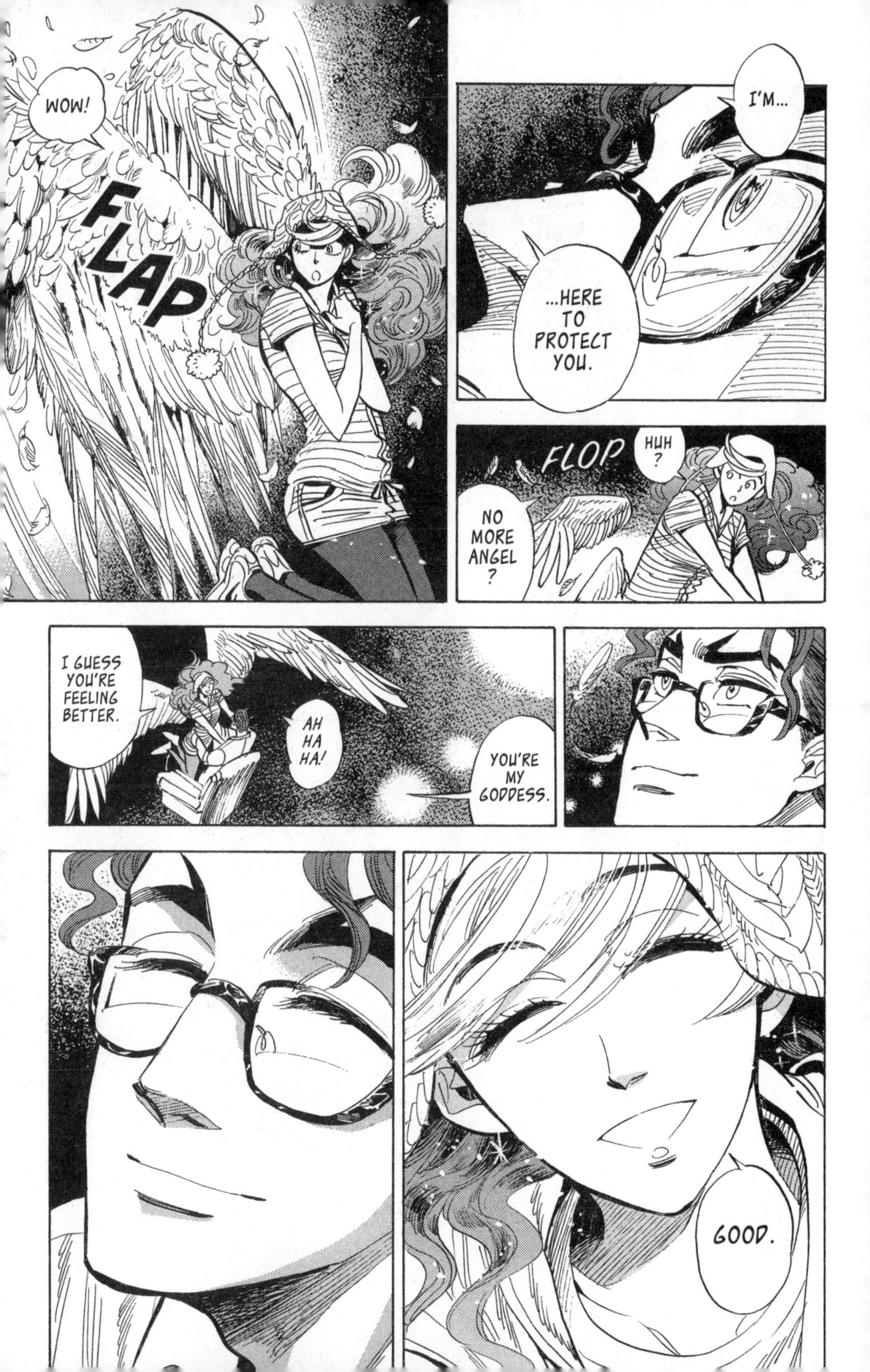
I'M...
...HERE TO PROTECT YOU.
HUH?
FLOP
NO MORE ANGEL?
WOW!
FLAP
YOU'RE MY GODDESS.
AH HA HA!
I GUESS YOU'RE FEELING BETTER.
GOOD.

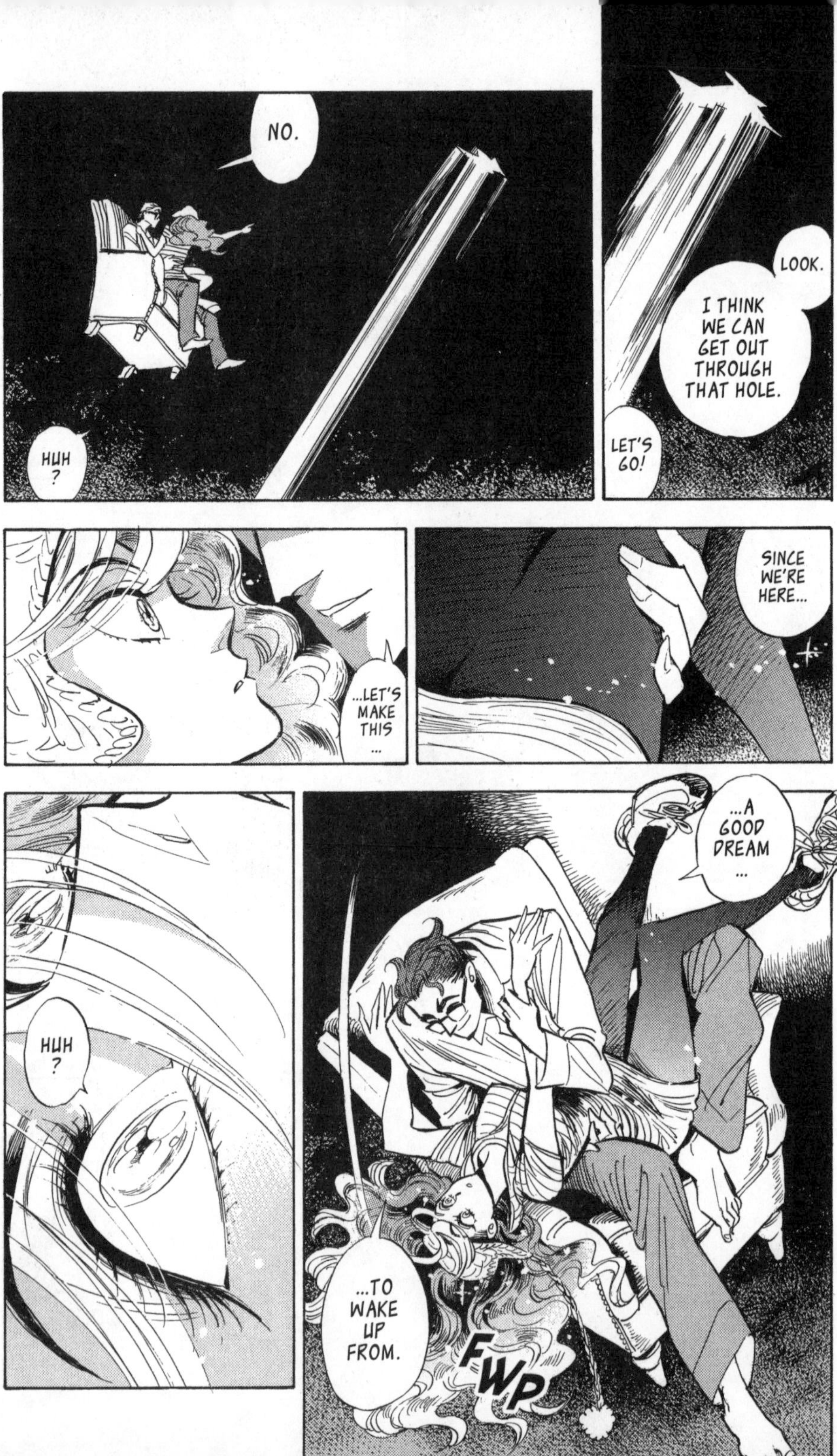
LOOK.
I THINK WE CAN GET OUT THROUGH THAT HOLE.
LET'S GO!
NO.
HUH?
SINCE WE'RE HERE...
...LET'S MAKE THIS...
...A GOOD DREAM...
...TO WAKE UP FROM.
FWP
HUH?

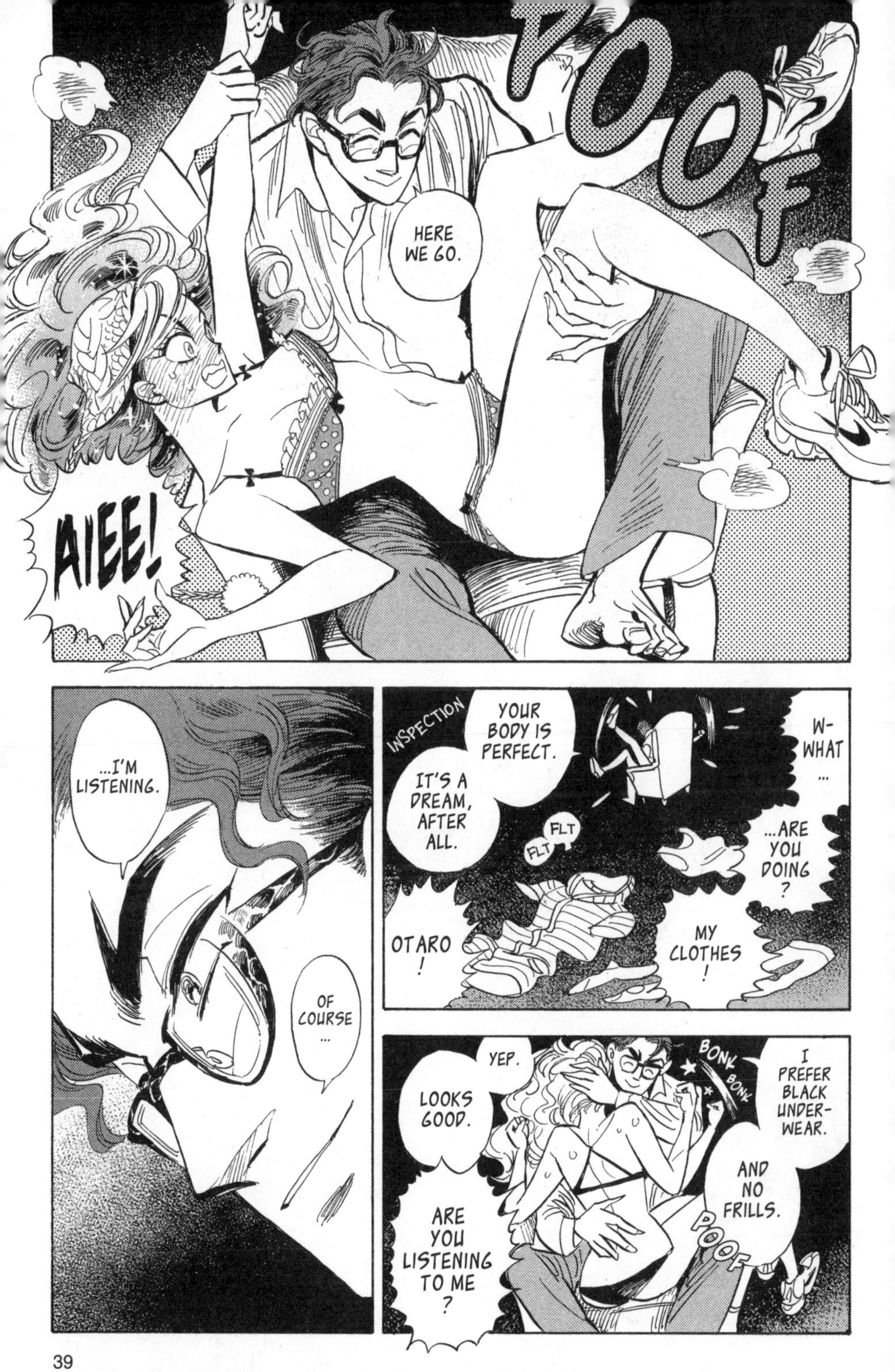
POOF
HERE WE GO.
AIEE!
W-WHAT...
...ARE YOU DOING?
YOUR BODY IS PERFECT.
INSPECTION
IT'S A DREAM, AFTER ALL.
FLT
FLT
MY CLOTHES!
OTARO!
I PREFER BLACK UNDER-WEAR.
BONK
BONK
YEP.
LOOKS GOOD.
AND NO FRILLS.
POOF
ARE YOU LISTENING TO ME?
...I'M LISTENING.
OF COURSE...

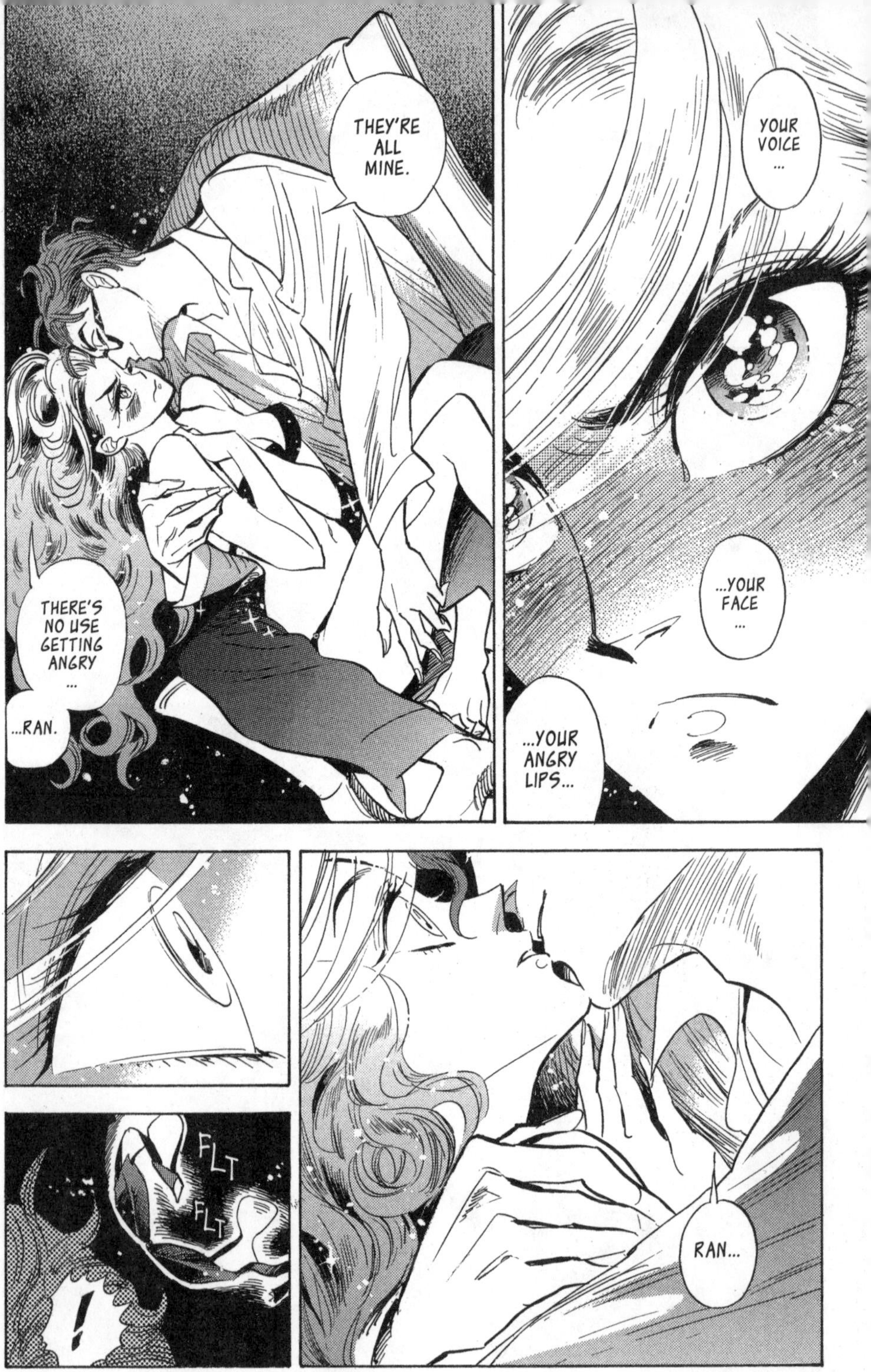
YOUR VOICE ...
...YOUR FACE ...
...YOUR ANGRY LIPS...
THEY'RE ALL MINE.
THERE'S NO USE GETTING ANGRY ...
...RAN.
RAN...
FLT
FLT
!

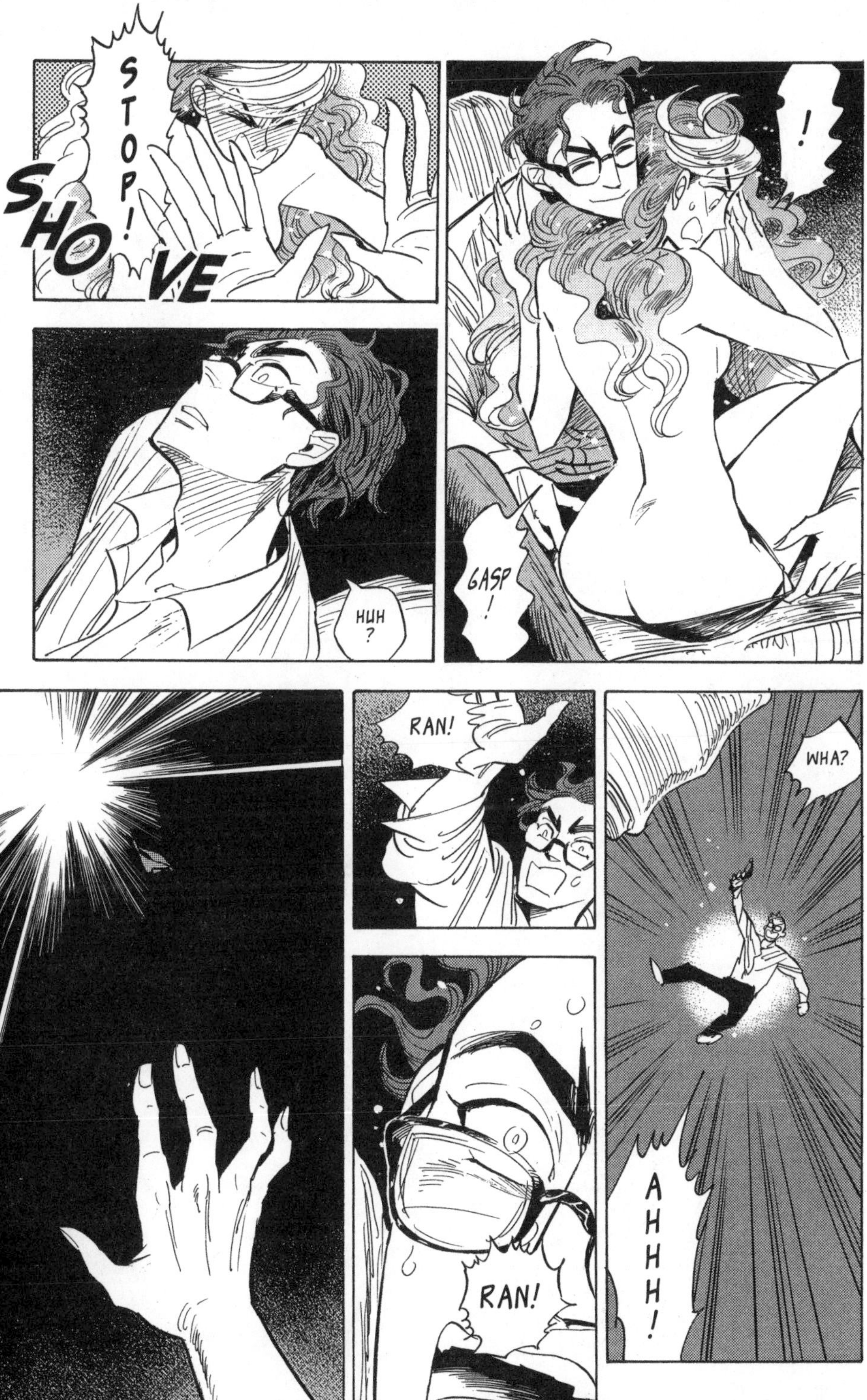
!
GASP!
STOP!
SHOVE
HUH?
WHA?
AHHHH!
RAN!
RAN!

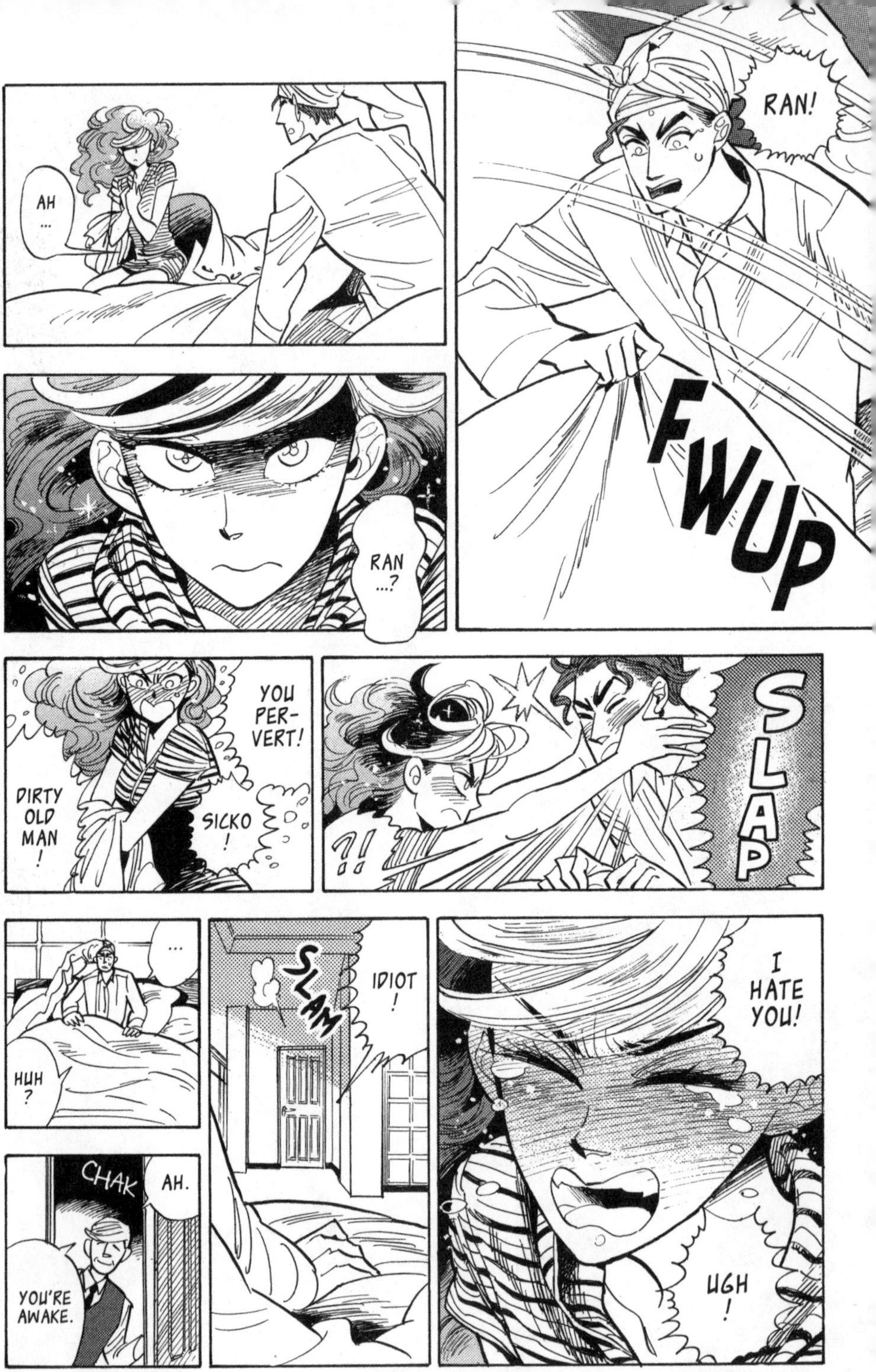
RAN!
FWUP
AH ...
RAN ...?
YOU PER-VERT!
SLAP
?!
SICKO!
DIRTY OLD MAN!
I HATE YOU!
UGH!
IDIOT!
SLAM
...
HUH?
AH.
CHAK
YOU'RE AWAKE.

Chapter 12 / The End

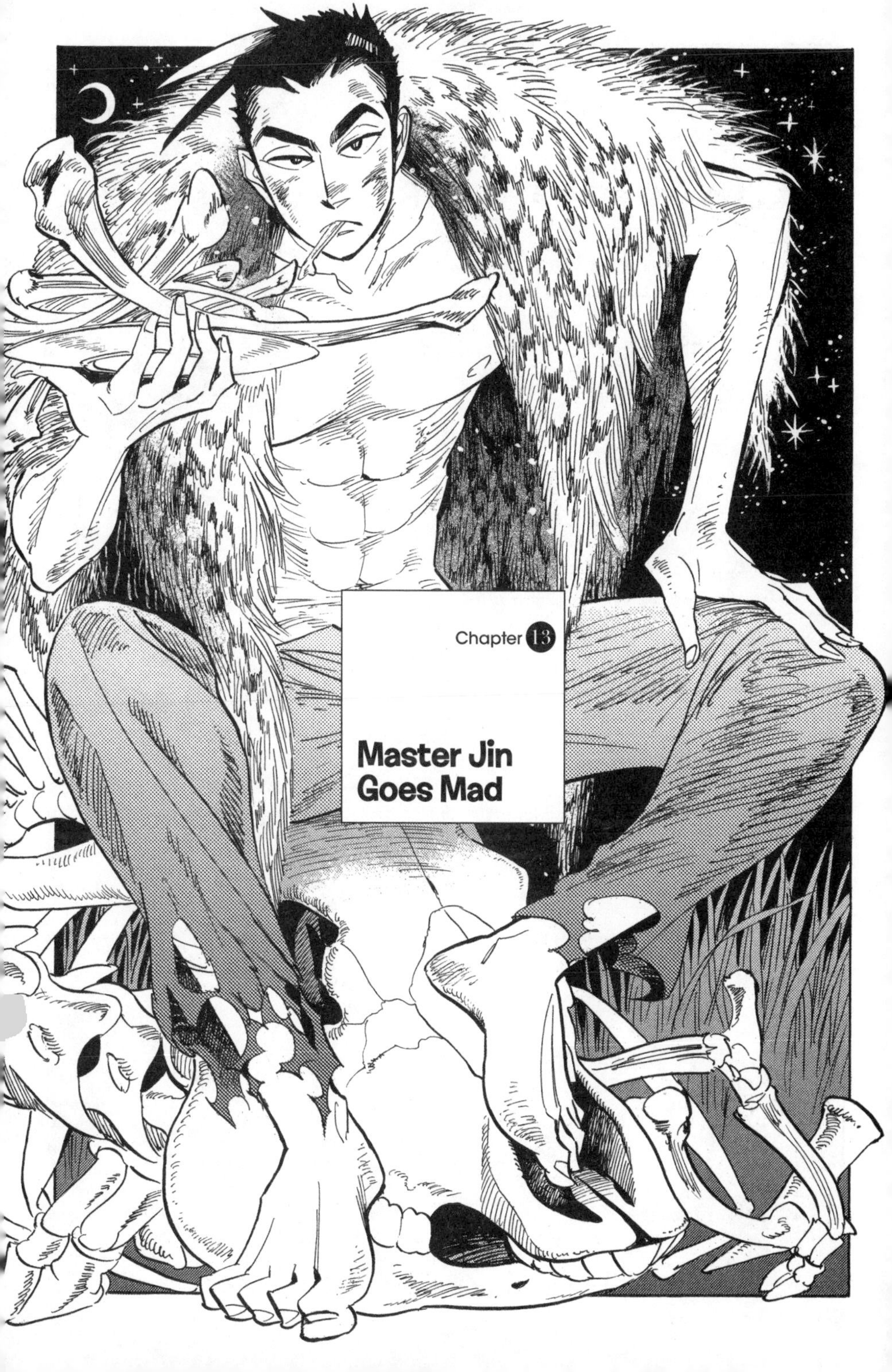
Chapter 13
Master Jin
Goes Mad

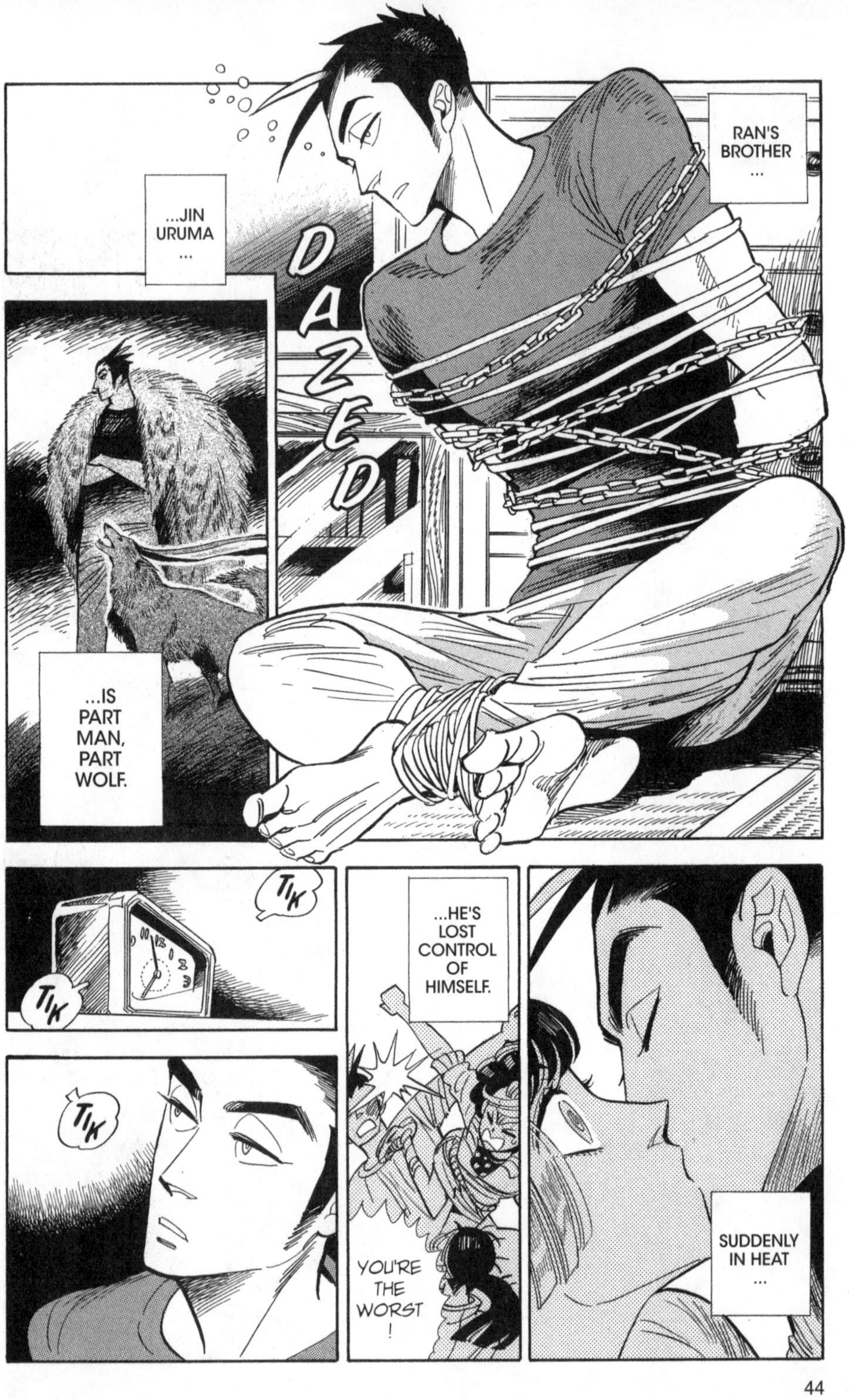
RAN'S BROTHER ...
...JIN URUMA ...
DAZED
...IS PART MAN, PART WOLF.
SUDDENLY IN HEAT ...
...HE'S LOST CONTROL OF HIMSELF.
YOU'RE THE WORST !
TIK
TIK
TIK

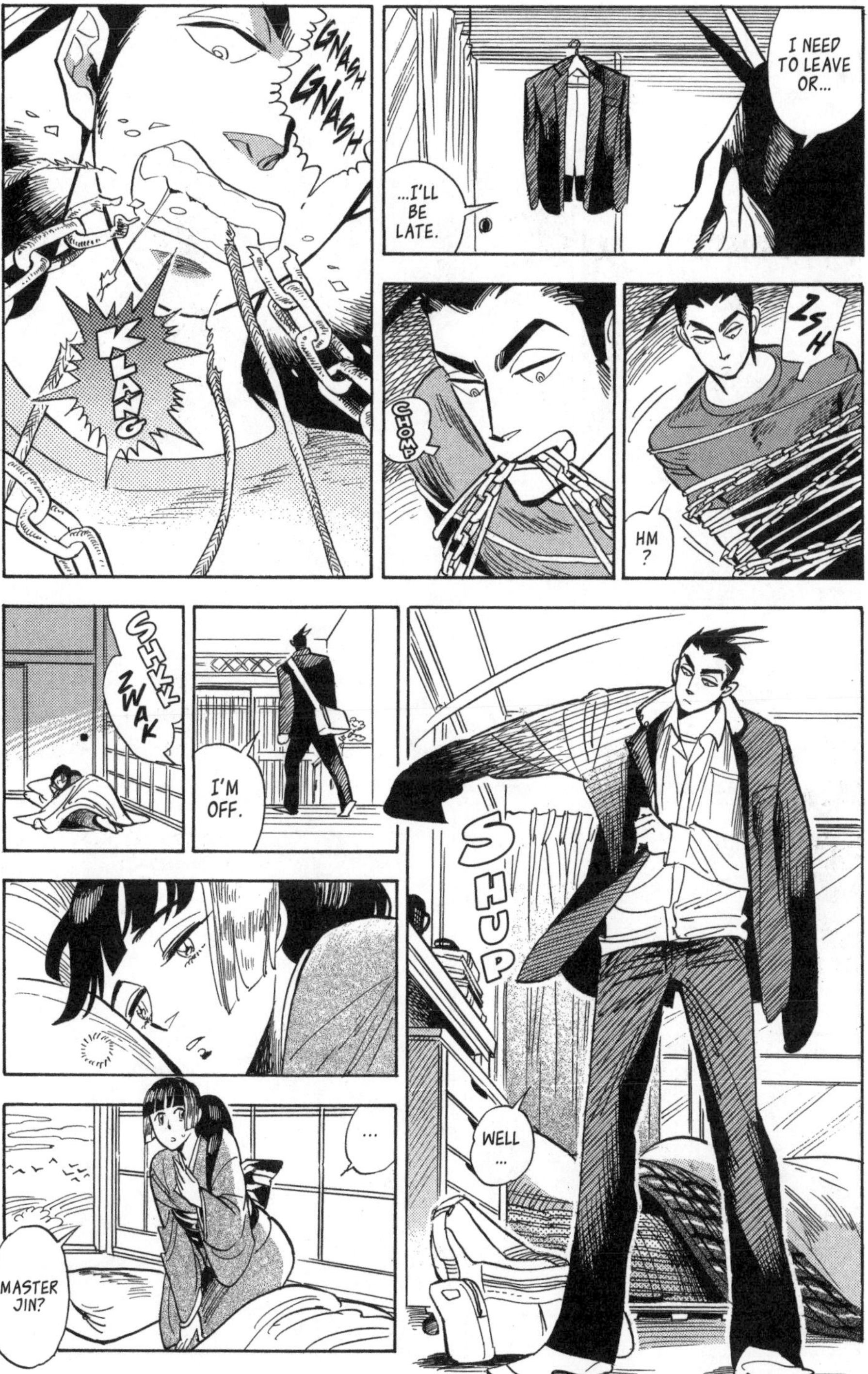
I NEED TO LEAVE OR...
...I'LL BE LATE.
ZSH
HM?
CHOMP
GNASH GNASH
KLANG
SHUP
WELL ...
I'M OFF.
SHHK ZWAK
...
MASTER JIN?

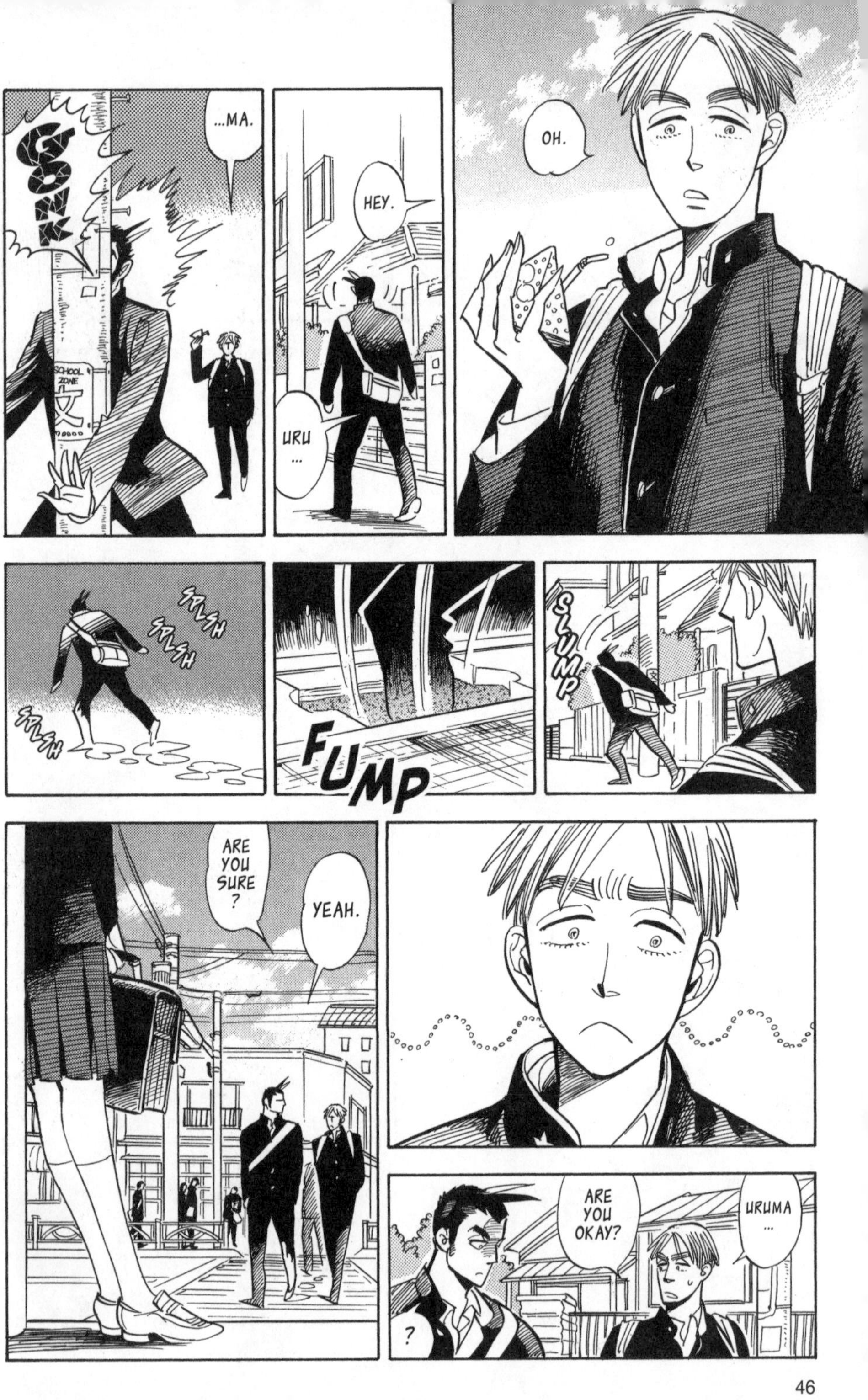
OH.
HEY.
URU ...
...MA.
GONK
SCHOOL ZONE
文
SLUMP
FUMP
SPLSH
SPLSH
SPLSH
URUMA ...
ARE YOU OKAY?
?
ARE YOU SURE?
YEAH.

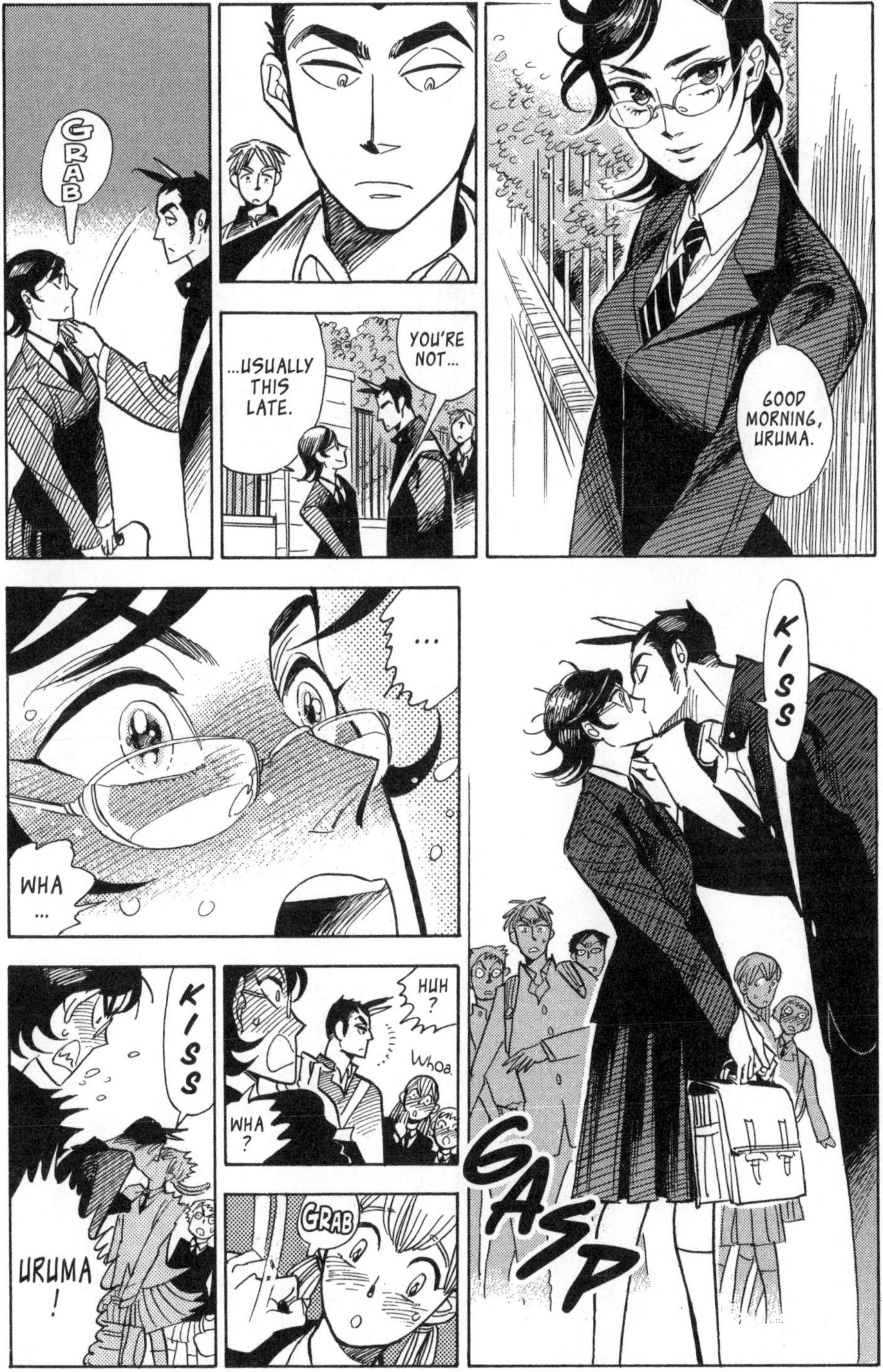
GOOD MORNING, URUMA.
YOU'RE NOT...
...USUALLY THIS LATE.
GRAB
KISS
GASP
...
WHA ...
HUH ?
Whoa.
WHA ?
GRAB
KISS
URUMA !

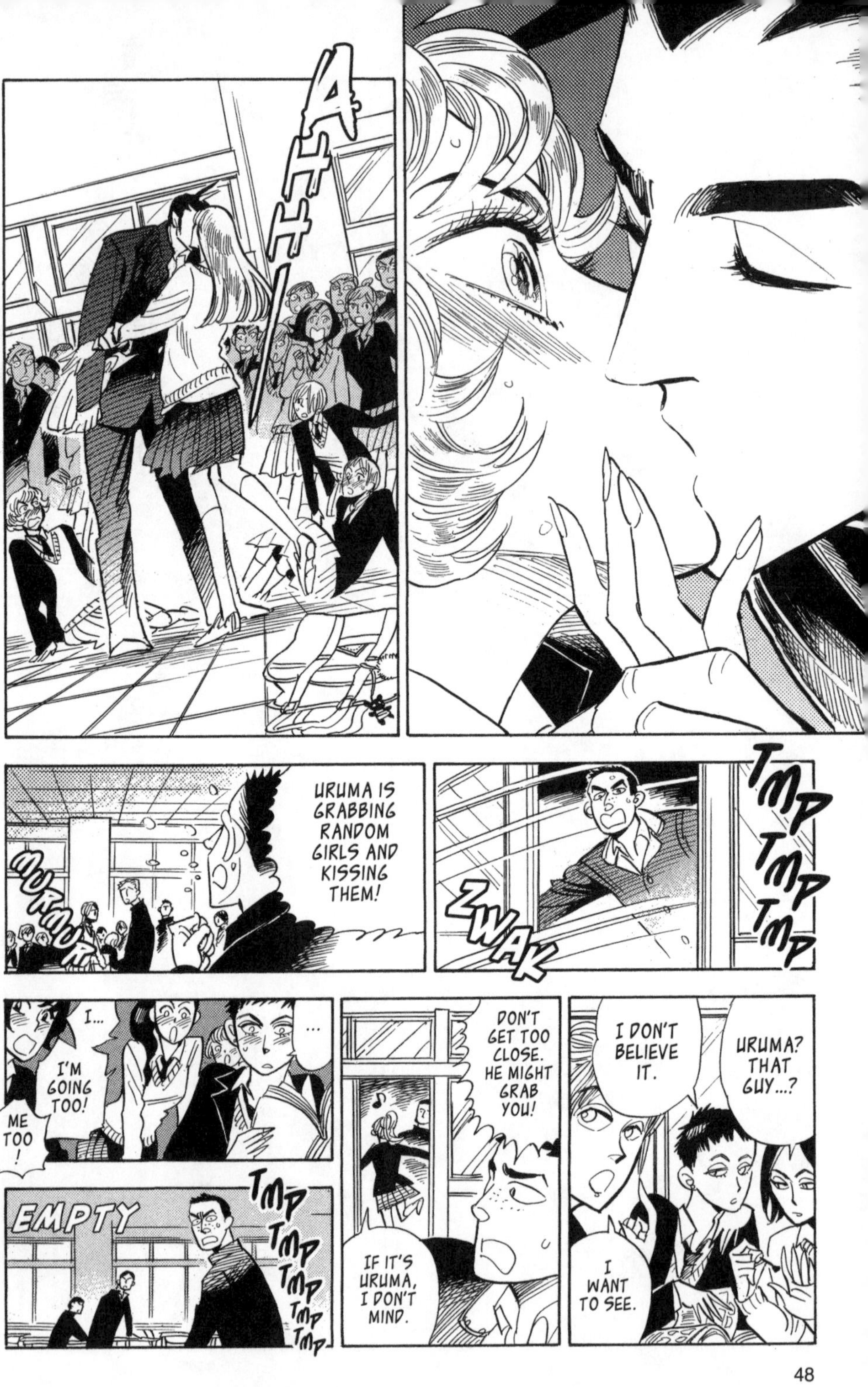
AHHH!
TMP TMP TMP TMP
ZWAK
URUMA IS GRABBING RANDOM GIRLS AND KISSING THEM!
MURMUR
URUMA? THAT GUY...?
I DON'T BELIEVE IT.
I WANT TO SEE.
DON'T GET TOO CLOSE. HE MIGHT GRAB YOU!
IF IT'S URUMA, I DON'T MIND.
...
I...
I'M GOING TOO!
ME TOO!
TMP TMP TMP TMP TMP TMP
EMPTY

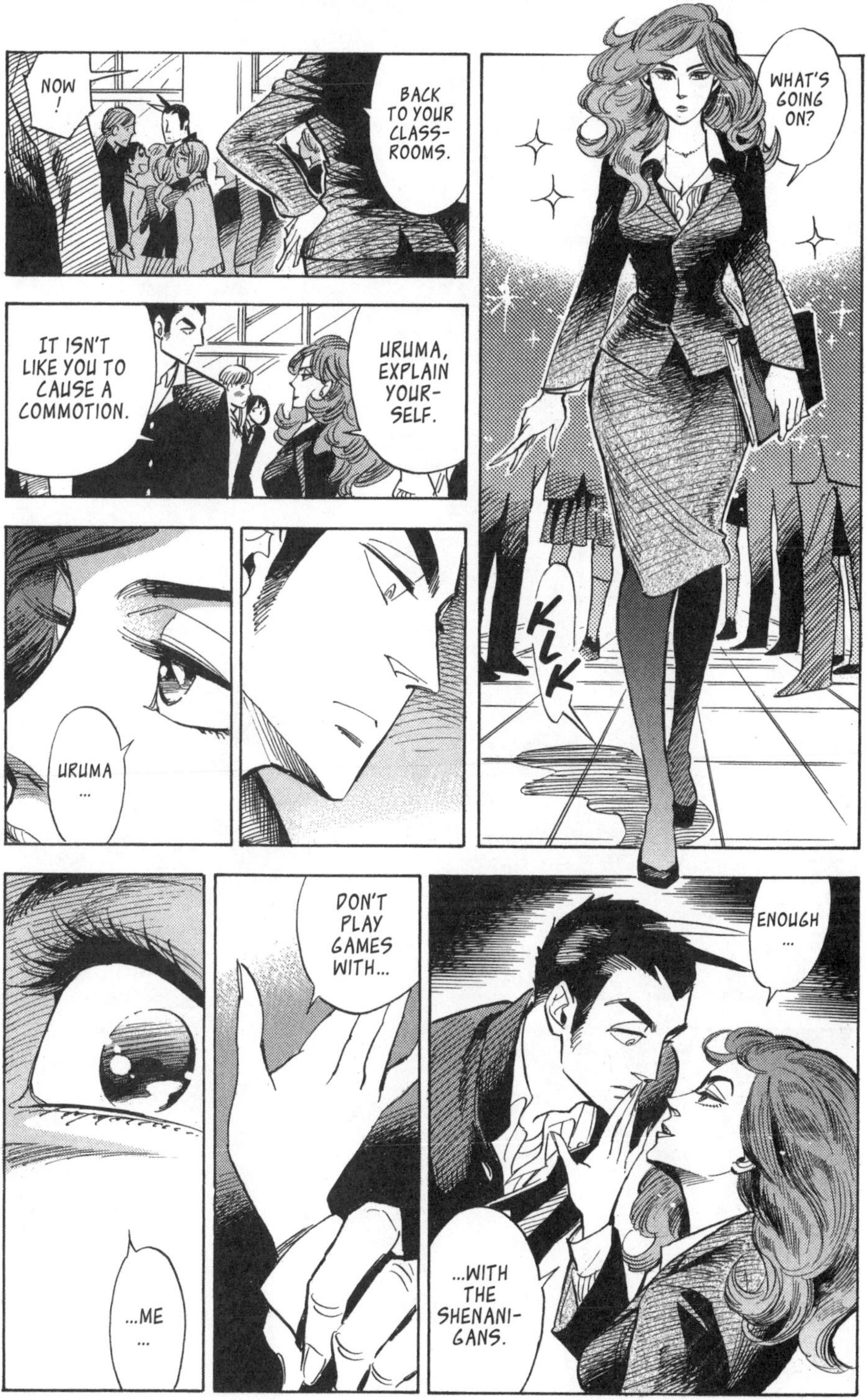
WHAT'S GOING ON?
KLK
BACK TO YOUR CLASS-ROOMS.
NOW!
URUMA, EXPLAIN YOUR-SELF.
IT ISN'T LIKE YOU TO CAUSE A COMMOTION.
URUMA...
ENOUGH...
...WITH THE SHENANI-GANS.
DON'T PLAY GAMES WITH...
...ME...

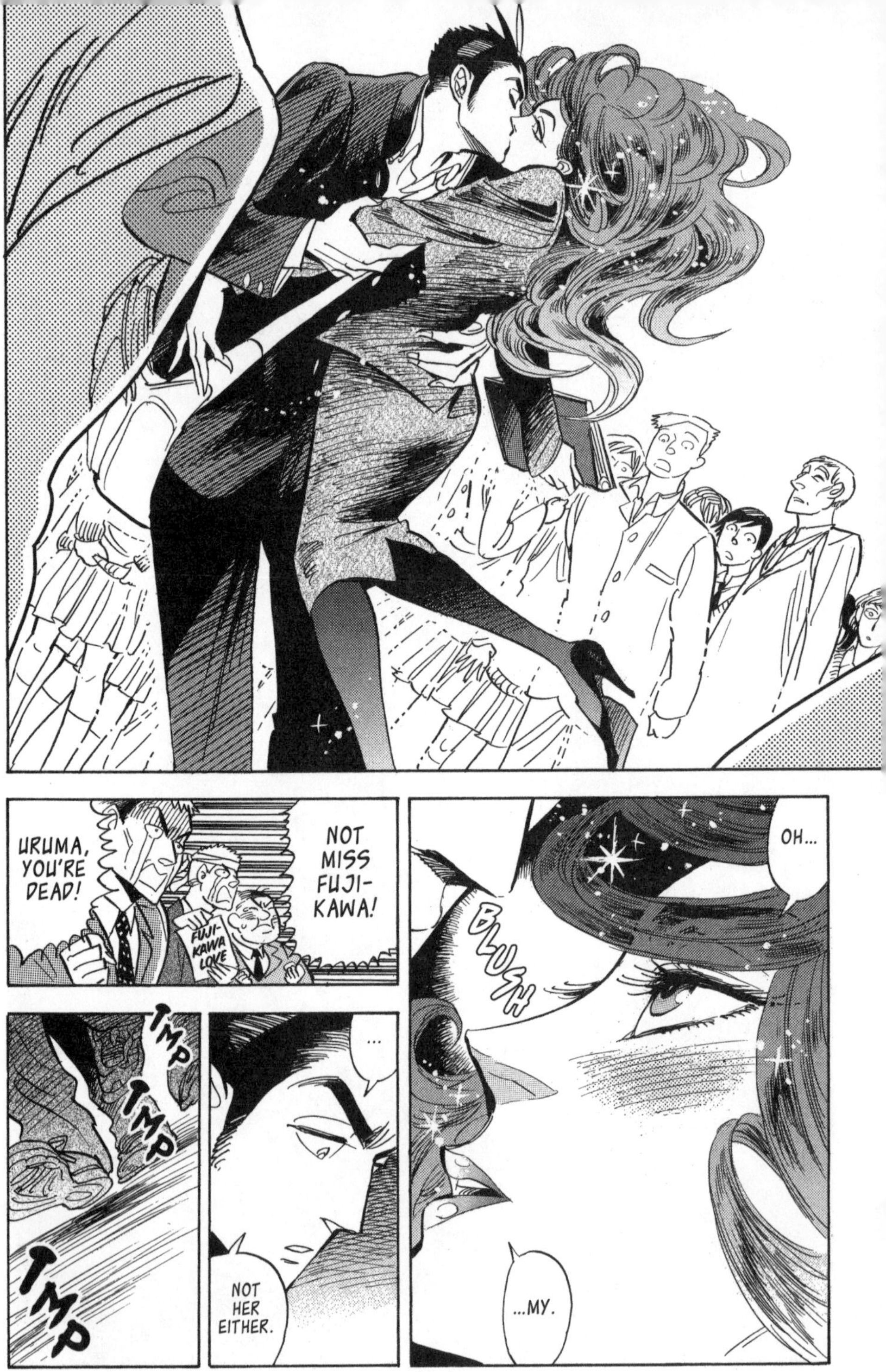
OH...
BLUSH
...MY.
NOT MISS FUJI-KAWA!
FUJI-KAWA LOVE
URUMA, YOU'RE DEAD!
...
NOT HER EITHER.
TMP
TMP
TMP
TMP

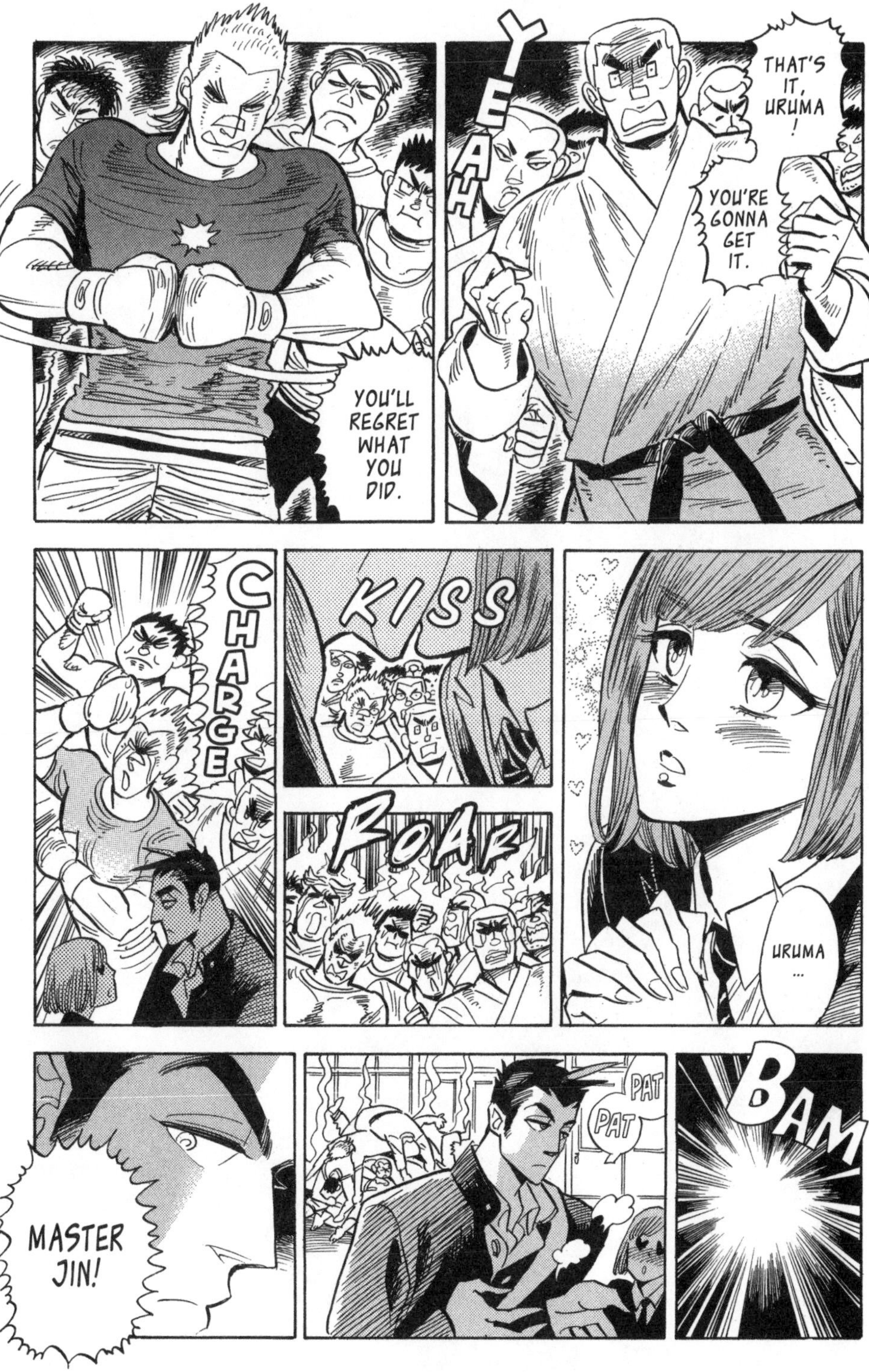
THAT'S IT, URUMA!
YEAH
YOU'RE GONNA GET IT.
YOU'LL REGRET WHAT YOU DID.
URUMA...
KISS
ROAR
CHARGE
BAM
PAT
PAT
MASTER JIN!

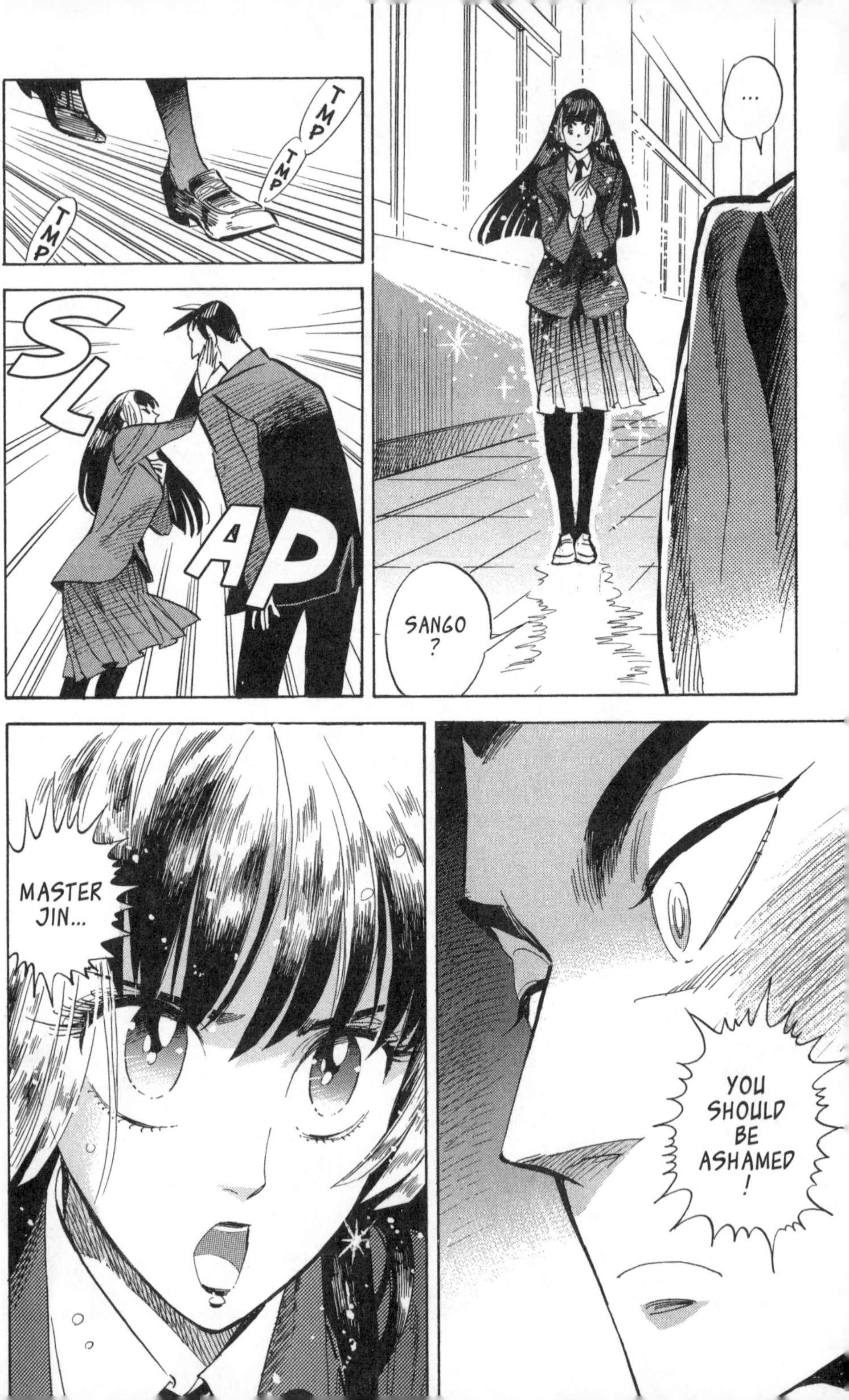
...
SANGO?
TMP TMP TMP
SLAP
YOU SHOULD BE ASHAMED!
MASTER JIN...

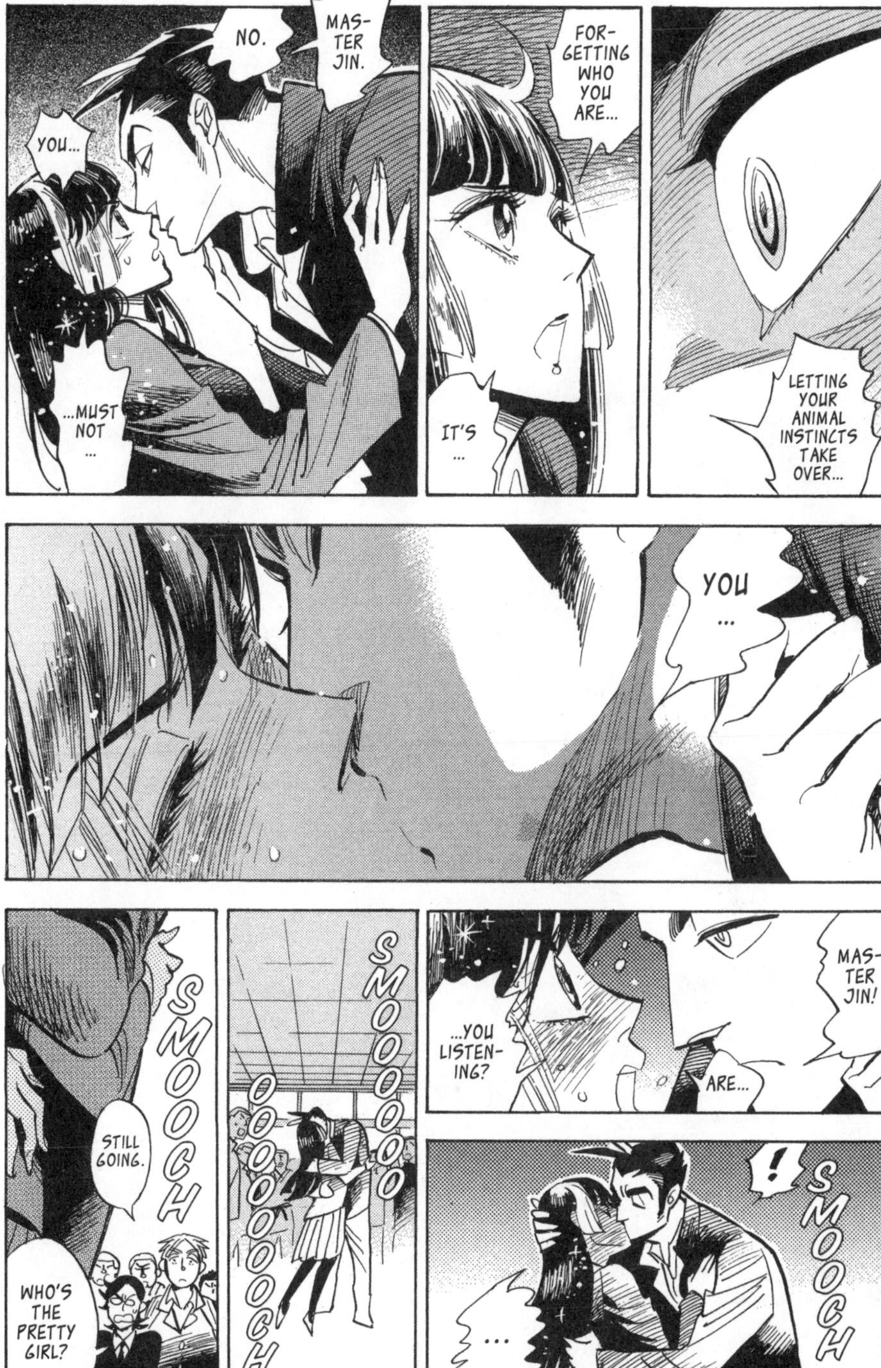
LETTING YOUR ANIMAL INSTINCTS TAKE OVER...
FOR-GETTING WHO YOU ARE...
IT'S ...
MAS-TER JIN.
NO.
YOU...
...MUST NOT ...
YOU ...
MAS-TER JIN!
ARE...
...YOU LISTEN-ING?
!
SMOOCH
...
SMOOOOOOOOOOOOOOOCH
SMOOOCH
STILL GOING.
WHO'S THE PRETTY GIRL?

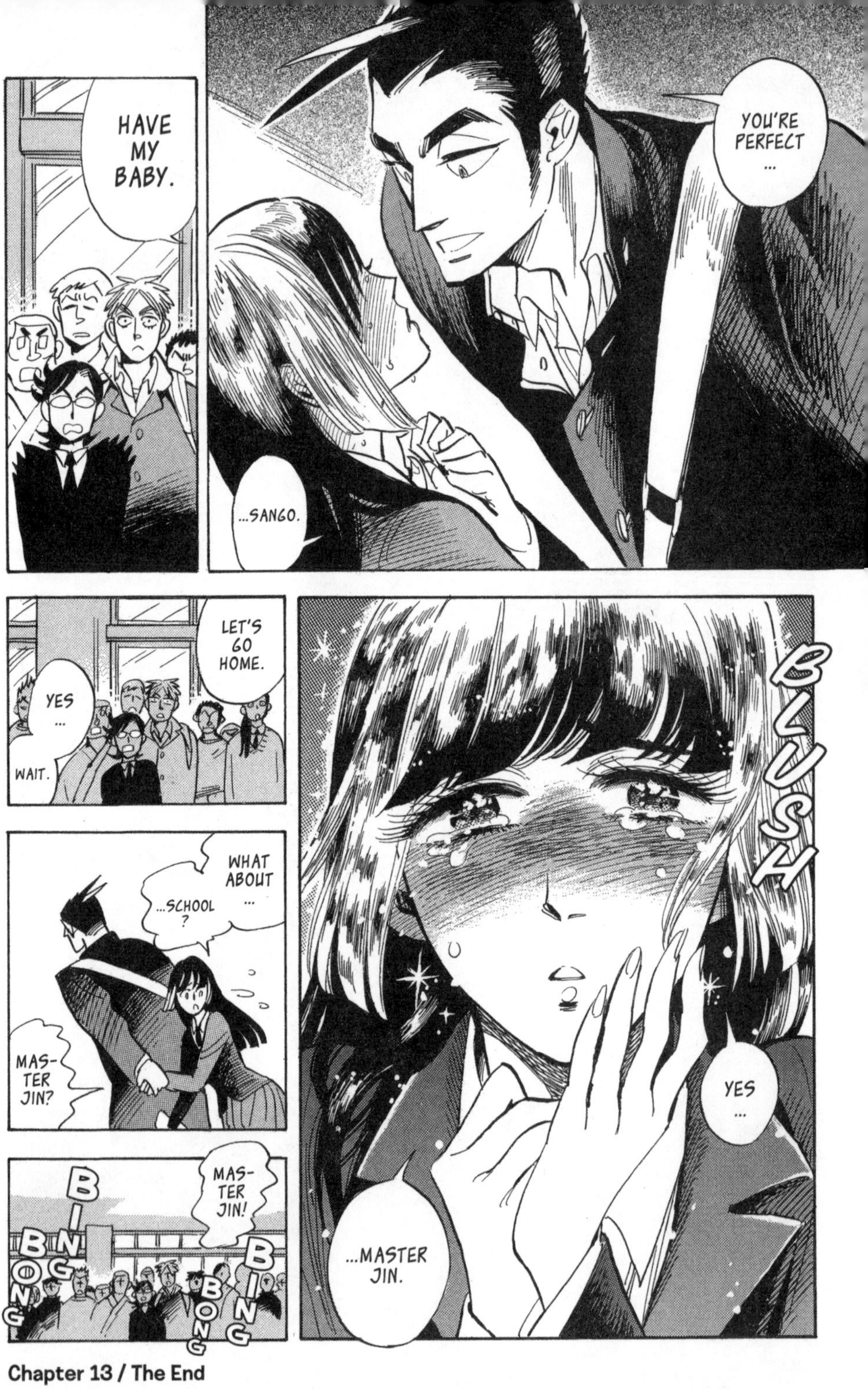
YOU'RE PERFECT ...
...SANGO.
HAVE MY BABY.
BLUSH
YES ...
...MASTER JIN.
LET'S GO HOME.
YES ...
WAIT.
WHAT ABOUT ...
...SCHOOL ?
MASTER JIN?
MASTER JIN!
BING
BONG
BING
BONG

Chapter 13 / The End

Chapter 14

Haimachi Neighbors

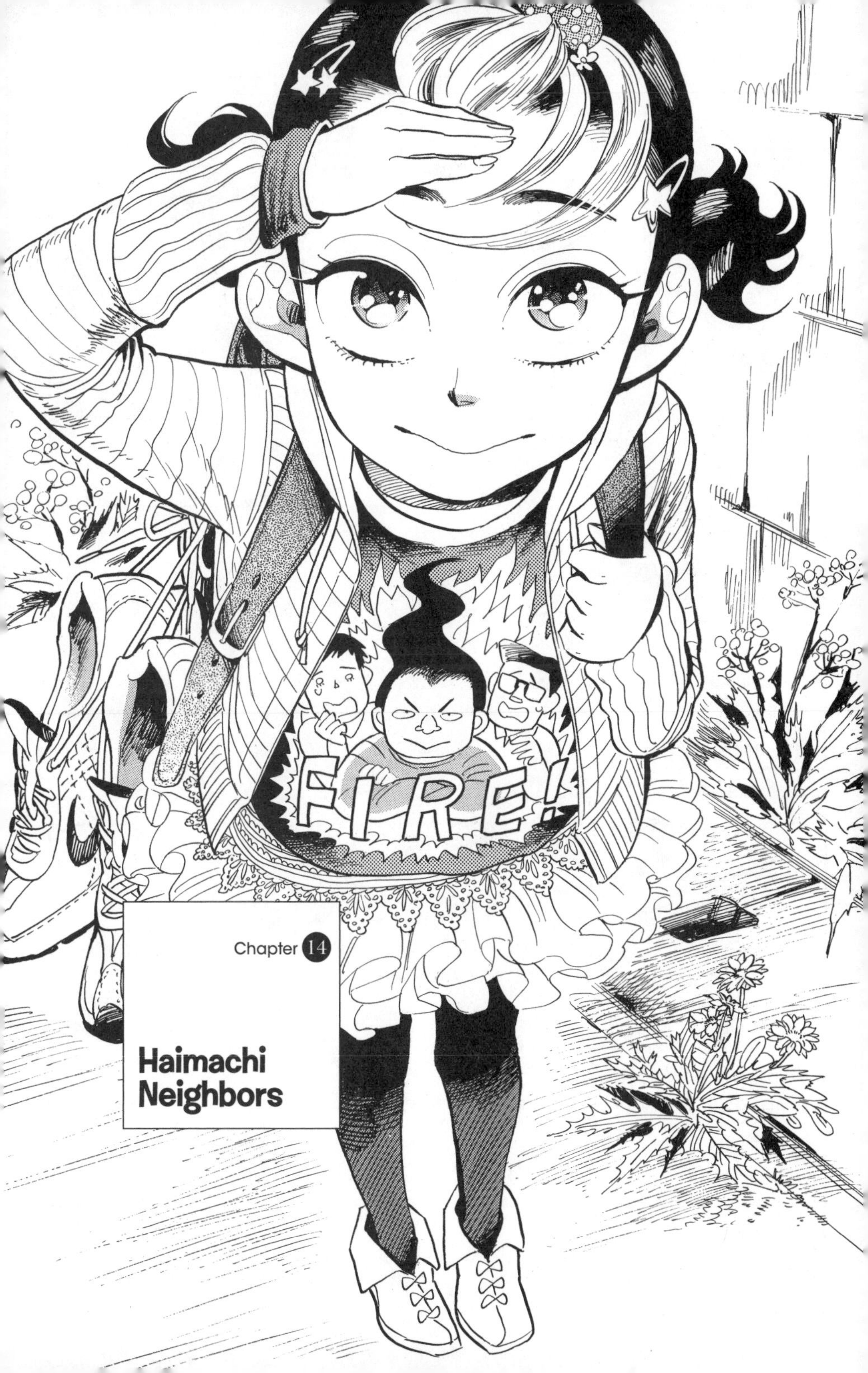
FIRE!

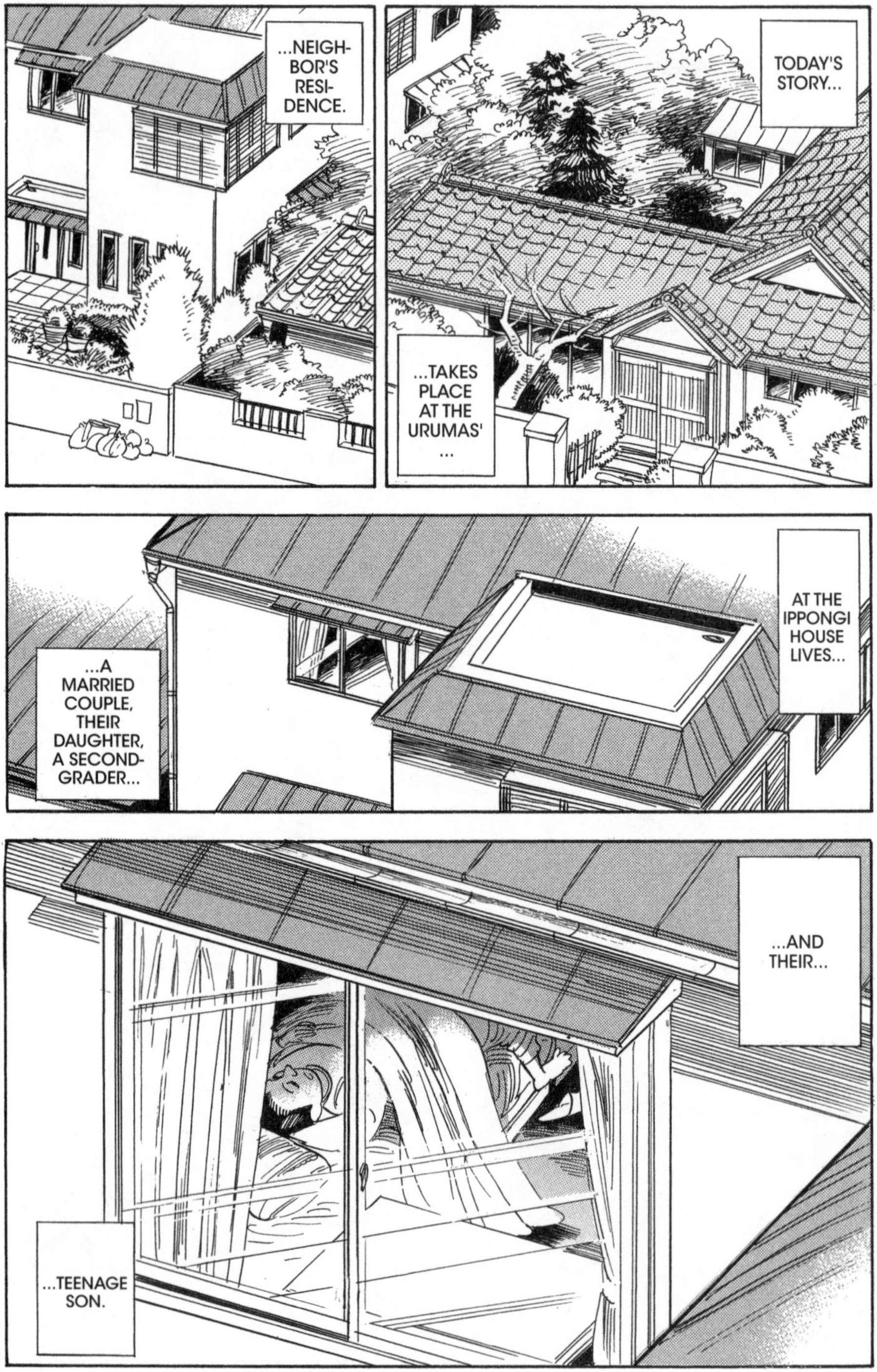
TODAY'S STORY...
...TAKES PLACE AT THE URUMAS' ...
...NEIGH-BOR'S RESI-DENCE.
AT THE IPPONGI HOUSE LIVES...
...A MARRIED COUPLE, THEIR DAUGHTER, A SECOND-GRADER...
...AND THEIR...
...TEENAGE SON.

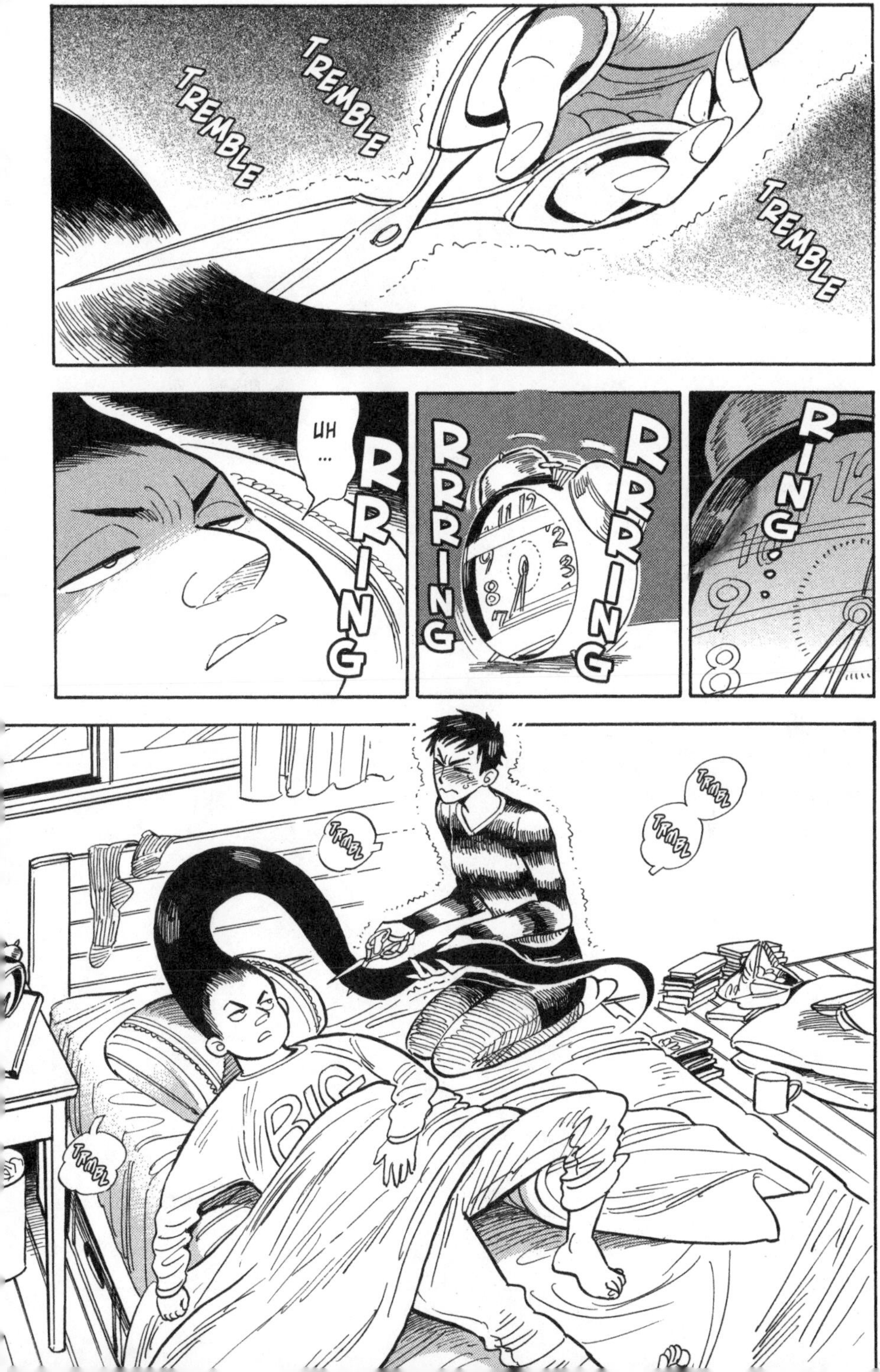
TREMBLE
TREMBLE
TREMBLE
RING...
RRRING
RRRING
UH ...
RRRING
TRMBL
TRMBL
TRMBL
TRMBL

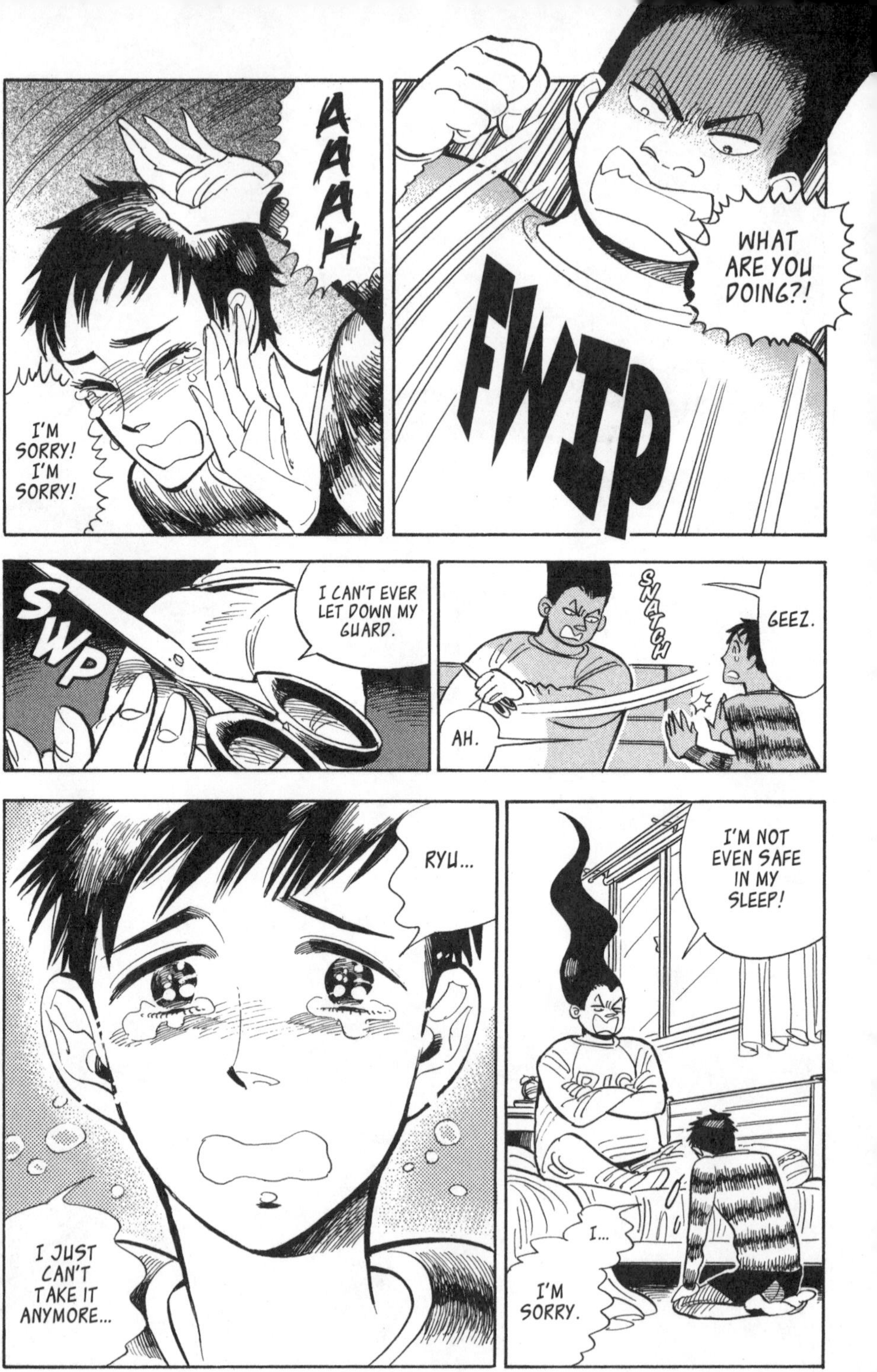
WHAT ARE YOU DOING?!
FWIP
AAAAH
I'M SORRY! I'M SORRY!
GEEZ.
SNATCH
AH.
I CAN'T EVER LET DOWN MY GUARD.
SWP
I'M NOT EVEN SAFE IN MY SLEEP!
I...
I'M SORRY.
RYU...
I JUST CAN'T TAKE IT ANYMORE...

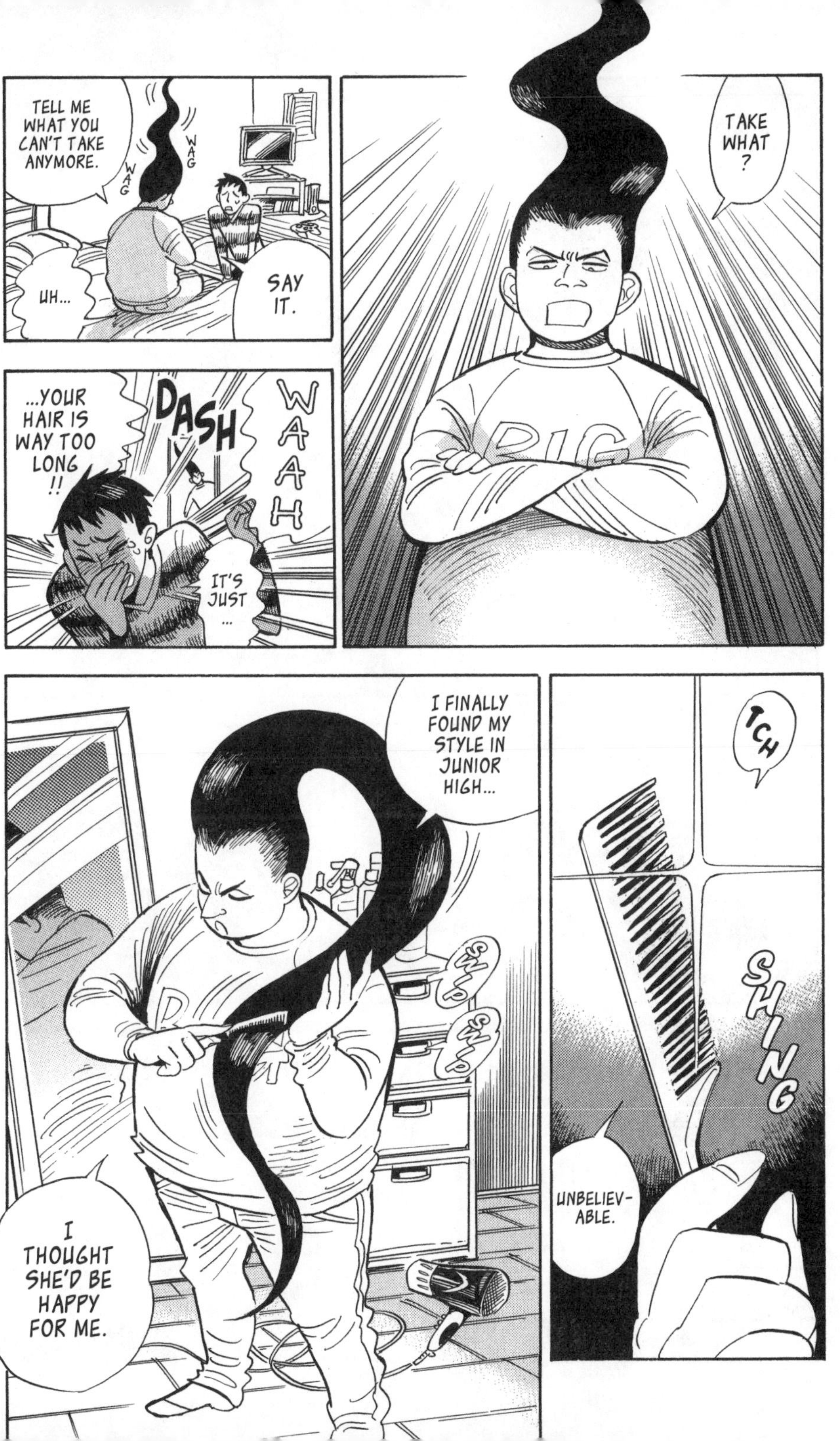
TAKE WHAT?
WAG
WAG
TELL ME WHAT YOU CAN'T TAKE ANYMORE.
SAY IT.
UH...
WAAAH
DASH
...YOUR HAIR IS WAY TOO LONG!!
IT'S JUST...
TCH
SHING
UNBELIEV-ABLE.
I FINALLY FOUND MY STYLE IN JUNIOR HIGH...
SWIP
SWIP
I THOUGHT SHE'D BE HAPPY FOR ME.

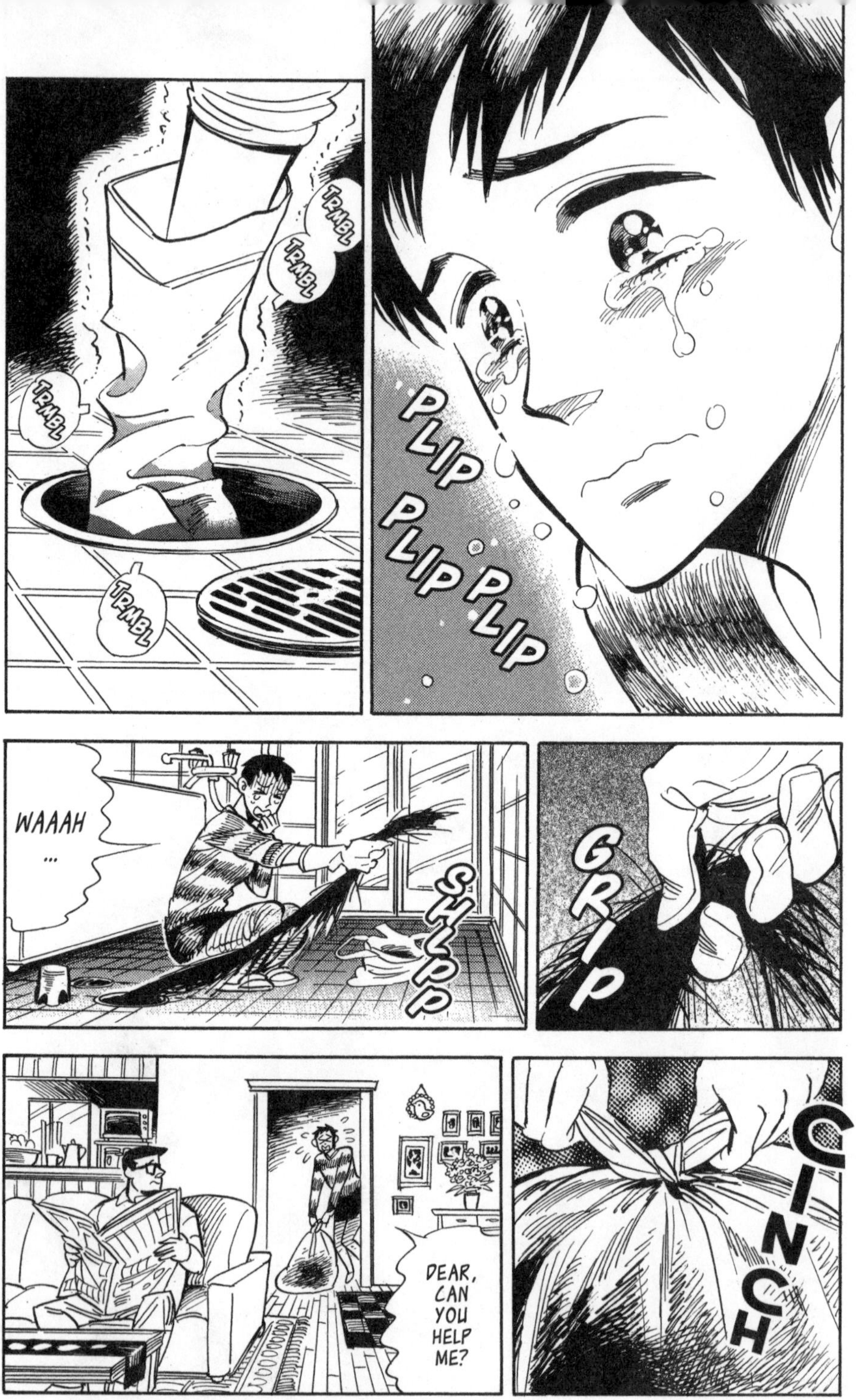
PLIP PLIP PLIP PLIP
TRMBL
TRMBL
TRMBL
TRMBL
GRIP
SHLPP
WAAAH ...
CINCH
DEAR, CAN YOU HELP ME?

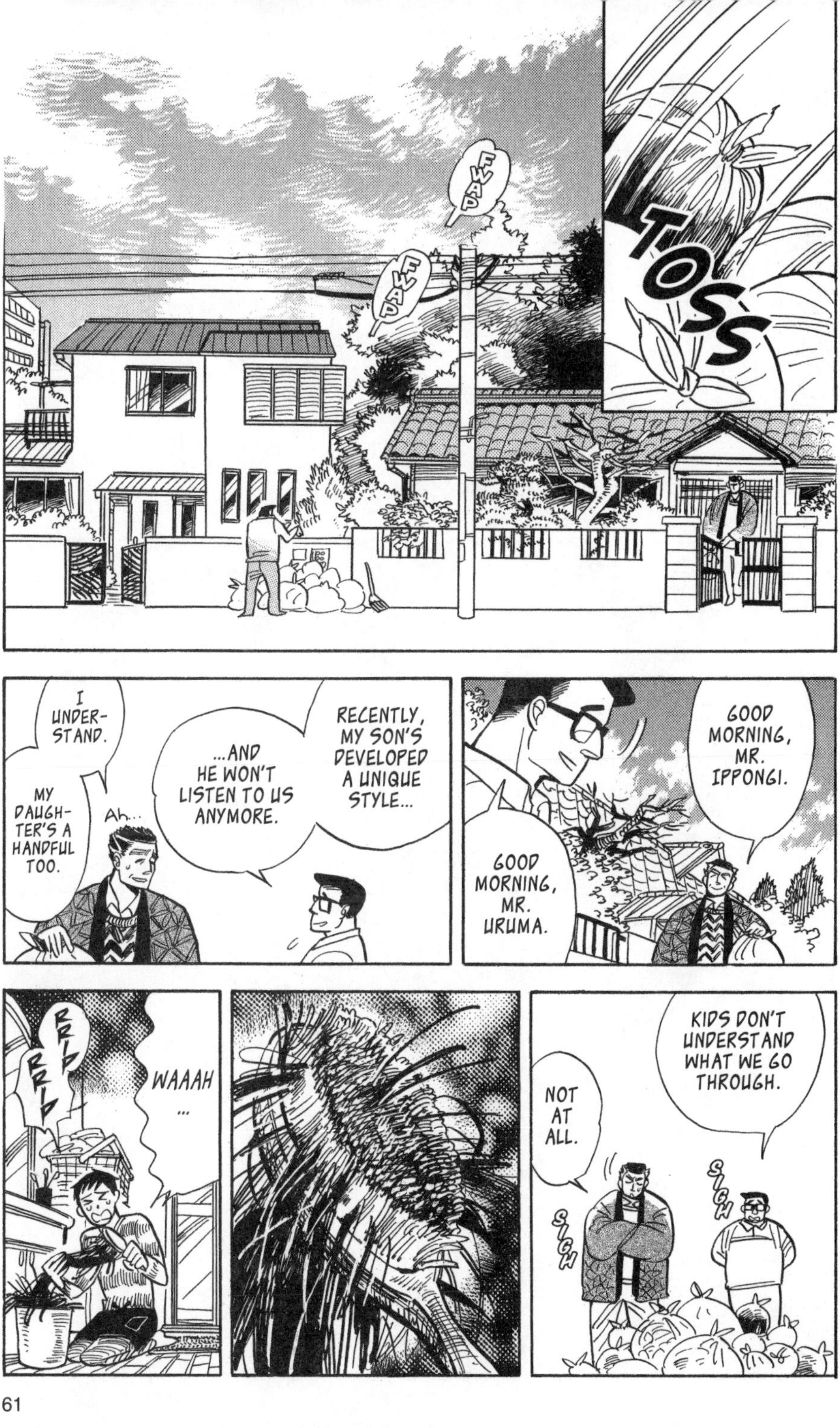
TOSS
FWAP
FWAP
GOOD MORNING, MR. IPPONGI.
GOOD MORNING, MR. URUMA.
RECENTLY, MY SON'S DEVELOPED A UNIQUE STYLE...
...AND HE WON'T LISTEN TO US ANYMORE.
I UNDER-STAND.
Ah...
MY DAUGHTER'S A HANDFUL TOO.
KIDS DON'T UNDERSTAND WHAT WE GO THROUGH.
NOT AT ALL.
SIGH
SIGH
RRIP
RRIP
WAAAH ...

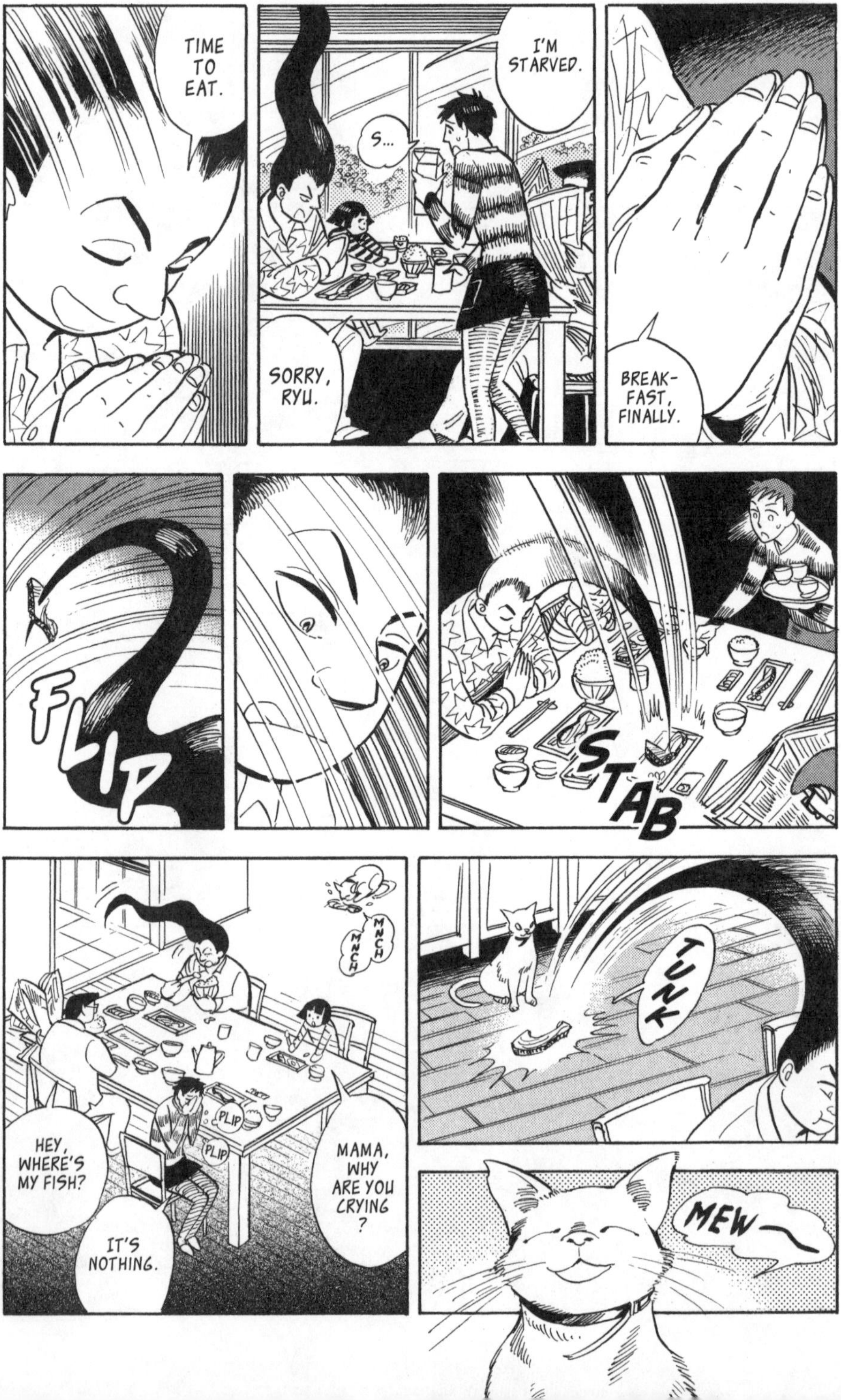
BREAK-FAST, FINALLY.
I'M STARVED.
S...
SORRY, RYU.
TIME TO EAT.
STAB
FLIP
TUNK
MEW—
MNCH
MNCH
MAMA, WHY ARE YOU CRYING?
PLIP
PLIP
HEY, WHERE'S MY FISH?
IT'S NOTHING.

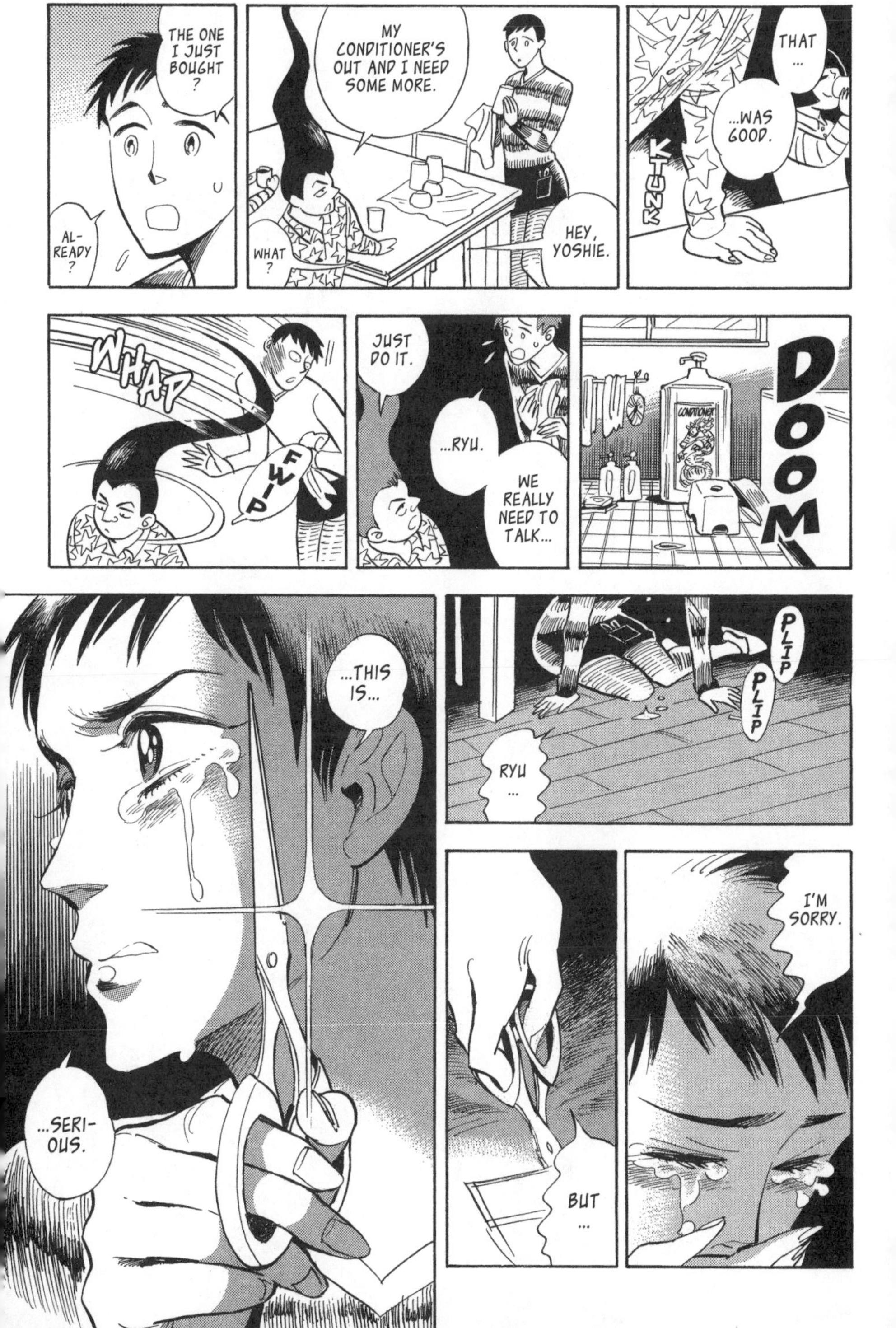
THAT ...
...WAS GOOD.
KTUNK
HEY, YOSHIE.
WHAT ?
MY CONDITIONER'S OUT AND I NEED SOME MORE.
THE ONE I JUST BOUGHT ?
AL-READY ?
DOOM
CONDITIONER
...RYU.
WE REALLY NEED TO TALK...
JUST DO IT.
WHAP
FWIP
PLIP
PLIP
RYU ...
I'M SORRY.
BUT ...
...THIS IS...
...SERI-OUS.

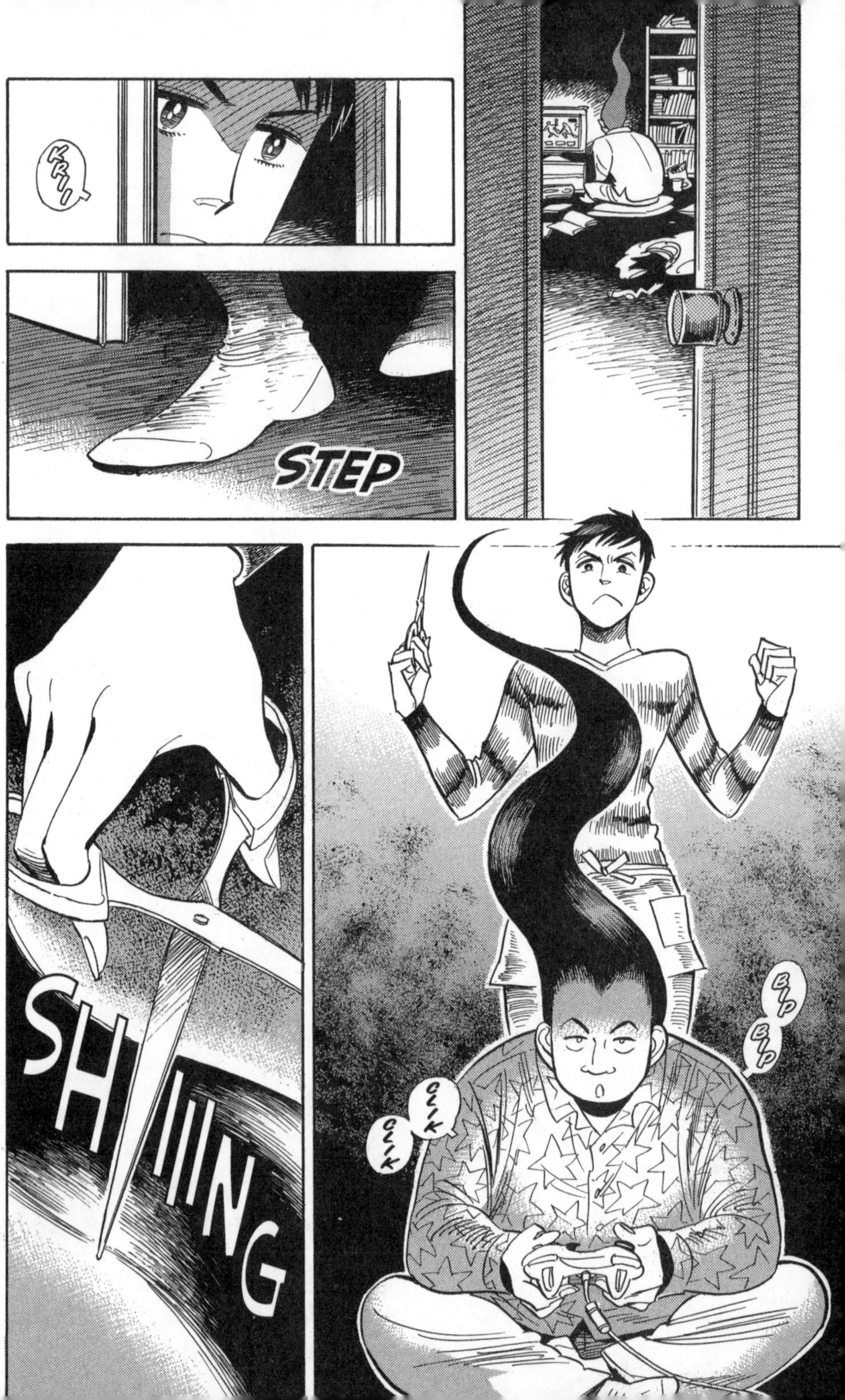
KRII
STEP
BIP BIP
CLIK CLIK
SHIIIING

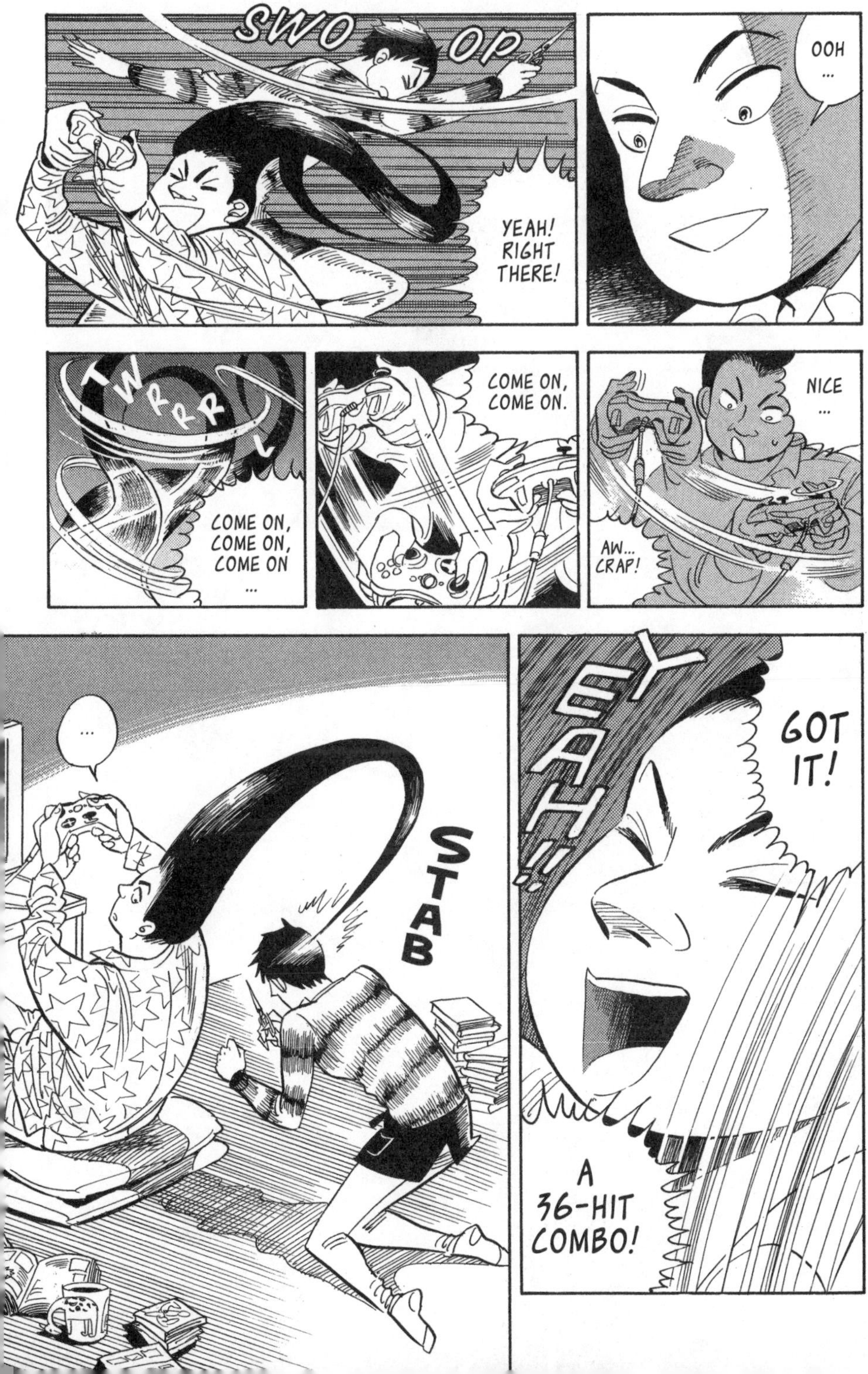
OOH ...
SWOOP
YEAH! RIGHT THERE!
NICE ...
AW... CRAP!
COME ON, COME ON.
TWRRRL
COME ON, COME ON, COME ON ...
YEAH!!
GOT IT!
A 36-HIT COMBO!
...
STAB

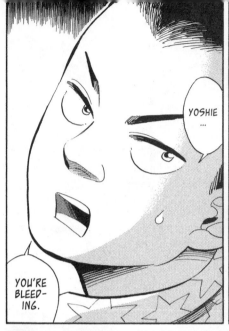

YOSHIE
...

YOU'RE BLEED- ING.

RYU ...

DRIP

FOR YOUR MOM...

...

RYU ...

PLEASE, WOULD YOU CUT YOUR HAIR?

OO-EE
OO-EE

SLUMP

YOSHIE !

YOSHIE !

IT'S RYU!

TMP
TMP
TMP

HAIMACHI HOSPITAL

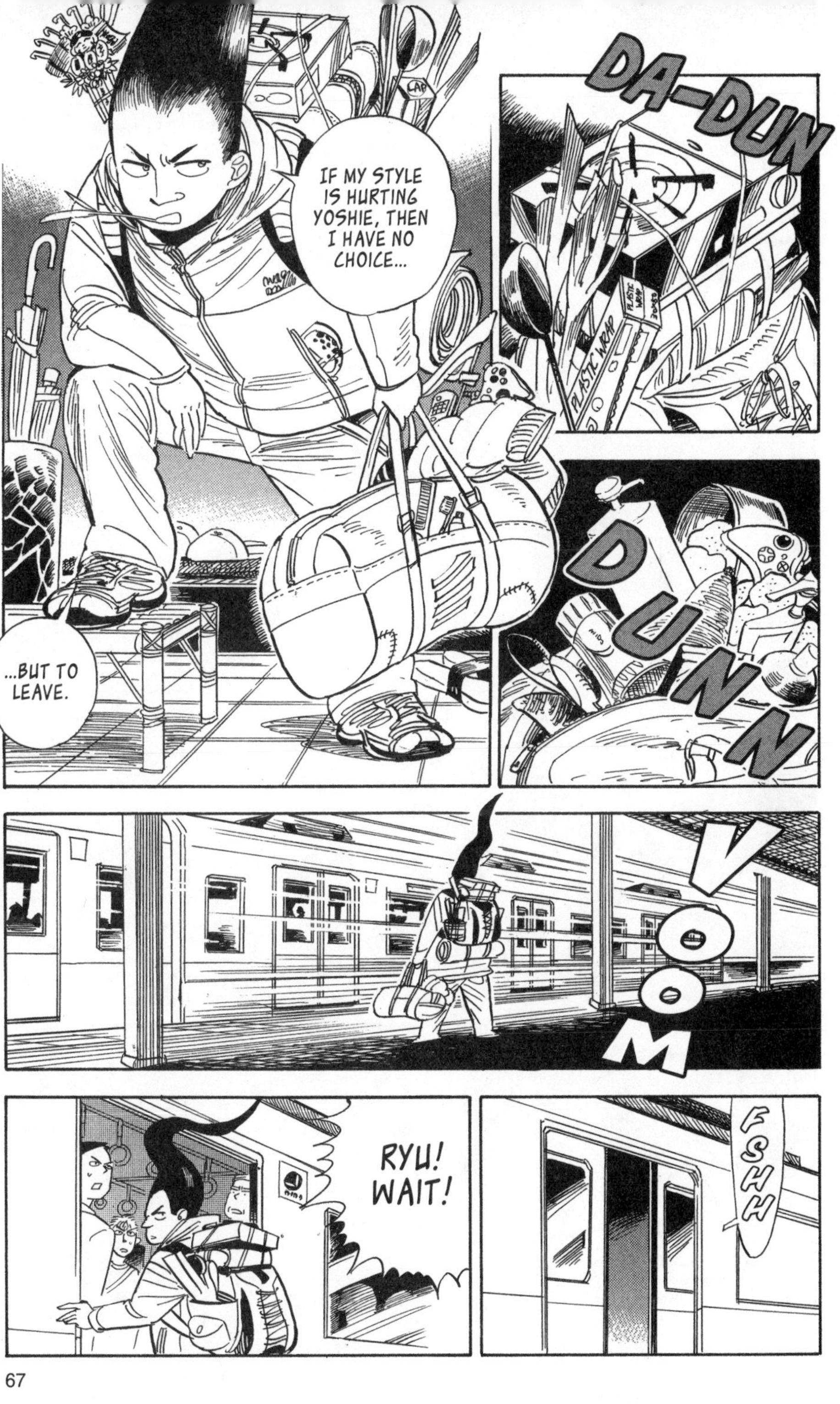
DA-DUN
PLASTIC WRAP
DUNN
IF MY STYLE IS HURTING YOSHIE, THEN I HAVE NO CHOICE...
...BUT TO LEAVE.
VOOOM
FSHH
RYU! WAIT!

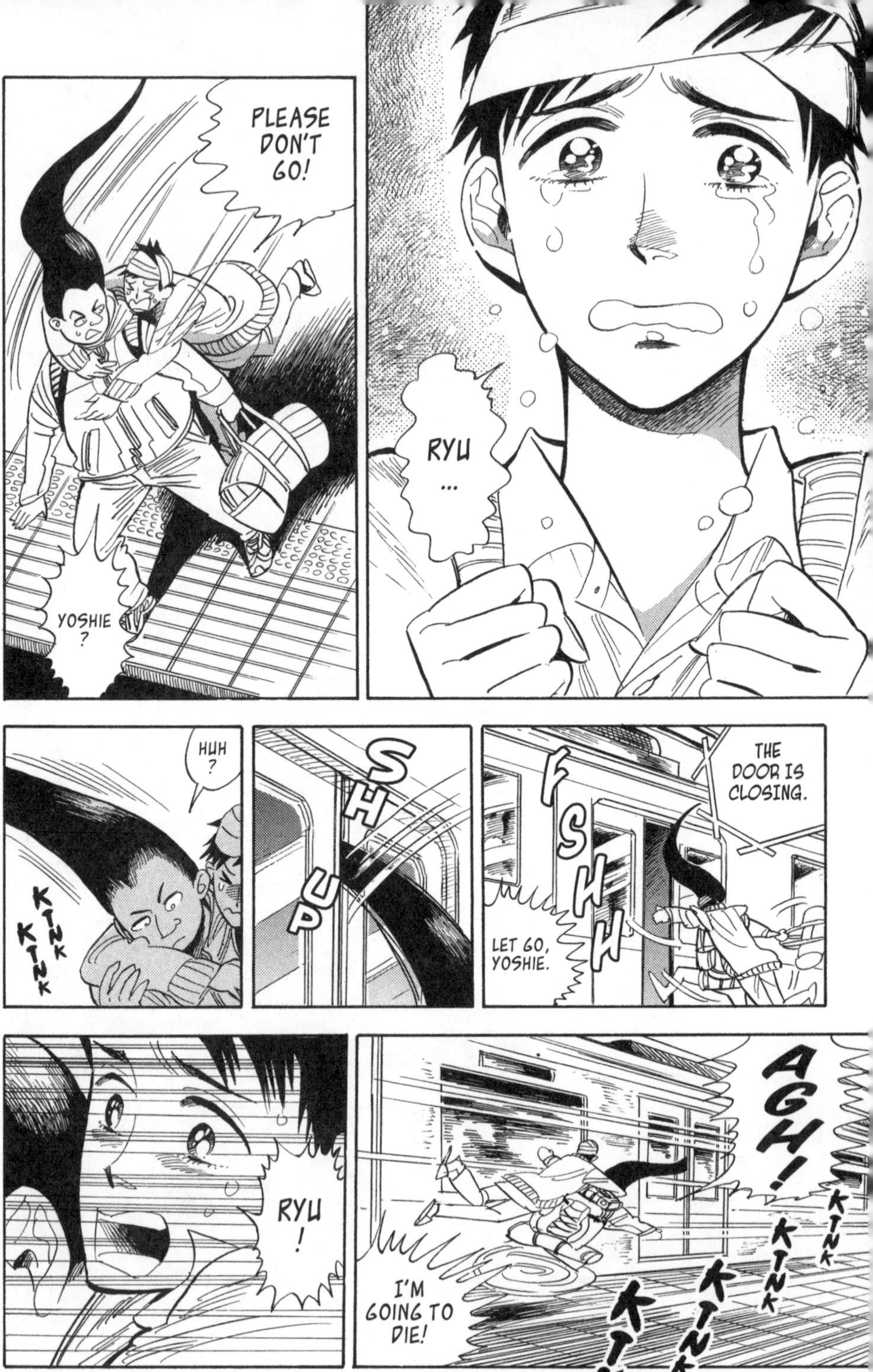
RYU ...
PLEASE DON'T GO!
YOSHIE ?
THE DOOR IS CLOSING.
FSHHH
LET GO, YOSHIE.
SHUP
HUH ?
KTNK KTNK
AGH!
I'M GOING TO DIE!
KTNK KTNK KTNK KTNK
RYU !

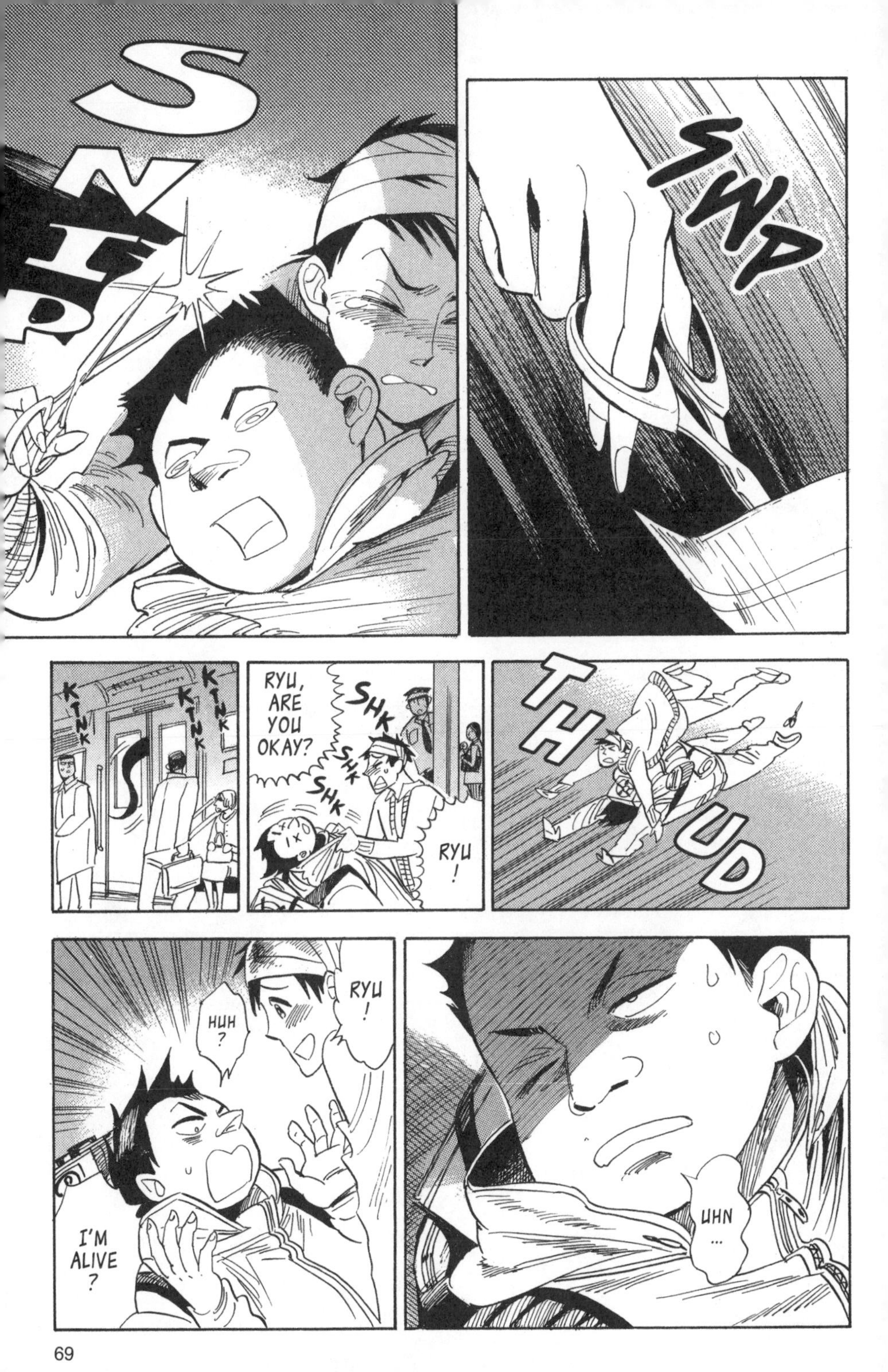
SWIP
SNIP
THUD
RYU, ARE YOU OKAY?
SHK
SHK
SHK
RYU!
KTINK
KTINK
KTINK
UHN...
RYU!
HUH?
I'M ALIVE?

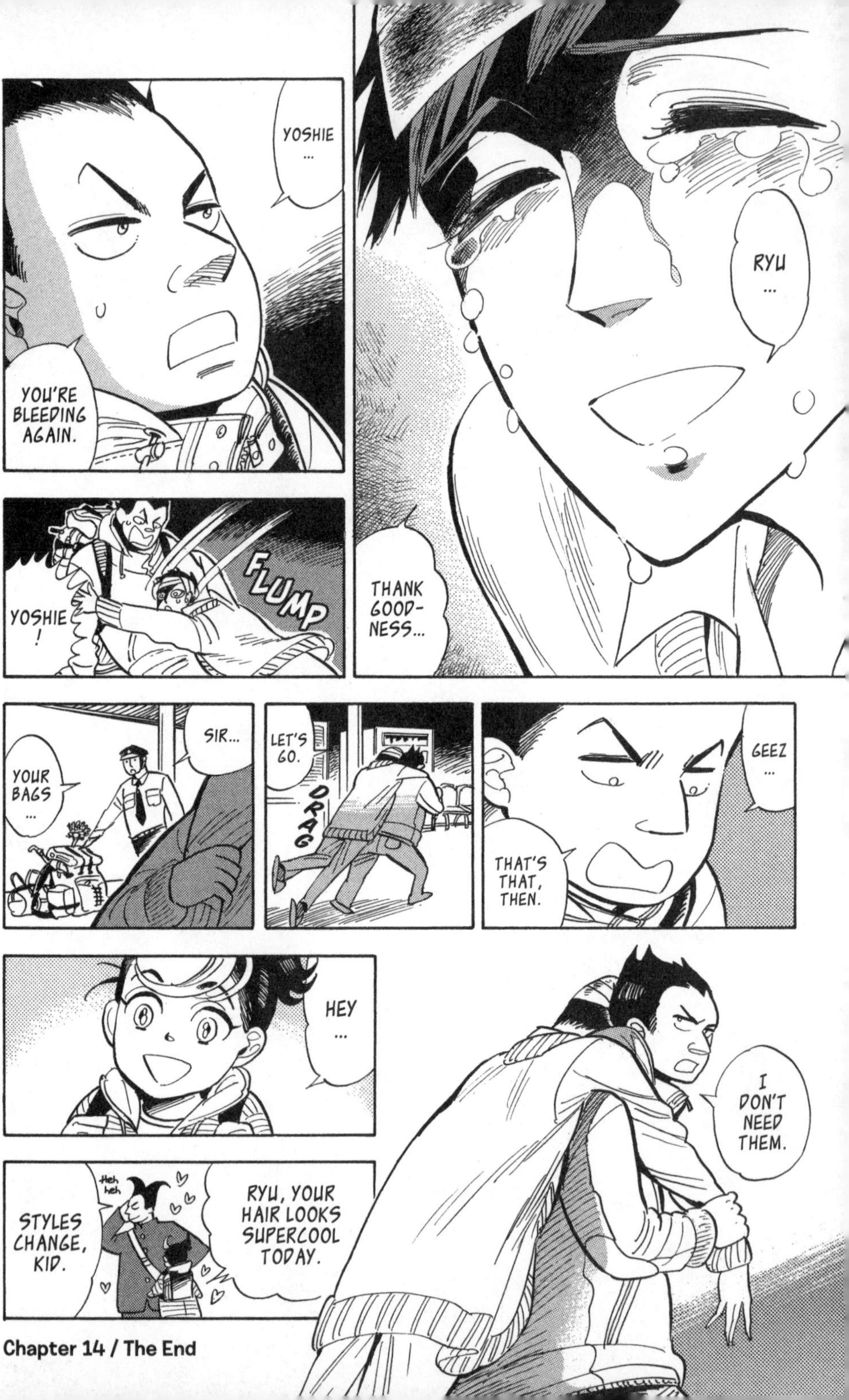
RYU ...
THANK GOOD-NESS...
YOSHIE ...
YOU'RE BLEEDING AGAIN.
FLUMP
YOSHIE !
GEEZ ...
THAT'S THAT, THEN.
LET'S GO.
DRAG
SIR...
YOUR BAGS ...
I DON'T NEED THEM.
HEY ...
RYU, YOUR HAIR LOOKS SUPERCOOL TODAY.
Heh heh
STYLES CHANGE, KID.

Chapter 14 / The End

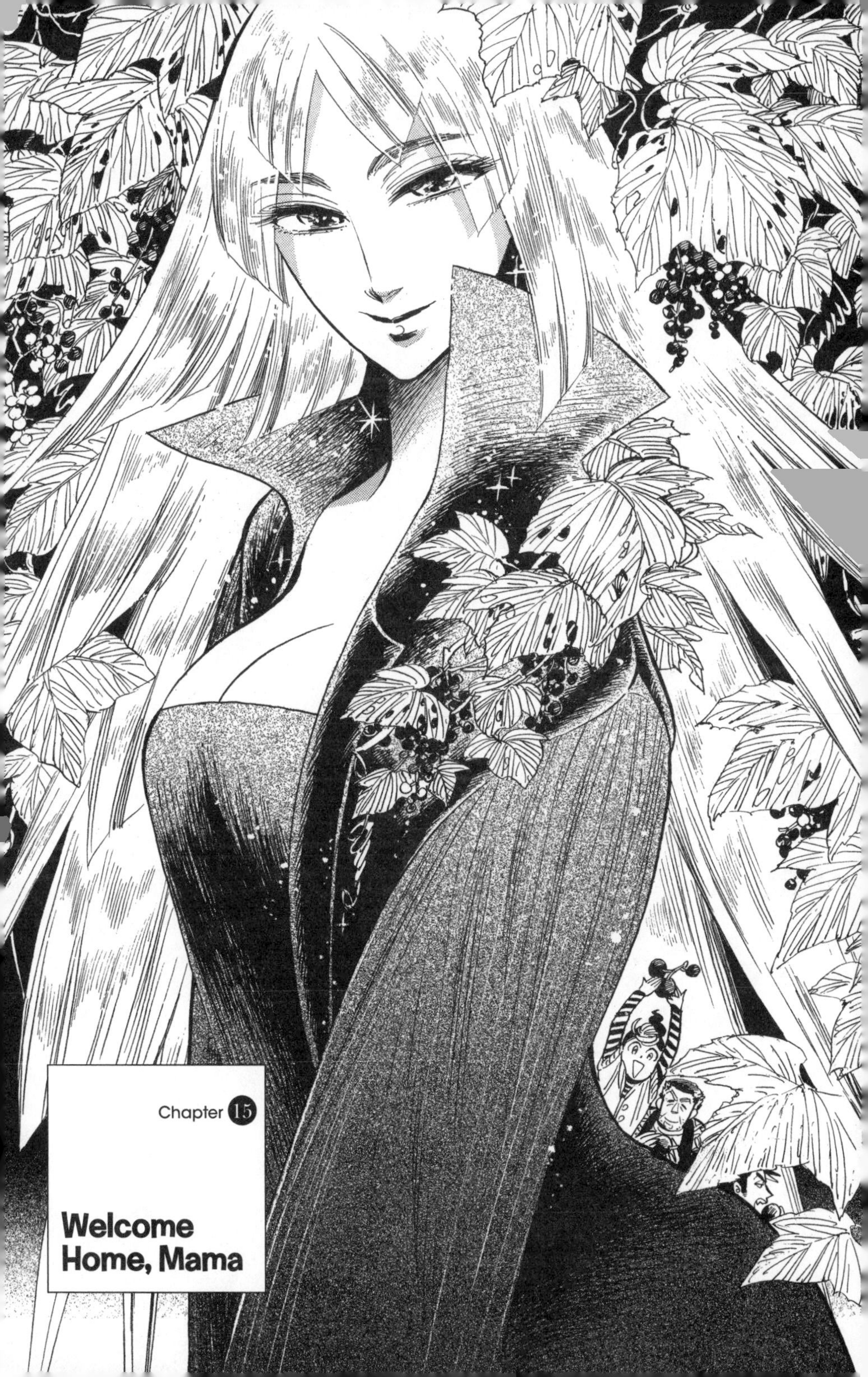
Chapter 15
Welcome Home, Mama

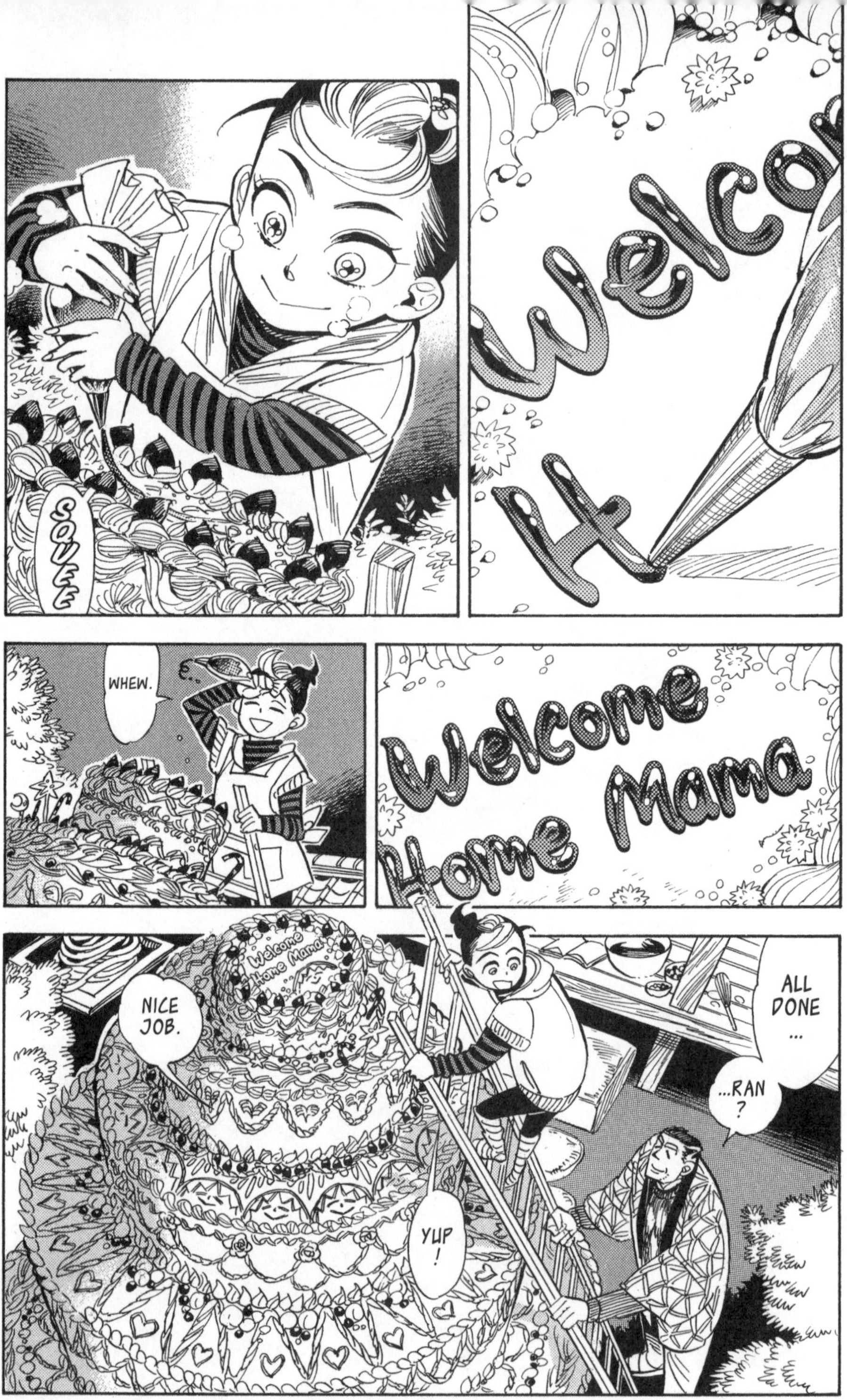
Welco
H
SQUEE
Welcome Home Mama
WHEW.
ALL DONE ...
...RAN ?
NICE JOB.
Welcome Home Mama
YUP !

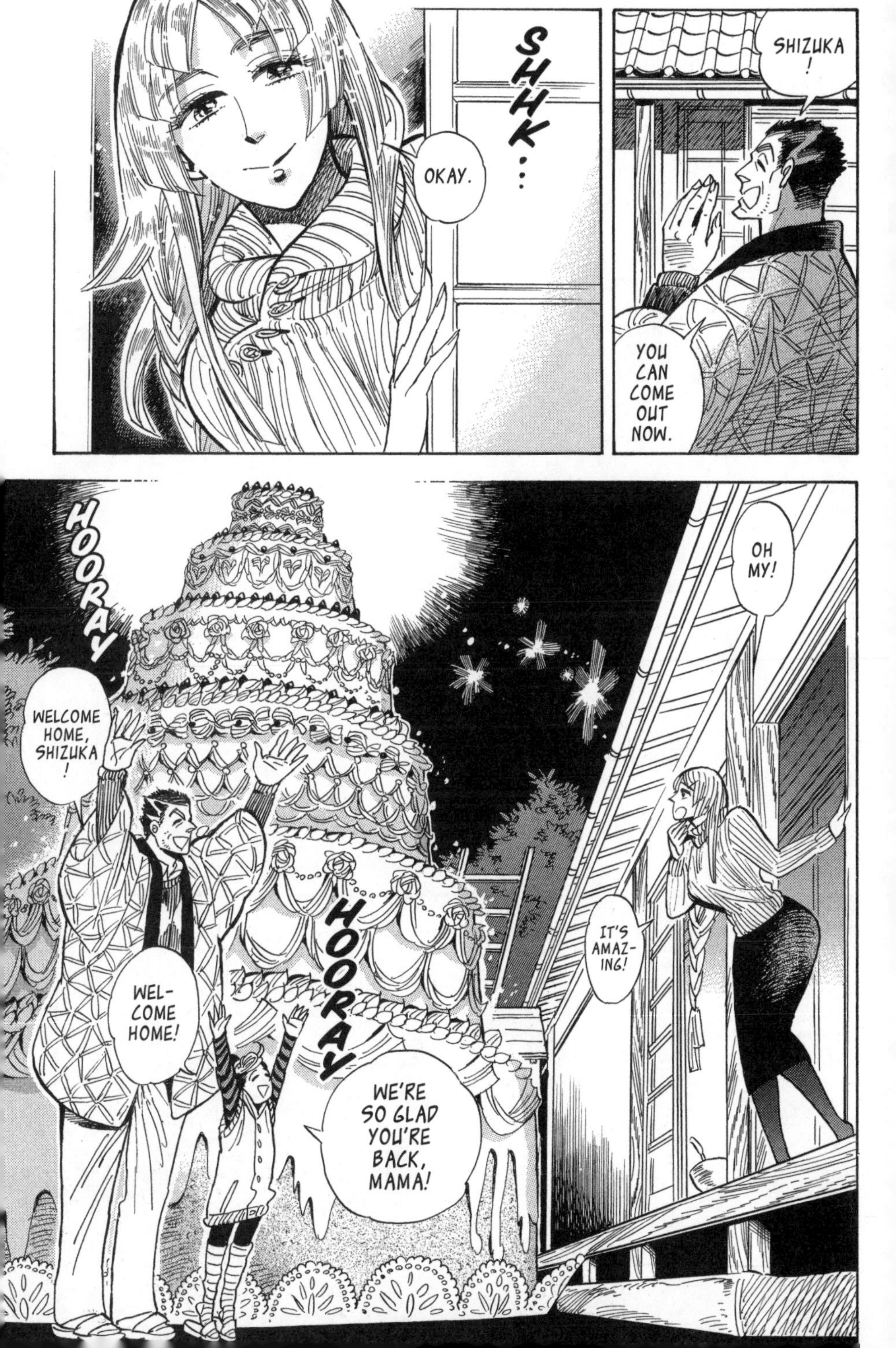
SHIZUKA!
YOU CAN COME OUT NOW.
OKAY.
SHHK...
OH MY!
IT'S AMAZ-ING!
HOORAY
WELCOME HOME, SHIZUKA!
HOORAY
WE'RE SO GLAD YOU'RE BACK, MAMA!
WEL-COME HOME!

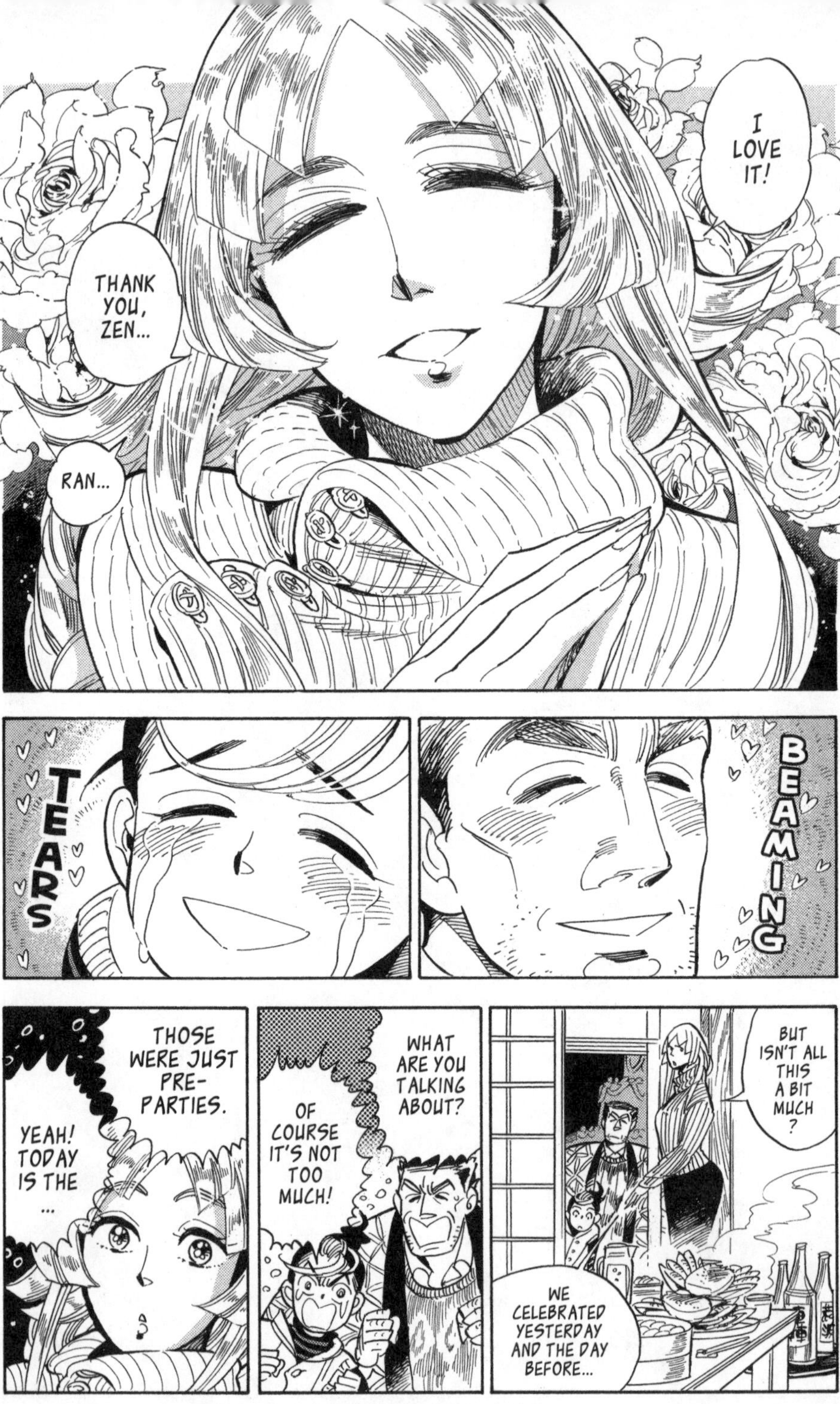
I LOVE IT!
THANK YOU, ZEN...
RAN...
BEAMING
TEARS
BUT ISN'T ALL THIS A BIT MUCH?
WE CELEBRATED YESTERDAY AND THE DAY BEFORE...
WHAT ARE YOU TALKING ABOUT?
OF COURSE IT'S NOT TOO MUCH!
THOSE WERE JUST PRE-PARTIES.
YEAH! TODAY IS THE ...

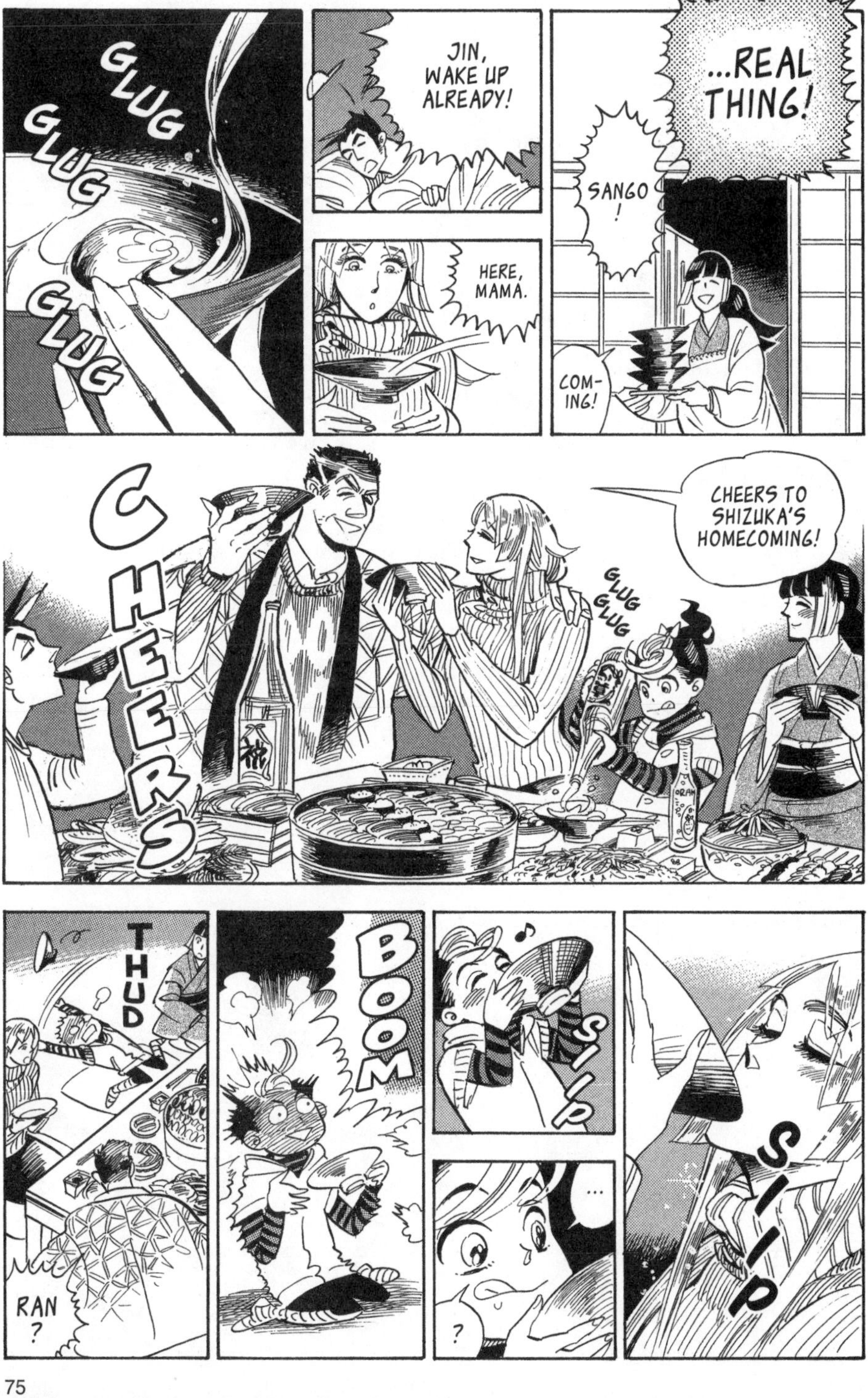
...REAL THING!
SANGO!
COMING!
JIN, WAKE UP ALREADY!
HERE, MAMA.
GLUG GLUG GLUG GLUG
CHEERS TO SHIZUKA'S HOMECOMING!
GLUG GLUG
CHEERS
SIIIP
SIIIP
...
?
BOOM
THUD
RAN?

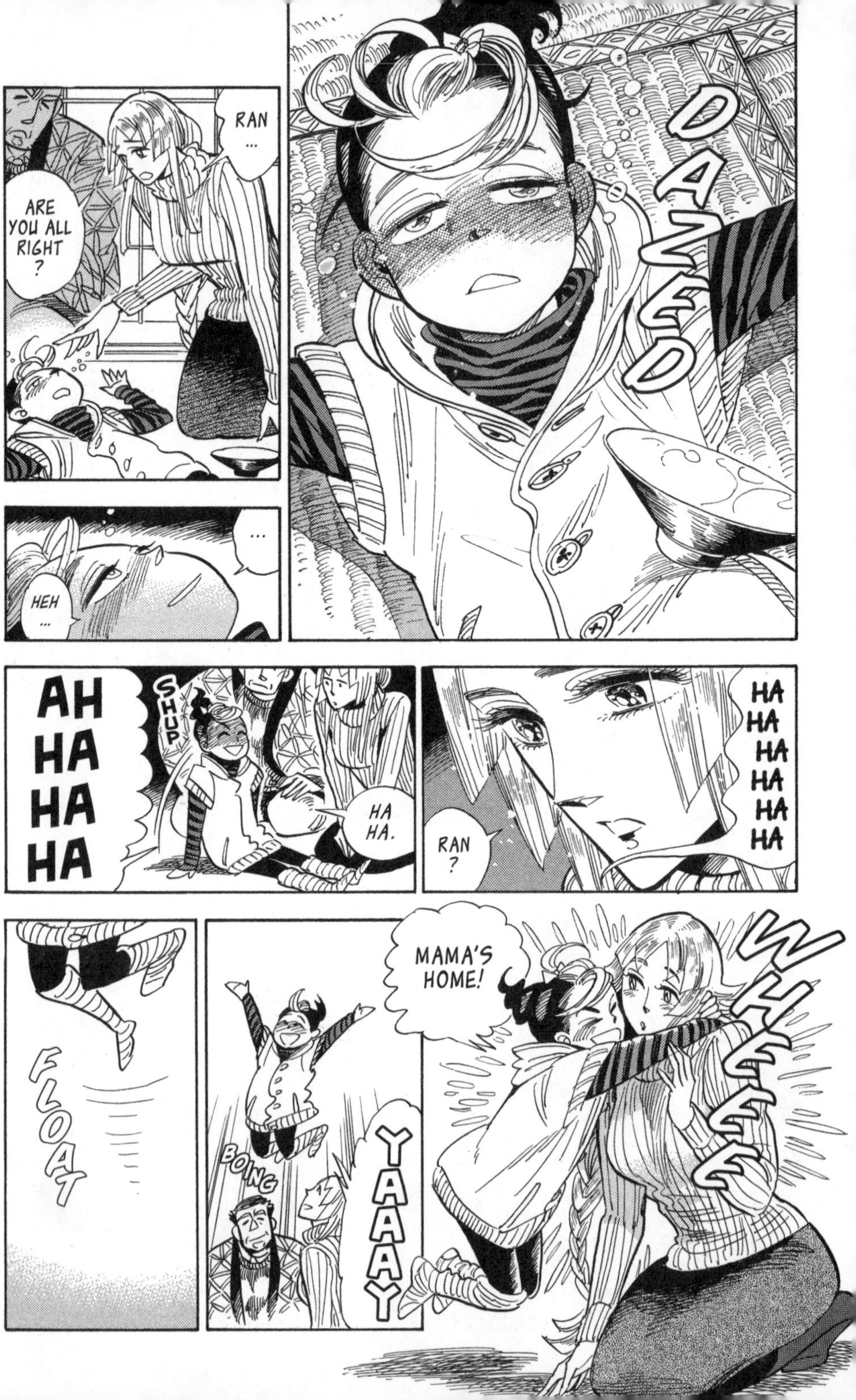
DAZED
RAN ...
ARE YOU ALL RIGHT ?
...
HEH ...
HA HA HA HA HA HA
RAN ?
AH HA HA HA HA
SHUP
HA HA.
WHEEEE
MAMA'S HOME!
YAAAY
BOING
FLOAT

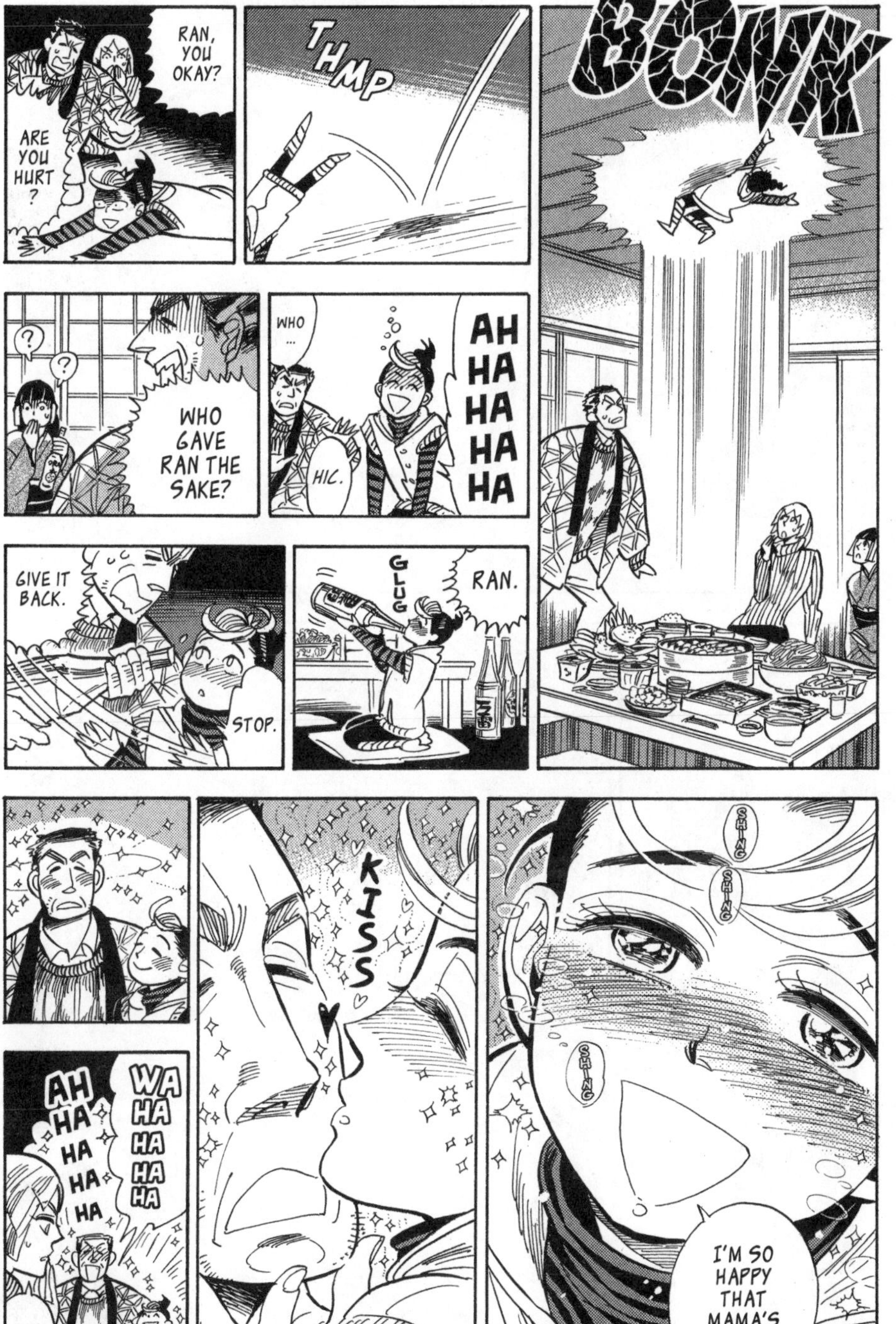
BONK
THMP
RAN, YOU OKAY?
ARE YOU HURT?
AH HA HA HA HA HA
WHO ...
HIC.
WHO GAVE RAN THE SAKE?
?
?
RAN.
GLUG
STOP.
GIVE IT BACK.
SHING
SHING
SHING
I'M SO HAPPY THAT MAMA'S BACK.
KISS
WA HA HA HA HA HA
AH HA HA HA HA HA
MY.

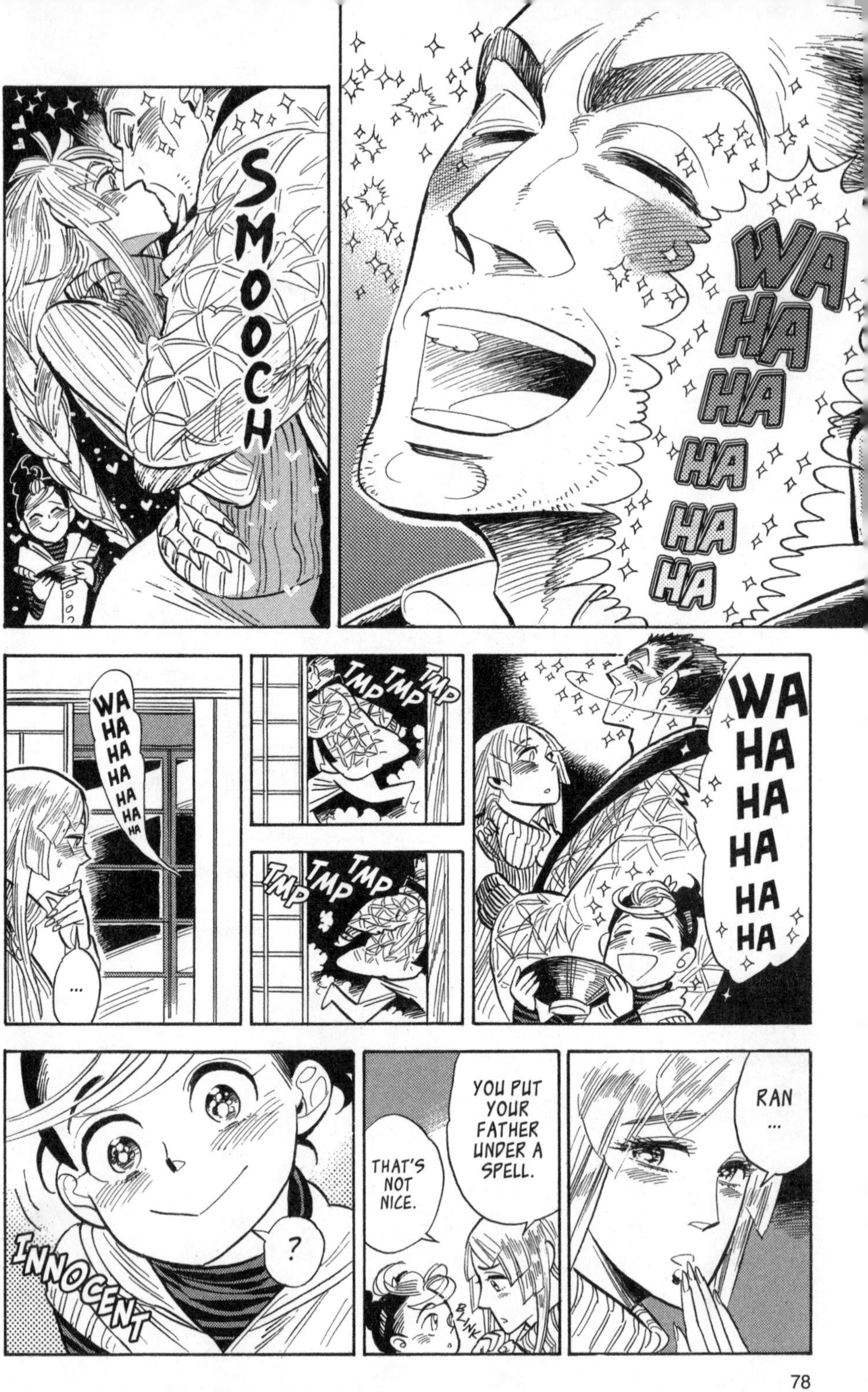
WA HA HA HA HA HA HA
SMOOCH
WA HA HA HA HA HA HA HA
TMP TMP TMP
TMP TMP TMP
WA HA HA HA HA HA HA
...
RAN ...
YOU PUT YOUR FATHER UNDER A SPELL.
THAT'S NOT NICE.
BLINK
?
INNOCENT

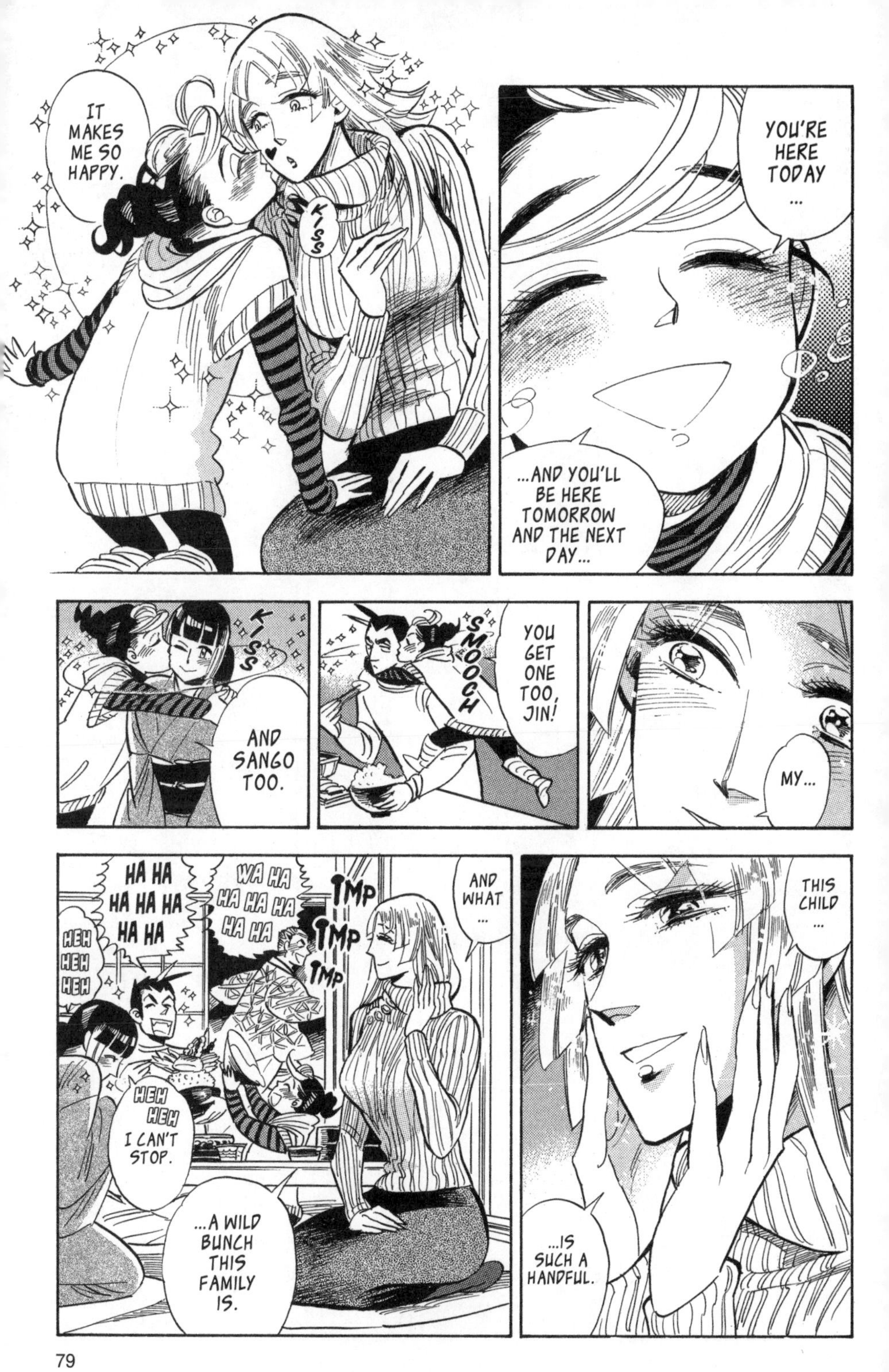
YOU'RE HERE TODAY ...
...AND YOU'LL BE HERE TOMORROW AND THE NEXT DAY...
IT MAKES ME SO HAPPY.
KISS
MY...
SMOOCH
YOU GET ONE TOO, JIN!
KISS
AND SANGO TOO.
THIS CHILD ...
...IS SUCH A HANDFUL.
AND WHAT ...
IMP
IMP
IMP
WA HA HA HA HA HA HA HA
HA HA HA HA HA HA HA
HEH HEH HEH
HEH HEH I CAN'T STOP.
...A WILD BUNCH THIS FAMILY IS.

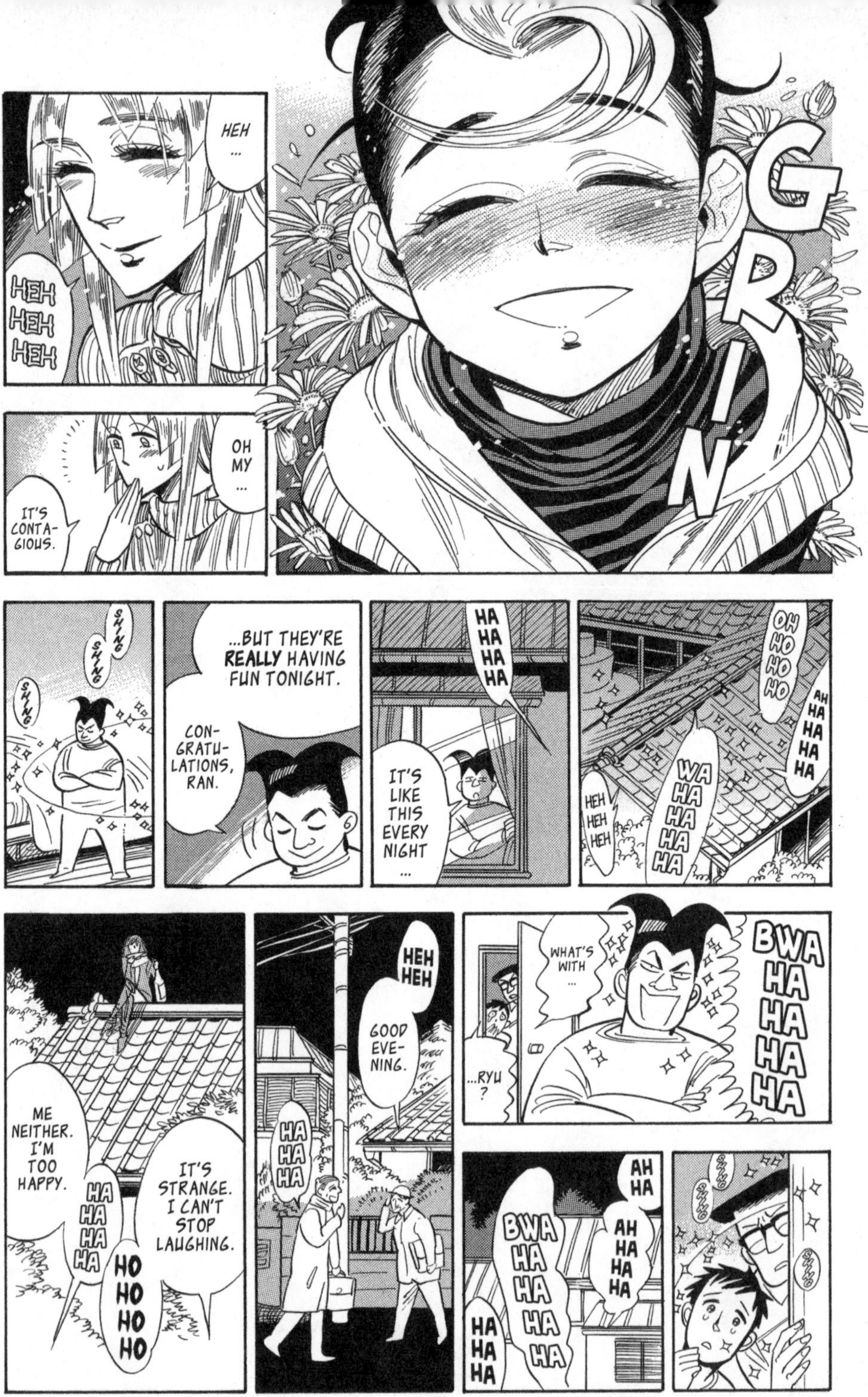
GRIN
HEH ...
HEH HEH HEH
OH MY ...
IT'S CONTAGIOUS.
OH HO HO HO HO
AH HA HA HA HA HA
WA HA HA HA HA HA
HEH HEH HEH
HA HA HA HA
IT'S LIKE THIS EVERY NIGHT ...
...BUT THEY'RE **REALLY** HAVING FUN TONIGHT.
CONGRATULATIONS, RAN.
SHING
SHING
SHING
BWA HA HA HA HA HA
WHAT'S WITH ...
...RYU ?
SHING
SHING
SHING
AH HA
AH HA HA HA HA
BWA HA HA HA HA HA
HA HA HA
HEH HEH
GOOD EVENING.
HA HA HA HA
IT'S STRANGE. I CAN'T STOP LAUGHING.
ME NEITHER. I'M TOO HAPPY.
HA HA HA HA
HO HO HO HO HO

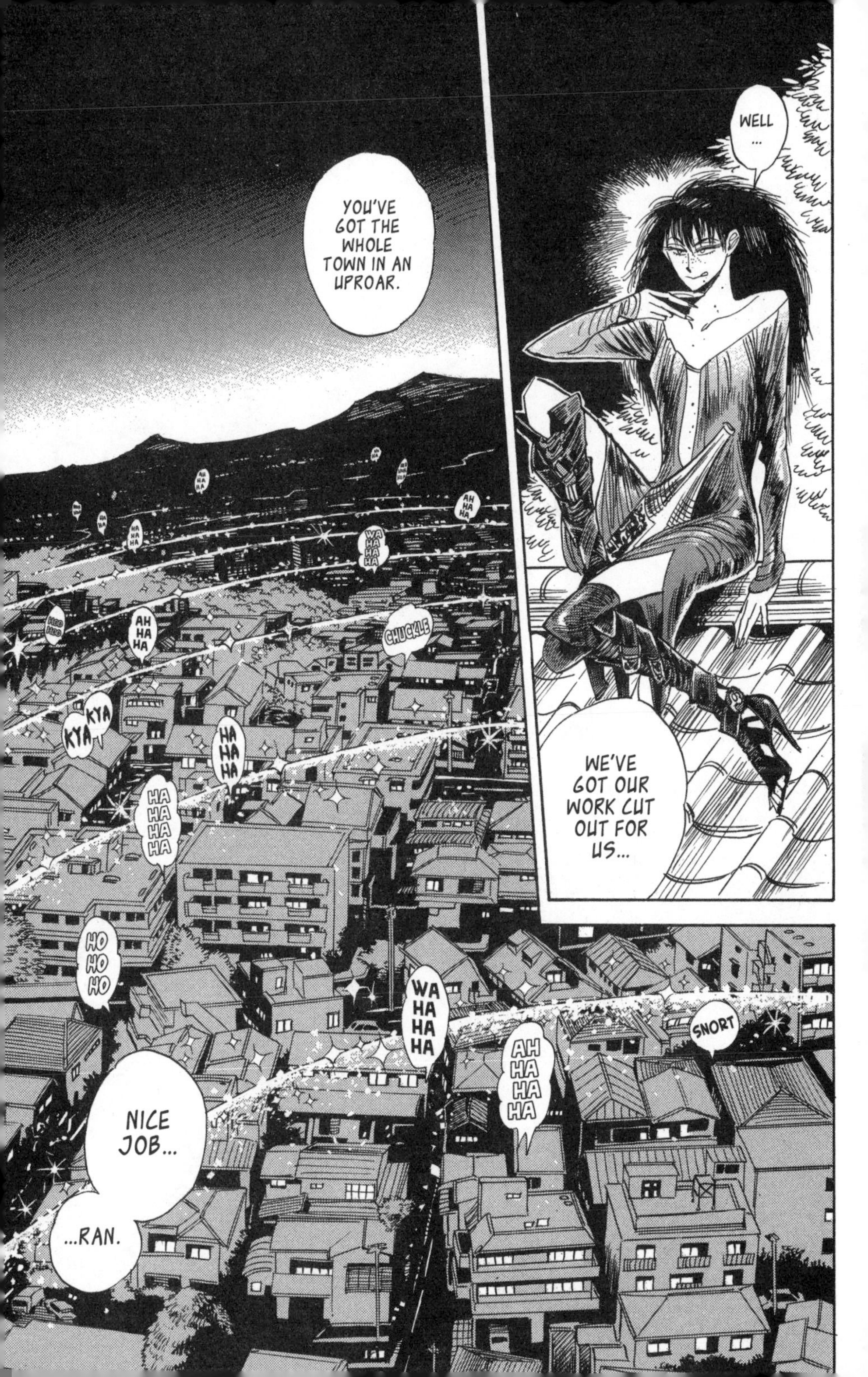
WELL ...
WE'VE GOT OUR WORK CUT OUT FOR US...
YOU'VE GOT THE WHOLE TOWN IN AN UPROAR.
AH HA HA
WA HA HA HA
CHUCKLE
AH HA HA
KYA KYA
HA HA HA
HA HA HA HA HA
HO HO HO
SNORT
AH HA HA HA HA
WA HA HA HA
NICE JOB...
...RAN.

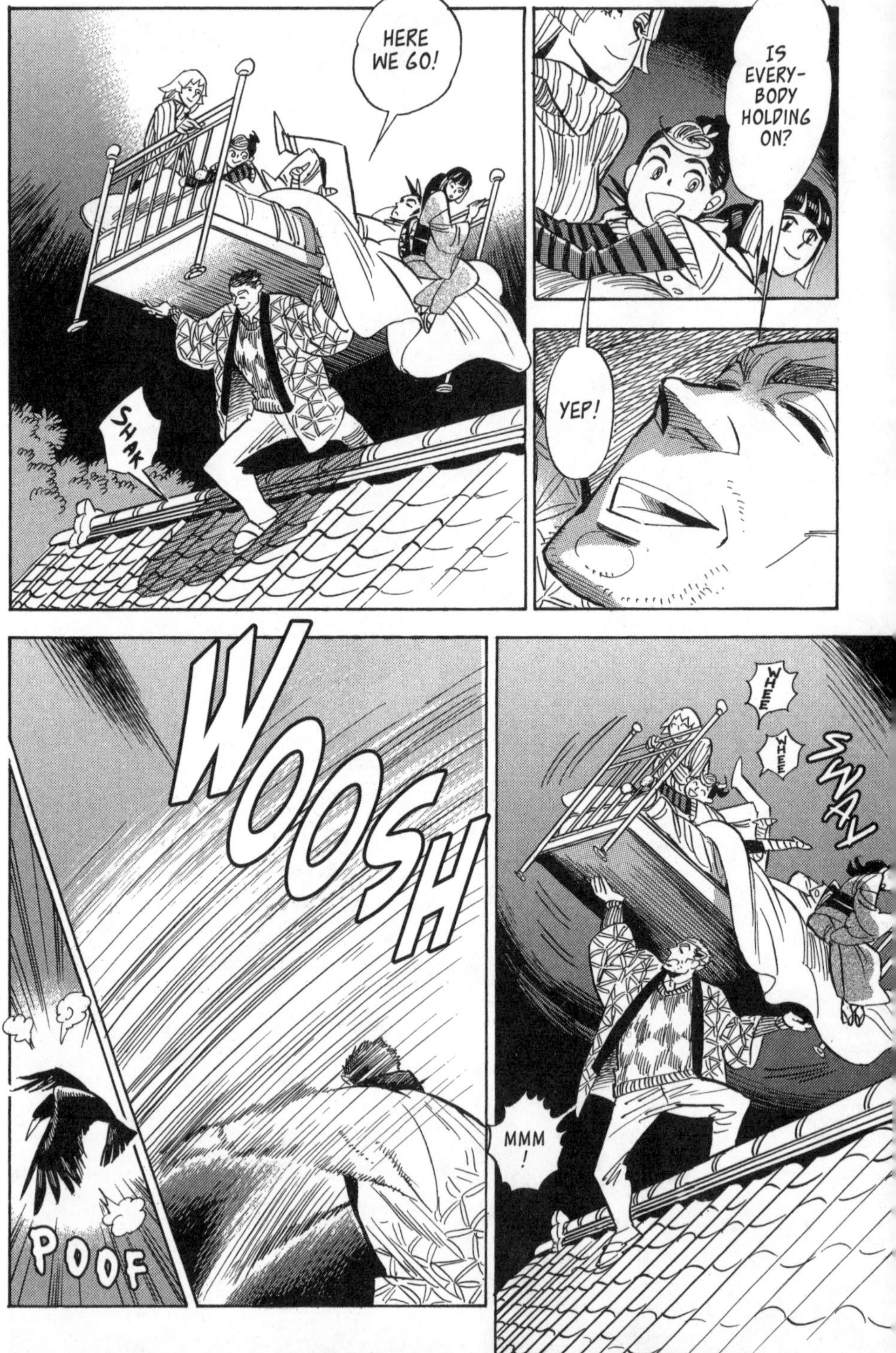
IS EVERY-BODY HOLDING ON?
YEP!
HERE WE GO!
SHAK
WHEE
WHEE
SWAY
MMM!
WOOSH
POOF

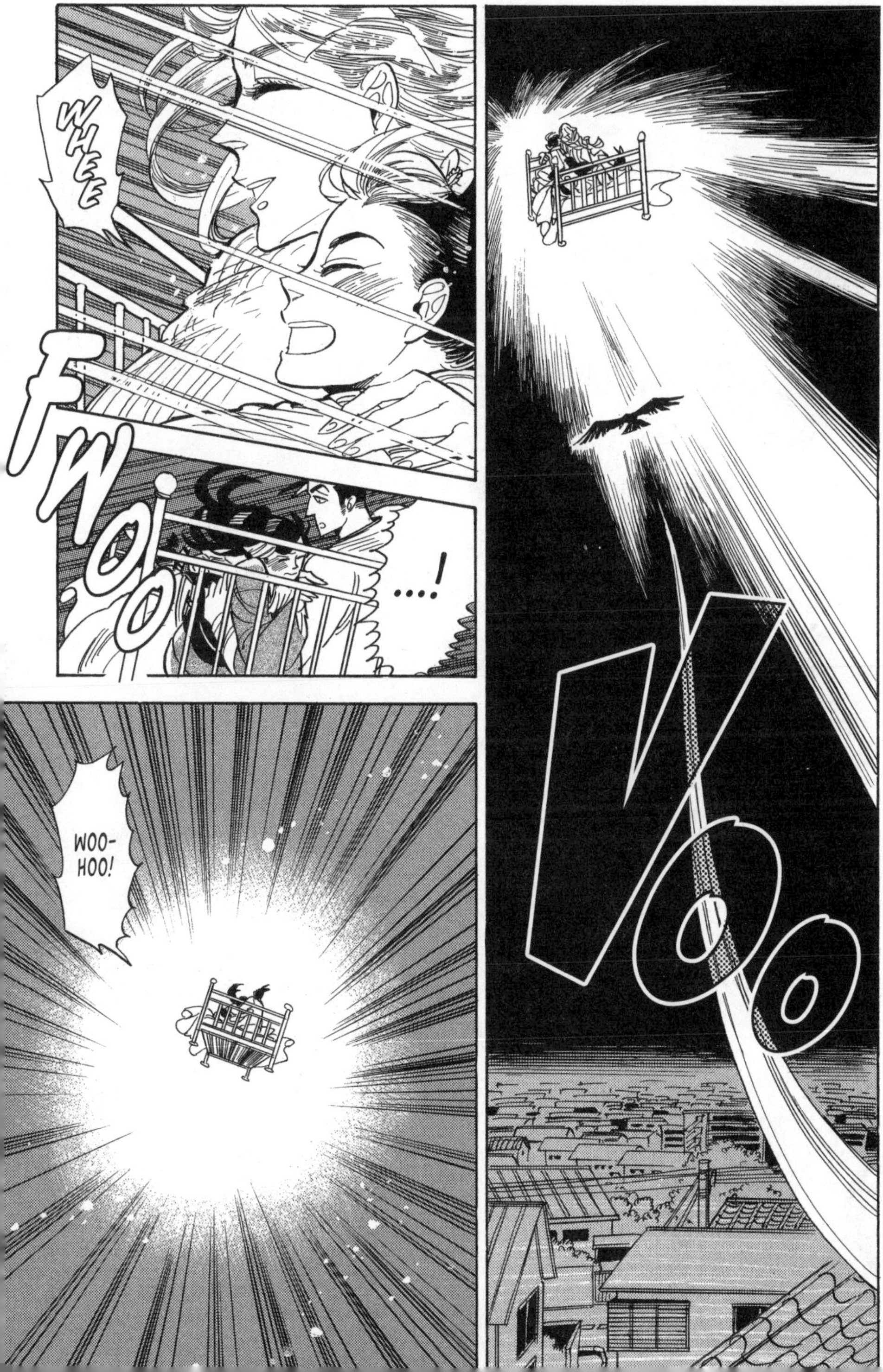
WOO
WHEE
FWOOO
...!
WOO-HOO!

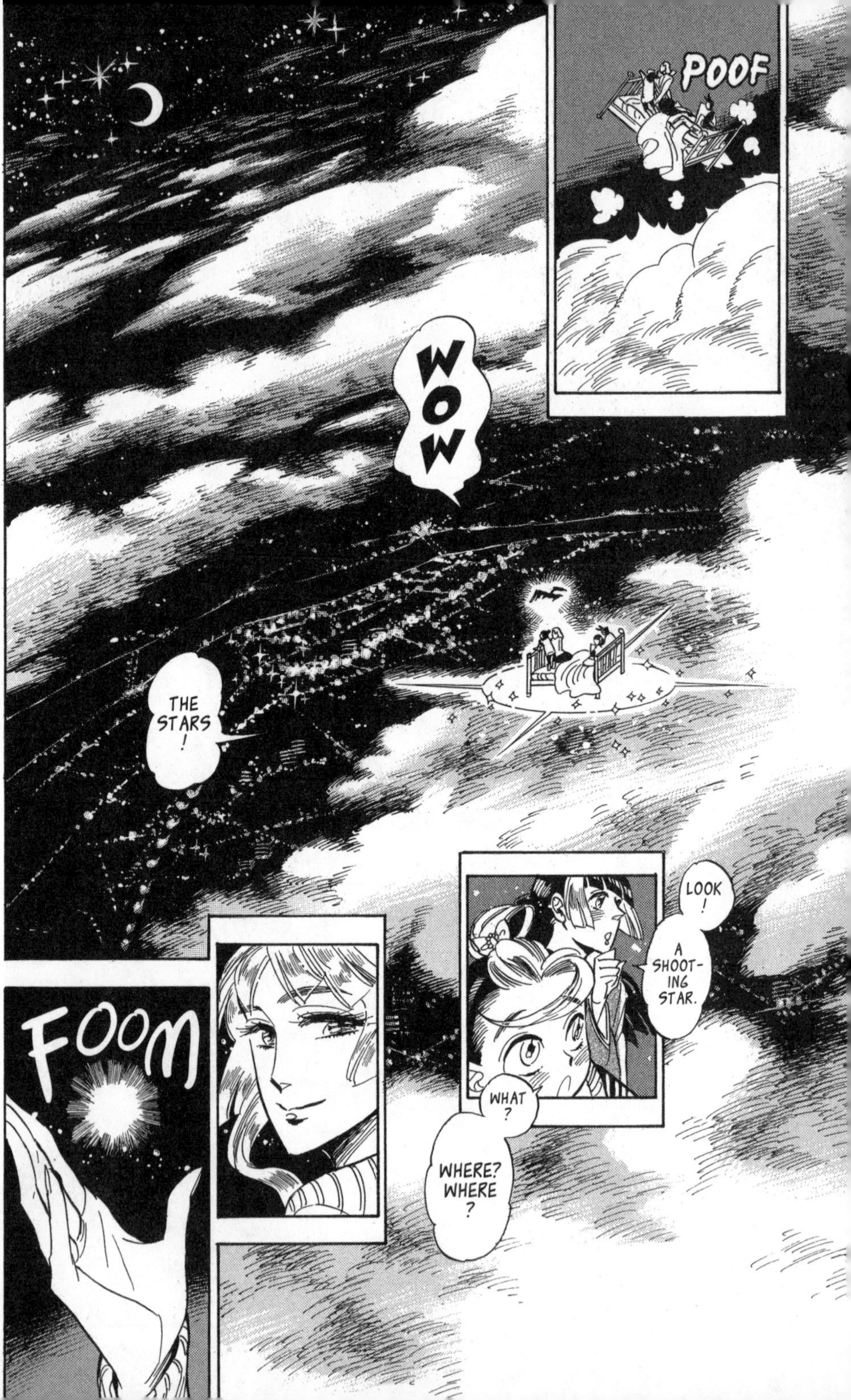
POOF
WOW
THE STARS!
LOOK!
A SHOOTING STAR.
WHAT?
WHERE? WHERE?
FOOM

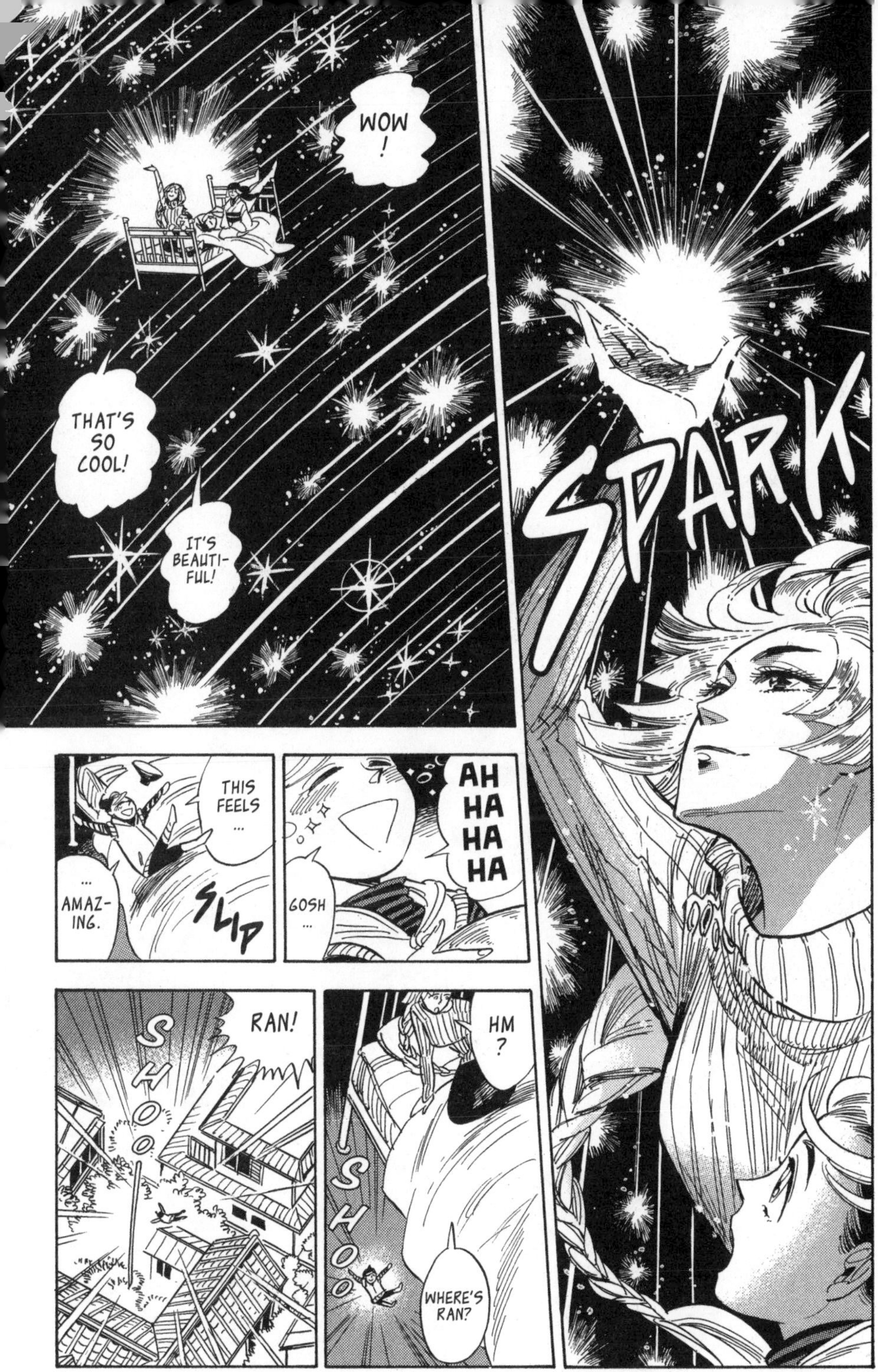
SPARK
WOW!
THAT'S SO COOL!
IT'S BEAUTIFUL!
AH HA HA HA
GOSH...
THIS FEELS...
...AMAZING.
SLIP
HM?
SHOO
WHERE'S RAN?
RAN!
SHOO

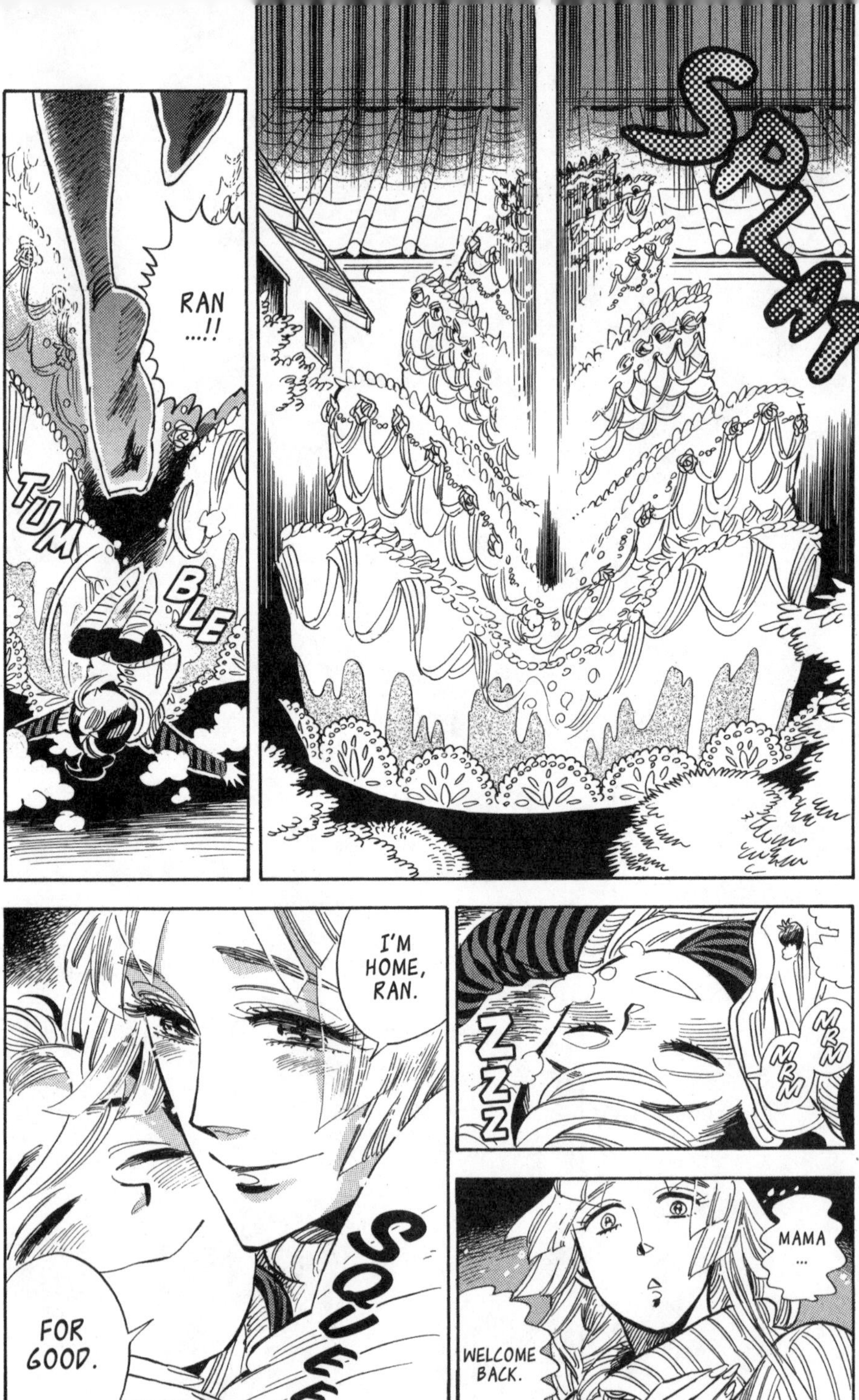
SPLAT
RAN ...!!
TUMBLE
ZZZ
MRM MRM
MAMA ...
WELCOME BACK.
I'M HOME, RAN.
SQUEE
FOR GOOD.

Chapter 15 / The End

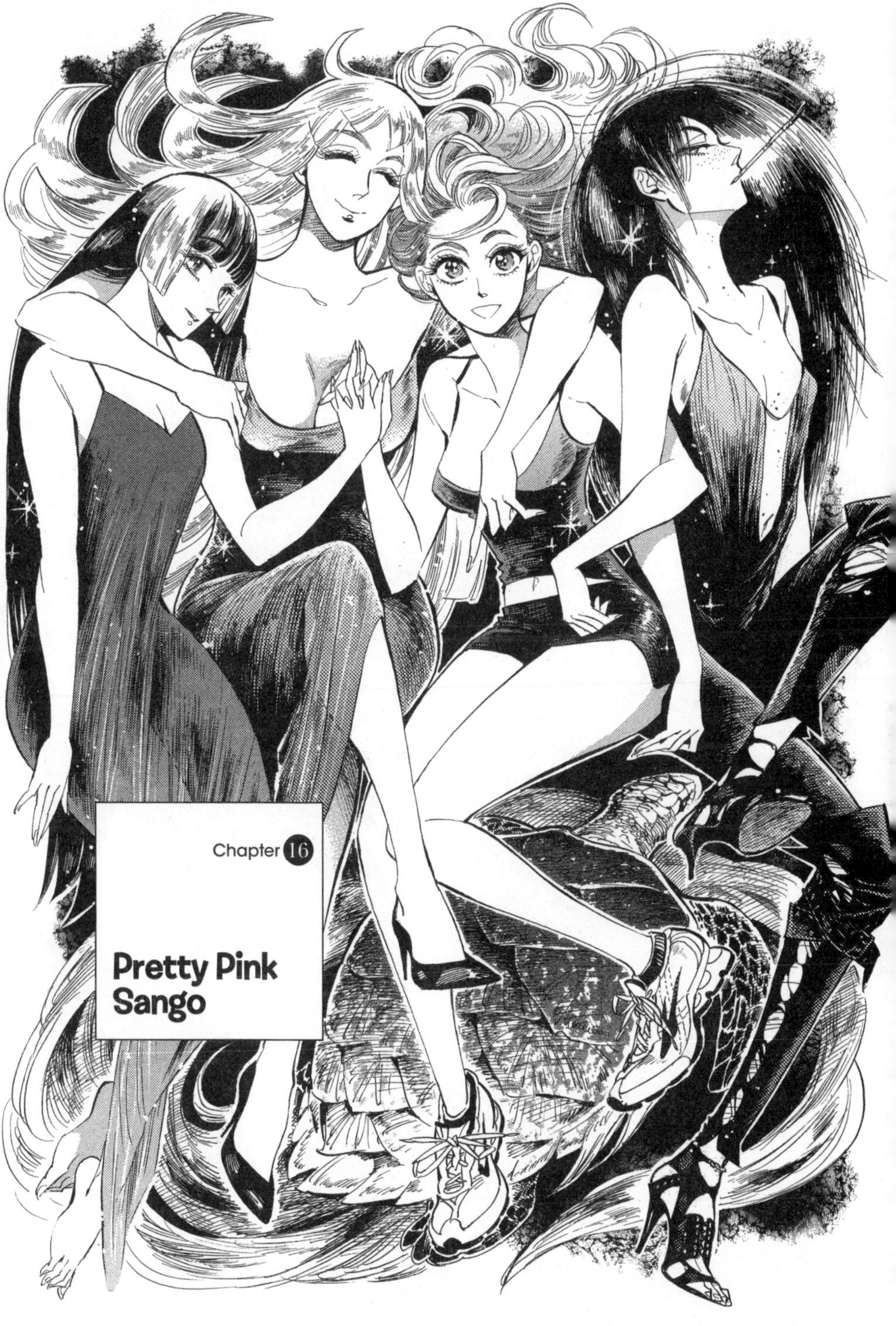
Chapter 16
Pretty Pink Sango

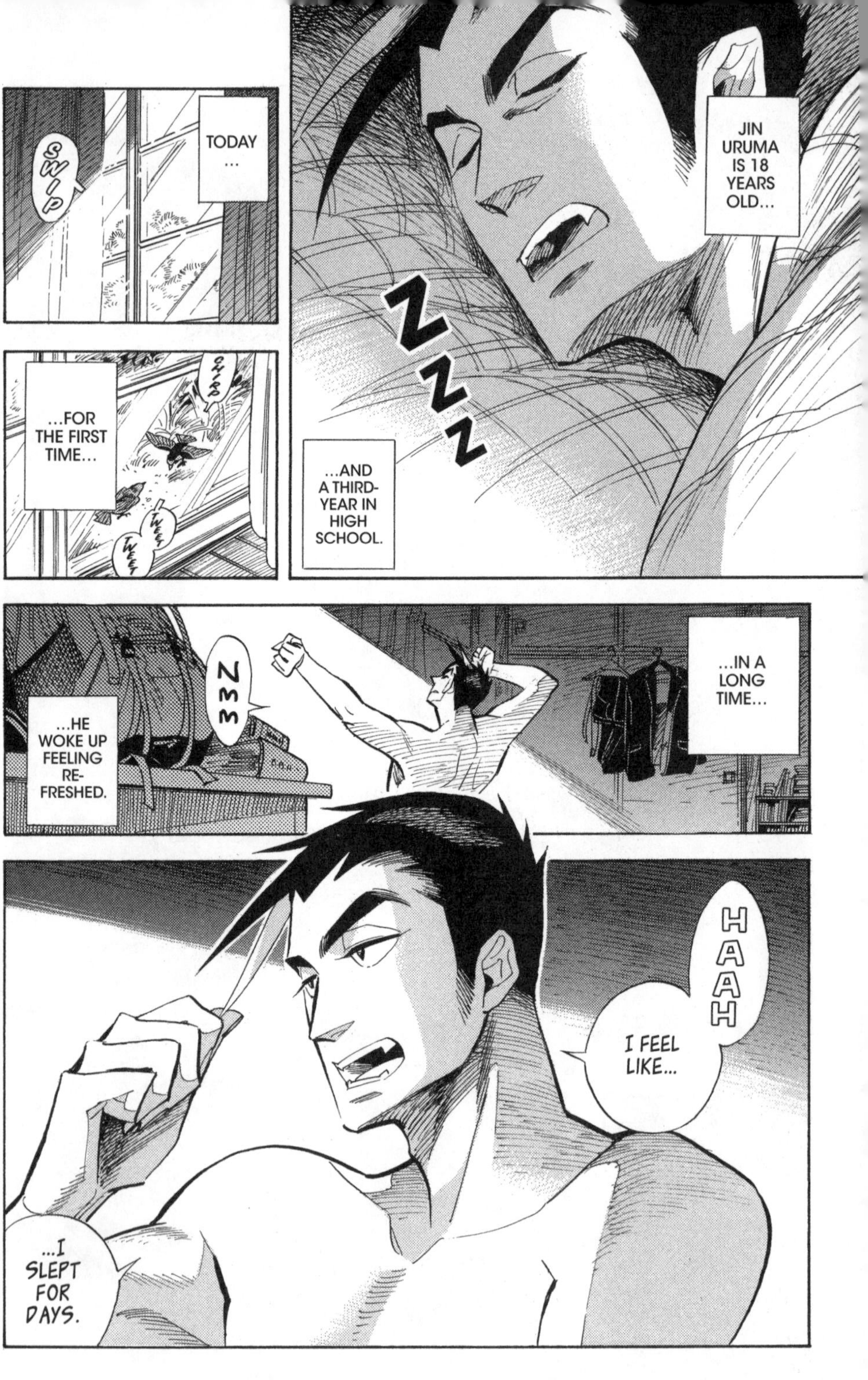
JIN URUMA IS 18 YEARS OLD…
ZZZ
…AND A THIRD-YEAR IN HIGH SCHOOL.
TODAY …
SWIP
…FOR THE FIRST TIME…
CHIRP
TWEET
TWEET
…IN A LONG TIME…
NMM
…HE WOKE UP FEELING RE-FRESHED.
HAAAH
I FEEL LIKE…
…I SLEPT FOR DAYS.

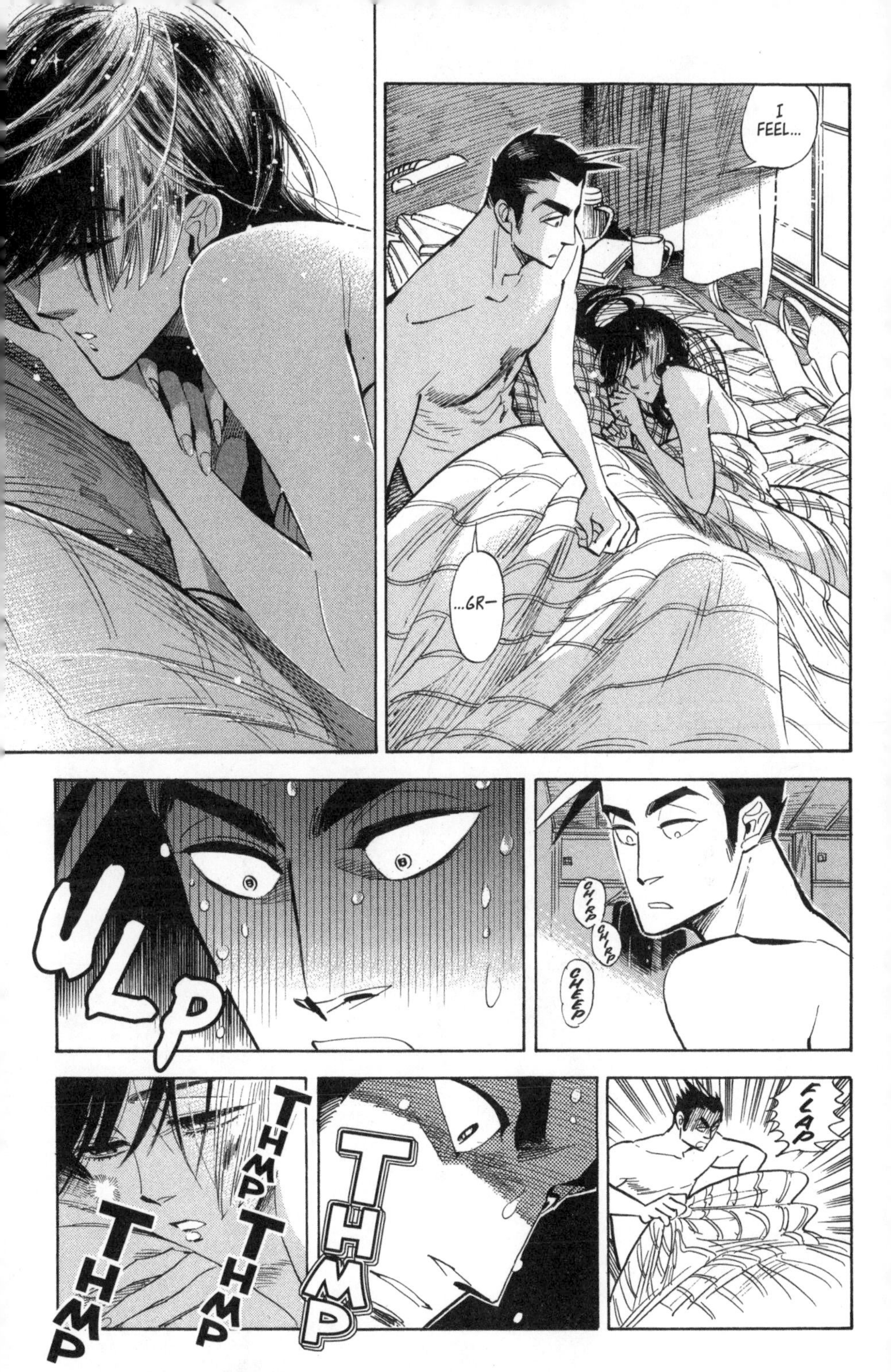
I FEEL...
...GR—
CHIRP CHIRP
CHEEP
ULP
FLAP
THMP
THMP THMP THMP

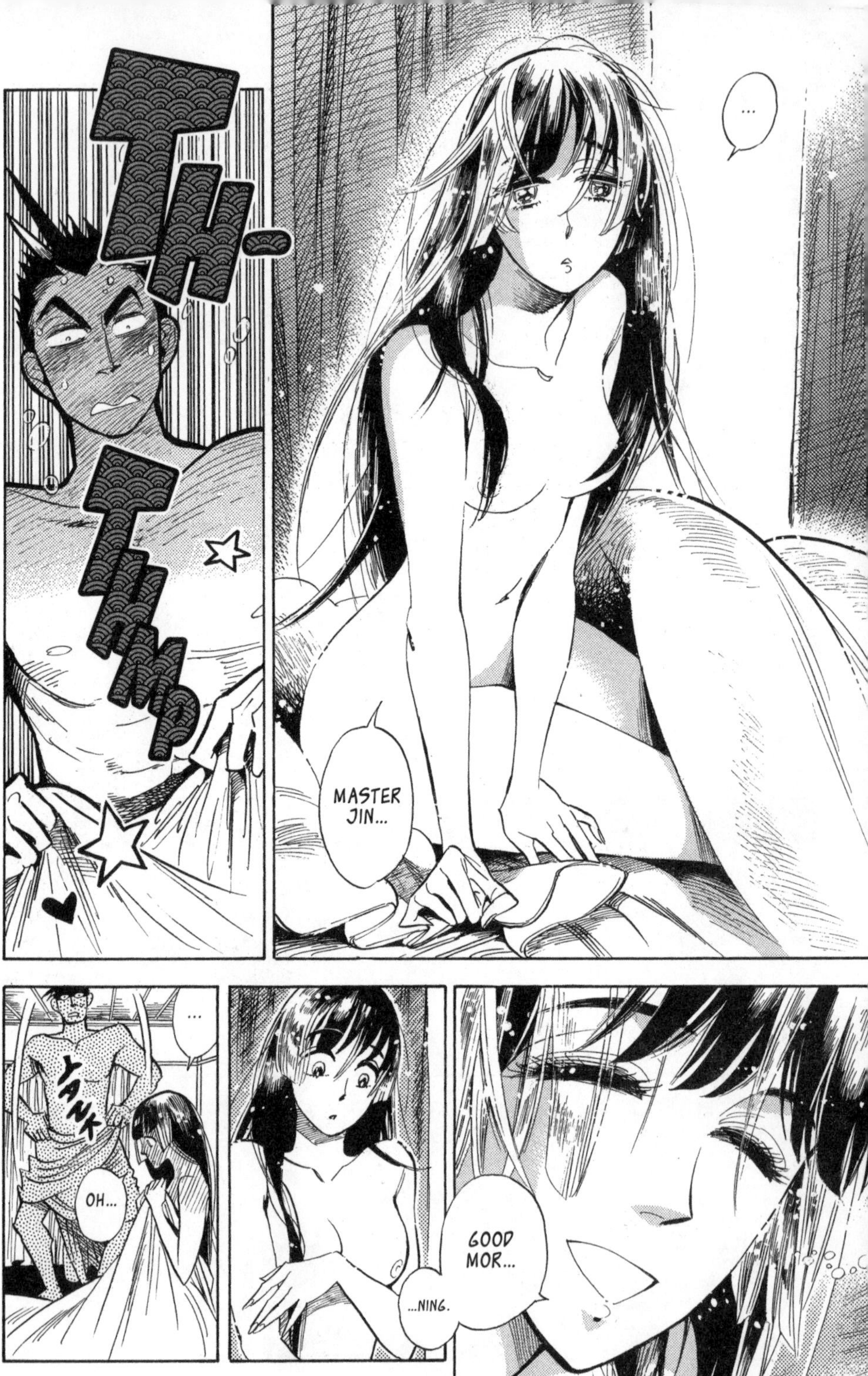
...
MASTER JIN...
TH-THUMP
GOOD MOR...
...NING.
...
YANK
OH...

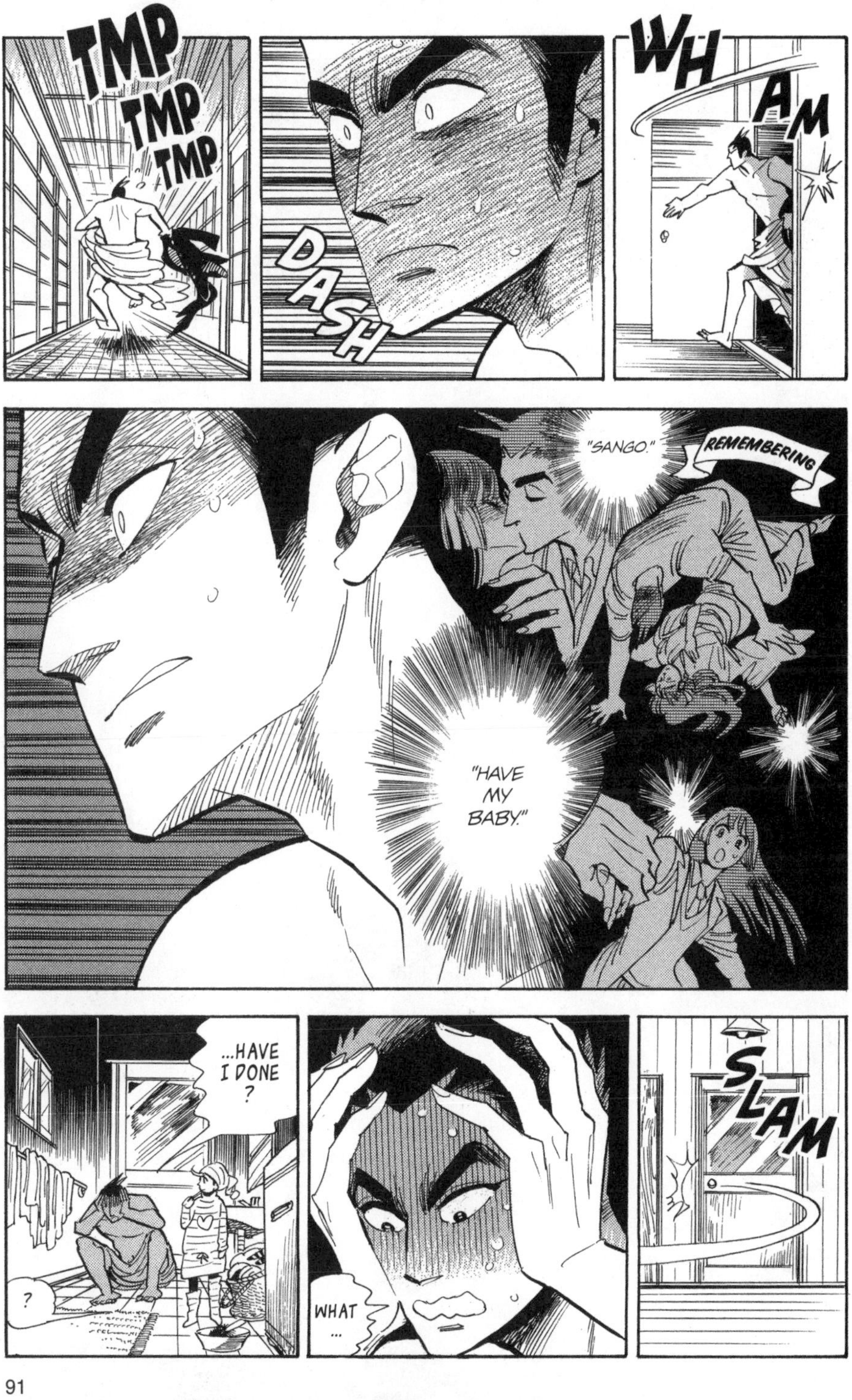
WHAM
DASH
TMP TMP TMP
REMEMBERING
"SANGO."
"HAVE MY BABY."
SLAM
WHAT ...
...HAVE I DONE ?
?

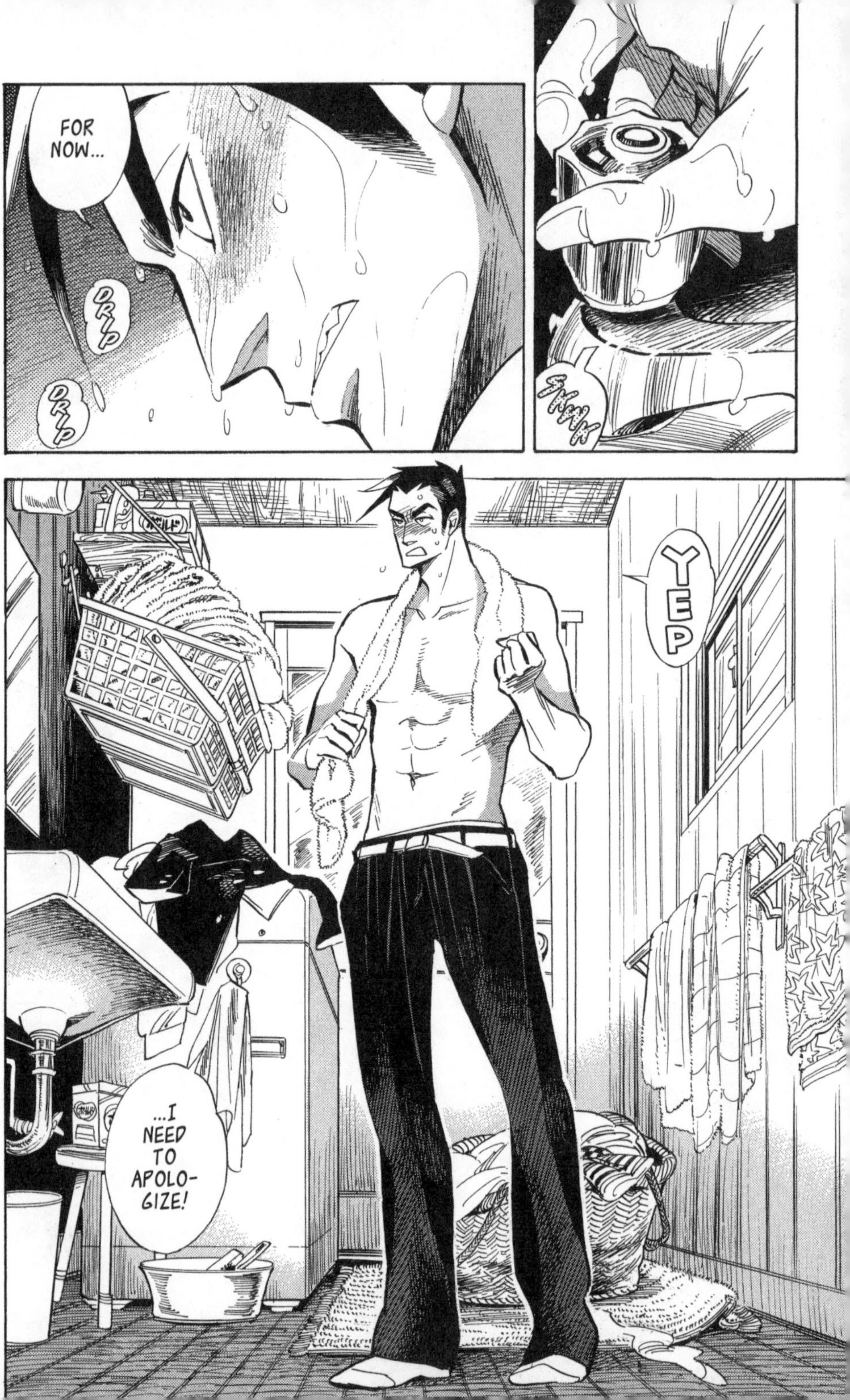
SKWK
FOR NOW...
DRIP
DRIP
YEP
...I NEED TO APOLOGIZE!

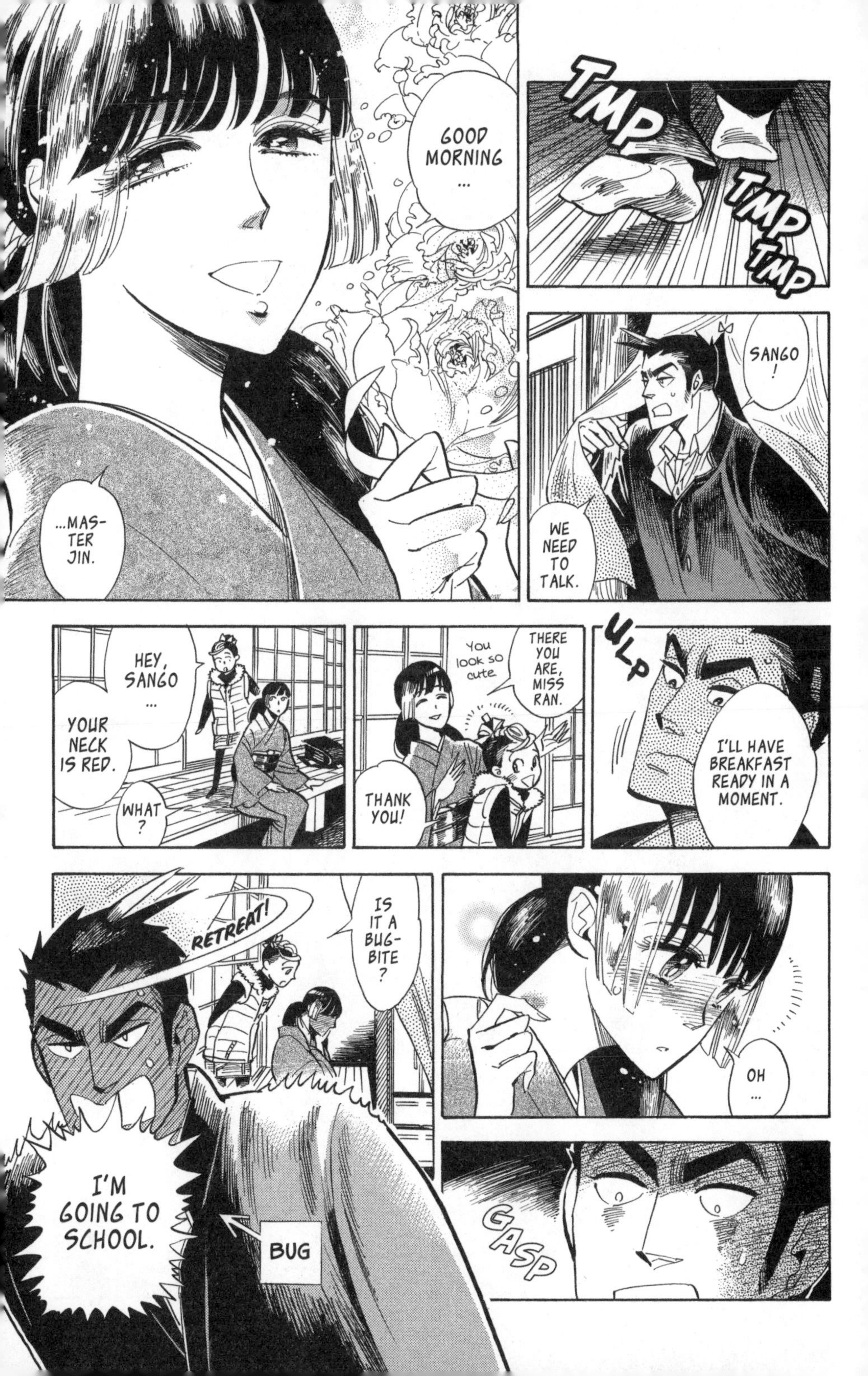
TMP
TMP
TMP
SANGO!
WE NEED TO TALK.
GOOD MORNING...
...MASTER JIN.
ULP
I'LL HAVE BREAKFAST READY IN A MOMENT.
THERE YOU ARE, MISS RAN.
You look so cute.
THANK YOU!
HEY, SANGO...
YOUR NECK IS RED.
WHAT?
OH...
GASP
IS IT A BUG-BITE?
RETREAT!
I'M GOING TO SCHOOL.
BUG

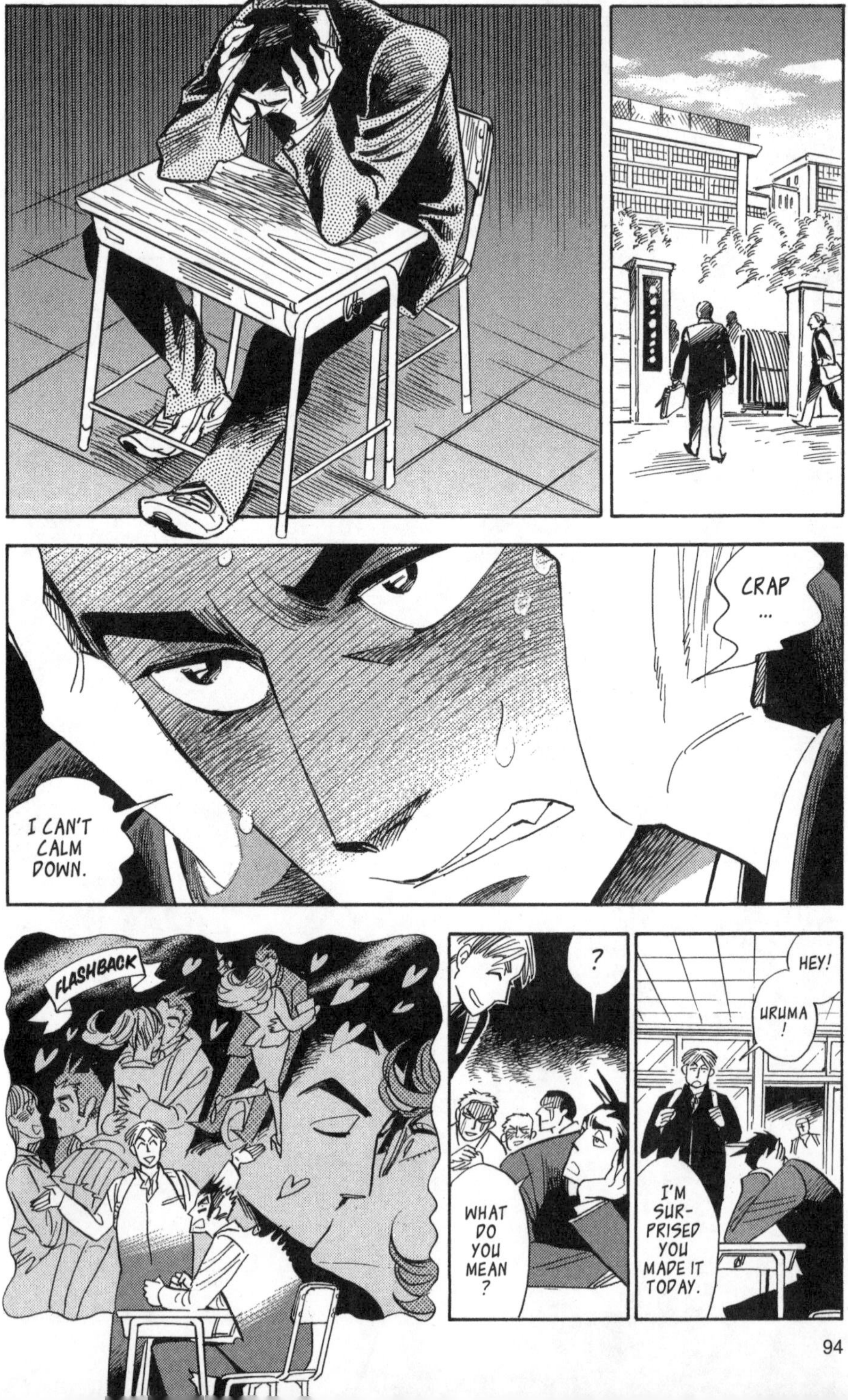
CRAP ...
I CAN'T CALM DOWN.
HEY!
URUMA!
I'M SUR-PRISED YOU MADE IT TODAY.
?
WHAT DO YOU MEAN?
FLASHBACK

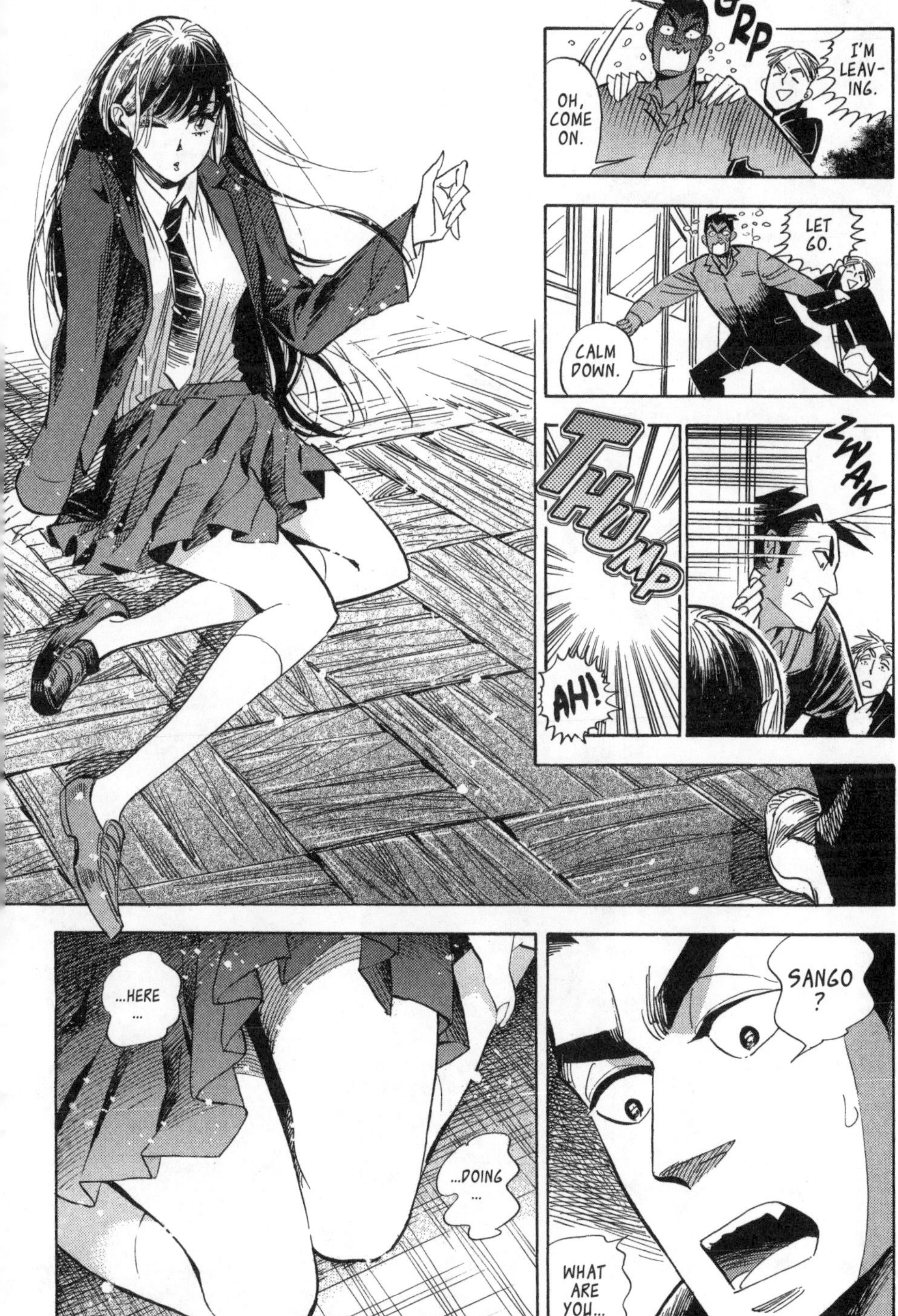
GRP
I'M LEAVING.
OH, COME ON.
LET GO.
CALM DOWN.
ZWAK
THUMP
AH!
SANGO?
WHAT ARE YOU...
...HERE...
...DOING...

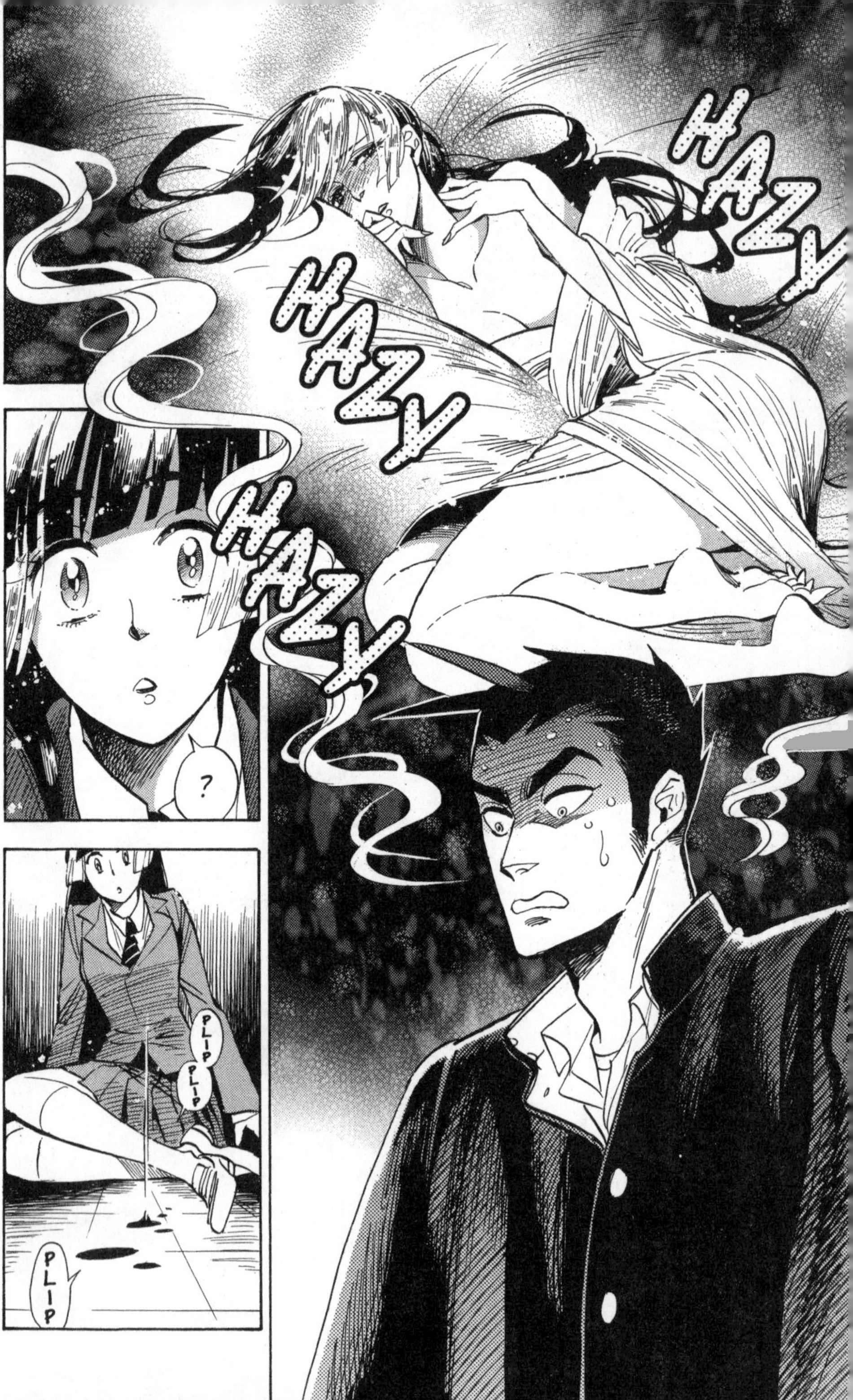
HAZY
HAZY
HAZY
?
PLIP PLIP
PLIP

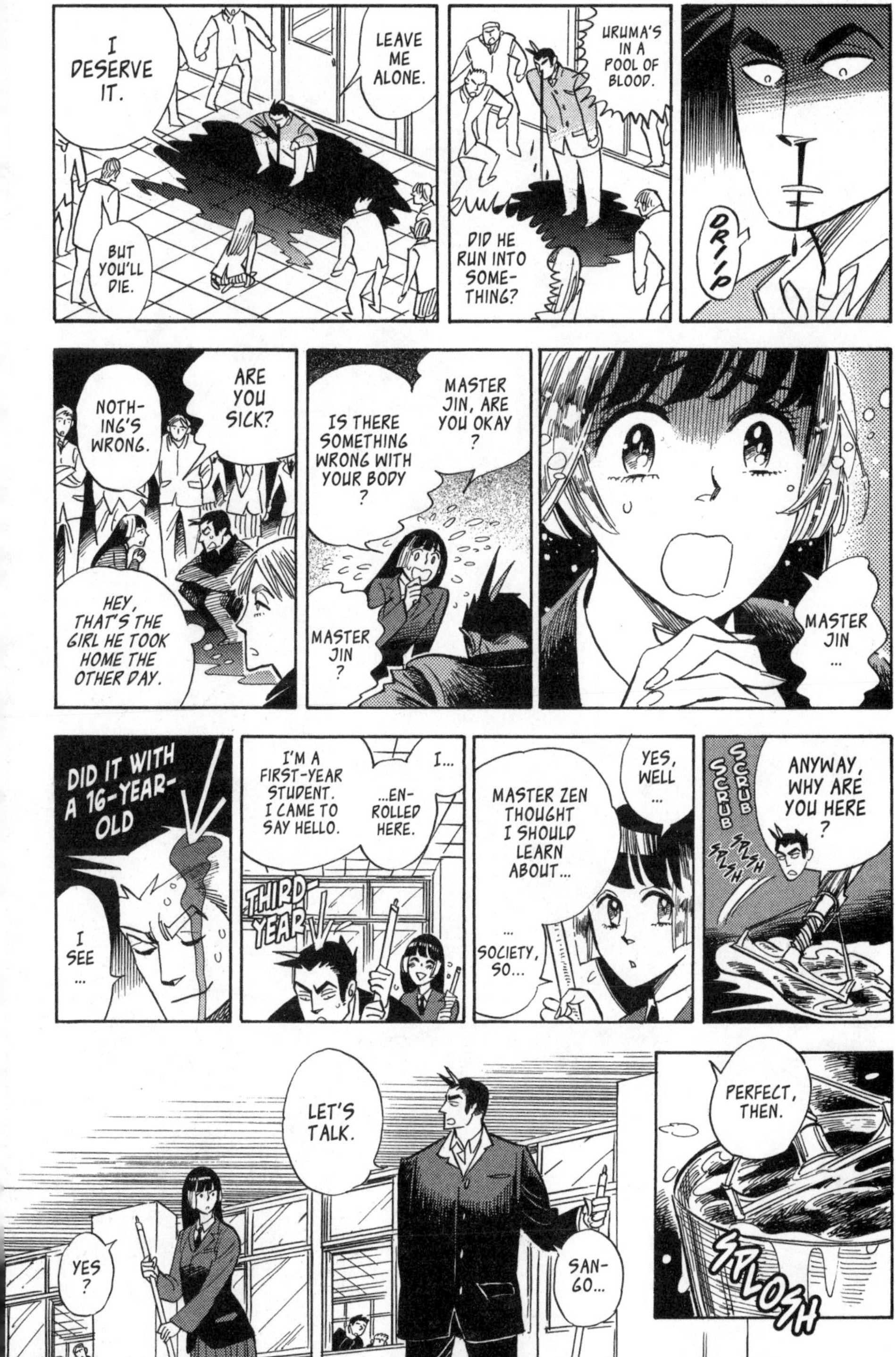
DRIP
URUMA'S IN A POOL OF BLOOD.
DID HE RUN INTO SOME-THING?
LEAVE ME ALONE.
I DESERVE IT.
BUT YOU'LL DIE.
MASTER JIN ...
MASTER JIN, ARE YOU OKAY ?
IS THERE SOMETHING WRONG WITH YOUR BODY ?
MASTER JIN ?
ARE YOU SICK?
NOTH-ING'S WRONG.
HEY, THAT'S THE GIRL HE TOOK HOME THE OTHER DAY.
SCRUB SCRUB
SPLSH SPLSH
ANYWAY, WHY ARE YOU HERE ?
YES, WELL ...
MASTER ZEN THOUGHT I SHOULD LEARN ABOUT...
... SOCIETY, SO...
I...
...EN-ROLLED HERE.
I'M A FIRST-YEAR STUDENT. I CAME TO SAY HELLO.
THIRD-YEAR
DID IT WITH A 16-YEAR-OLD
I SEE ...
PERFECT, THEN.
SPLOSH
LET'S TALK.
SAN-GO...
YES ?

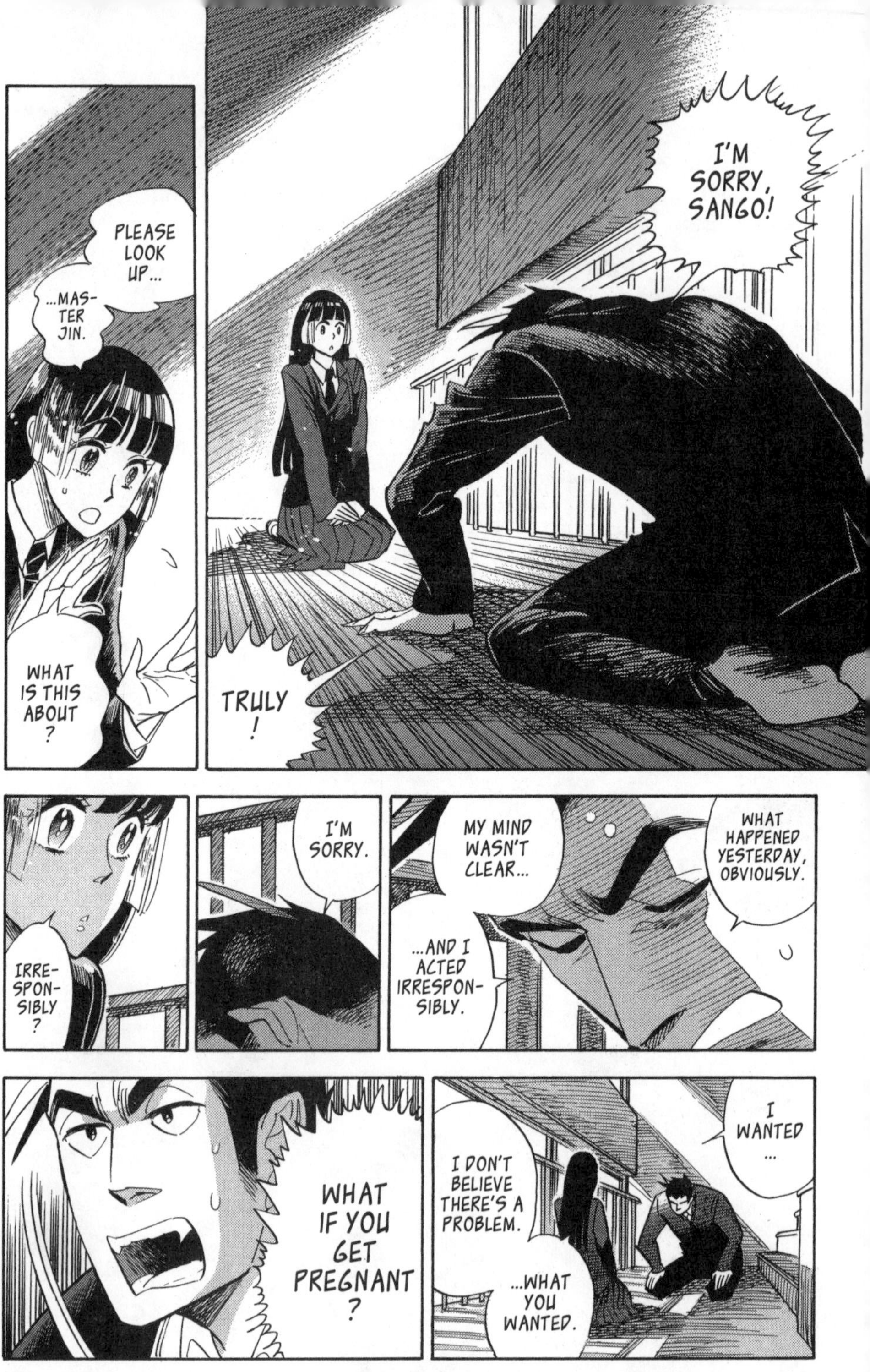
I'M SORRY, SANGO!
TRULY!
PLEASE LOOK UP...
...MASTER JIN.
WHAT IS THIS ABOUT?
WHAT HAPPENED YESTERDAY, OBVIOUSLY.
MY MIND WASN'T CLEAR...
...AND I ACTED IRRESPONSIBLY.
I'M SORRY.
IRRESPONSIBLY?
I WANTED...
I DON'T BELIEVE THERE'S A PROBLEM.
...WHAT YOU WANTED.
WHAT IF YOU GET PREGNANT?

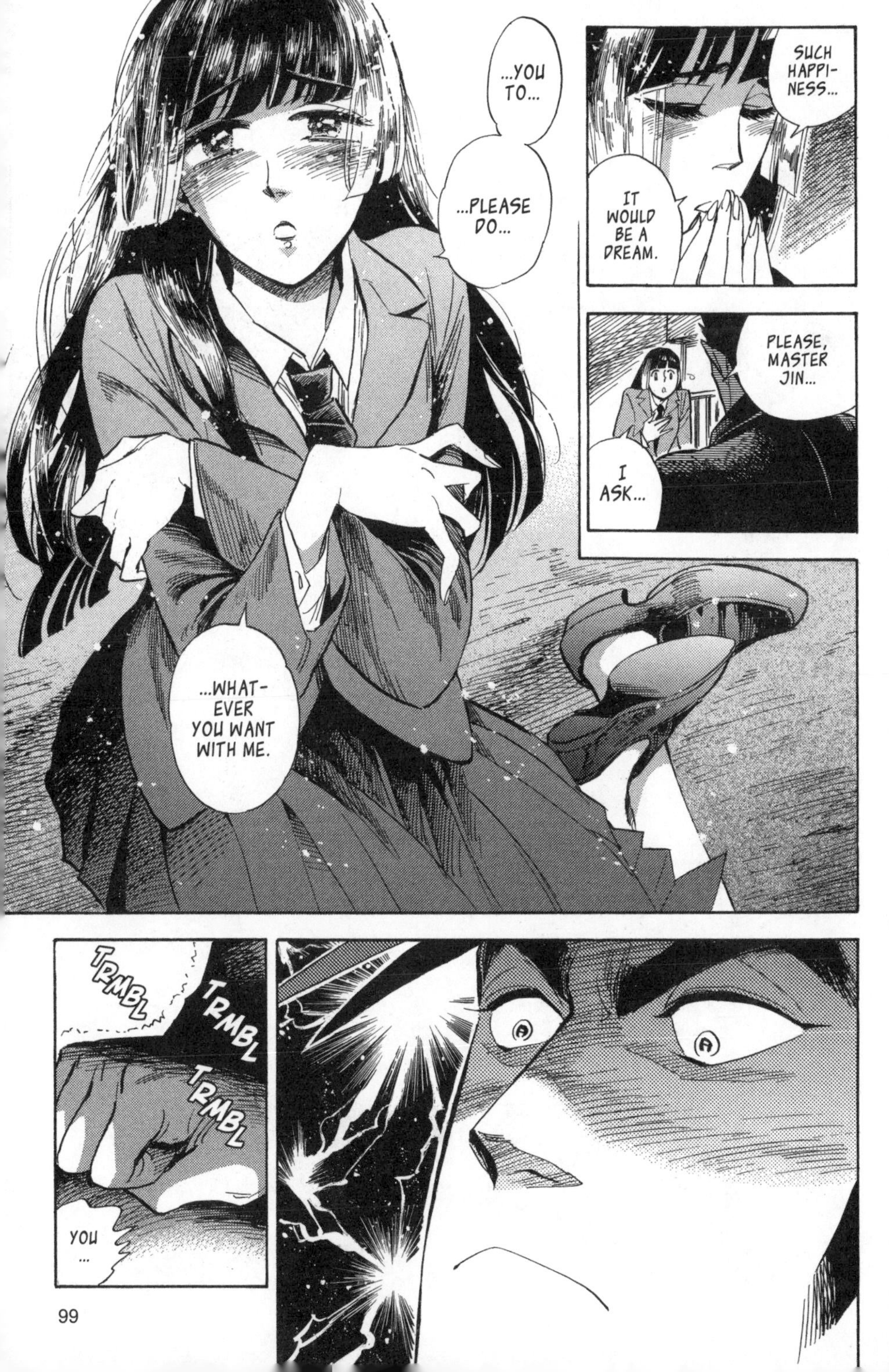
SUCH HAPPINESS...
IT WOULD BE A DREAM.
PLEASE, MASTER JIN...
I ASK...
...YOU TO...
...PLEASE DO...
...WHATEVER YOU WANT WITH ME.
TRMBL
TRMBL
TRMBL
YOU ...

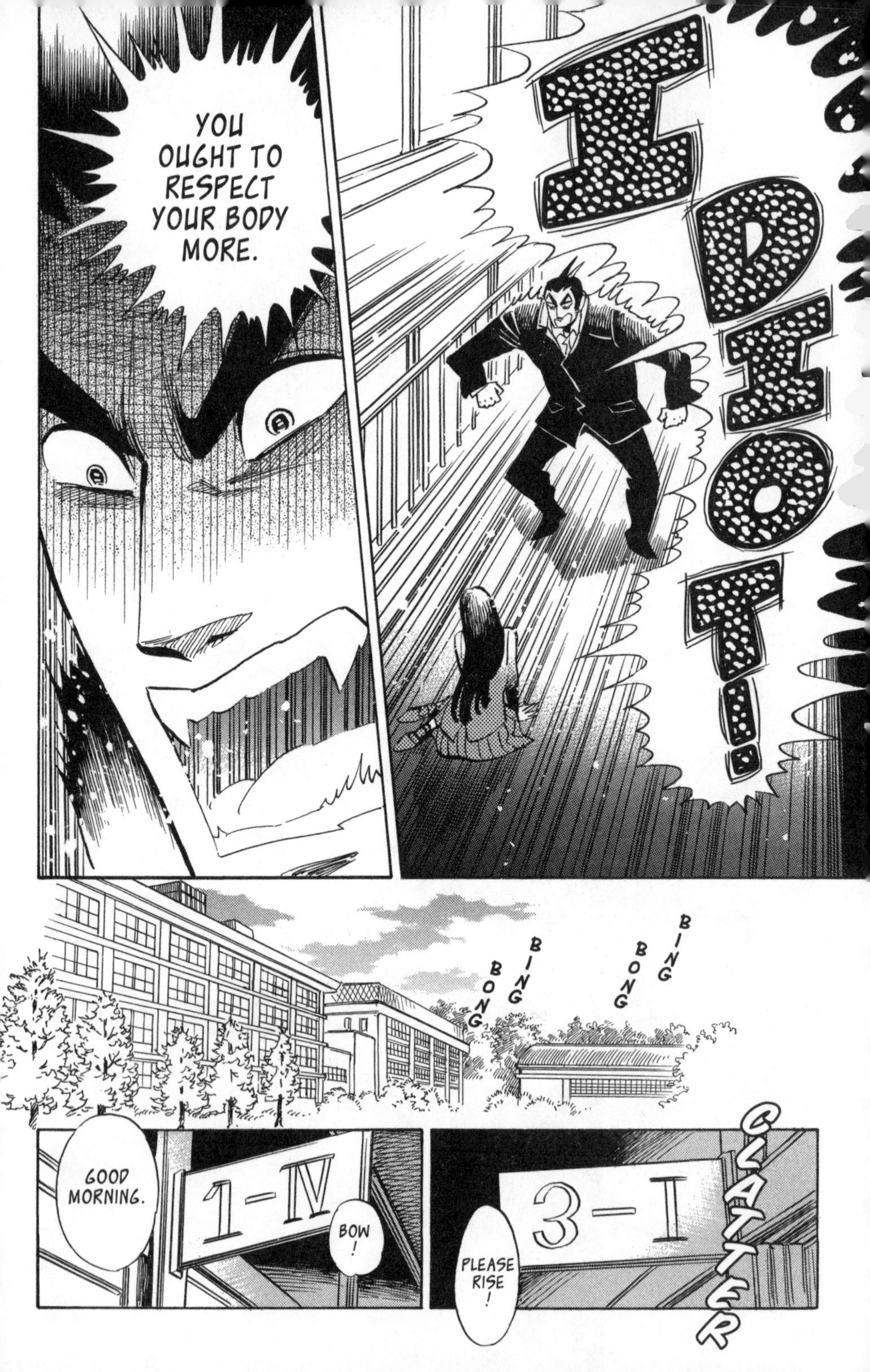
IDIOT!!
YOU OUGHT TO RESPECT YOUR BODY MORE.
BING BONG
BING BONG
3-I
CLATTER
PLEASE RISE!
1-IV
BOW!
GOOD MORNING.

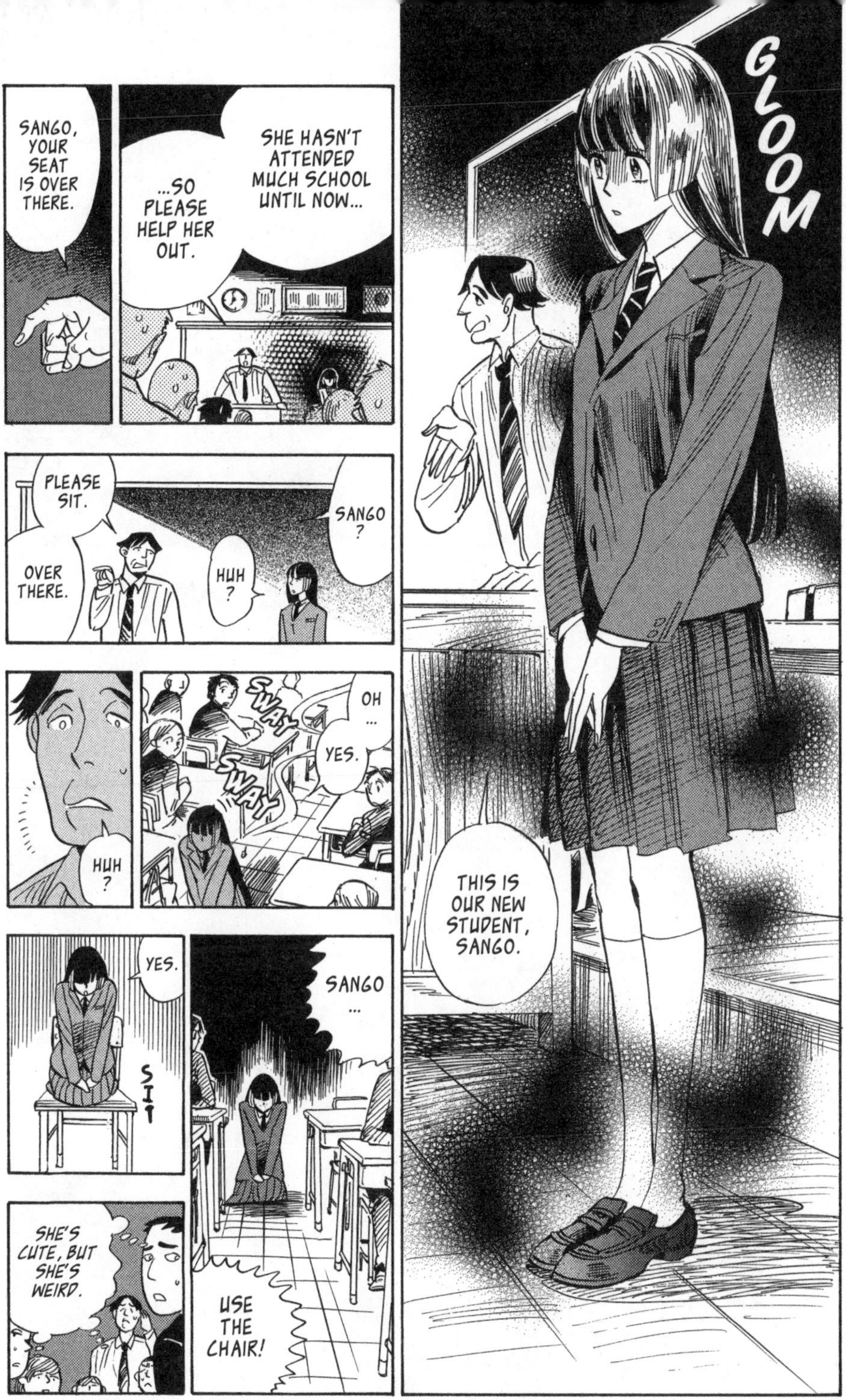
GLOOM
THIS IS OUR NEW STUDENT, SANGO.
SHE HASN'T ATTENDED MUCH SCHOOL UNTIL NOW...
...SO PLEASE HELP HER OUT.
SANGO, YOUR SEAT IS OVER THERE.
SANGO?
PLEASE SIT.
HUH?
OVER THERE.
SWAY
SWAY
OH... YES.
HUH?
SANGO...
USE THE CHAIR!
YES.
SIT
SHE'S CUTE, BUT SHE'S WEIRD.

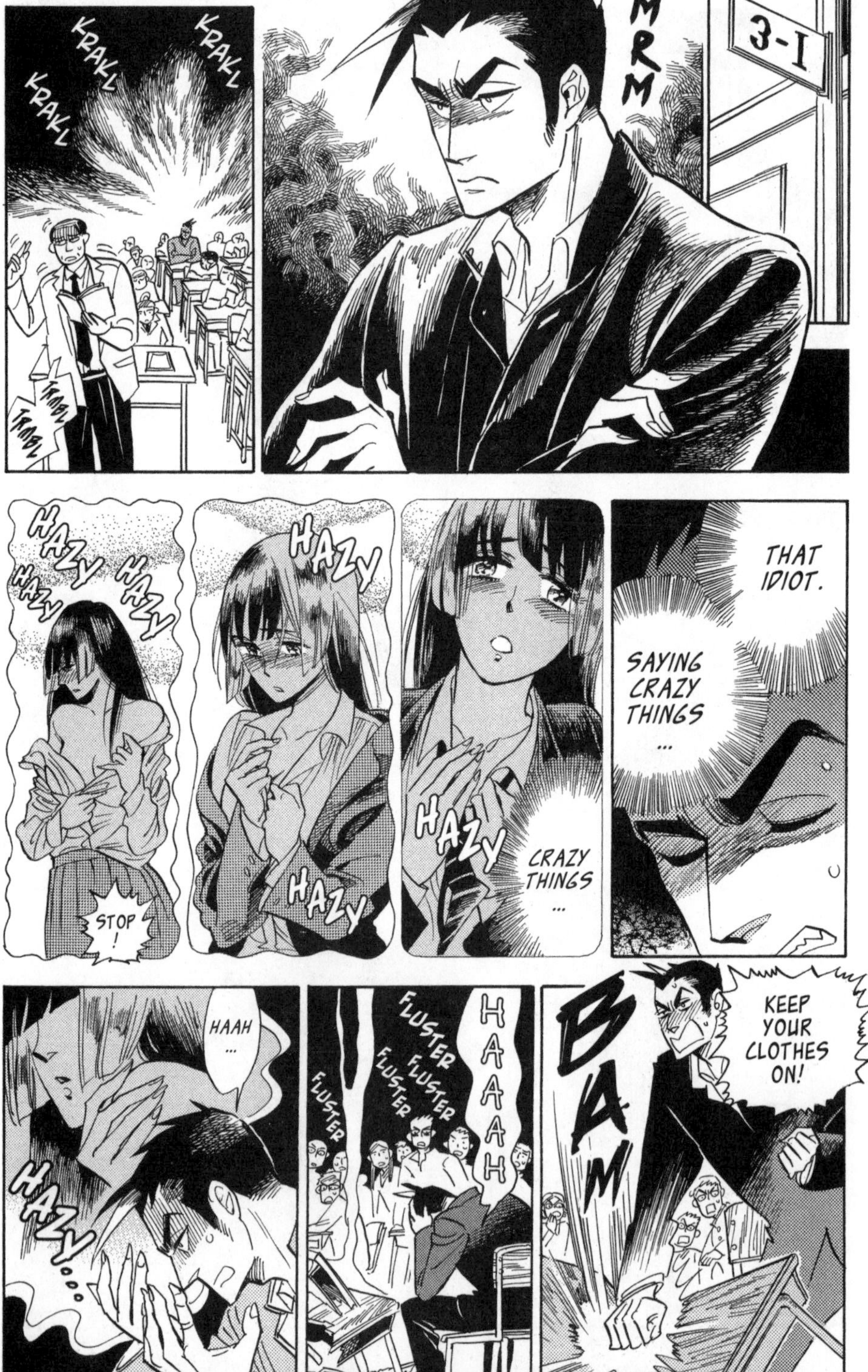
3-I
MRM
KRAKL
KRAKL
KRAKL
TREMBL
TREMBL
THAT IDIOT.
SAYING CRAZY THINGS ...
HAZY
CRAZY THINGS ...
HAZY
HAZY
HAZY
HAZY
HAZY
STOP!
BAM
KEEP YOUR CLOTHES ON!
FLUSTER
FLUSTER
FLUSTER
HAAAAH
HAAH ...
HAZY...

"MASTER JIN..."

"AAH..."

"AH!"

SLUMP

FLUSH....!

JOLT

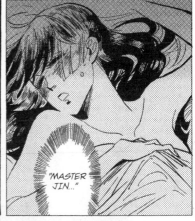

"MASTER JIN..."

DAMMIT...

SANGO...

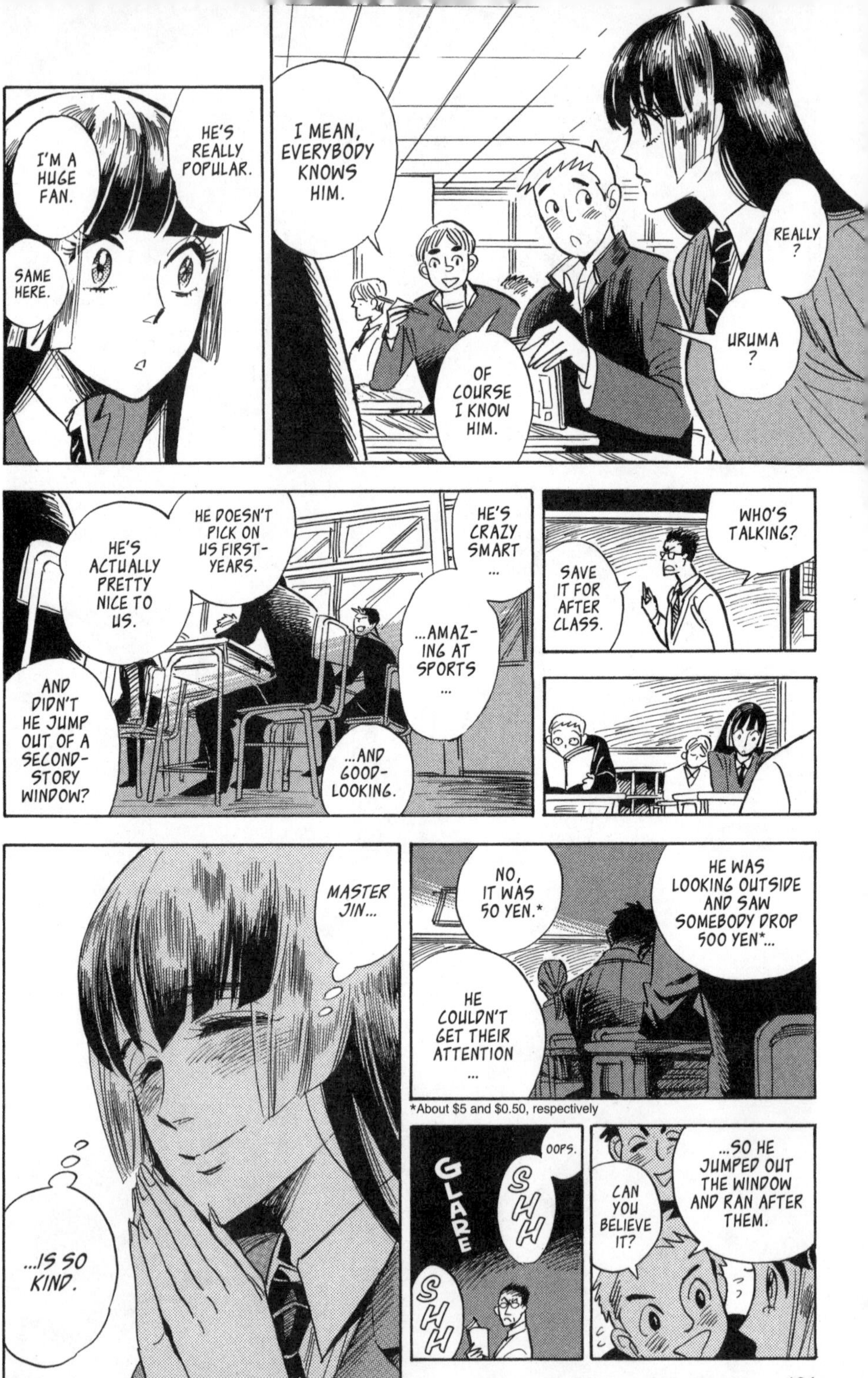
REALLY?
URUMA?
I MEAN, EVERYBODY KNOWS HIM.
OF COURSE I KNOW HIM.
HE'S REALLY POPULAR.
I'M A HUGE FAN.
SAME HERE.
WHO'S TALKING?
SAVE IT FOR AFTER CLASS.
HE'S CRAZY SMART...
...AMAZING AT SPORTS...
...AND GOOD-LOOKING.
HE DOESN'T PICK ON US FIRST-YEARS.
HE'S ACTUALLY PRETTY NICE TO US.
AND DIDN'T HE JUMP OUT OF A SECOND-STORY WINDOW?
HE WAS LOOKING OUTSIDE AND SAW SOMEBODY DROP 500 YEN*...
NO, IT WAS 50 YEN.*
HE COULDN'T GET THEIR ATTENTION...
...SO HE JUMPED OUT THE WINDOW AND RAN AFTER THEM.
CAN YOU BELIEVE IT?
OOPS.
SHH
GLARE
SHH
MASTER JIN...
...IS SO KIND.

*About $5 and $0.50, respectively

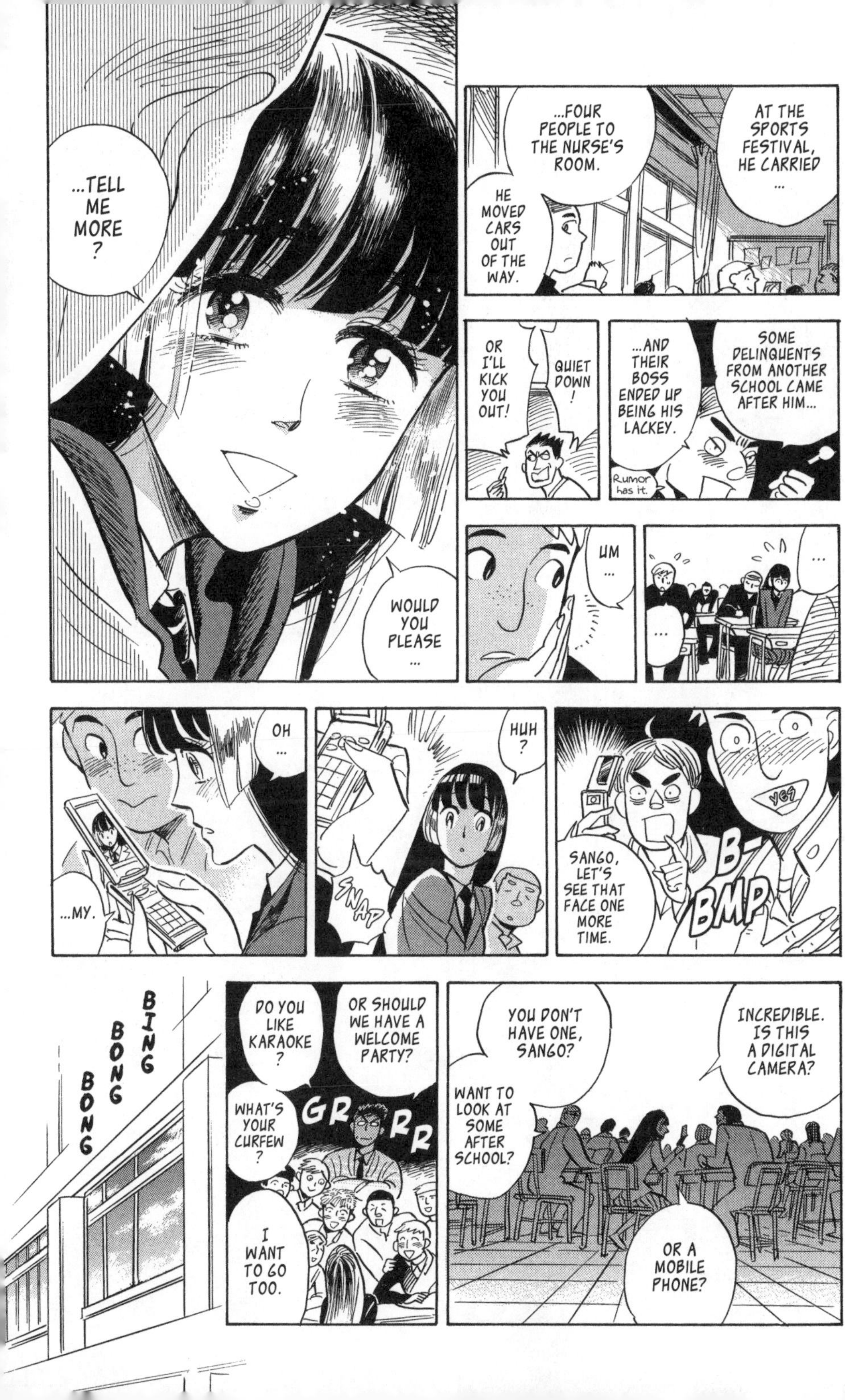
AT THE SPORTS FESTIVAL, HE CARRIED ...
...FOUR PEOPLE TO THE NURSE'S ROOM.
HE MOVED CARS OUT OF THE WAY.
SOME DELINQUENTS FROM ANOTHER SCHOOL CAME AFTER HIM...
...AND THEIR BOSS ENDED UP BEING HIS LACKEY.
Rumor has it.
QUIET DOWN!
OR I'LL KICK YOU OUT!
...
...
UM ...
WOULD YOU PLEASE ...
...TELL ME MORE?
YES
B-BMP
SANGO, LET'S SEE THAT FACE ONE MORE TIME.
HUH?
SNAP
OH ...
...MY.
INCREDIBLE. IS THIS A DIGITAL CAMERA?
YOU DON'T HAVE ONE, SANGO?
WANT TO LOOK AT SOME AFTER SCHOOL?
OR A MOBILE PHONE?
OR SHOULD WE HAVE A WELCOME PARTY?
DO YOU LIKE KARAOKE?
GRRR
WHAT'S YOUR CURFEW?
I WANT TO GO TOO.
BING
BONG
BONG

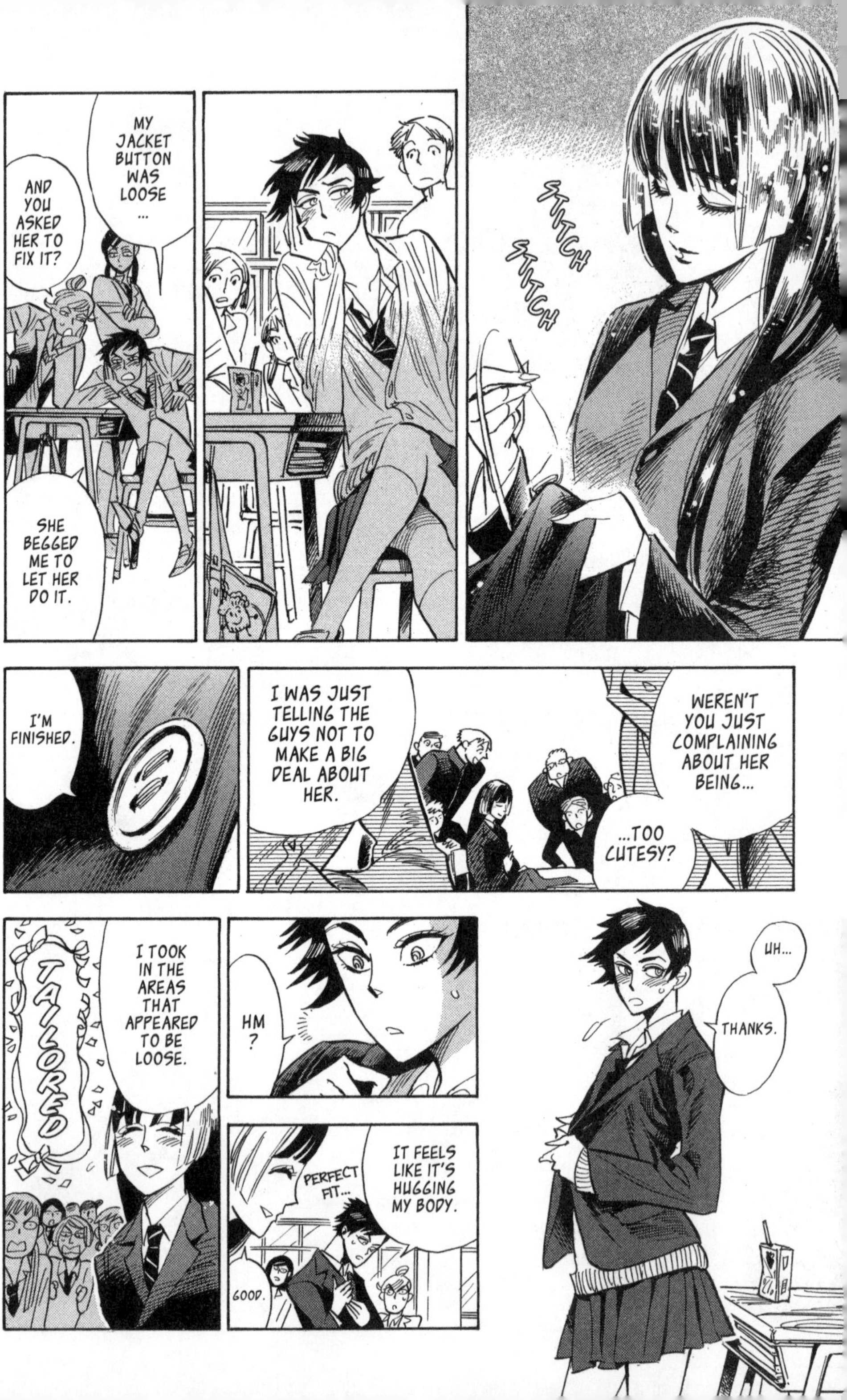
STITCH
STITCH
MY JACKET BUTTON WAS LOOSE ...
AND YOU ASKED HER TO FIX IT?
SHE BEGGED ME TO LET HER DO IT.
WEREN'T YOU JUST COMPLAINING ABOUT HER BEING...
I WAS JUST TELLING THE GUYS NOT TO MAKE A BIG DEAL ABOUT HER.
...TOO CUTESY?
I'M FINISHED.
UH...
THANKS.
HM ?
IT FEELS LIKE IT'S HUGGING MY BODY.
PERFECT FIT...
GOOD.
I TOOK IN THE AREAS THAT APPEARED TO BE LOOSE.
TAILORED

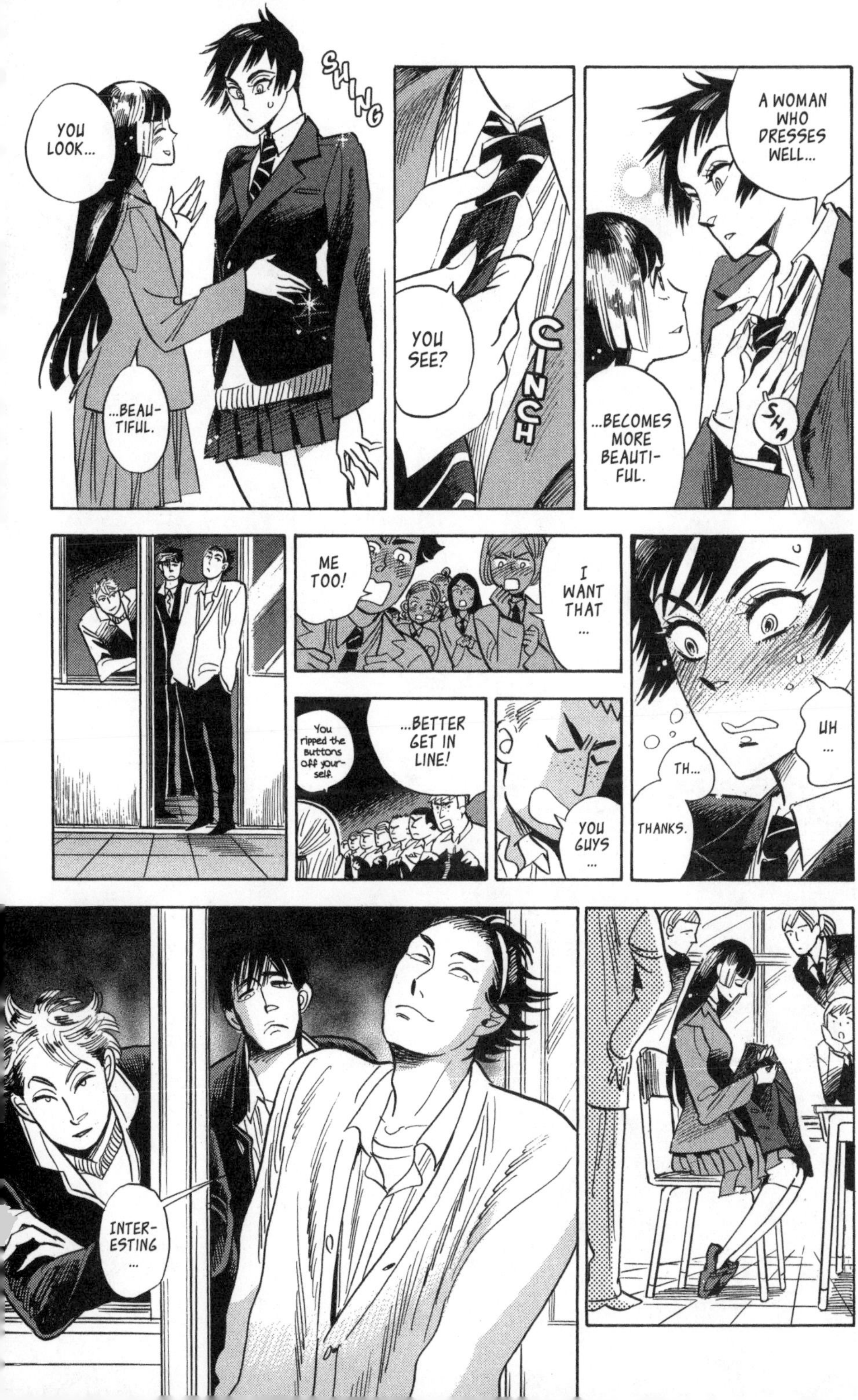
A WOMAN WHO DRESSES WELL...
...BECOMES MORE BEAUTIFUL.
SHA
YOU SEE?
CINCH
SHING
YOU LOOK...
...BEAUTIFUL.
UH ...
TH... THANKS.
I WANT THAT ...
ME TOO!
YOU GUYS ...
...BETTER GET IN LINE!
You ripped the buttons off yourself.
INTERESTING ...

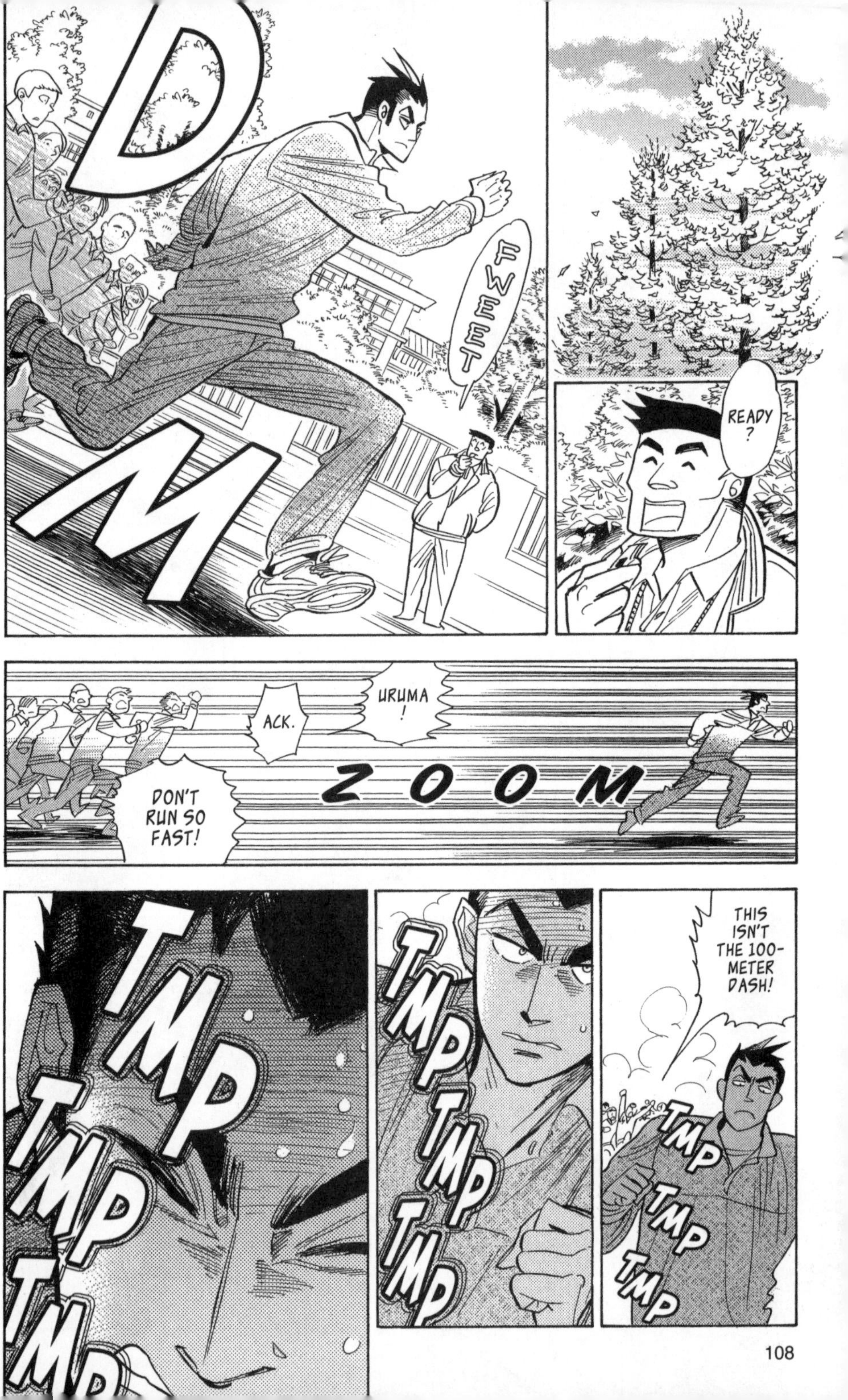
READY?
FWEET
DM
URUMA!
ACK.
ZOOM
DON'T RUN SO FAST!
THIS ISN'T THE 100-METER DASH!
TMP TMP TMP TMP
TMP TMP TMP TMP
TMP TMP TMP

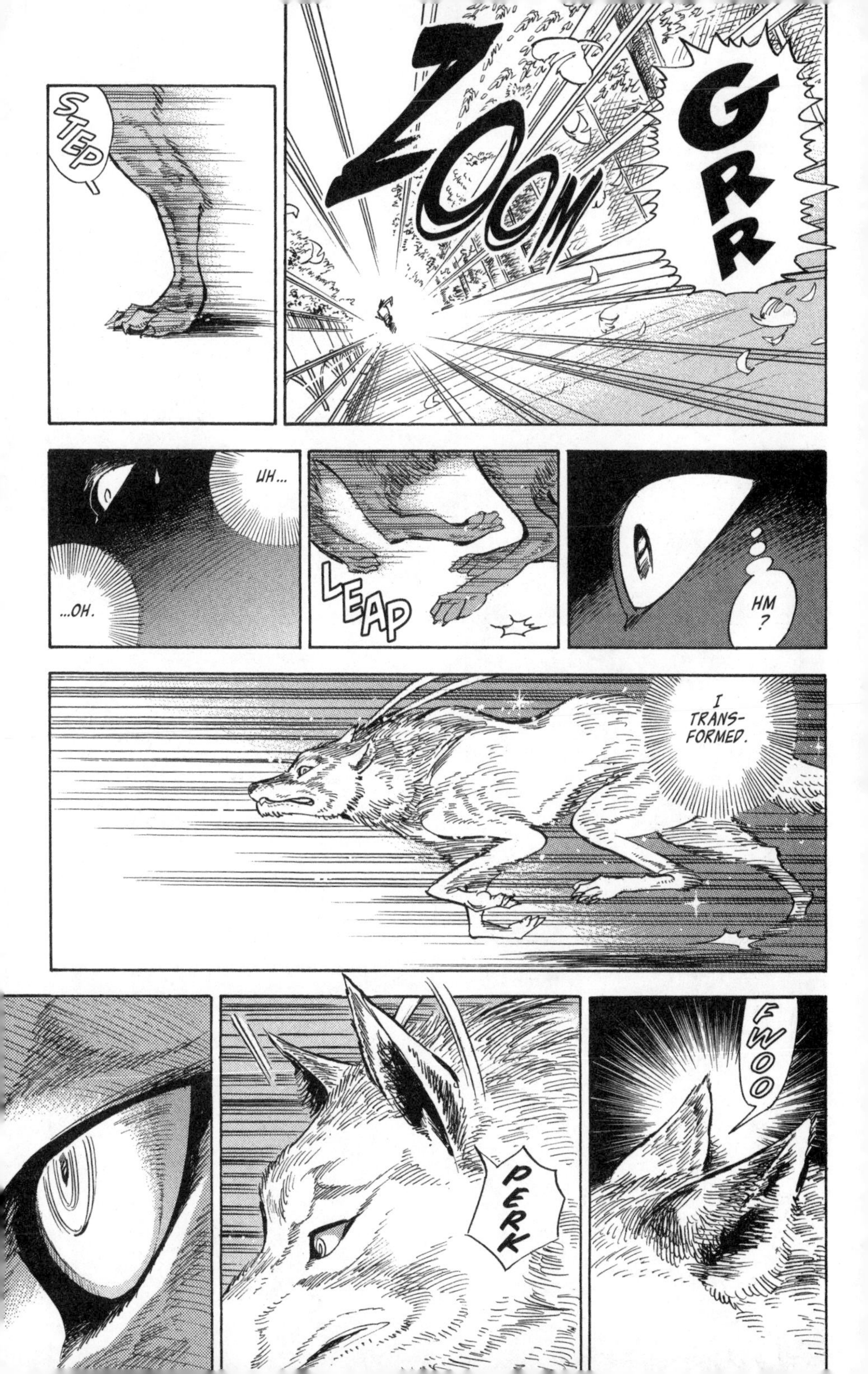
GRR
ZOOM
STEP
HM?
LEAP
UH...
...OH.
I TRANS-FORMED.
FWOO
PERK

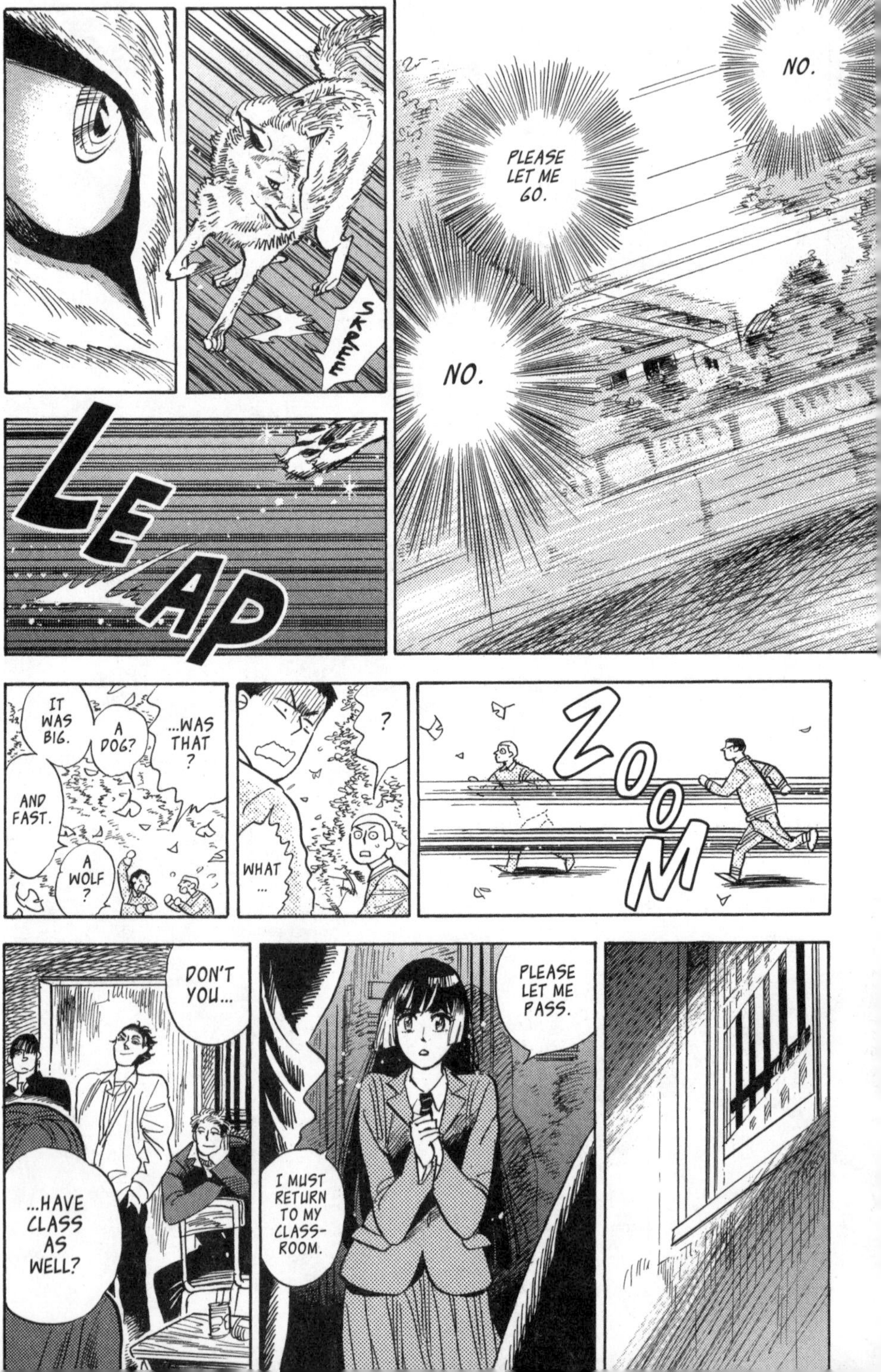
NO.
PLEASE LET ME GO.
NO.
SKREE
LEAP
ZOOM
?
WHAT...
...WAS THAT?
A DOG?
IT WAS BIG.
AND FAST.
A WOLF?
PLEASE LET ME PASS.
I MUST RETURN TO MY CLASS-ROOM.
DON'T YOU...
...HAVE CLASS AS WELL?

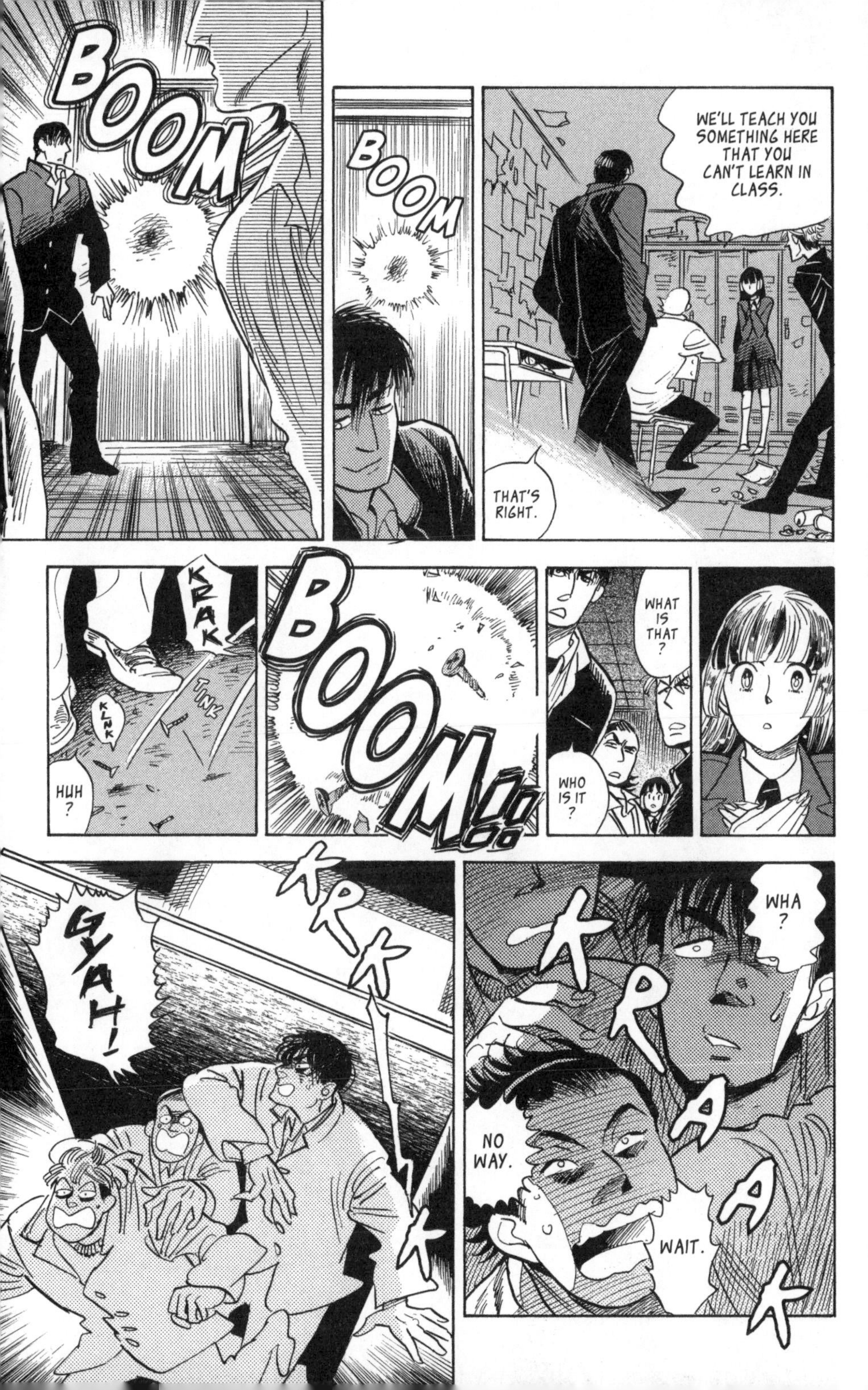
WE'LL TEACH YOU SOMETHING HERE THAT YOU CAN'T LEARN IN CLASS.
THAT'S RIGHT.
BOOM
BOOM
WHAT IS THAT?
WHO IS IT?
BOOM!!
KRAK
TINK
KLNK
HUH?
WHA?
KRAAK
NO WAY.
WAIT.
KRKK
GYAH!

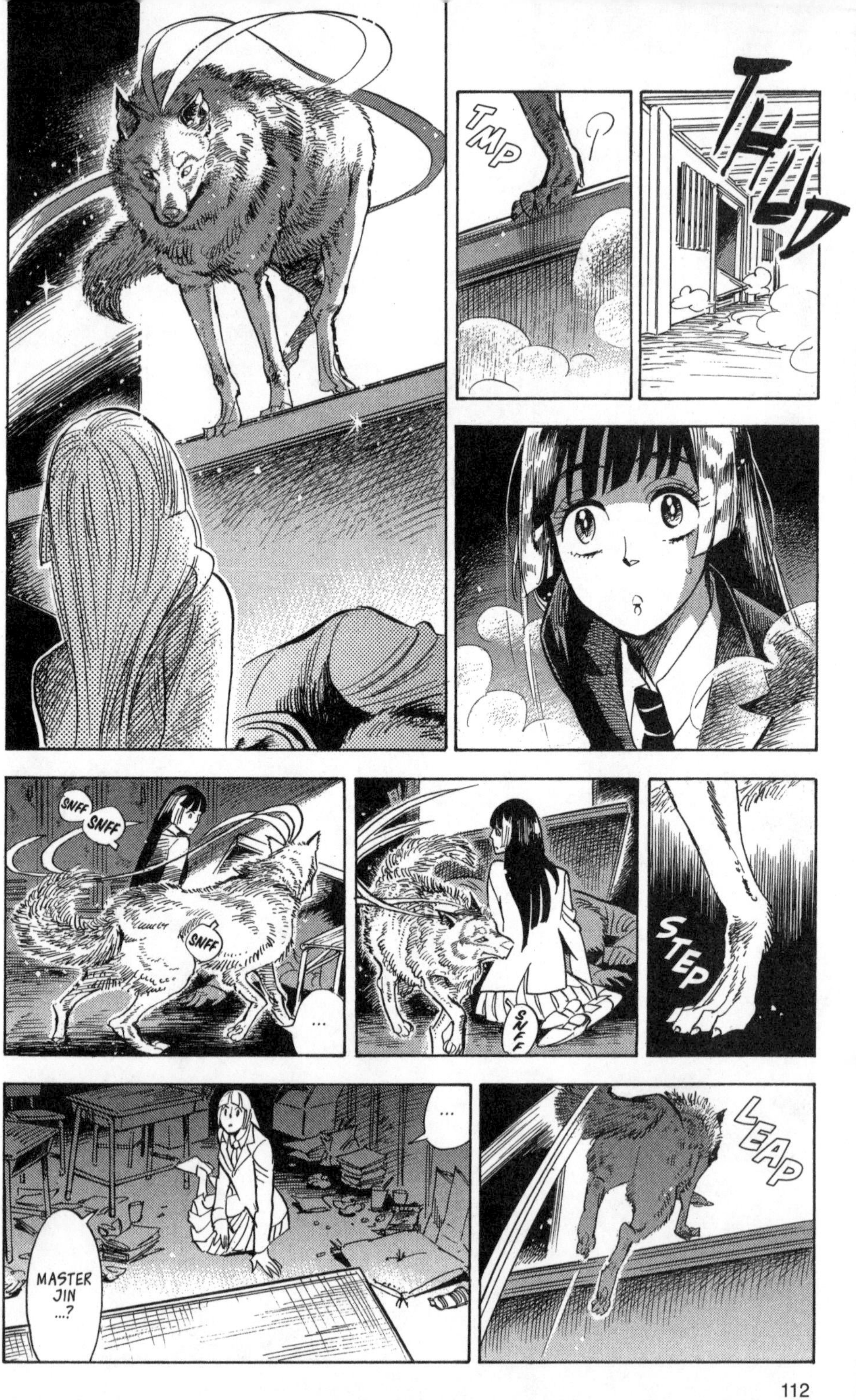
THUD
TMP
STEP
SNFF
SNFF
SNFF
SNFF
...
LEAP
...
MASTER JIN ...?

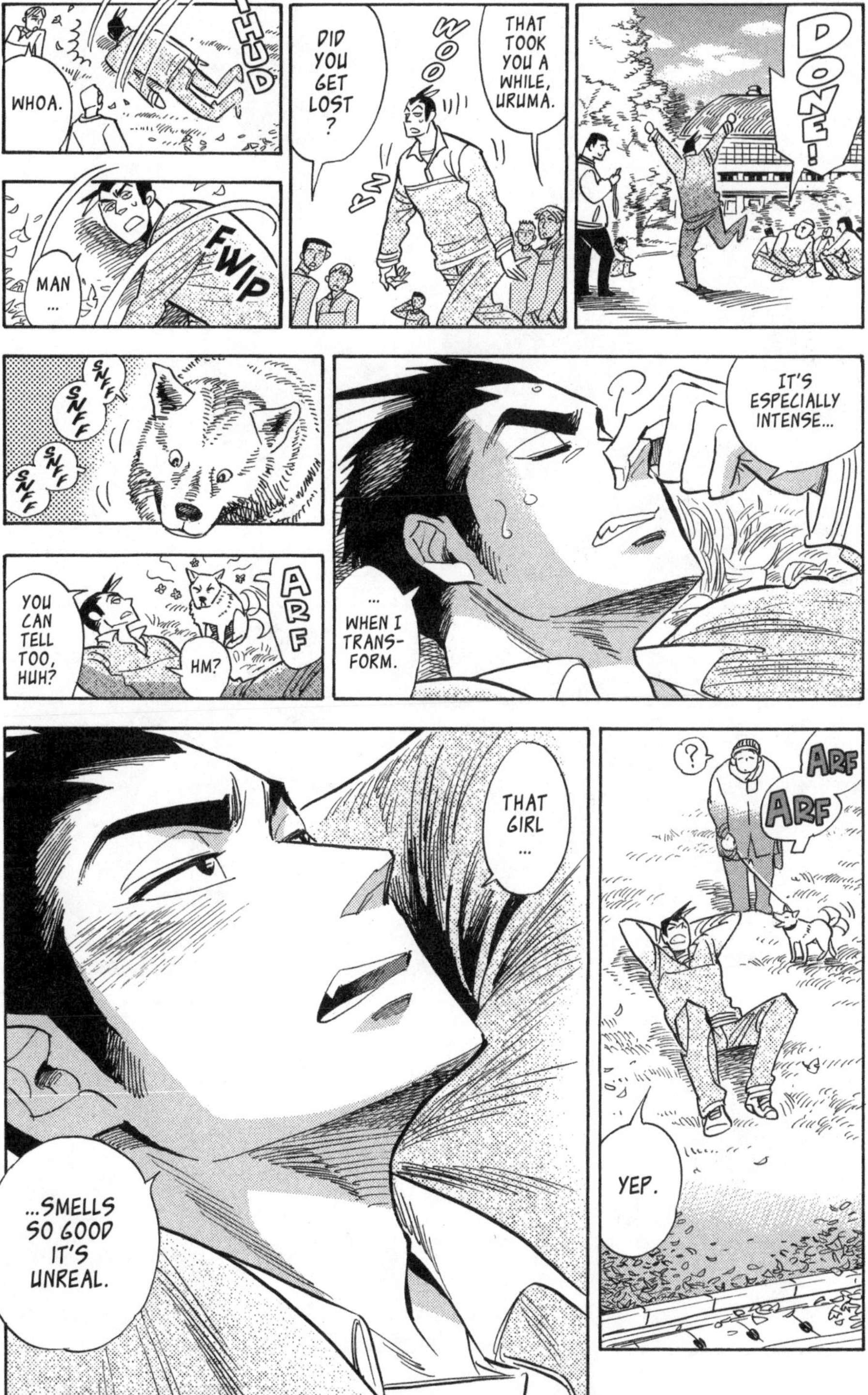
DONE!
THAT TOOK YOU A WHILE, URUMA.
WOOO
DID YOU GET LOST?
THUD
WHOA.
FWIP
MAN...
IT'S ESPECIALLY INTENSE...
...WHEN I TRANSFORM.
SNFF SNFF
SNFF SNFF
ARF
HM?
YOU CAN TELL TOO, HUH?
ARF
ARF
?
YEP.
THAT GIRL...
...SMELLS SO GOOD IT'S UNREAL.

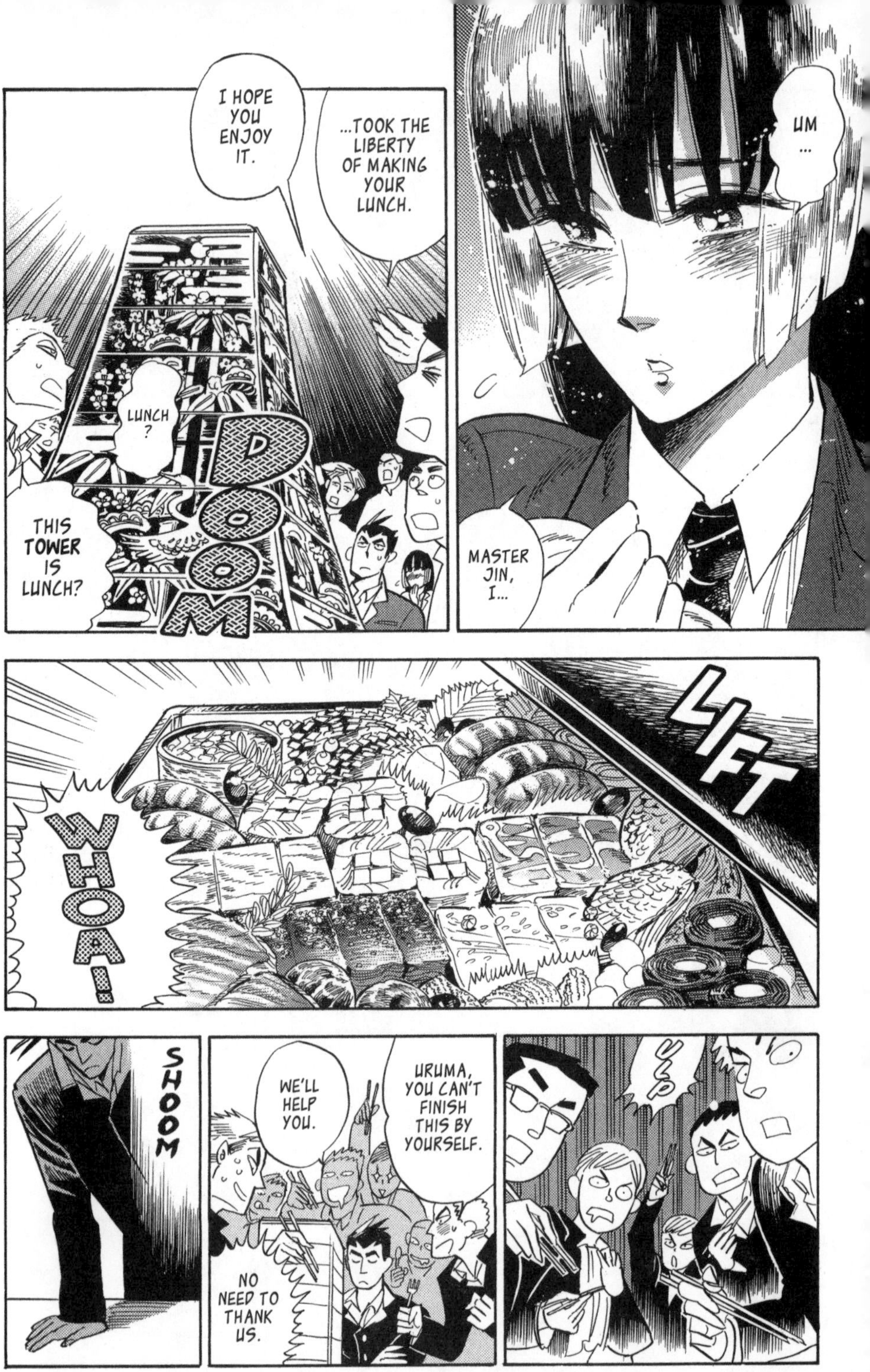
UM ...
MASTER JIN, I...
...TOOK THE LIBERTY OF MAKING YOUR LUNCH.
I HOPE YOU ENJOY IT.
LUNCH ?
DOOM
THIS TOWER IS LUNCH?
LIFT
WHOA!!
ULP
URUMA, YOU CAN'T FINISH THIS BY YOURSELF.
WE'LL HELP YOU.
NO NEED TO THANK US.
SHOOM

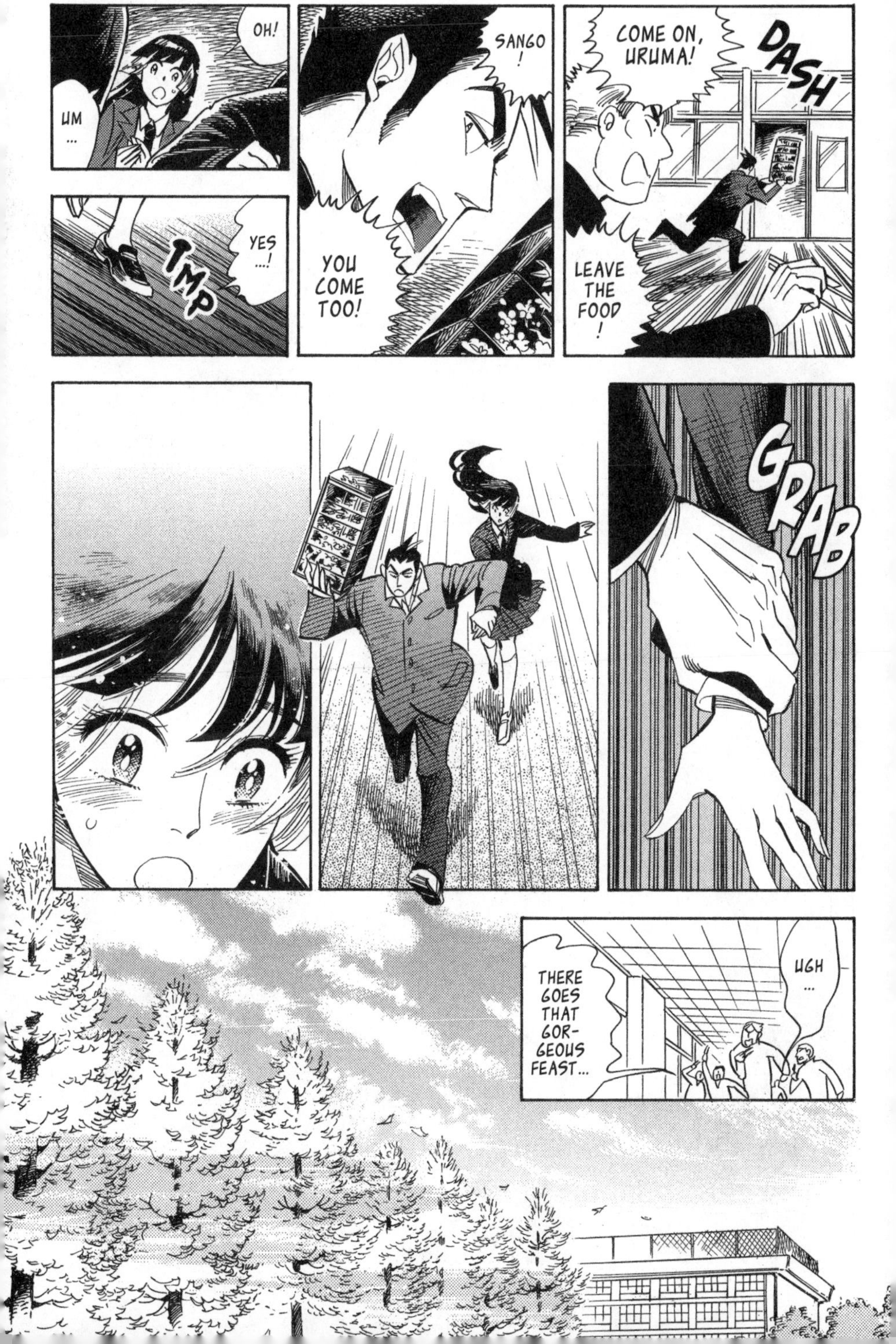
COME ON, URUMA!
DASH
LEAVE THE FOOD!
SANGO!
YOU COME TOO!
OH!
UM...
YES...!
TMP
GRAB
UGH...
THERE GOES THAT GORGEOUS FEAST...

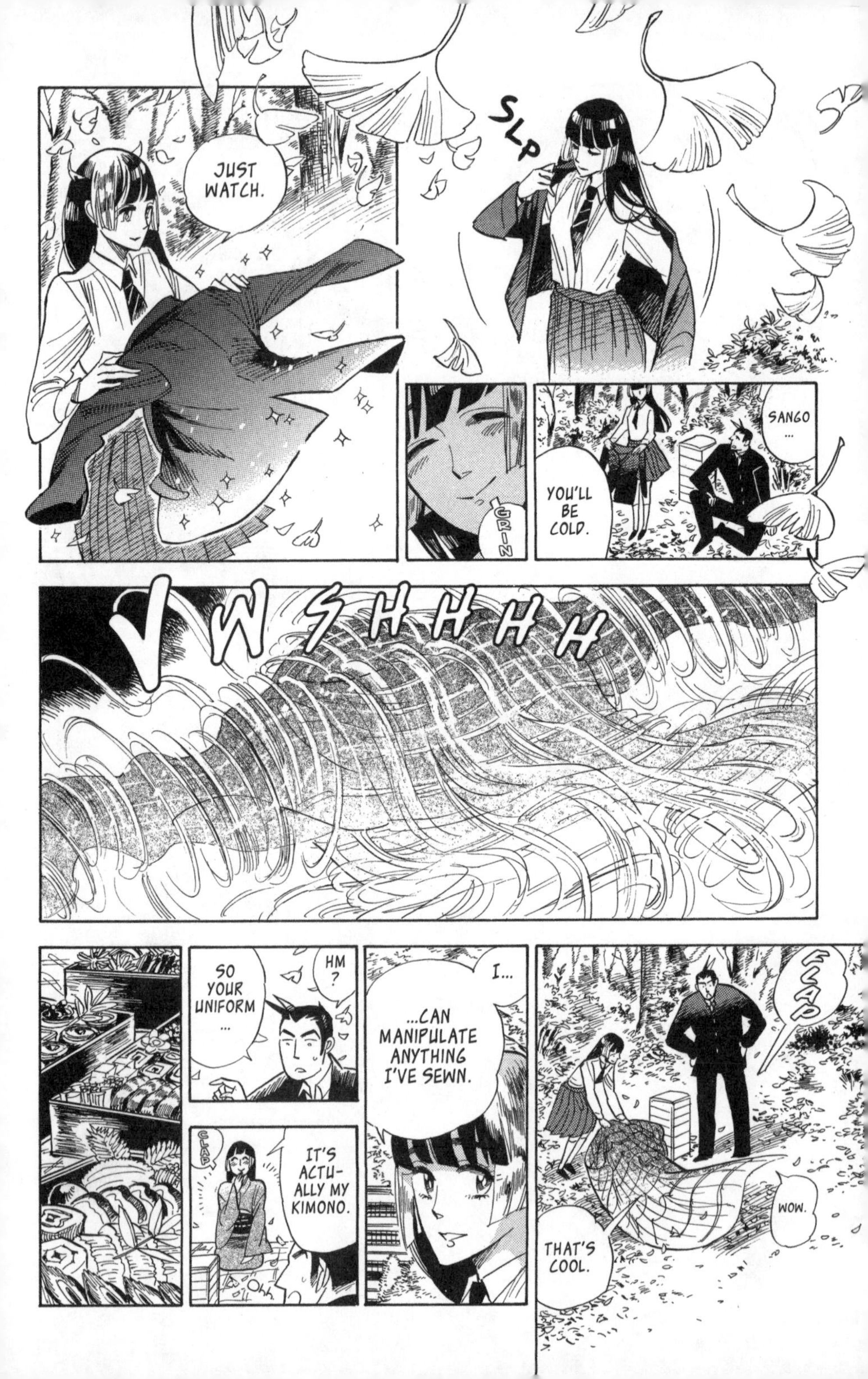
SLP
SANGO...
YOU'LL BE COLD.
GRIN
JUST WATCH.
VWSHHHHH
FLAP
WOW.
THAT'S COOL.
I...
...CAN MANIPULATE ANYTHING I'VE SEWN.
HM?
SO YOUR UNIFORM...
CLAP
IT'S ACTU-ALLY MY KIMONO.
Ohh

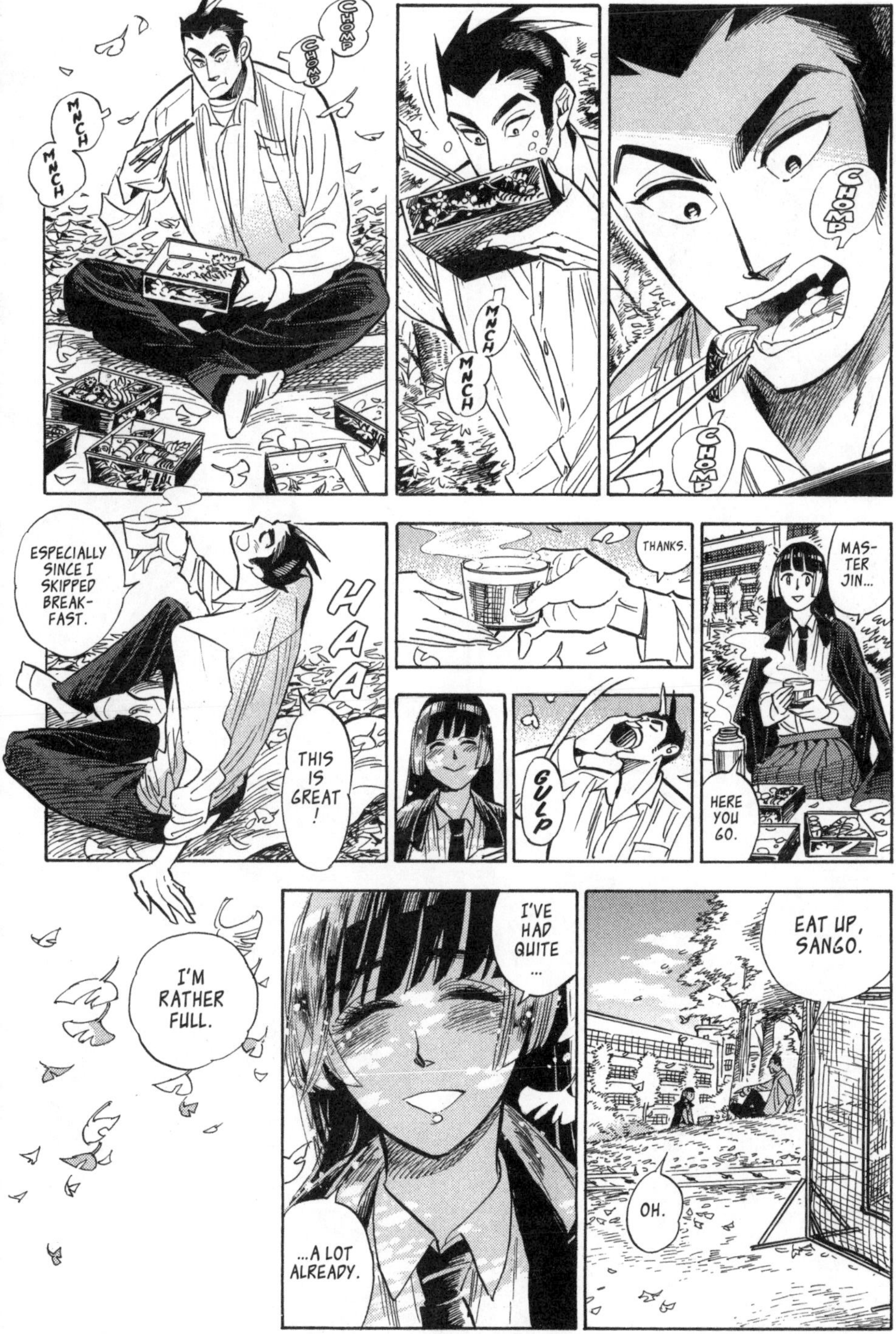
CHOMP
CHOMP
MNCH
MNCH
CHOMP
CHOMP
MNCH
MNCH
MAS-TER JIN...
HERE YOU GO.
THANKS.
GULP
HAA
THIS IS GREAT!
ESPECIALLY SINCE I SKIPPED BREAK-FAST.
EAT UP, SANGO.
OH.
I'VE HAD QUITE...
...A LOT ALREADY.
I'M RATHER FULL.

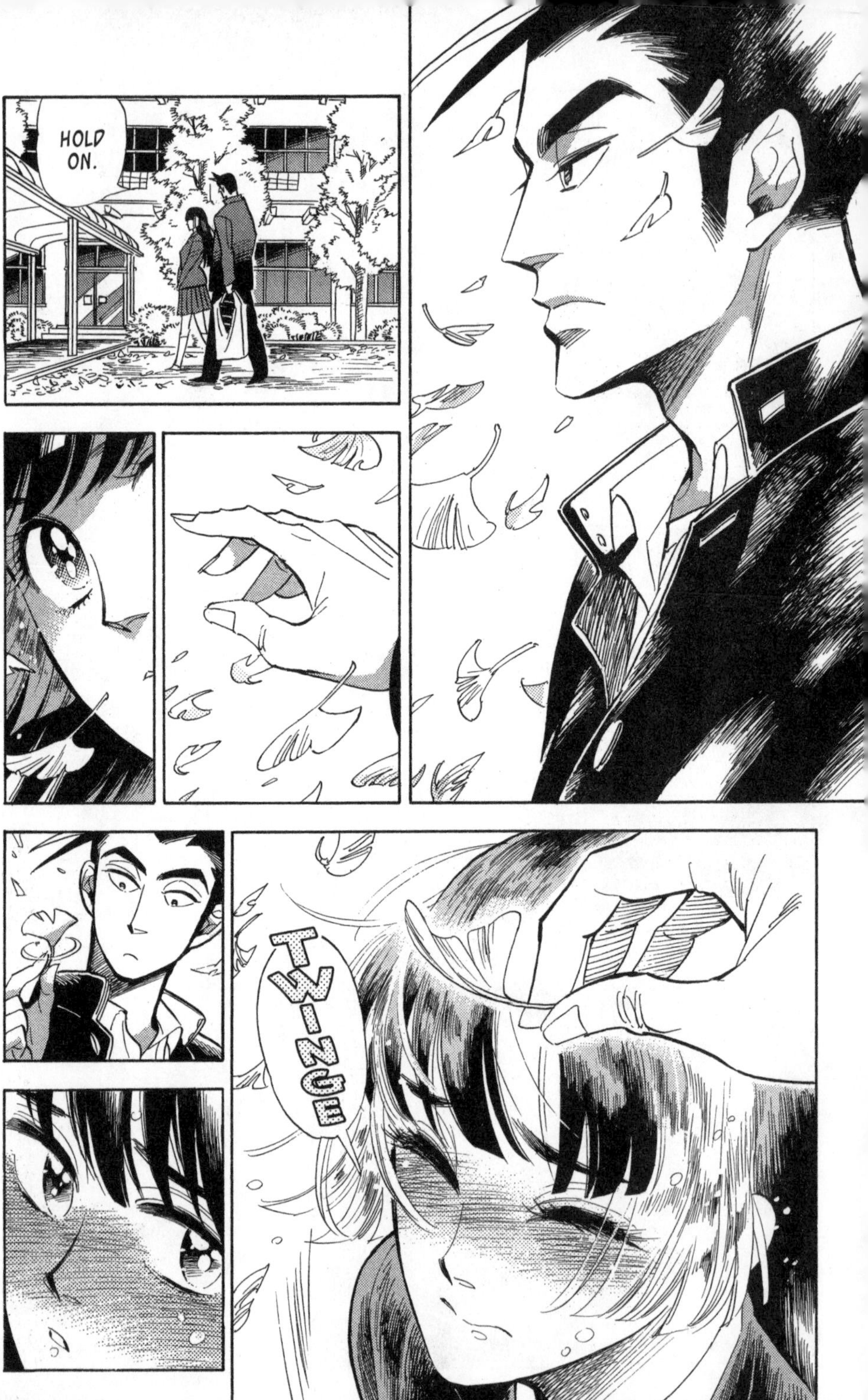
HOLD ON.
TWINGE

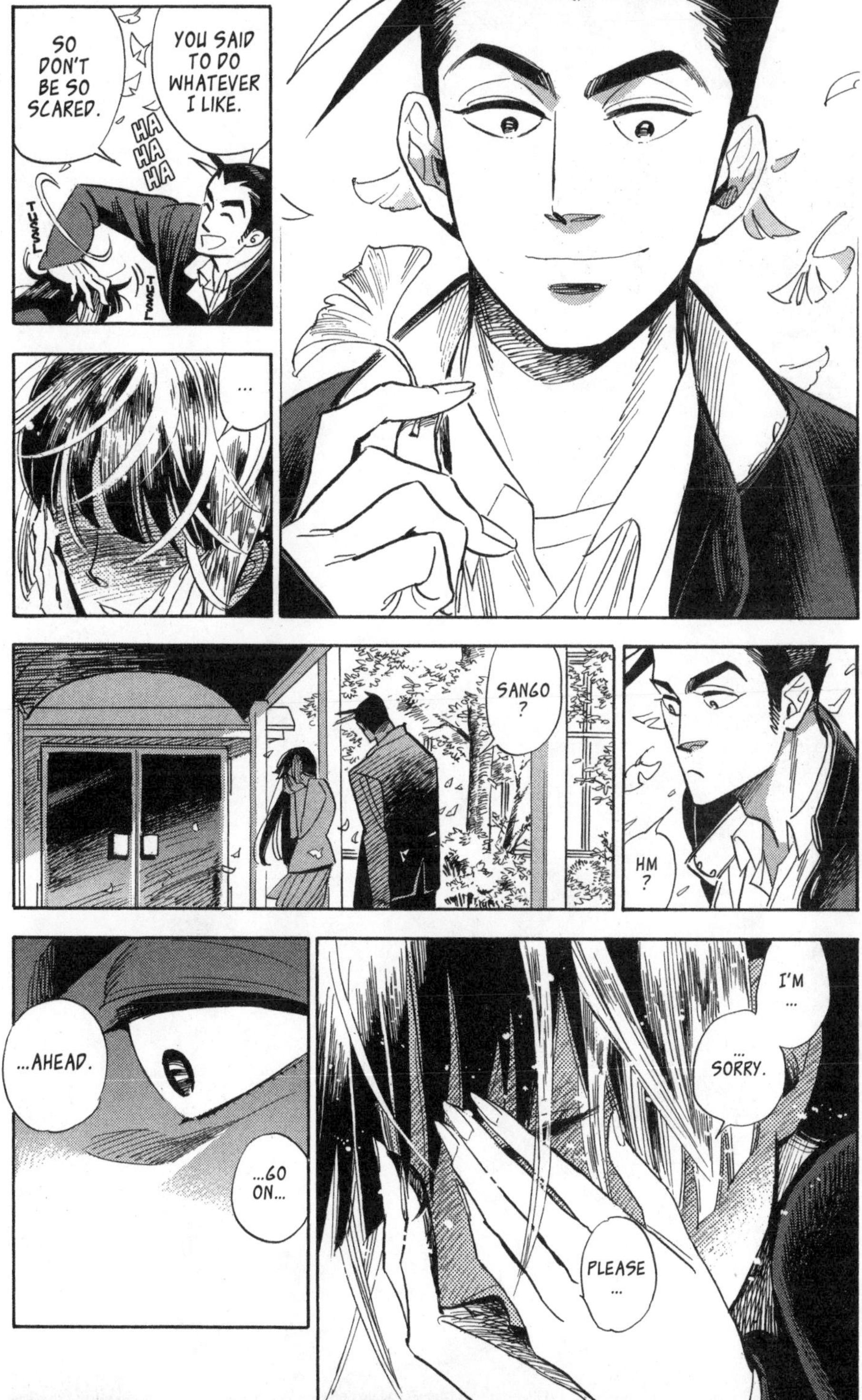
YOU SAID TO DO WHATEVER I LIKE.
HA HA HA
SO DON'T BE SO SCARED.
TUSSL
TUSSL
...
HM ?
SANGO ?
I'M ...
... SORRY.
PLEASE ...
...GO ON...
...AHEAD.

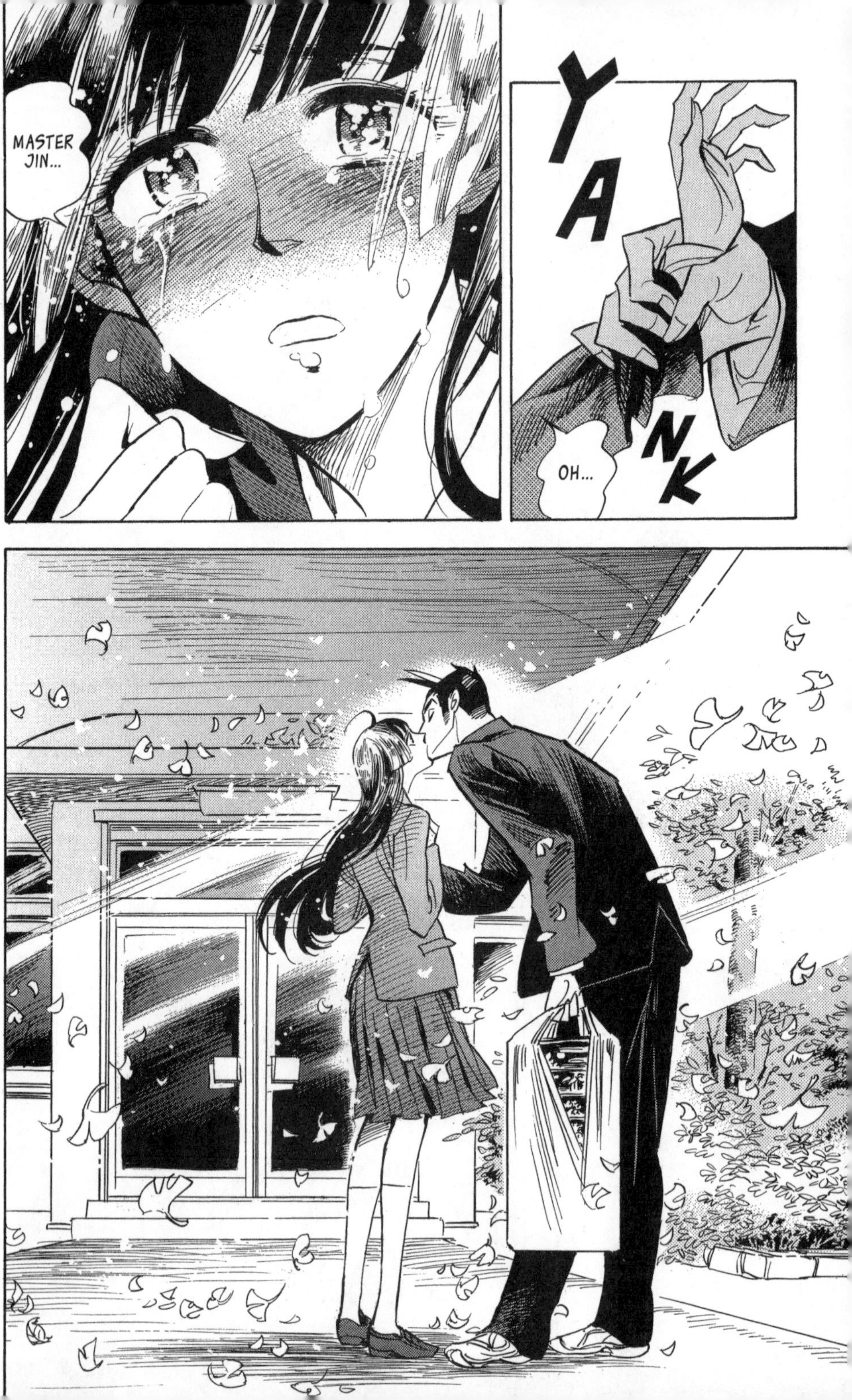
YANK
OH...
MASTER JIN...

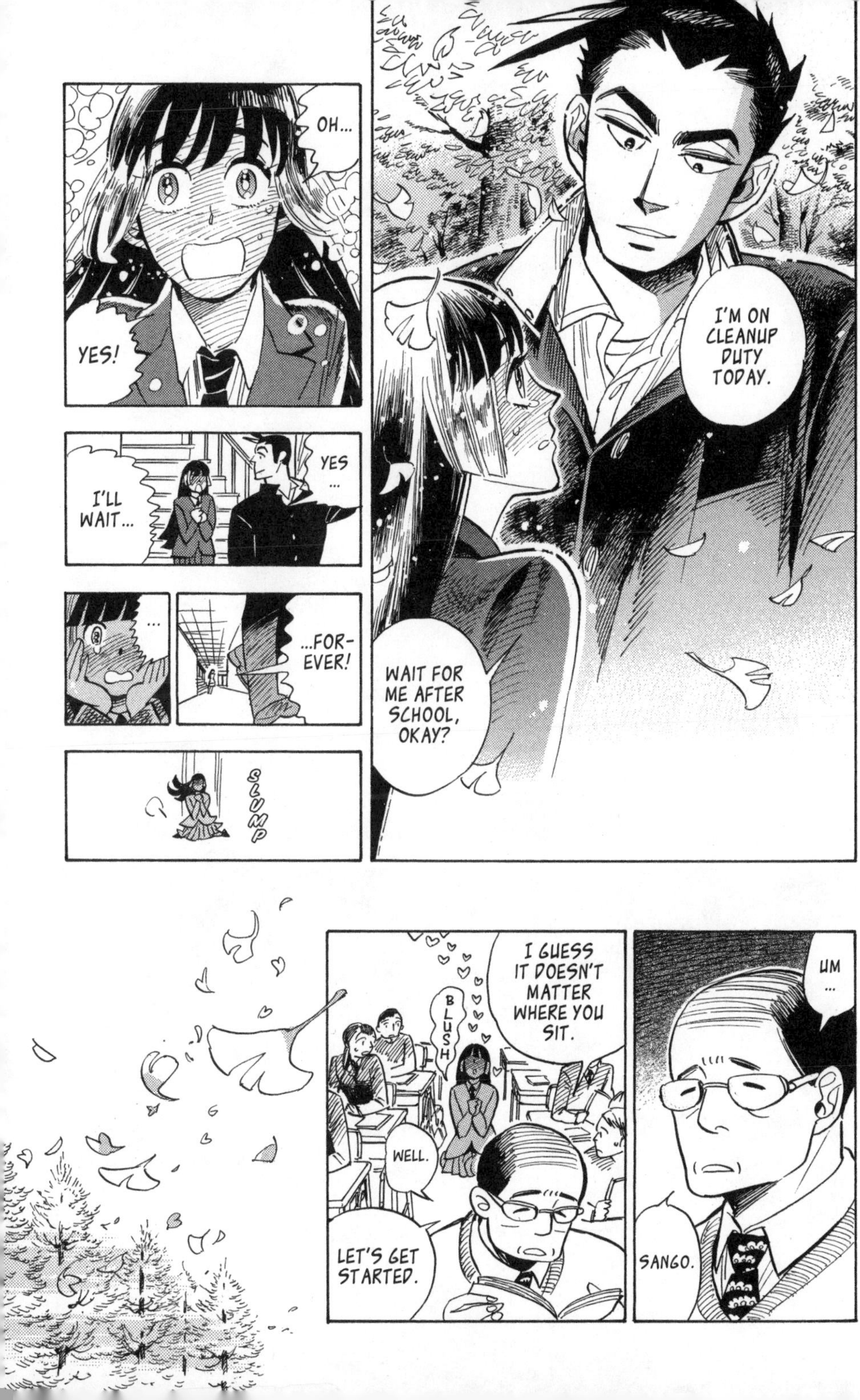
I'M ON CLEANUP DUTY TODAY.
WAIT FOR ME AFTER SCHOOL, OKAY?
OH...
YES!
YES ...
I'LL WAIT...
...FOR-EVER!
...
SLUMP
UM ...
SANGO.
I GUESS IT DOESN'T MATTER WHERE YOU SIT.
BLUSH
WELL.
LET'S GET STARTED.

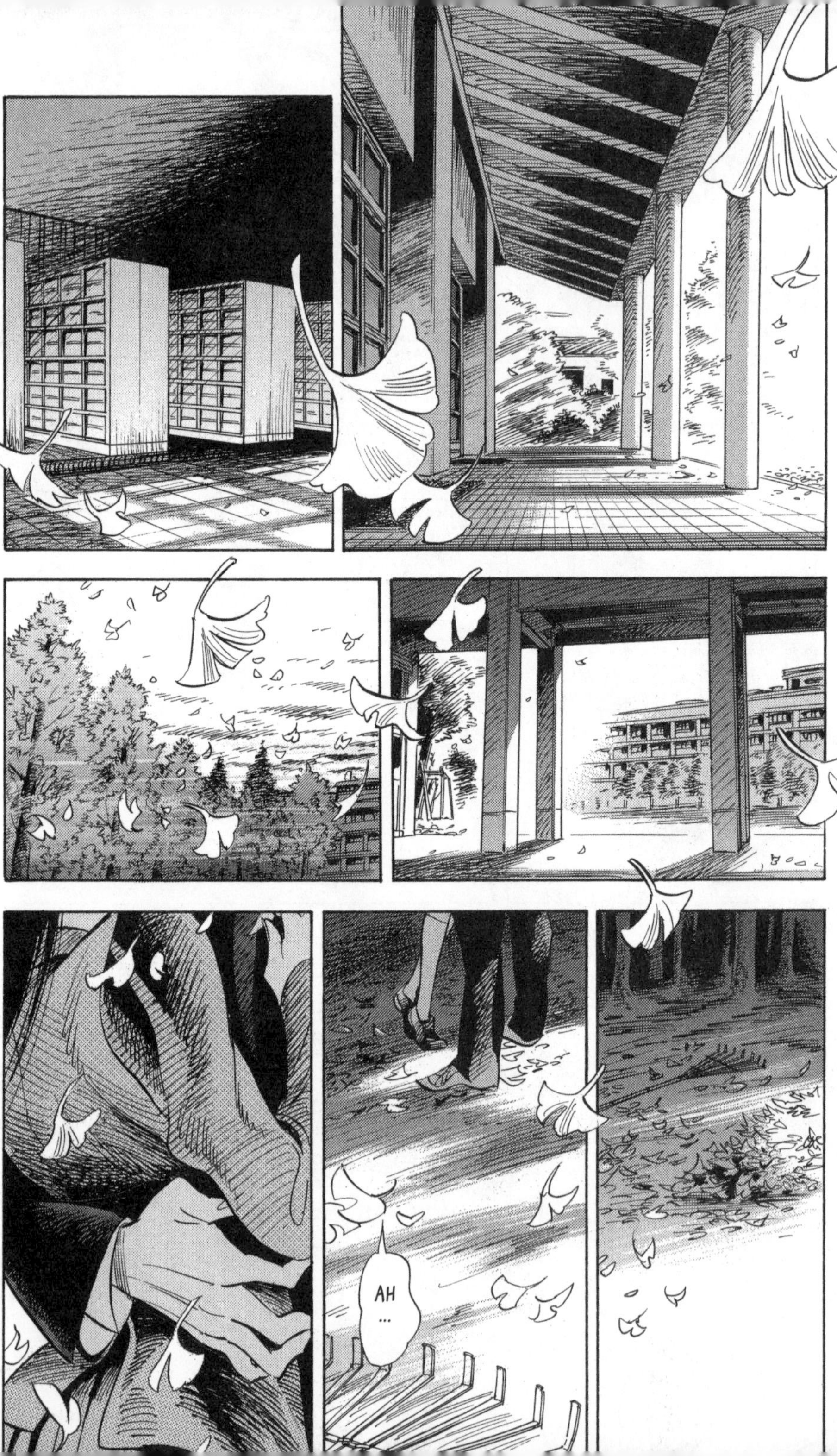
AH ...

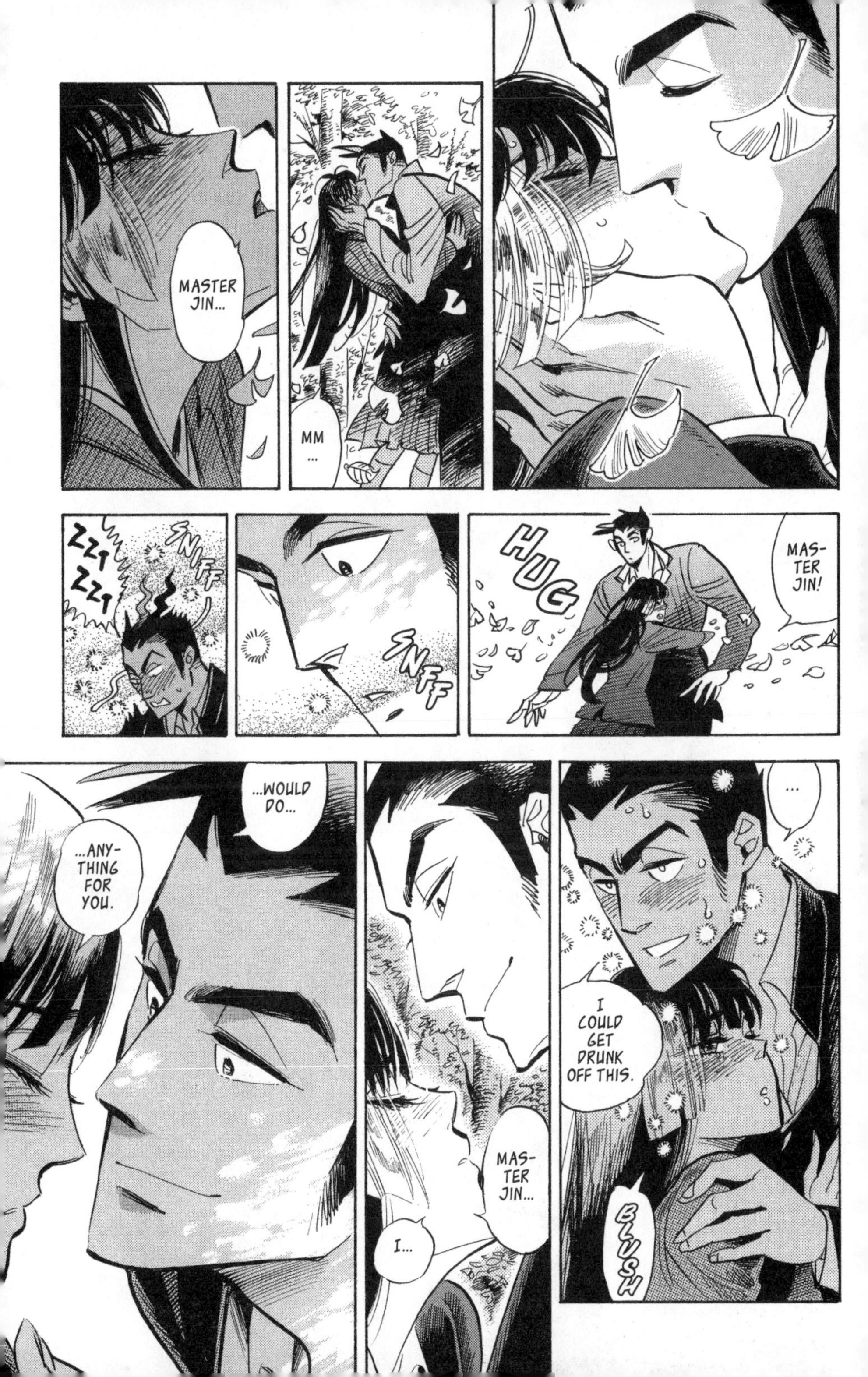
MM ...
MASTER JIN...
HUG
MAS-TER JIN!
SNIFF
SNIFF
ZZT
ZZT
...
I COULD GET DRUNK OFF THIS.
BLUSH
MAS-TER JIN...
I...
...WOULD DO...
...ANY-THING FOR YOU.

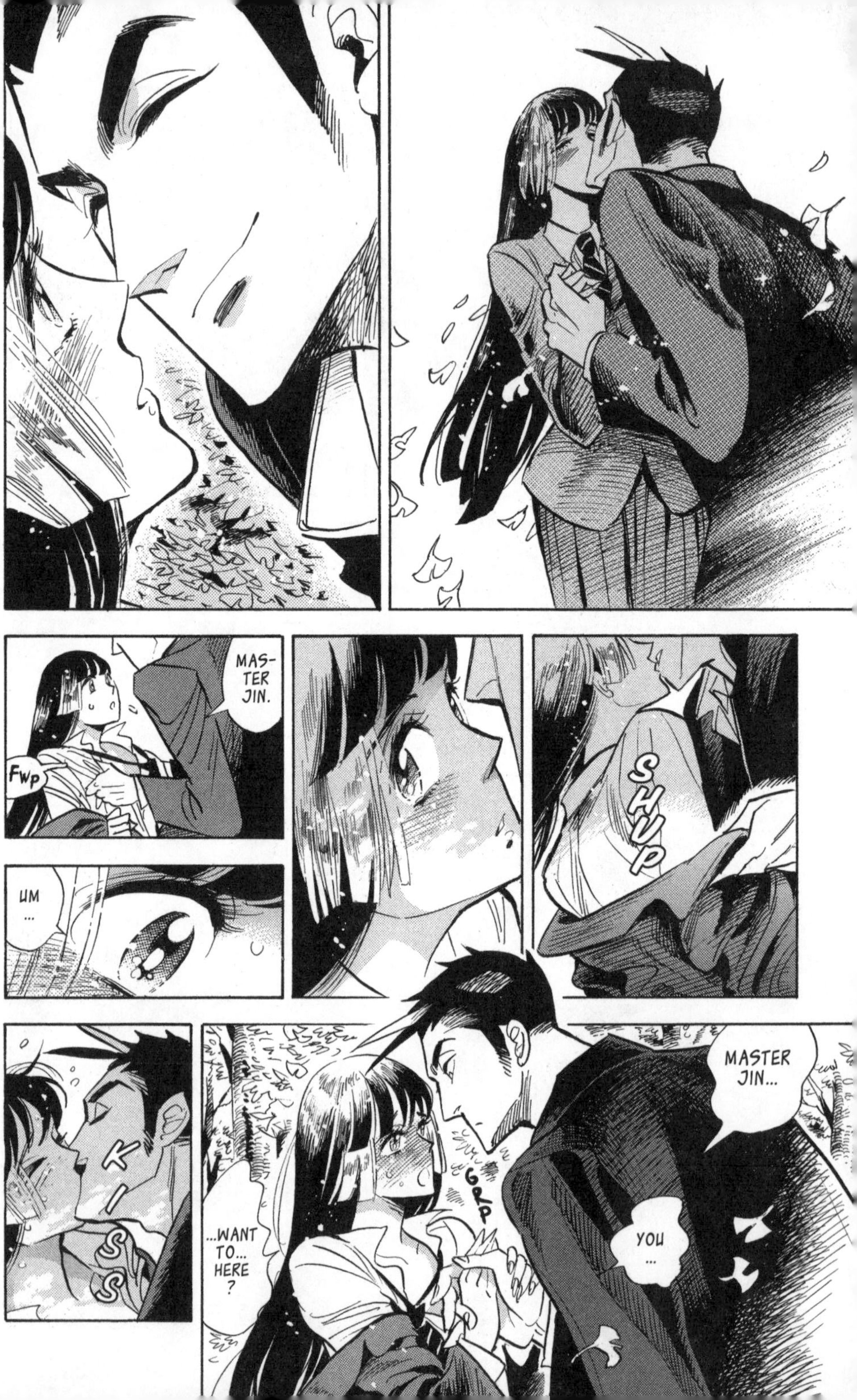
SHUP
MAS-TER JIN.
FWP
UM ...
MASTER JIN...
GRP
YOU ...
...WANT TO... HERE ?
KISS

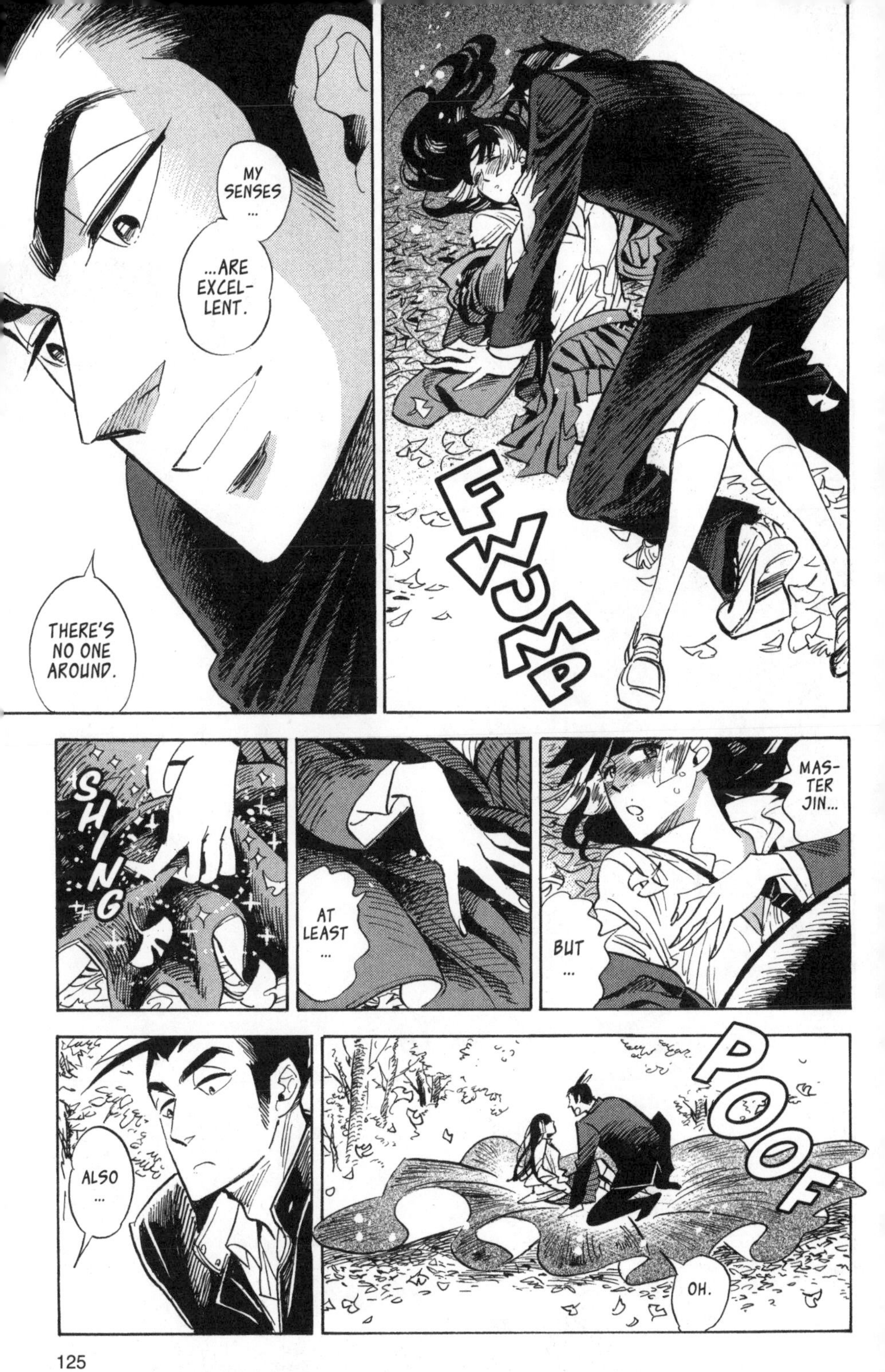
FWUMP
MY SENSES ...
...ARE EXCEL-LENT.
THERE'S NO ONE AROUND.
MAS-TER JIN...
BUT ...
AT LEAST ...
SHING
POOF
OH.
ALSO ...

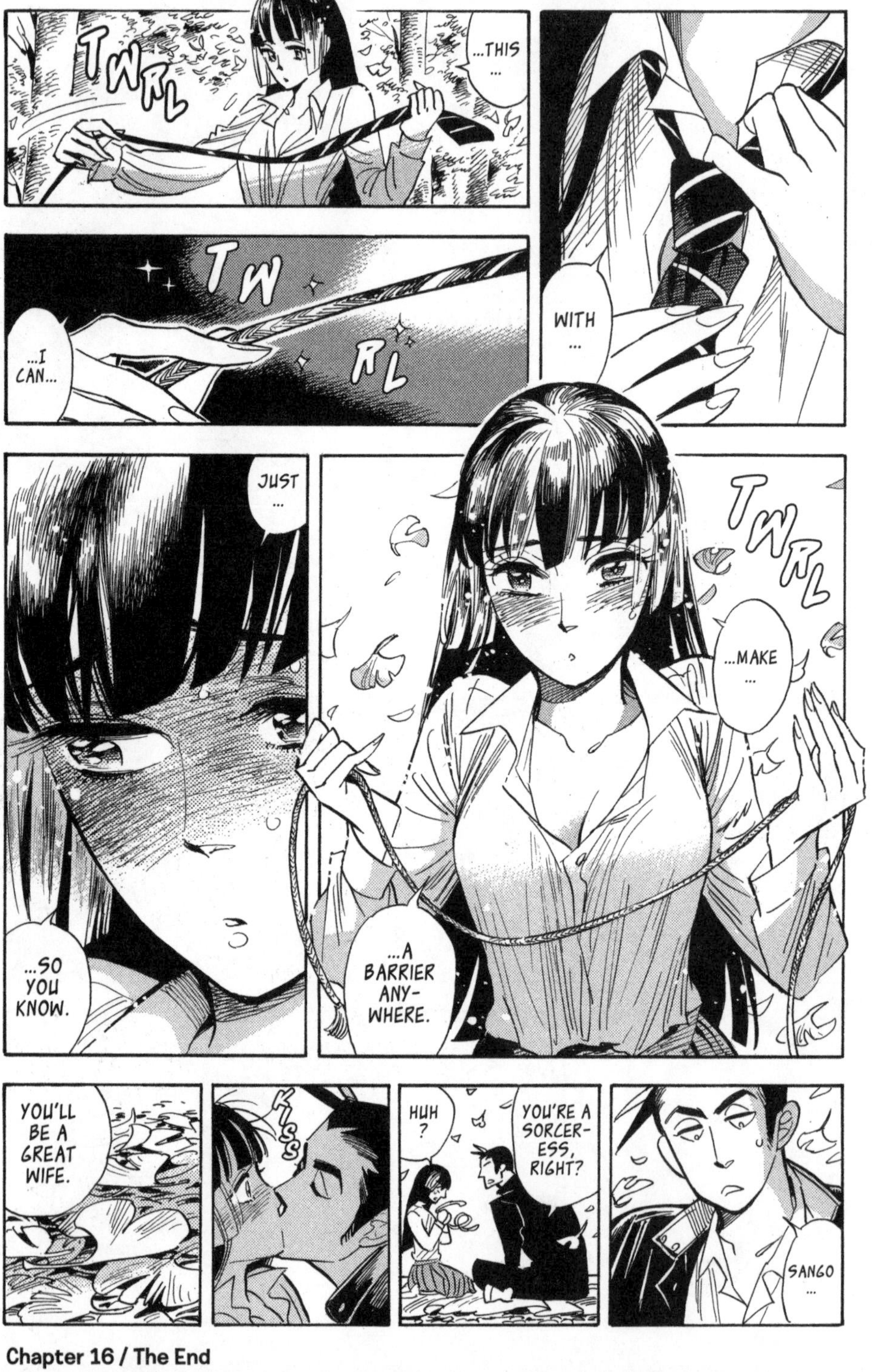
WITH ...
TWRL
...THIS ...
TW RL
...I CAN...
TWRL
...MAKE ...
...A BARRIER ANYWHERE.
JUST ...
...SO YOU KNOW.
SANGO ...
YOU'RE A SORCERESS, RIGHT?
HUH ?
KISS
YOU'LL BE A GREAT WIFE.

Chapter 16 / The End

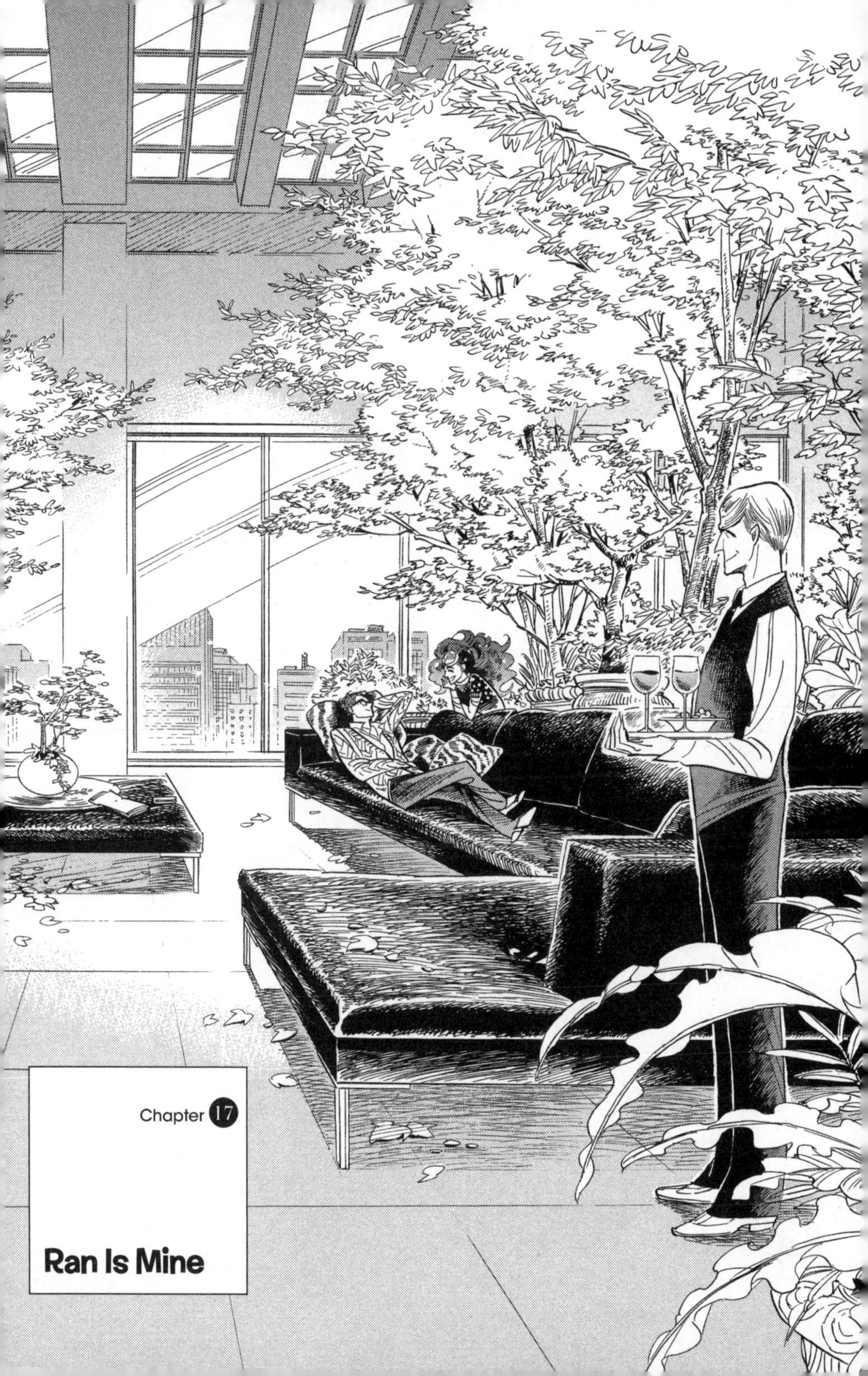
Chapter 17
Ran Is Mine

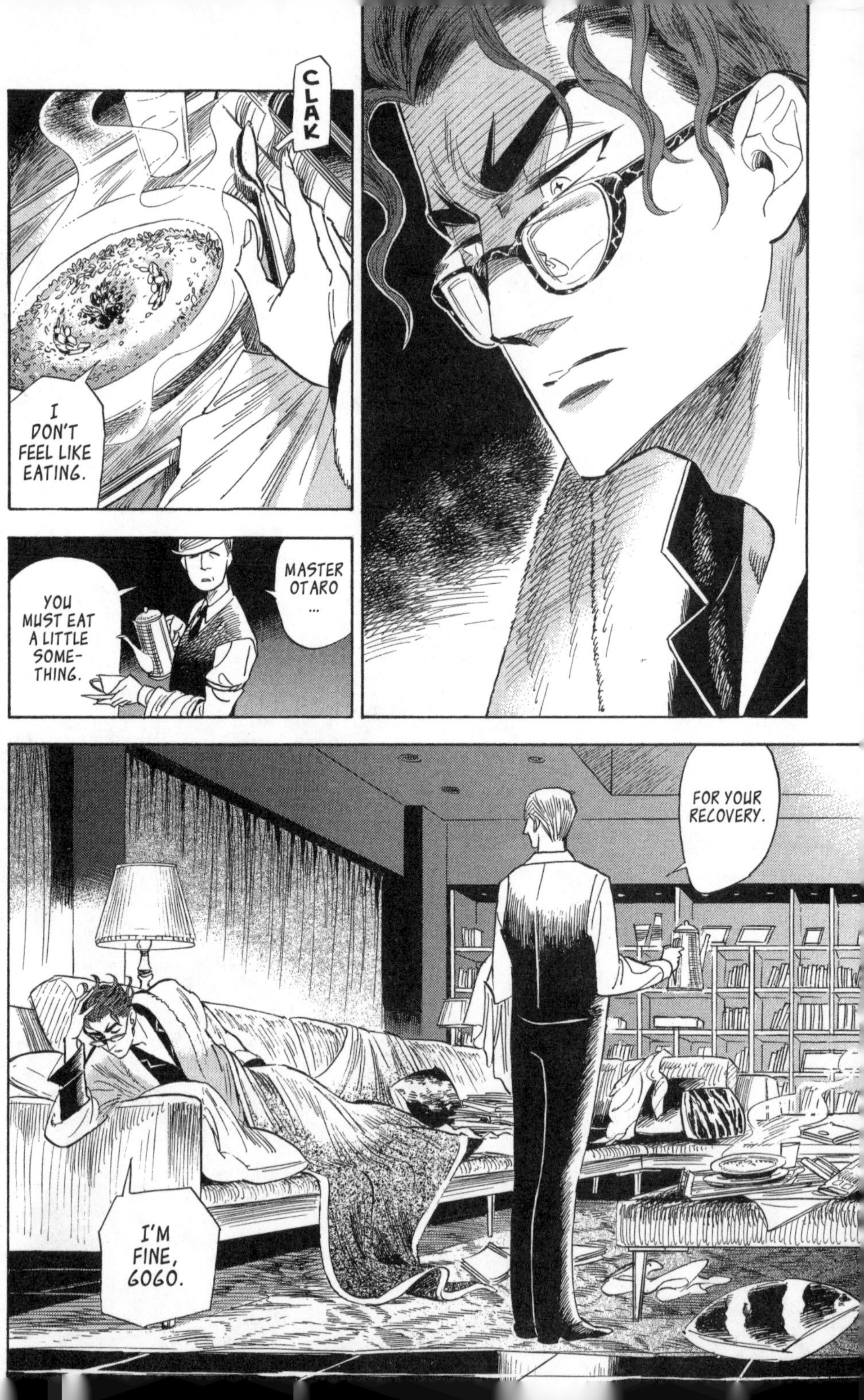
CLAK
I DON'T FEEL LIKE EATING.
MASTER OTARO...
YOU MUST EAT A LITTLE SOMETHING.
FOR YOUR RECOVERY.
I'M FINE, GOGO.

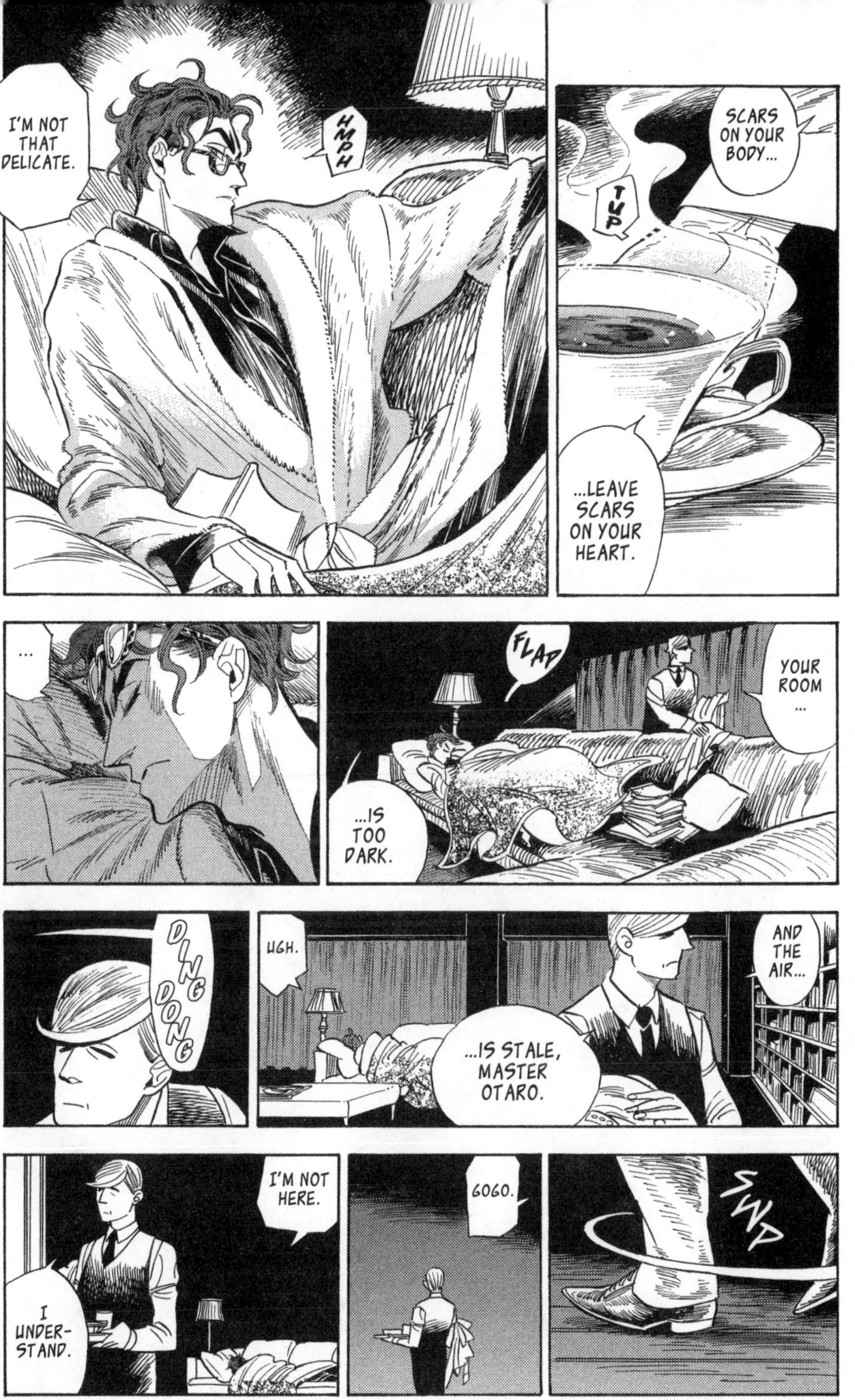

SCARS ON YOUR BODY...
TUP
...LEAVE SCARS ON YOUR HEART.
HMPH
I'M NOT THAT DELICATE.
YOUR ROOM...
FLAP
...IS TOO DARK.
...
AND THE AIR...
UGH.
...IS STALE, MASTER OTARO.
DING DONG
SWP
GOGO.
I'M NOT HERE.
I UNDERSTAND.

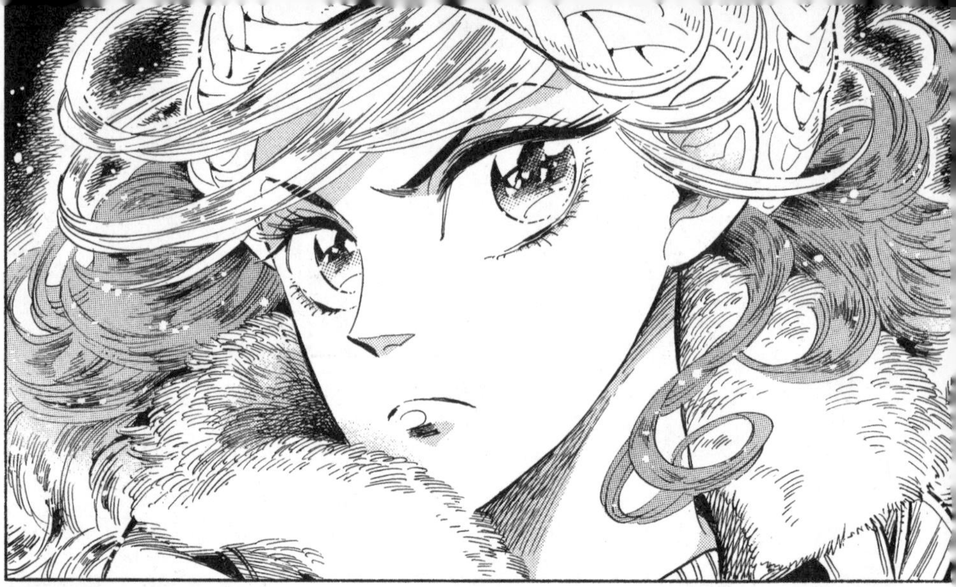
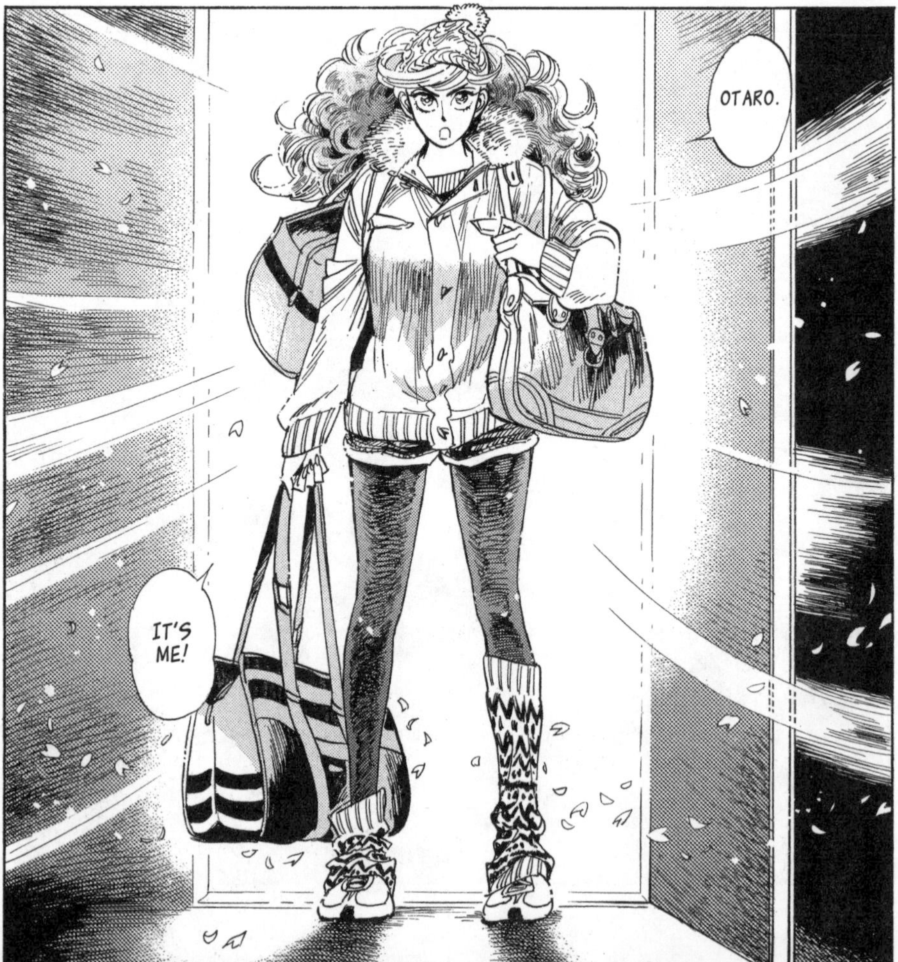
OTARO.
IT'S ME!

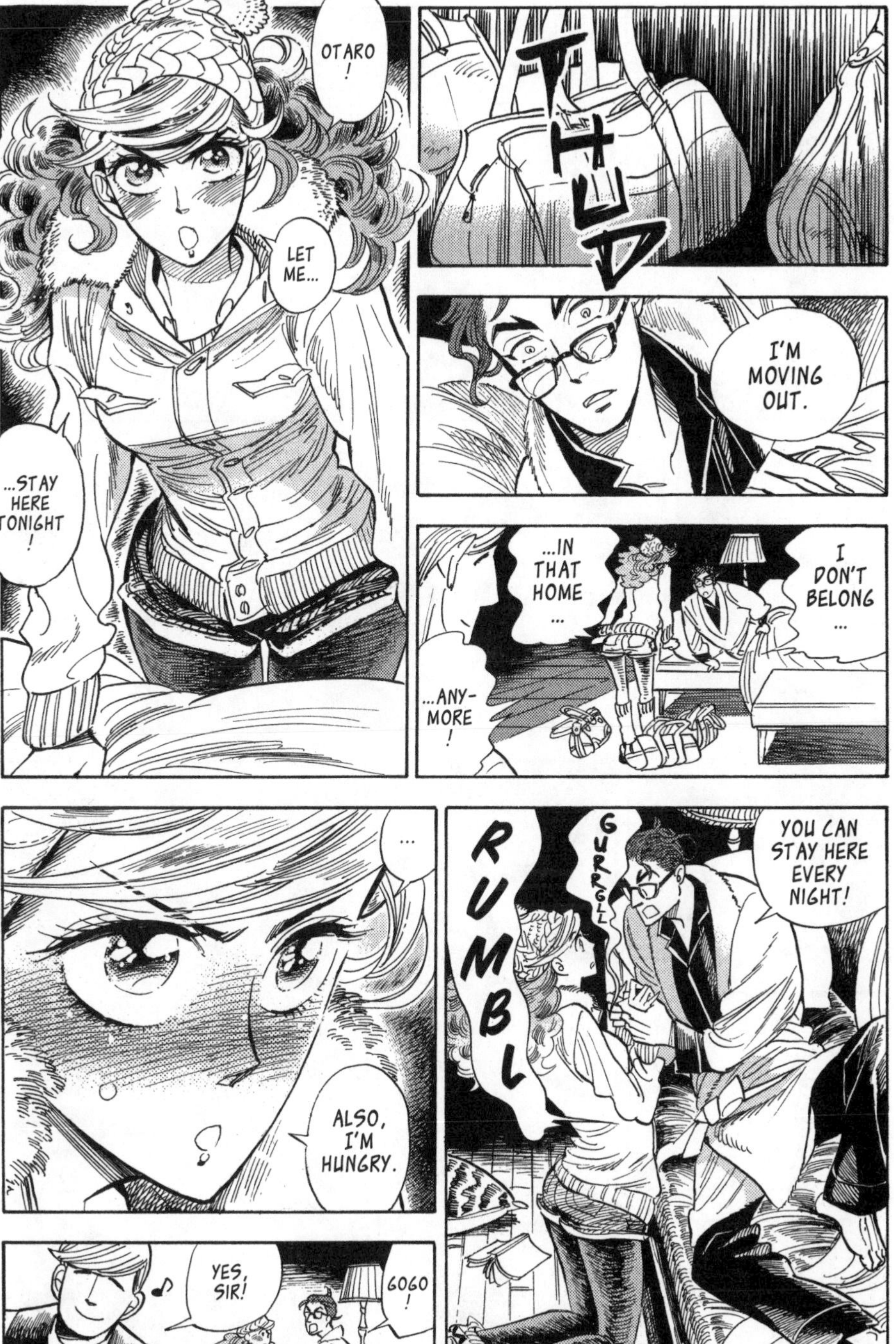
THUD
I'M MOVING OUT.
I DON'T BELONG ...
...IN THAT HOME ...
...ANY-MORE !
OTARO !
LET ME...
...STAY HERE TONIGHT !
YOU CAN STAY HERE EVERY NIGHT!
GURRGLL
RUMBL
...
ALSO, I'M HUNGRY.
GOGO !
YES, SIR!

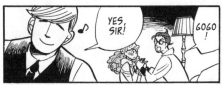

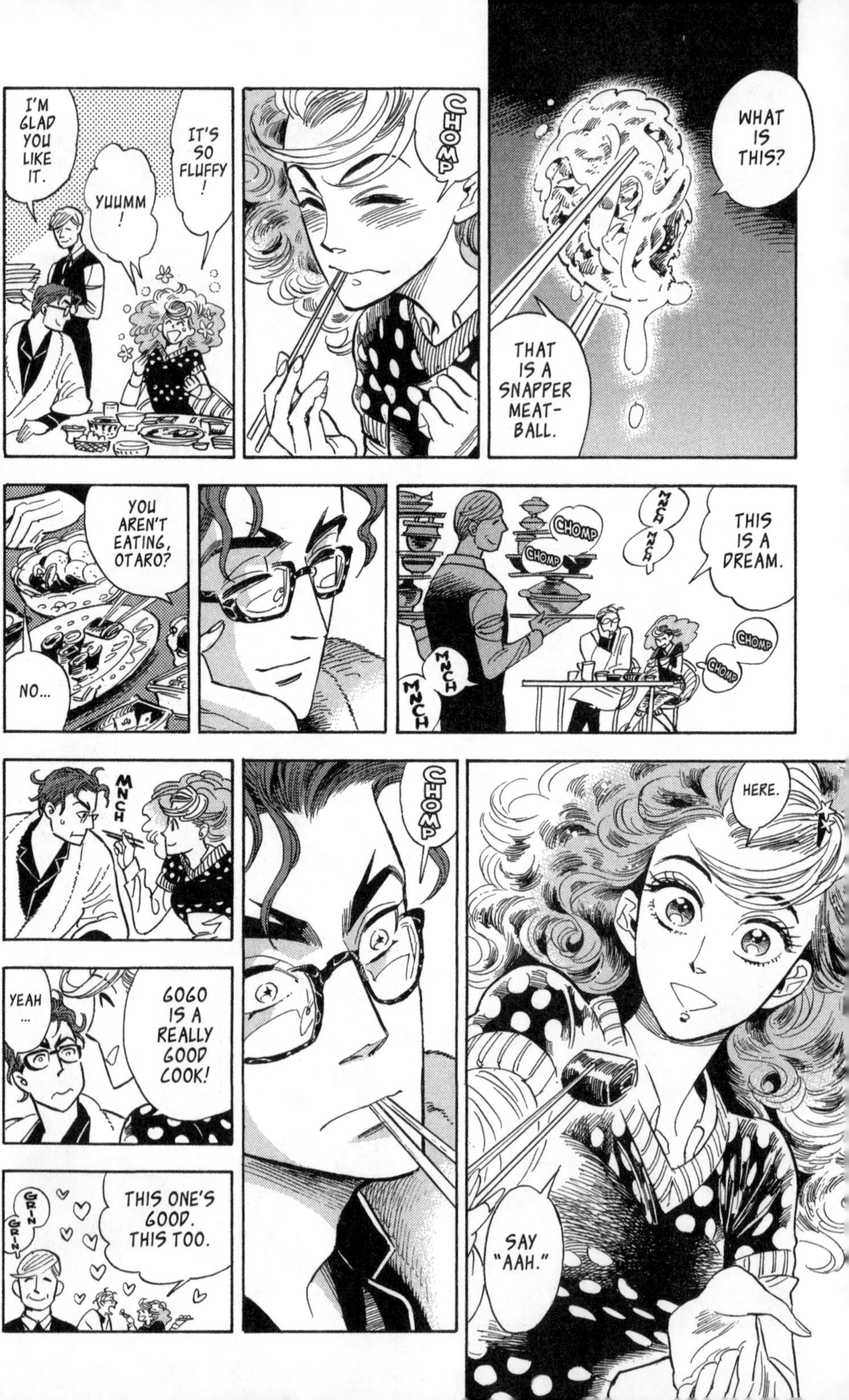
WHAT IS THIS?
THAT IS A SNAPPER MEAT-BALL.
CHOMP
IT'S SO FLUFFY!
I'M GLAD YOU LIKE IT.
YUUMM!
THIS IS A DREAM.
MNCH MNCH
CHOMP
CHOMP
CHOMP
CHOMP
MNCH MNCH
YOU AREN'T EATING, OTARO?
NO...
HERE.
SAY "AAH."
CHOMP
MNCH
GOGO IS A REALLY GOOD COOK!
YEAH ...
THIS ONE'S GOOD. THIS TOO.
GRIN GRIN

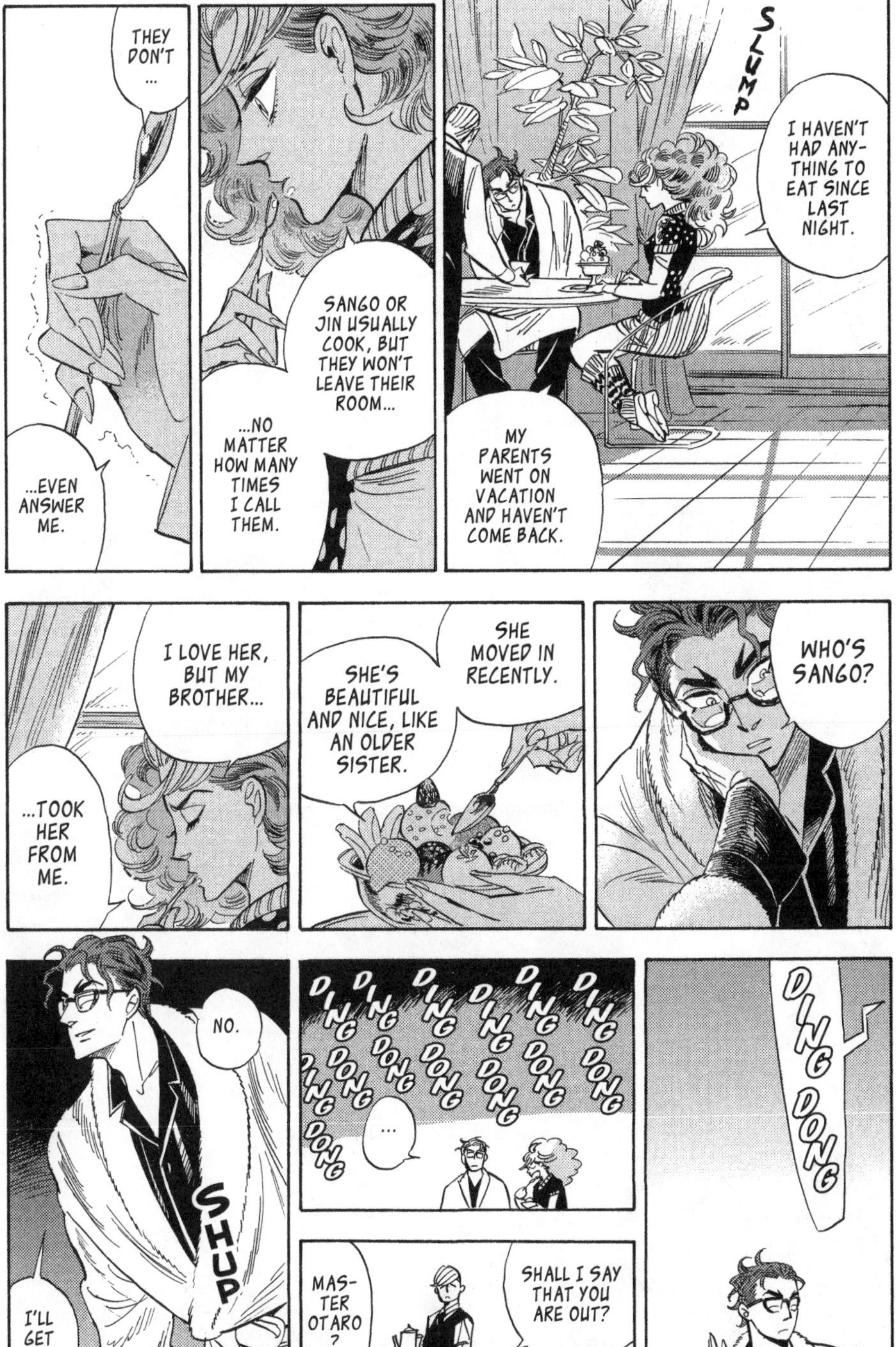
SLUMP
I HAVEN'T HAD ANYTHING TO EAT SINCE LAST NIGHT.
MY PARENTS WENT ON VACATION AND HAVEN'T COME BACK.
SANGO OR JIN USUALLY COOK, BUT THEY WON'T LEAVE THEIR ROOM...
...NO MATTER HOW MANY TIMES I CALL THEM.
THEY DON'T...
...EVEN ANSWER ME.
WHO'S SANGO?
SHE MOVED IN RECENTLY.
SHE'S BEAUTIFUL AND NICE, LIKE AN OLDER SISTER.
I LOVE HER, BUT MY BROTHER...
...TOOK HER FROM ME.
DING DONG
DING DONG DING DONG DING DONG DING DONG DING DONG DING DONG DING DONG
...
SHALL I SAY THAT YOU ARE OUT?
MASTER OTARO?
NO.
SHUP
I'LL GET IT.

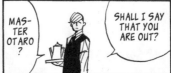

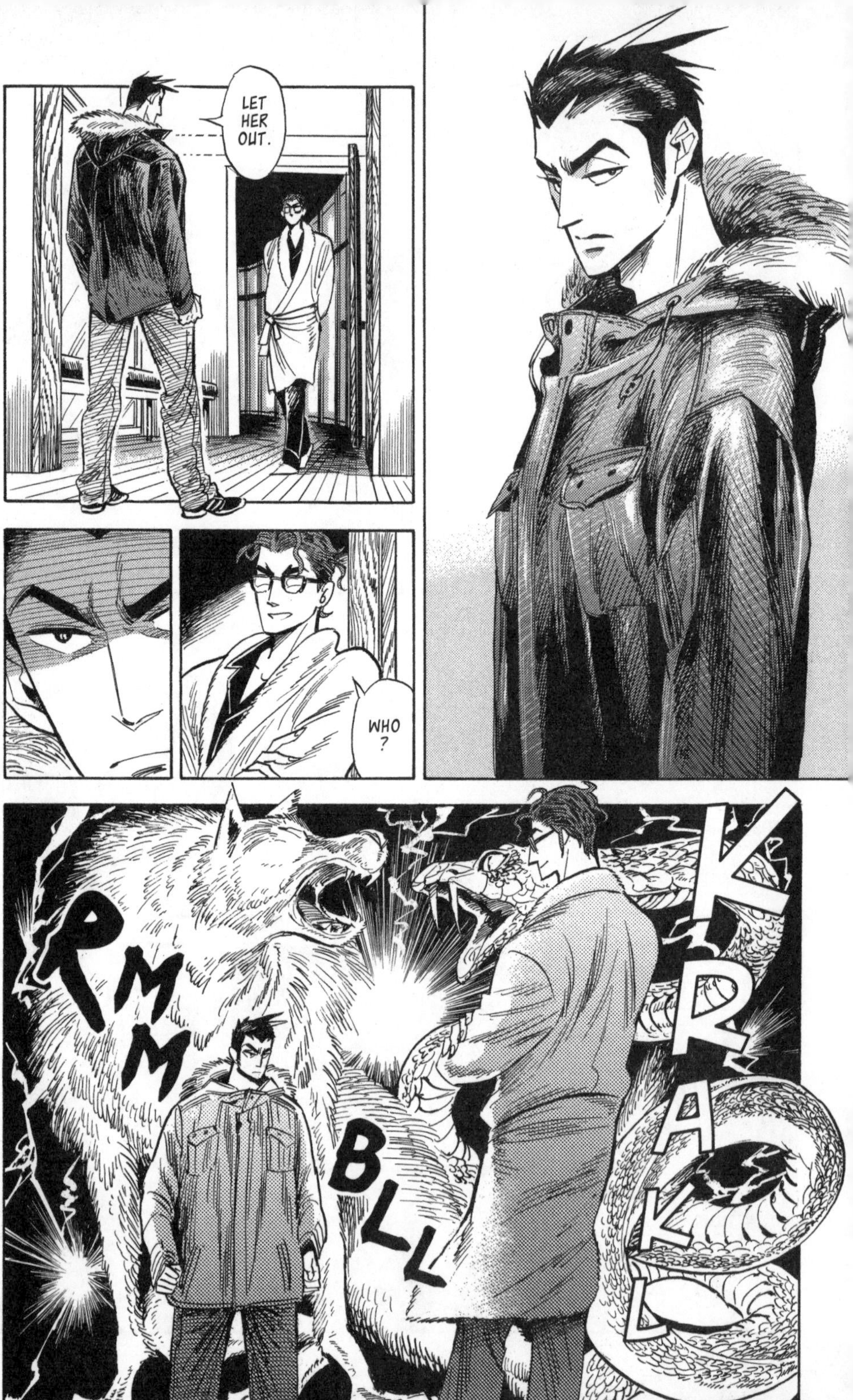
LET HER OUT.
WHO?
KRAKL
RMMBLL

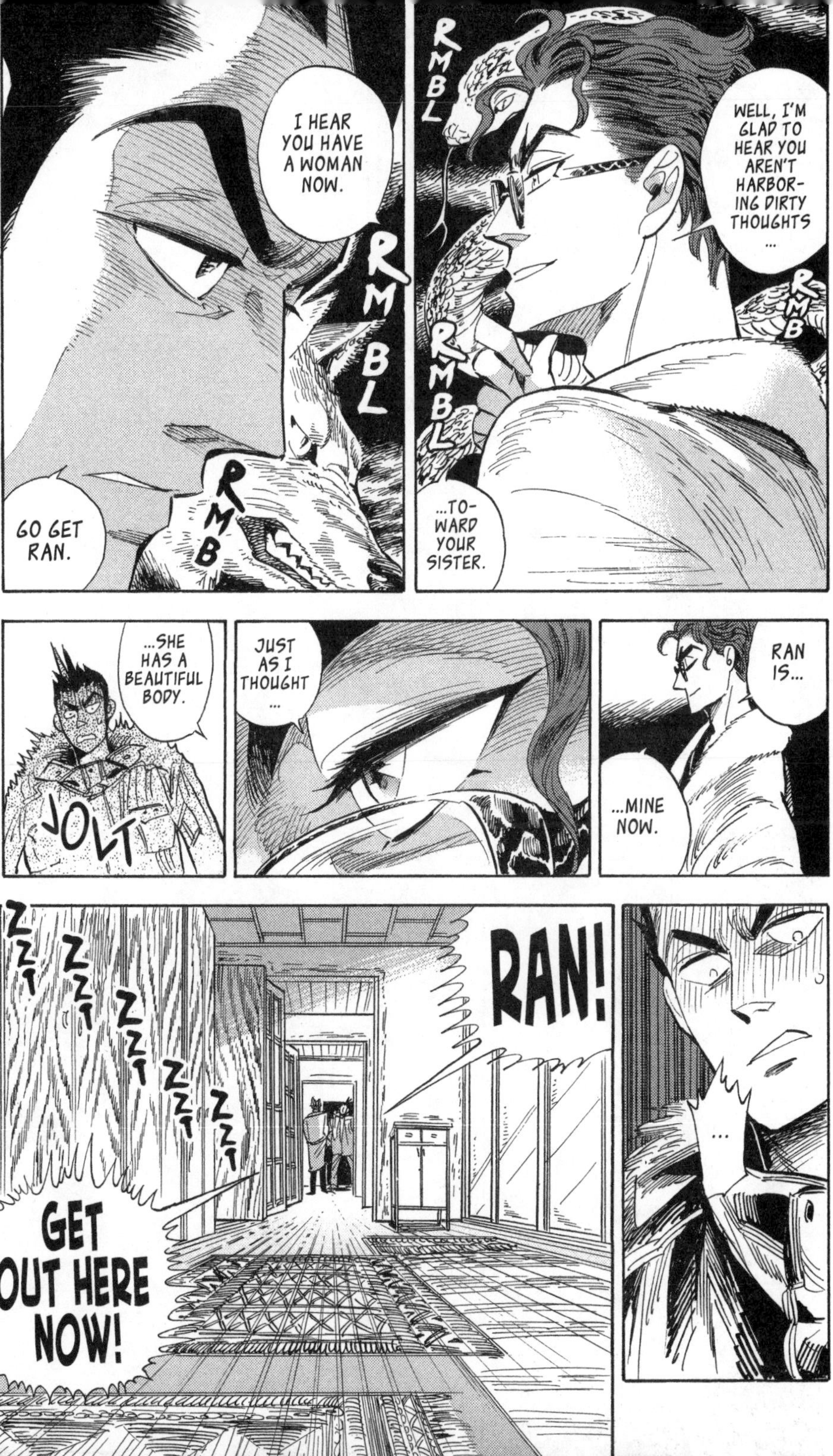
RMBL
WELL, I'M GLAD TO HEAR YOU AREN'T HARBORING DIRTY THOUGHTS ...
RMB
RMBL
...TOWARD YOUR SISTER.
I HEAR YOU HAVE A WOMAN NOW.
RMBL
RMB
GO GET RAN.
RAN IS...
...MINE NOW.
JUST AS I THOUGHT ...
...SHE HAS A BEAUTIFUL BODY.
JOLT
...
RAN!
ZZZT ZZZT ZZZT ZZZT ZZZT
GET OUT HERE NOW!

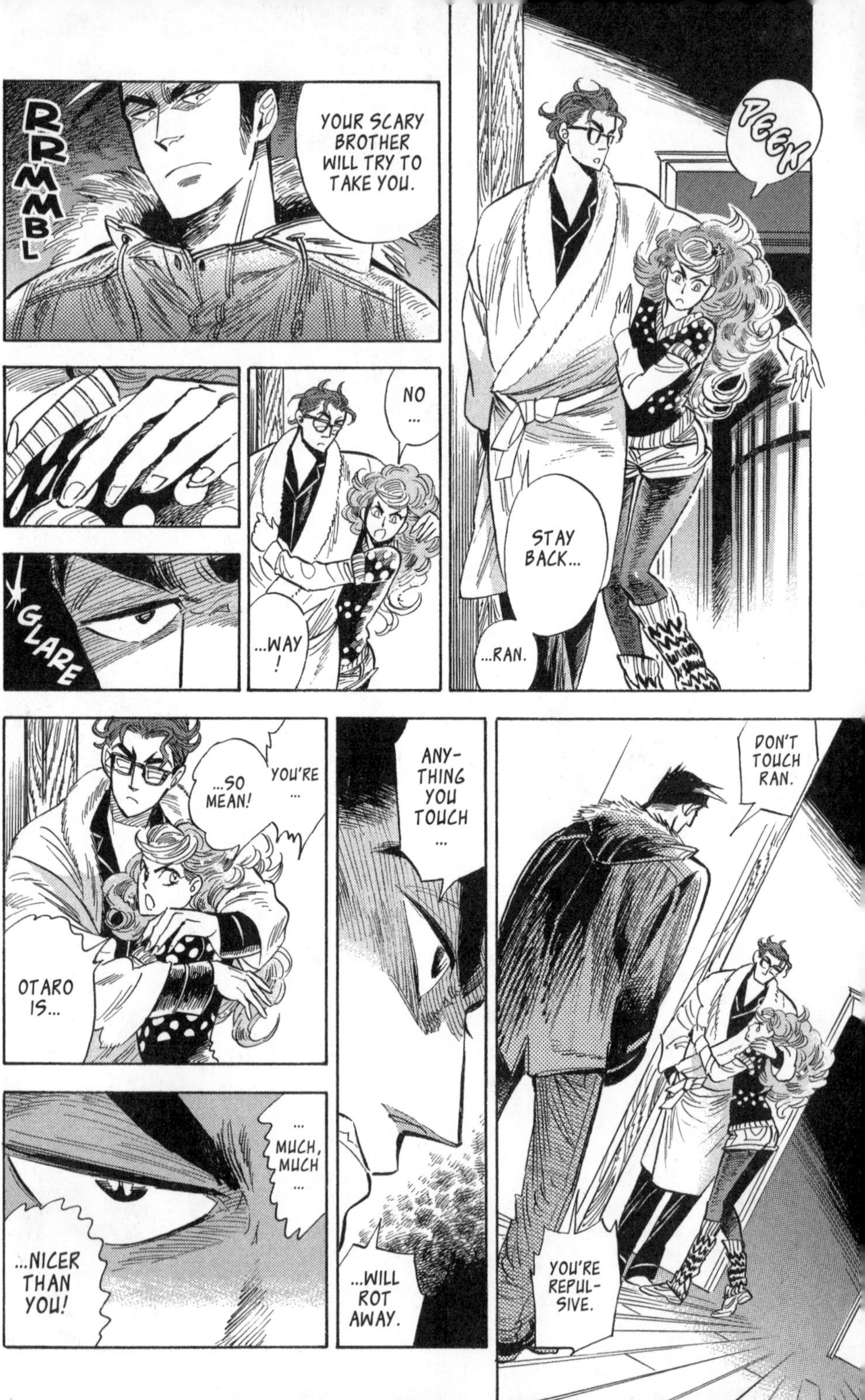
PEEK
STAY BACK...
...RAN.
RRMMBL
YOUR SCARY BROTHER WILL TRY TO TAKE YOU.
NO ...
...WAY !
GLARE
DON'T TOUCH RAN.
YOU'RE REPUL-SIVE.
ANY-THING YOU TOUCH ...
...WILL ROT AWAY.
YOU'RE ...
...SO MEAN!
OTARO IS...
... MUCH, MUCH ...
...NICER THAN YOU!

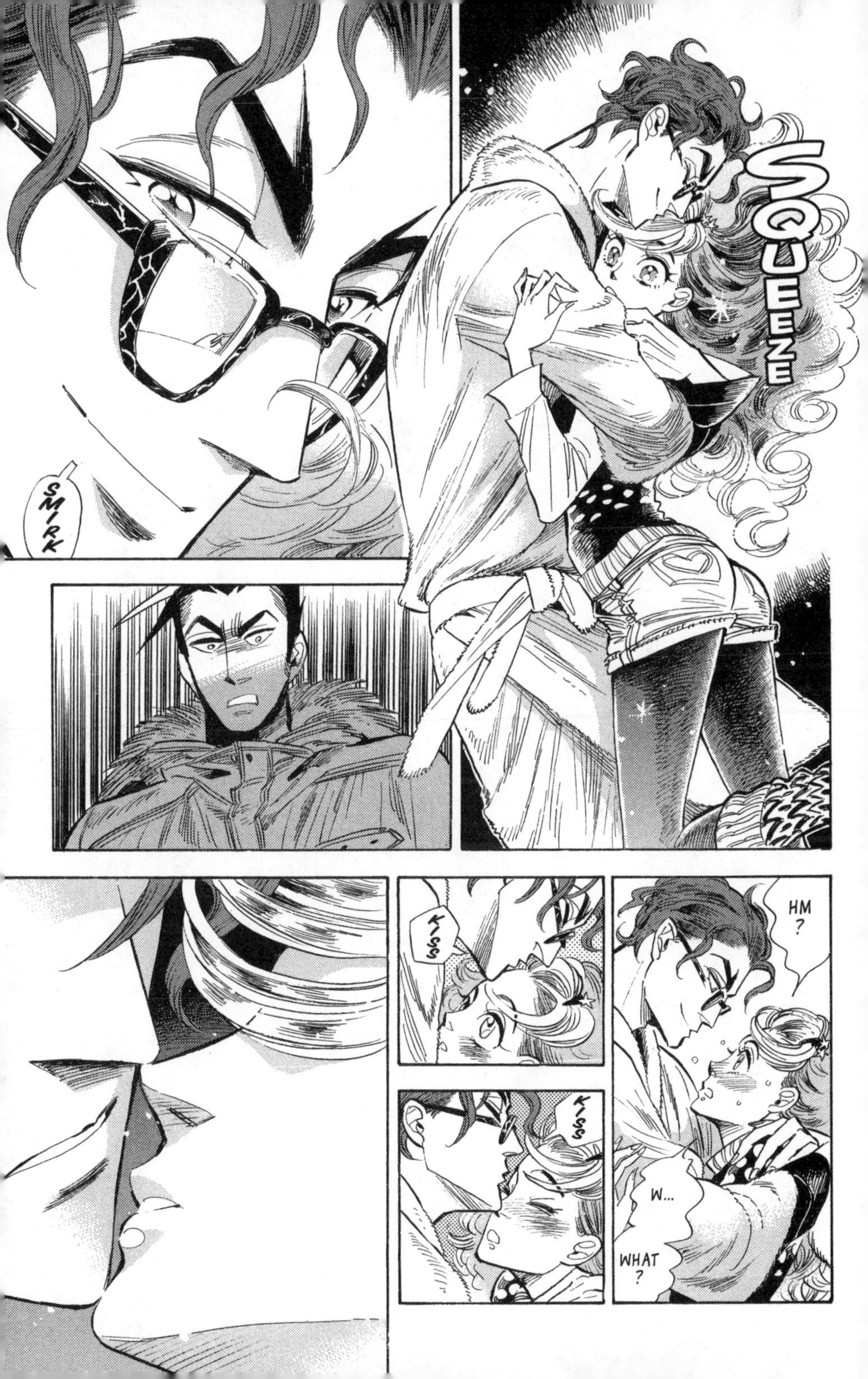
SQUEEZE
SMIRK
HM?
W...
WHAT?
KISS
KISS

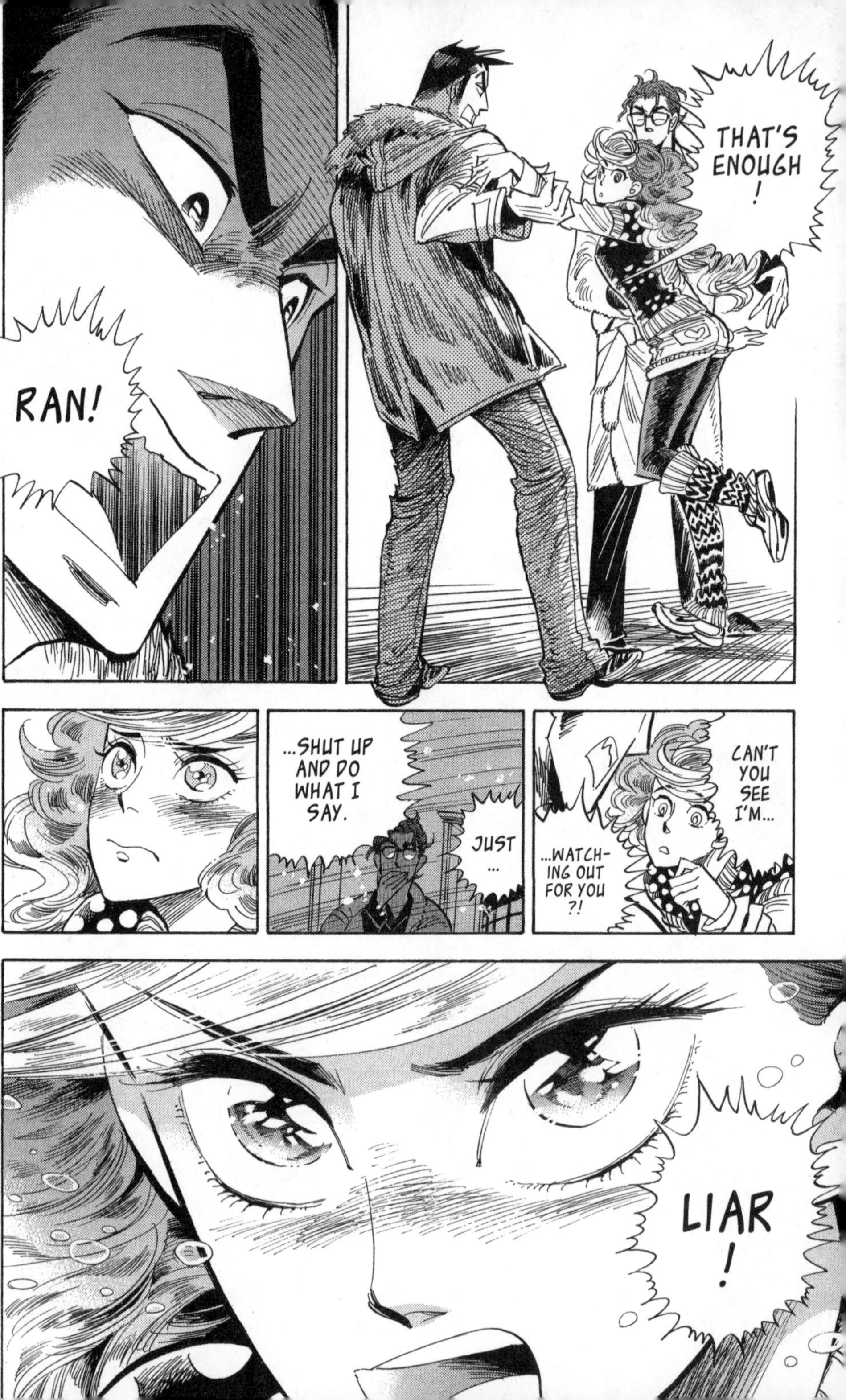
THAT'S ENOUGH!
RAN!
CAN'T YOU SEE I'M...
...WATCHING OUT FOR YOU?!
JUST...
...SHUT UP AND DO WHAT I SAY.
LIAR!

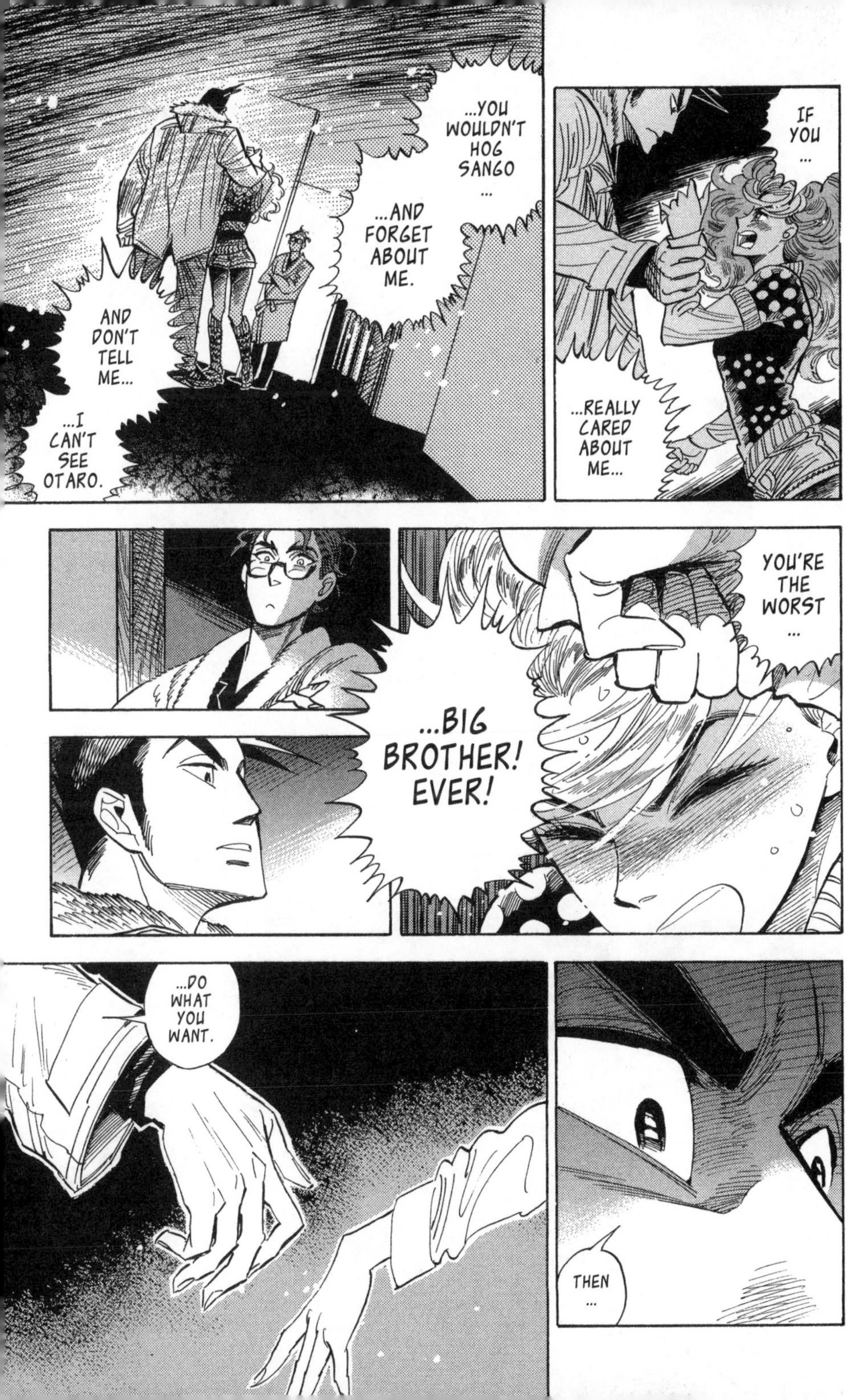
IF YOU...
...REALLY CARED ABOUT ME...
...YOU WOULDN'T HOG SANGO...
...AND FORGET ABOUT ME.
AND DON'T TELL ME...
...I CAN'T SEE OTARO.
YOU'RE THE WORST...
...BIG BROTHER! EVER!
THEN...
...DO WHAT YOU WANT.

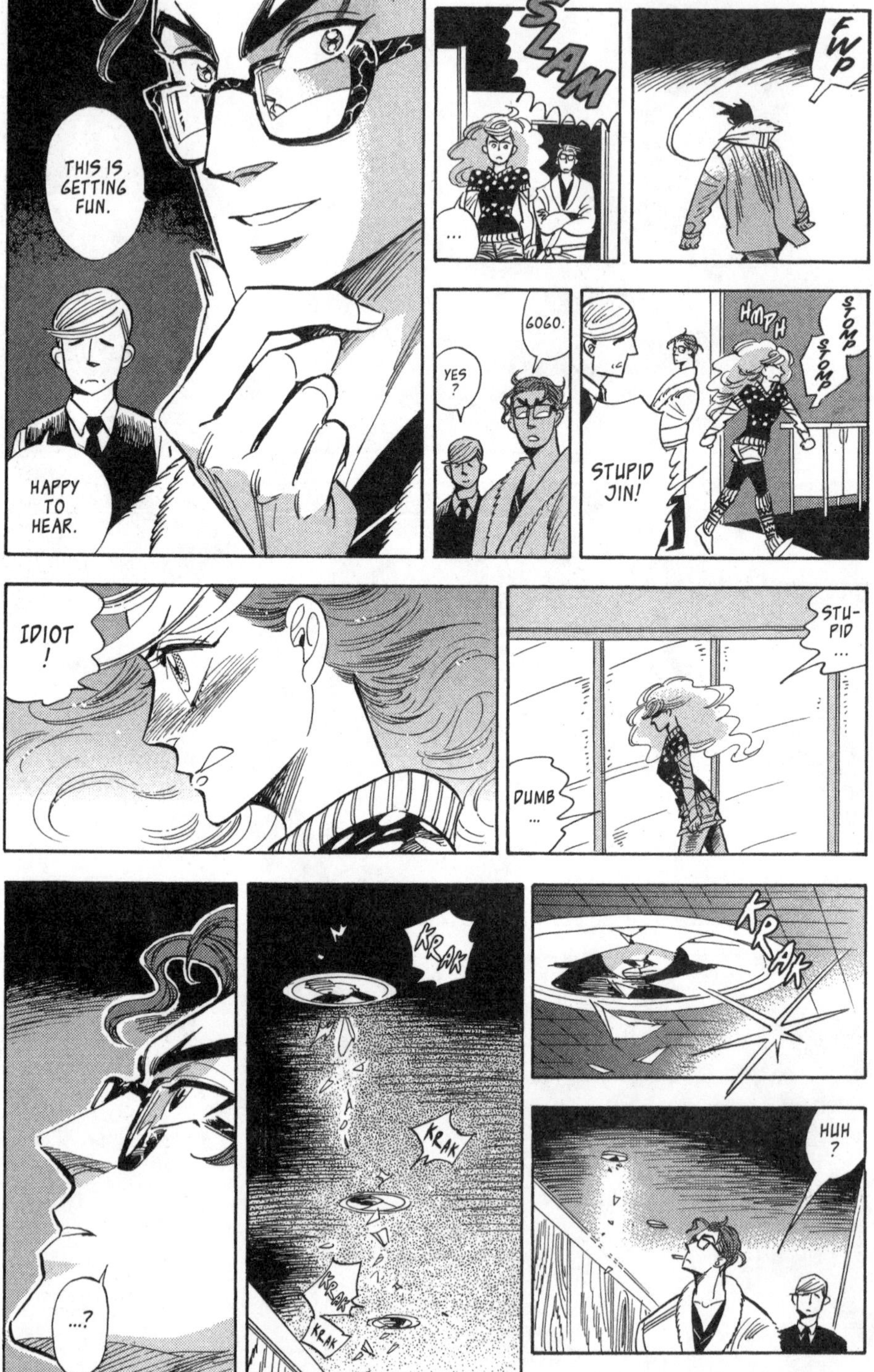
FWP
SLAM
...
STOMP STOMP
HMPH
STUPID JIN!
GOGO.
YES?
THIS IS GETTING FUN.
HAPPY TO HEAR.
STUPID...
DUMB...
IDIOT!
KRAK
HUH?
KRAK
KRAK
KRAK
KRAK
...?

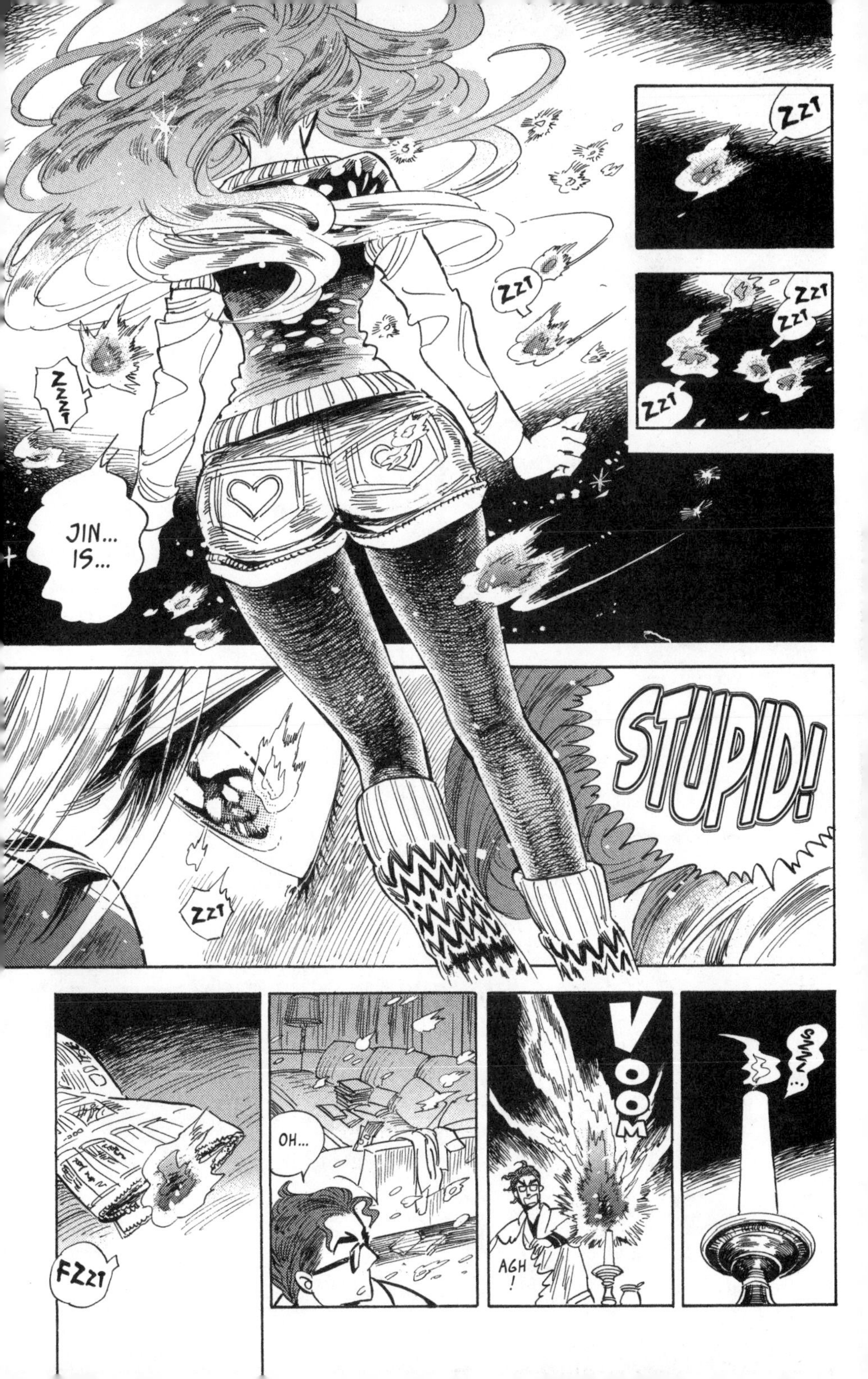

ZZT
ZZT
ZZT
ZZT
ZZT
ZZZZT
JIN... IS...
STUPID!
ZZT
VOOM
AGH!
OH...
FZZT

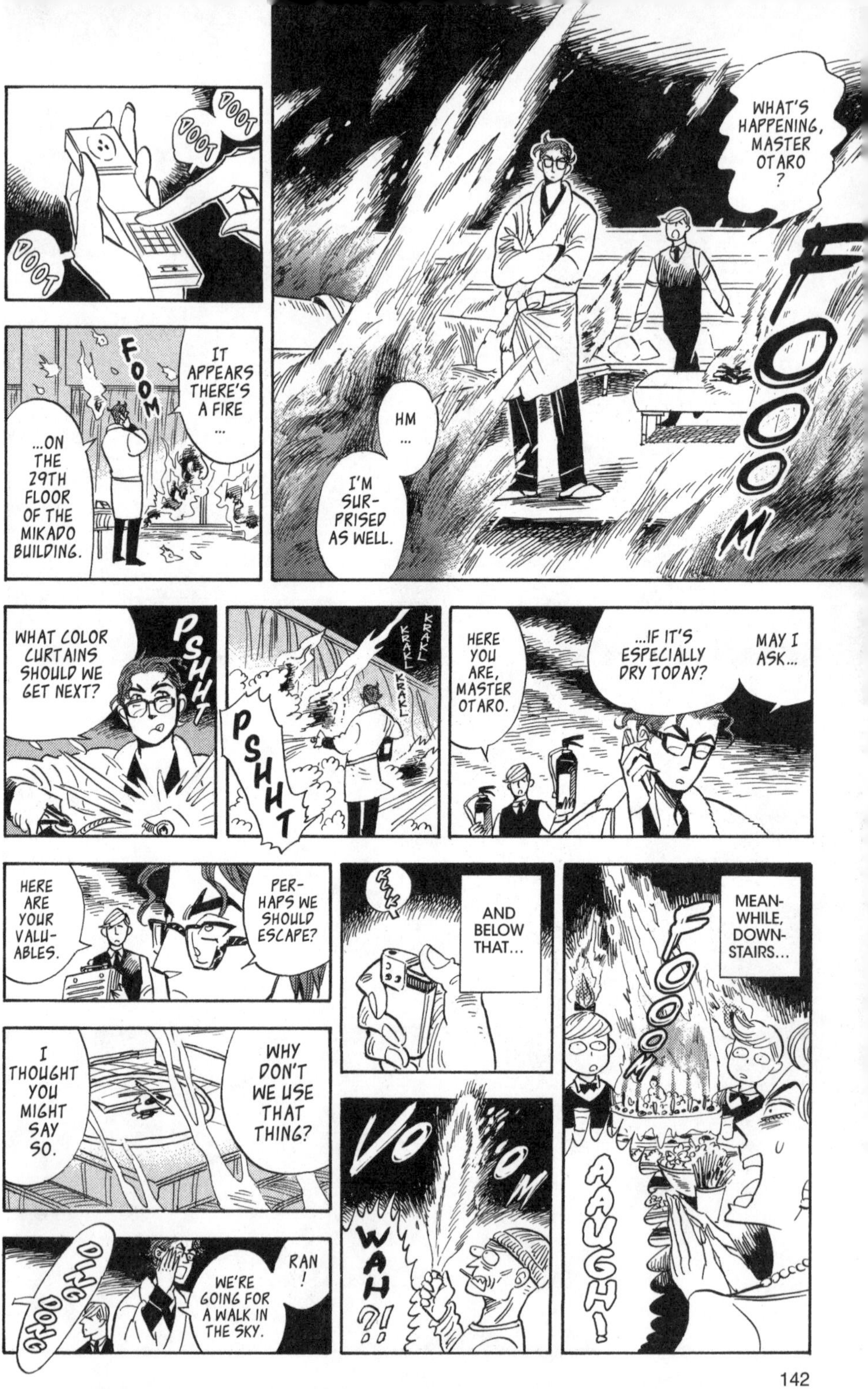
WHAT'S HAPPENING, MASTER OTARO?
FOOOOOM
HM...
I'M SURPRISED AS WELL.
DOOT
DOOT
DOOT
IT APPEARS THERE'S A FIRE...
FOOM
...ON THE 29TH FLOOR OF THE MIKADO BUILDING.
MAY I ASK...
...IF IT'S ESPECIALLY DRY TODAY?
HERE YOU ARE, MASTER OTARO.
KRAKL
KRAKL
KRAKL
PSHHT
PSHHT
WHAT COLOR CURTAINS SHOULD WE GET NEXT?
MEANWHILE, DOWNSTAIRS...
FOOOOM
AAUGH!
AND BELOW THAT...
KLIK
VOOOM
WAH?!
PERHAPS WE SHOULD ESCAPE?
HERE ARE YOUR VALUABLES.
WHY DON'T WE USE THAT THING?
I THOUGHT YOU MIGHT SAY SO.
RAN!
WE'RE GOING FOR A WALK IN THE SKY.
DING DONG
DING DONG

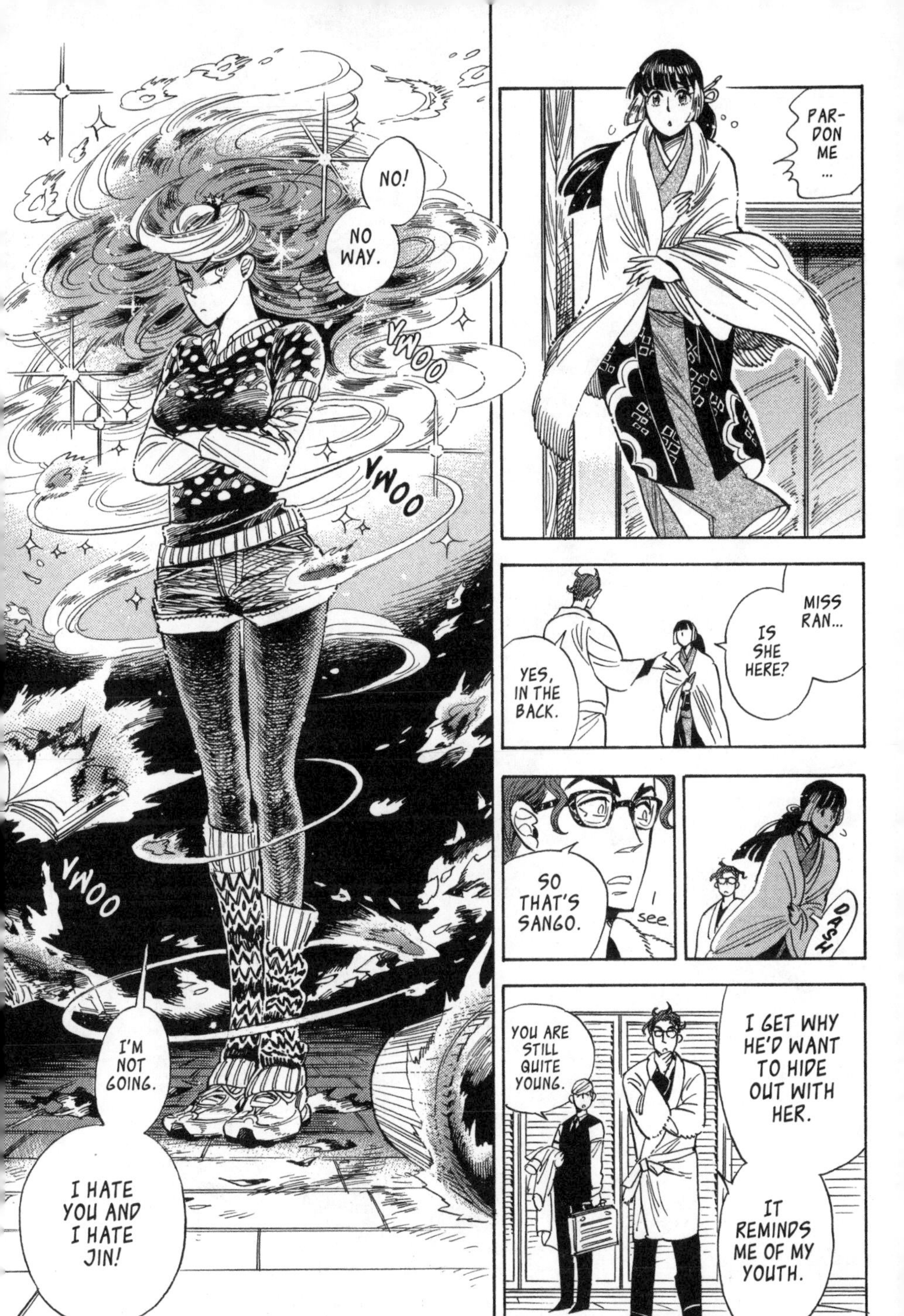
PAR-DON ME ...
MISS RAN... IS SHE HERE?
YES, IN THE BACK.
DASH
SO THAT'S SANGO.
I see.
I GET WHY HE'D WANT TO HIDE OUT WITH HER.
IT REMINDS ME OF MY YOUTH.
YOU ARE STILL QUITE YOUNG.
NO!
NO WAY.
VWOO
VWOO
VWOO
I'M NOT GOING.
I HATE YOU AND I HATE JIN!

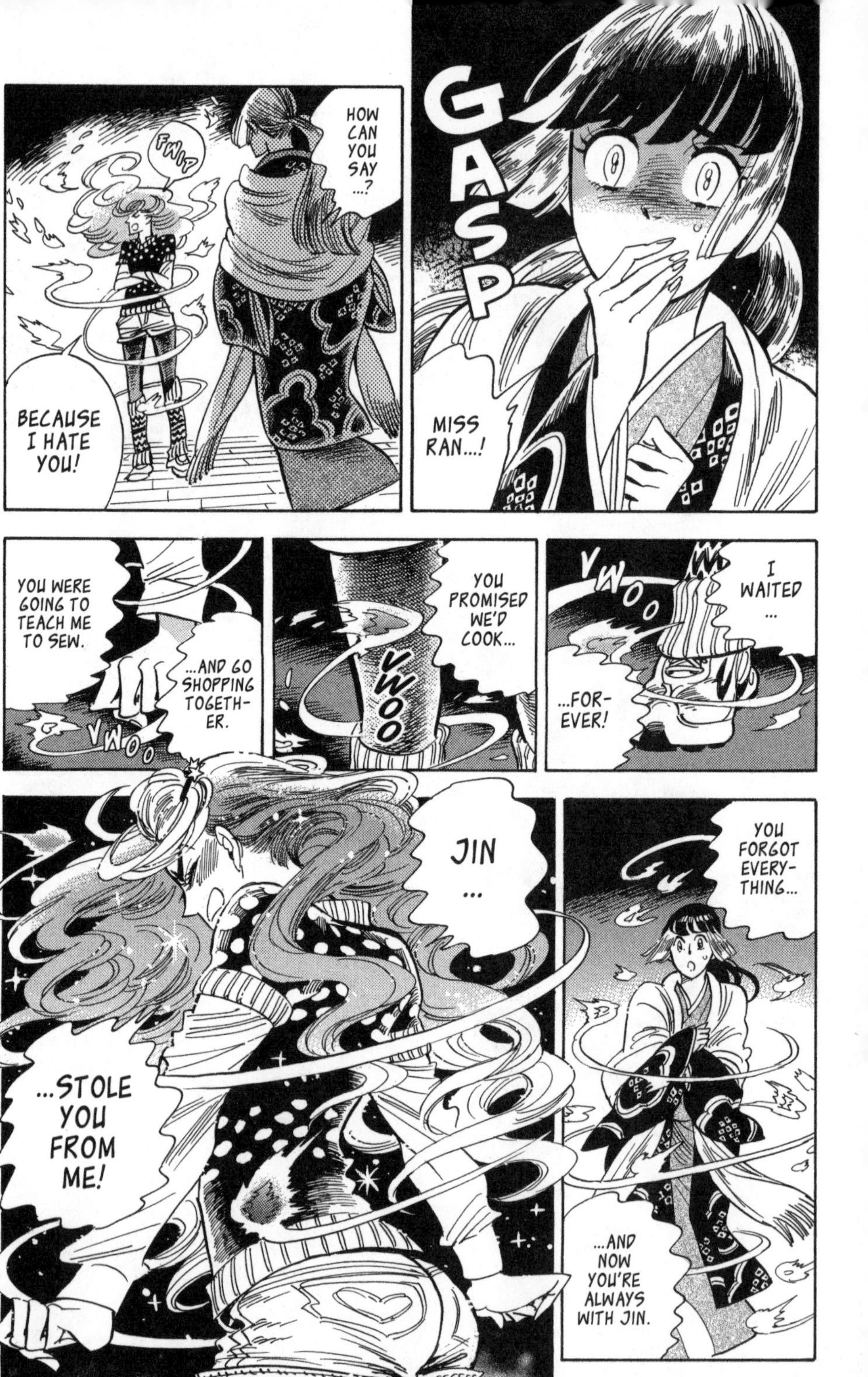
GASP
MISS RAN...!
FWIP
HOW CAN YOU SAY ...?
BECAUSE I HATE YOU!
VWOO
I WAITED ...
...FOR-EVER!
YOU PROMISED WE'D COOK...
VWOO
YOU WERE GOING TO TEACH ME TO SEW.
...AND GO SHOPPING TOGETH-ER.
VWOO
YOU FORGOT EVERY-THING...
...AND NOW YOU'RE ALWAYS WITH JIN.
JIN ...
...STOLE YOU FROM ME!

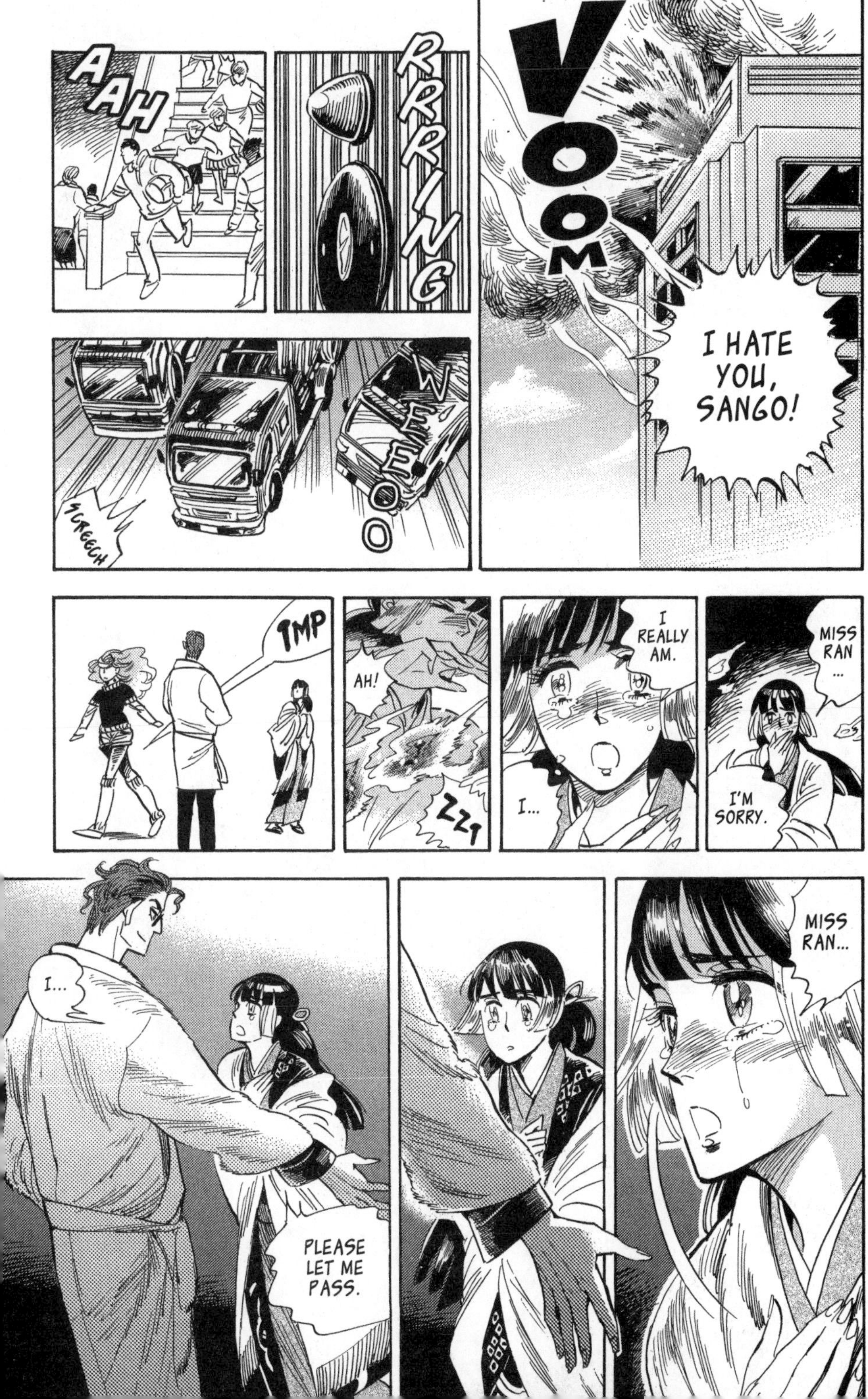
VOOM
I HATE YOU, SANGO!
RRRING
AAH
WEEOOO
SCREECH
MISS RAN ...
I'M SORRY.
I REALLY AM.
I...
AH!
ZZT
TMP
MISS RAN...
I...
PLEASE LET ME PASS.

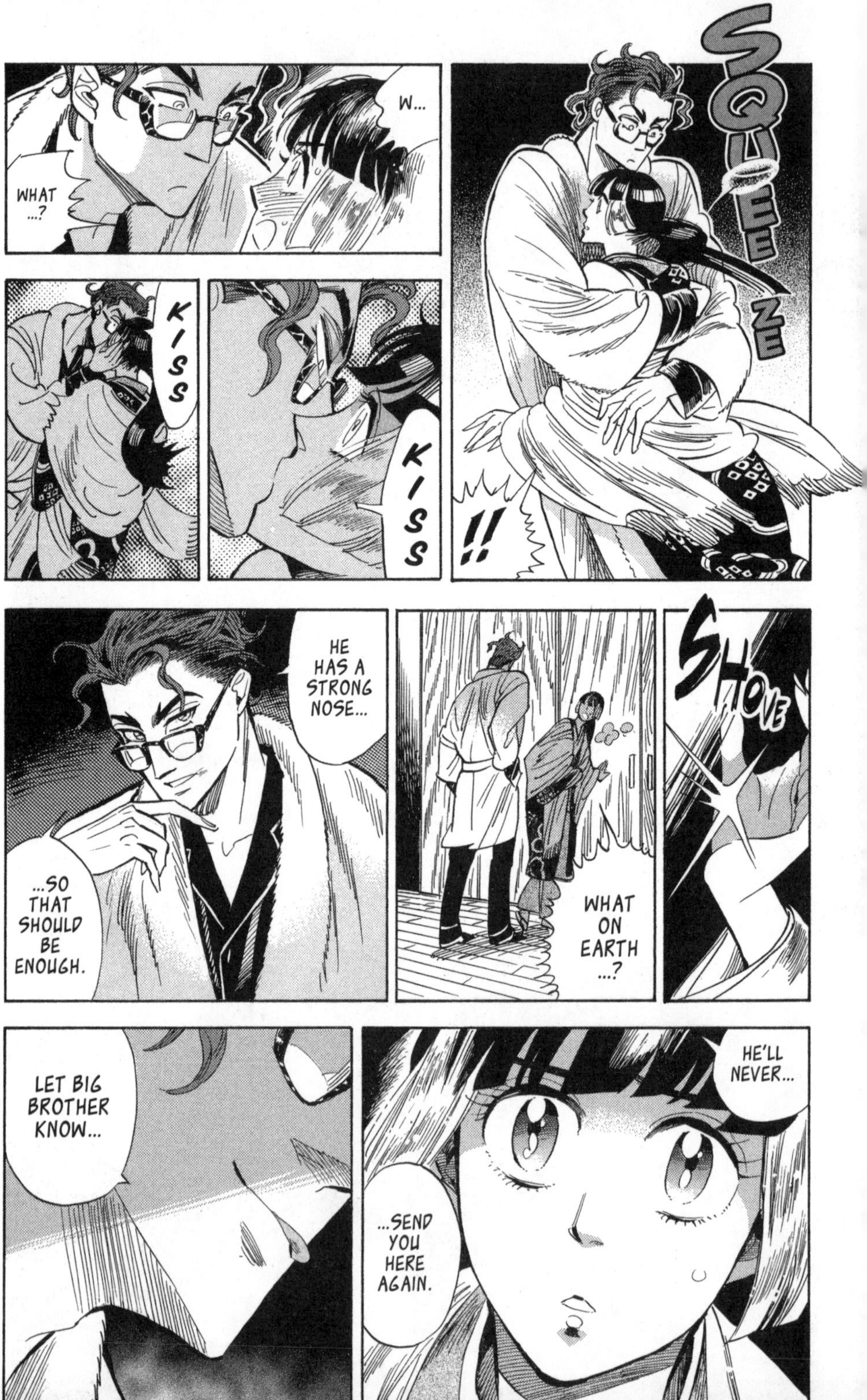
SQUEEZE
!!
W...
WHAT ...?
KISS
KISS
SHOVE
WHAT ON EARTH ...?
HE HAS A STRONG NOSE...
...SO THAT SHOULD BE ENOUGH.
HE'LL NEVER...
...SEND YOU HERE AGAIN.
LET BIG BROTHER KNOW...

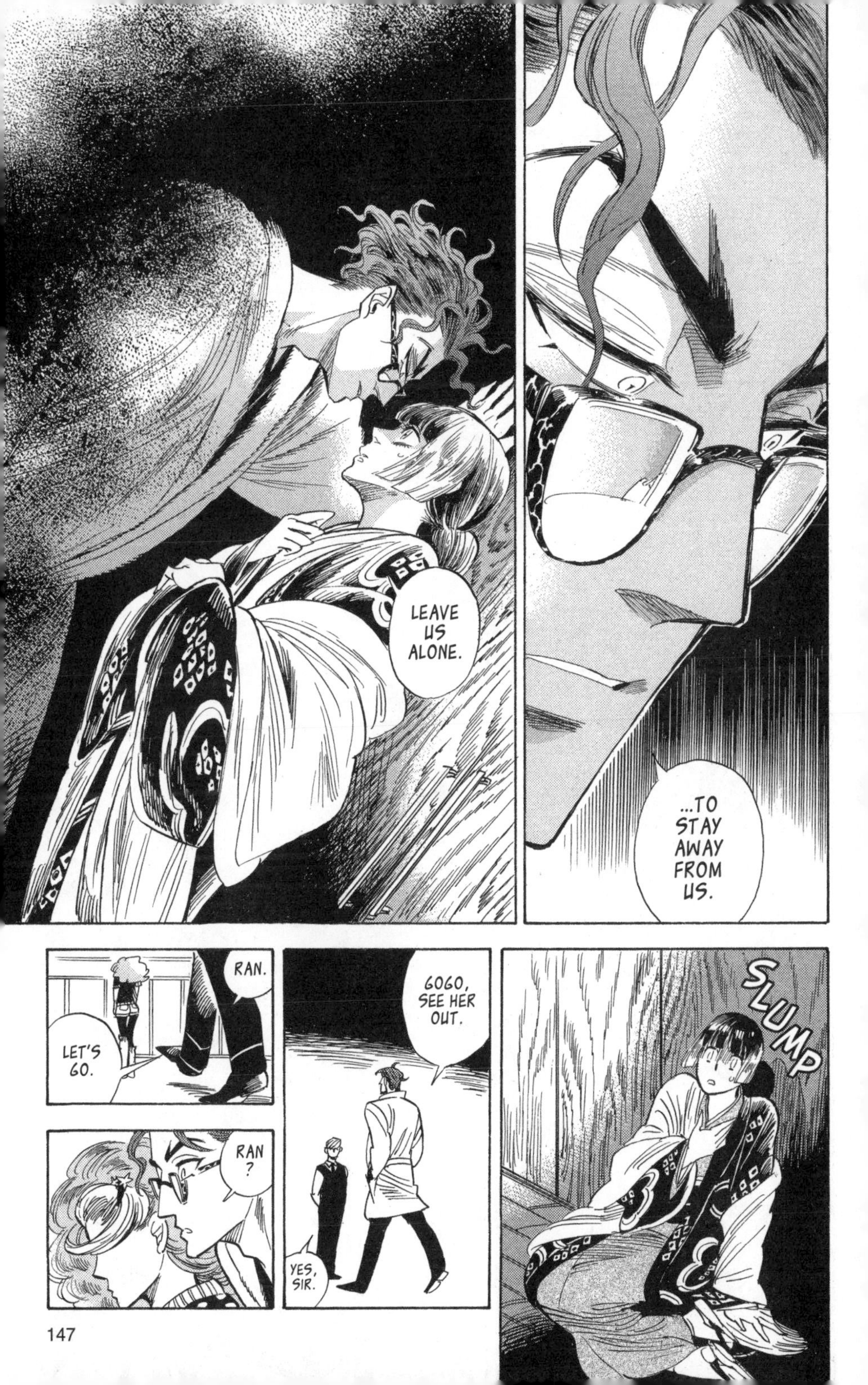

...TO STAY AWAY FROM US.
LEAVE US ALONE.
SLUMP
GOGO, SEE HER OUT.
YES, SIR.
RAN.
LET'S GO.
RAN ?

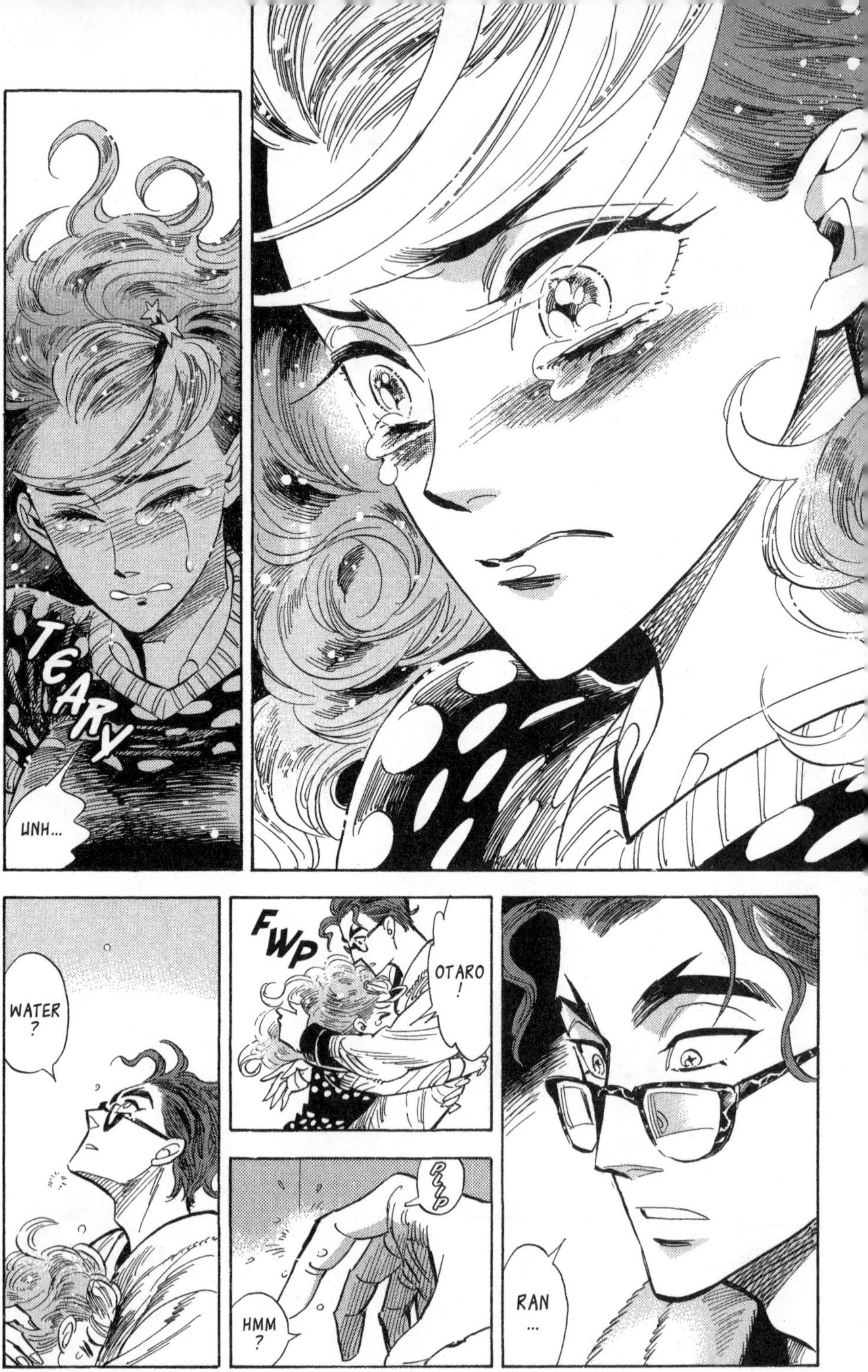
TEARY
UNH...
RAN ...
FWP
OTARO !
PLIP
HMM ?
WATER ?

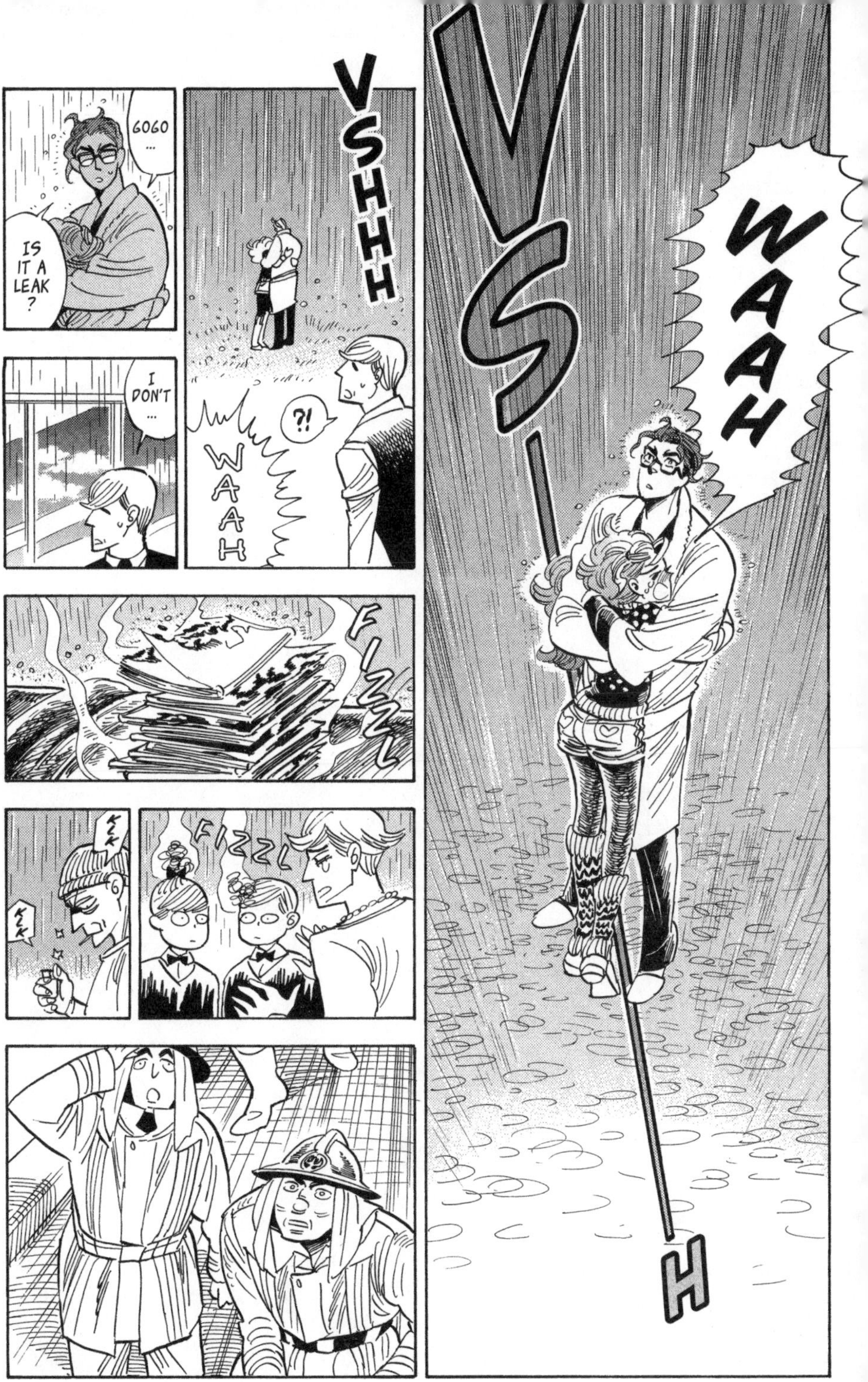

VSH
WAAH
VSHHH
?!
WAAH
GOGO ...
IS IT A LEAK?
I DON'T ...
FIZZL
FIZZL
KIK
KIK

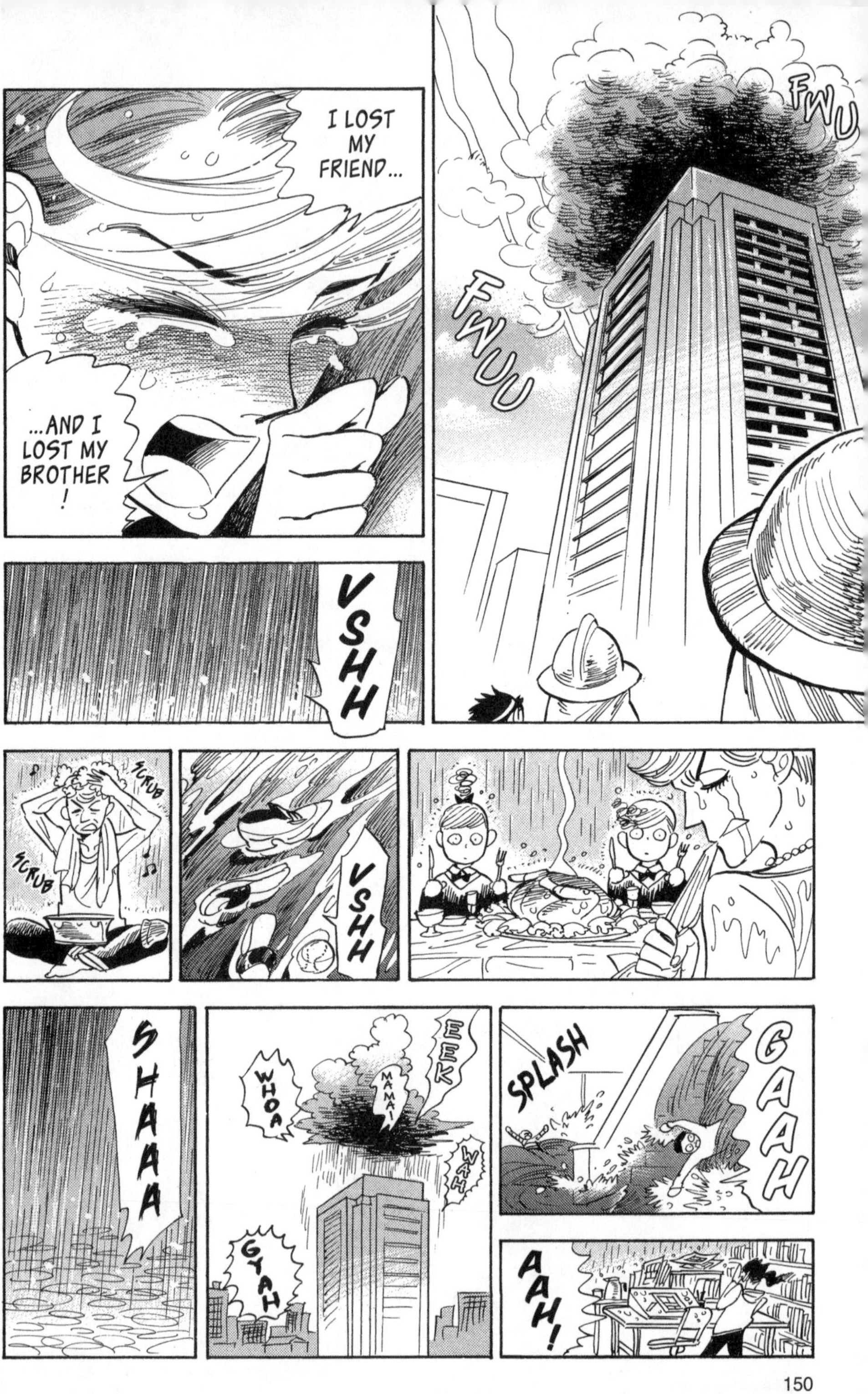
FWU
FWUU
I LOST MY FRIEND...
...AND I LOST MY BROTHER!
VSHH
VSHH
SCRUB
SCRUB
GAAAH
SPLASH
AAH!
EEK
MAMA!
WHOA
WAH
GYAH
SHAAAA

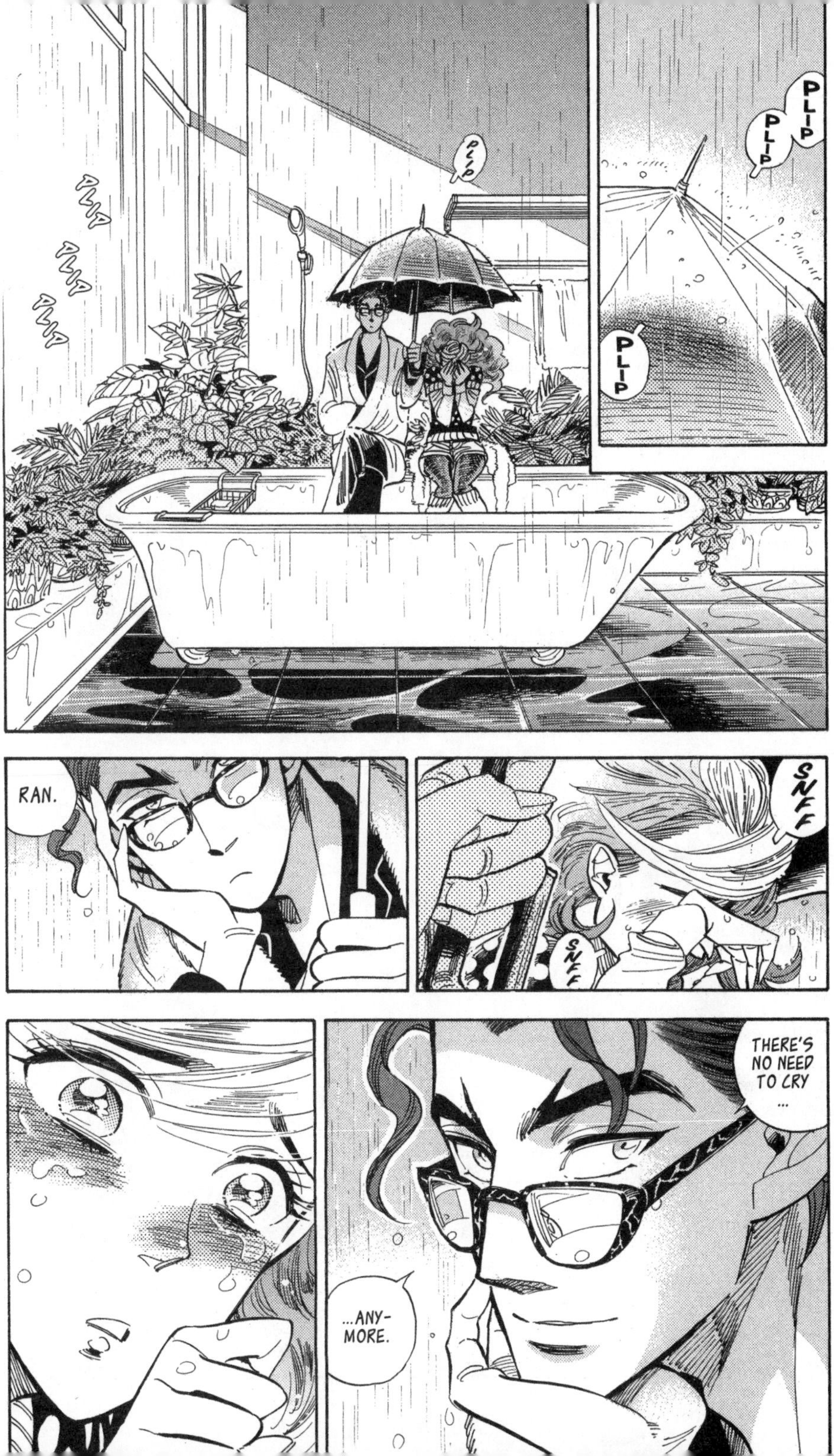
PLIP
PLIP
PLIP
PLIP
PLIP
PLIP
PLIP
SNFF
SNFF
RAN.
THERE'S NO NEED TO CRY ...
...ANY-MORE.

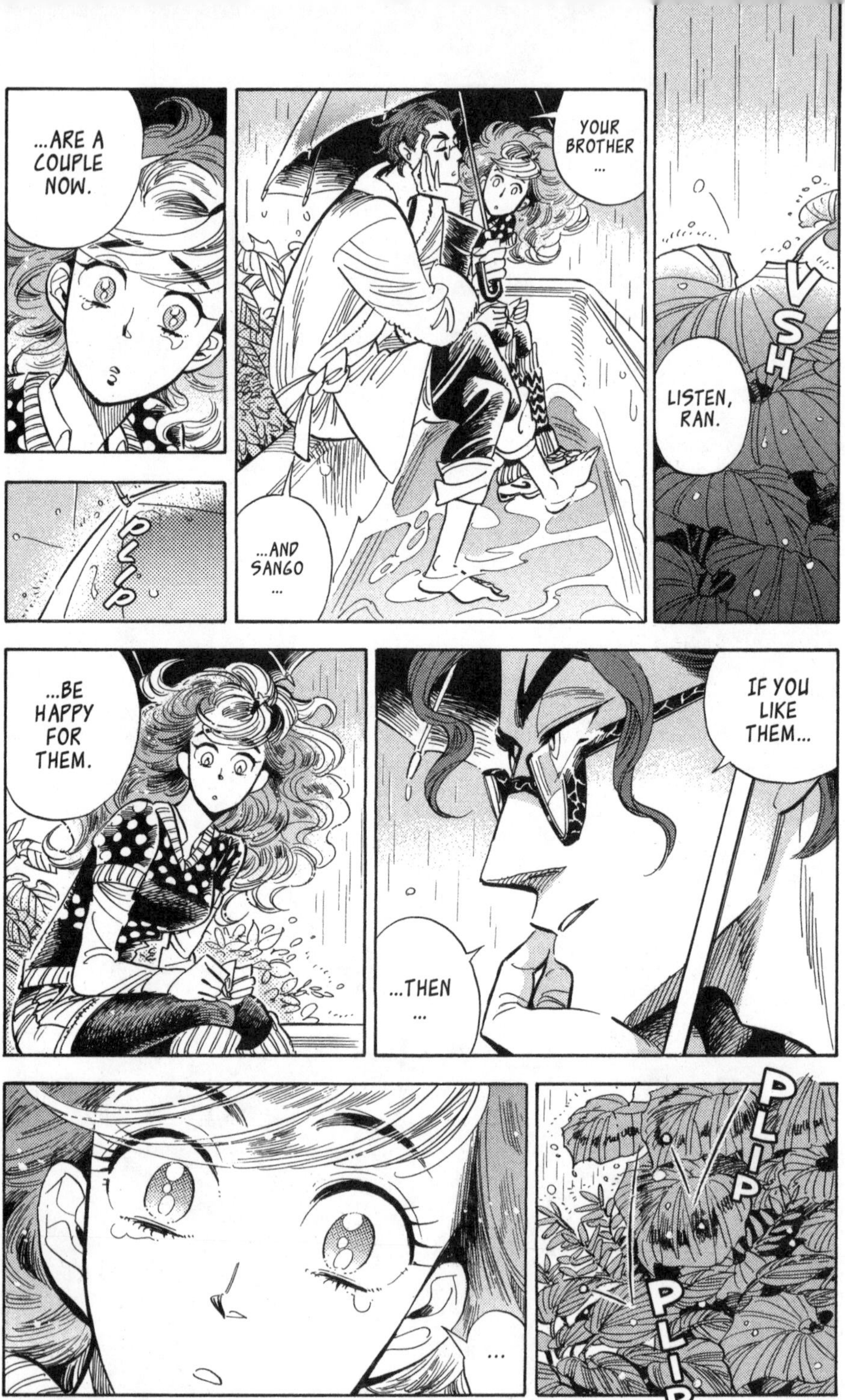
VSH
LISTEN, RAN.
YOUR BROTHER ...
...AND SANGO ...
...ARE A COUPLE NOW.
PLIP
IF YOU LIKE THEM...
...THEN ...
...BE HAPPY FOR THEM.
PLIP
PLIP
...

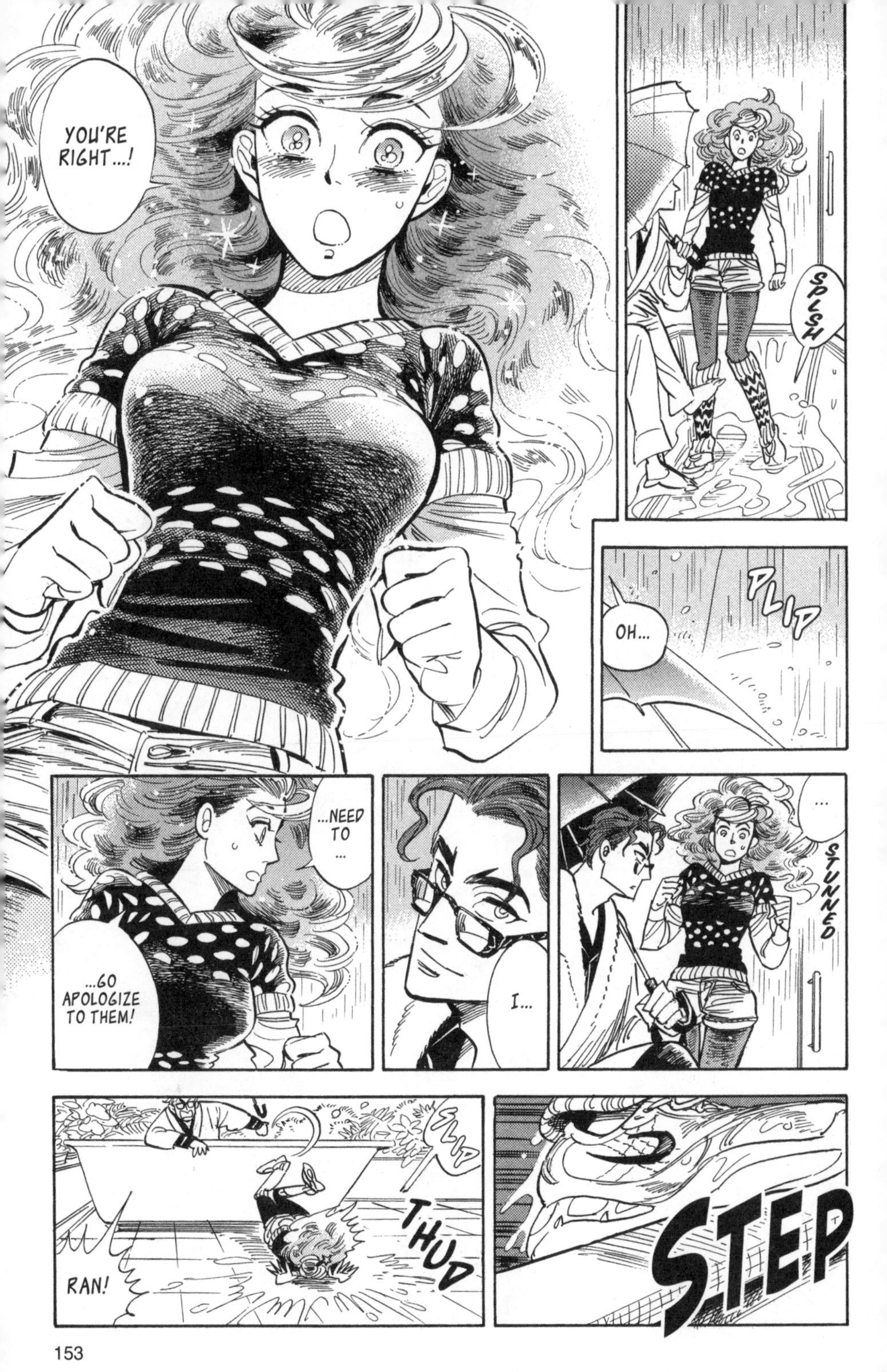
SPLISH
OH...
PLIP
YOU'RE RIGHT...!
...
STUNNED
I...
...NEED TO ...
...GO APOLOGIZE TO THEM!
S.T.E.P
SLIP
THUD
RAN!

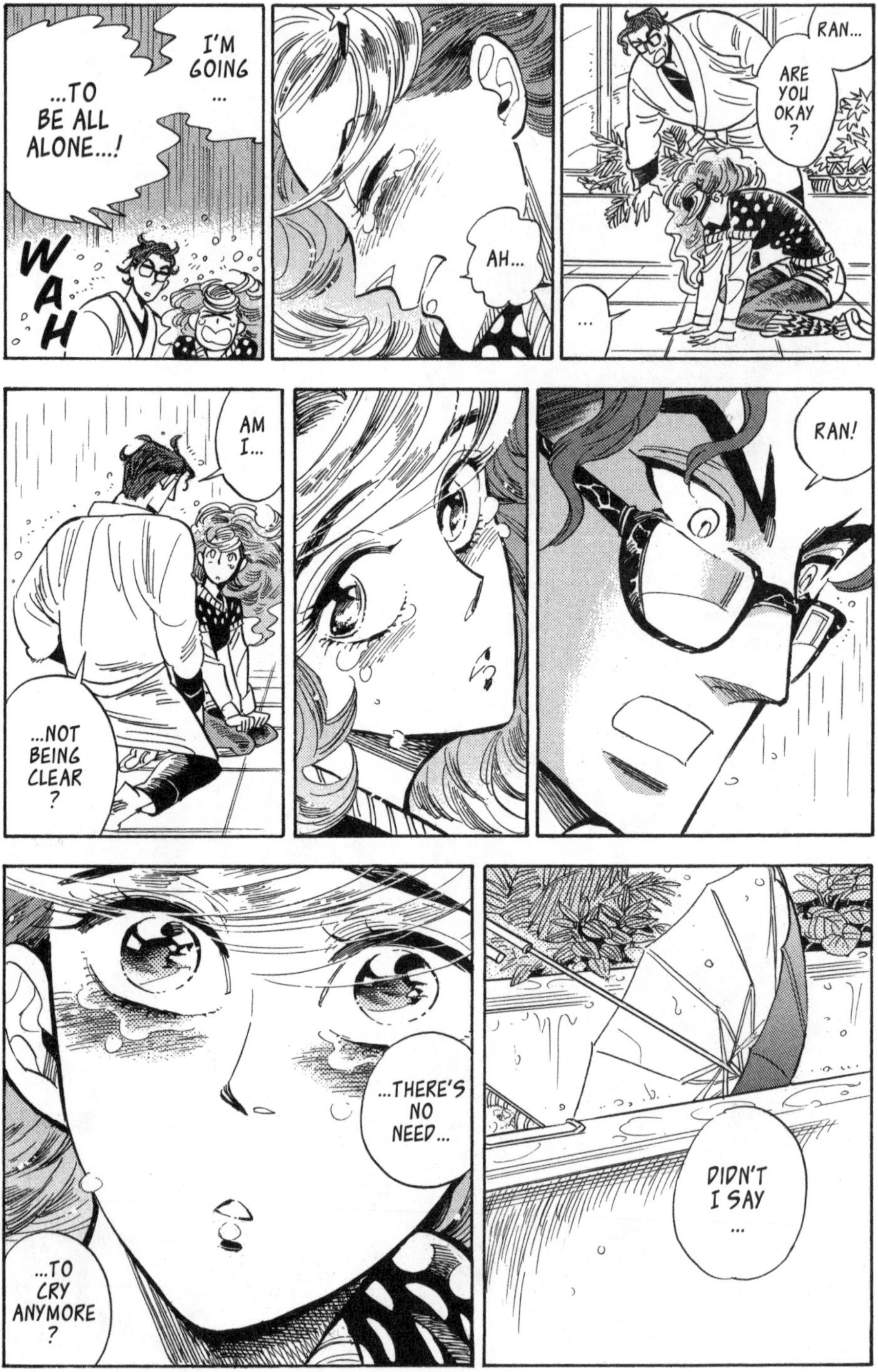
RAN...
ARE YOU OKAY?
...
AH...
I'M GOING...
...TO BE ALL ALONE...!
WAH
RAN!
AM I...
...NOT BEING CLEAR?
DIDN'T I SAY...
...THERE'S NO NEED...
...TO CRY ANYMORE?

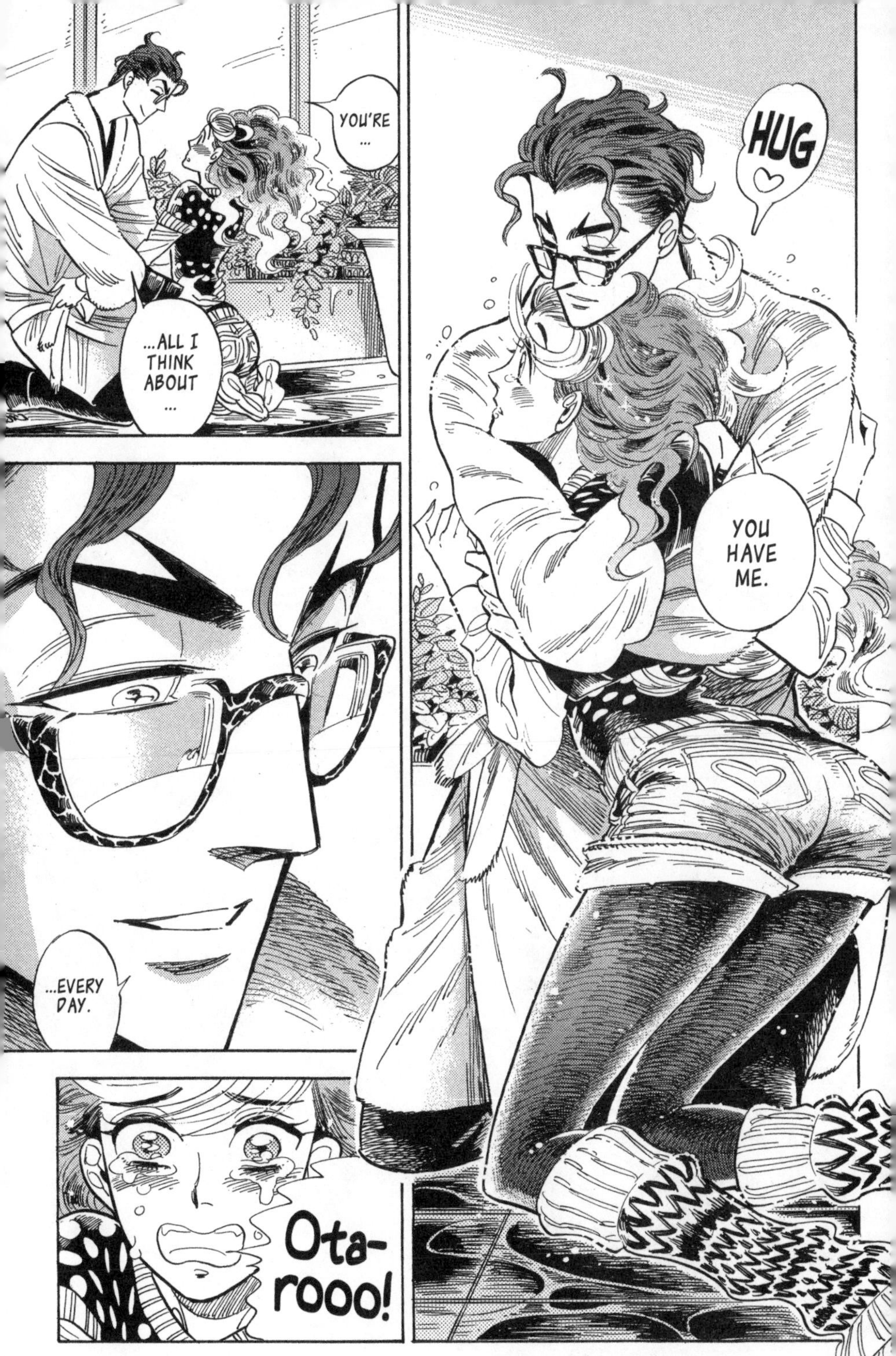
HUG
YOU HAVE ME.
YOU'RE ...
...ALL I THINK ABOUT ...
...EVERY DAY.
Ota-rooo!

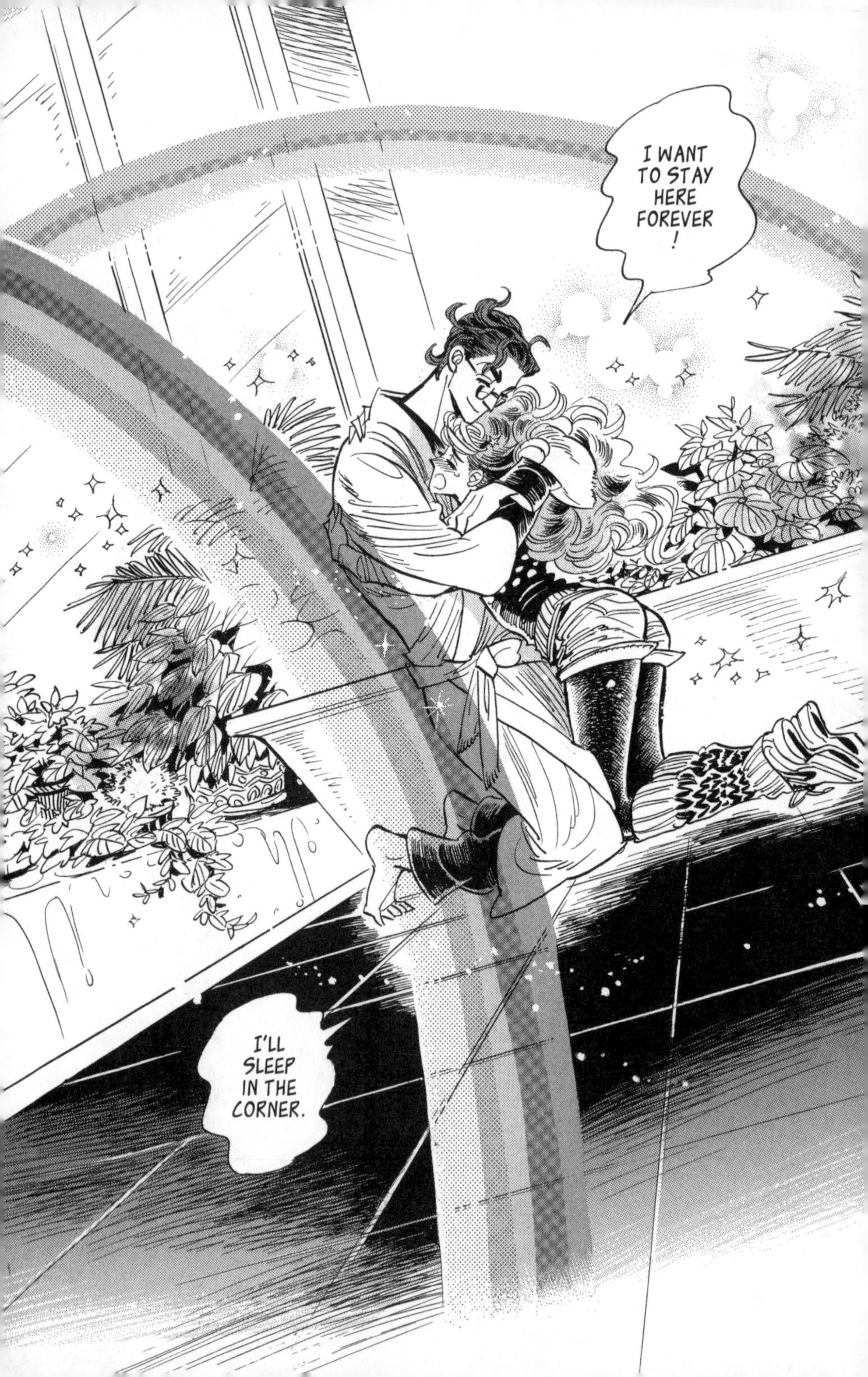
I WANT TO STAY HERE FOREVER!
I'LL SLEEP IN THE CORNER.

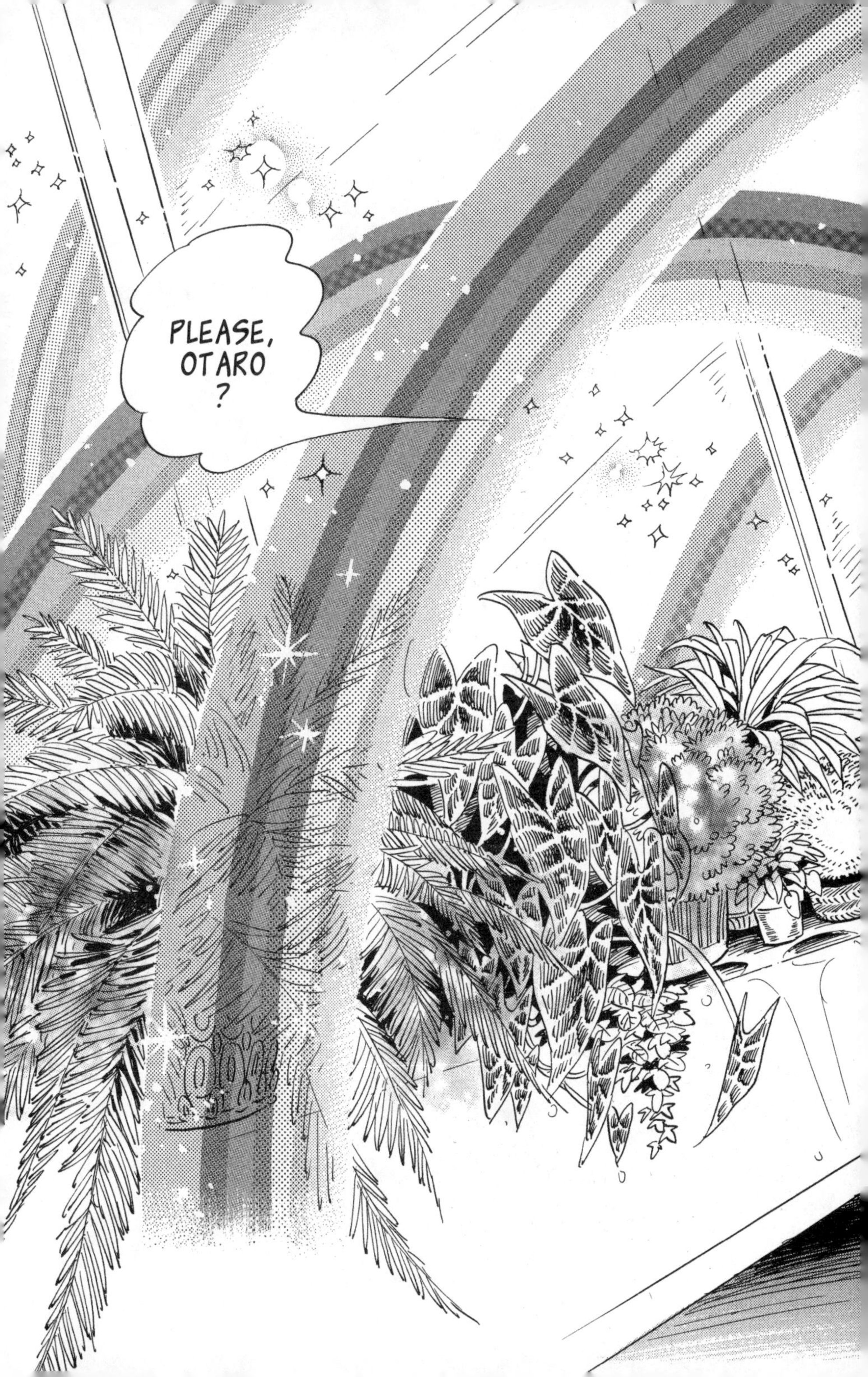
PLEASE, OTARO ?

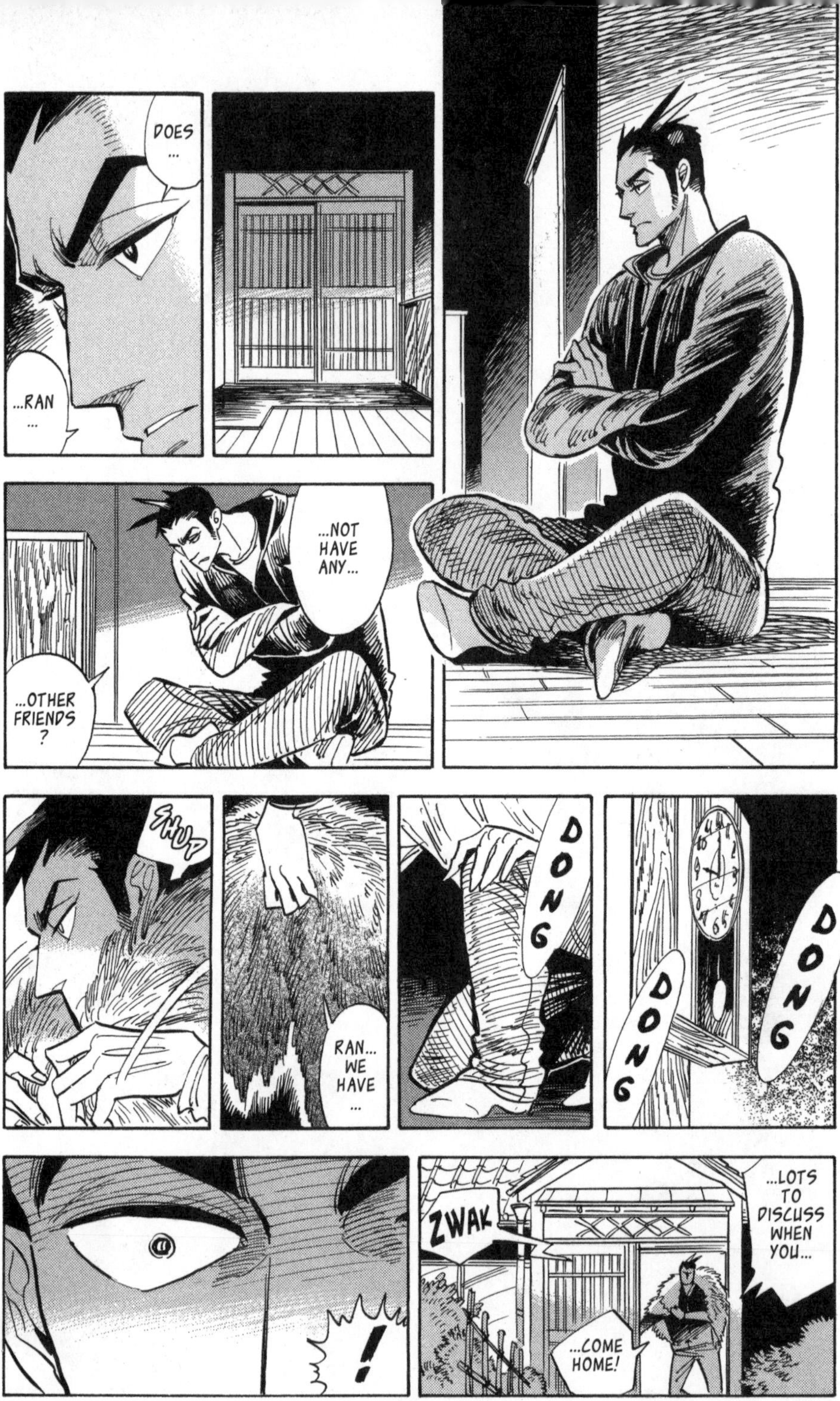
DOES ...
...RAN ...
...NOT HAVE ANY...
...OTHER FRIENDS ?
DONG
DONG
DONG
RAN... WE HAVE ...
SHUP
...LOTS TO DISCUSS WHEN YOU...
ZWAK
...COME HOME!
!

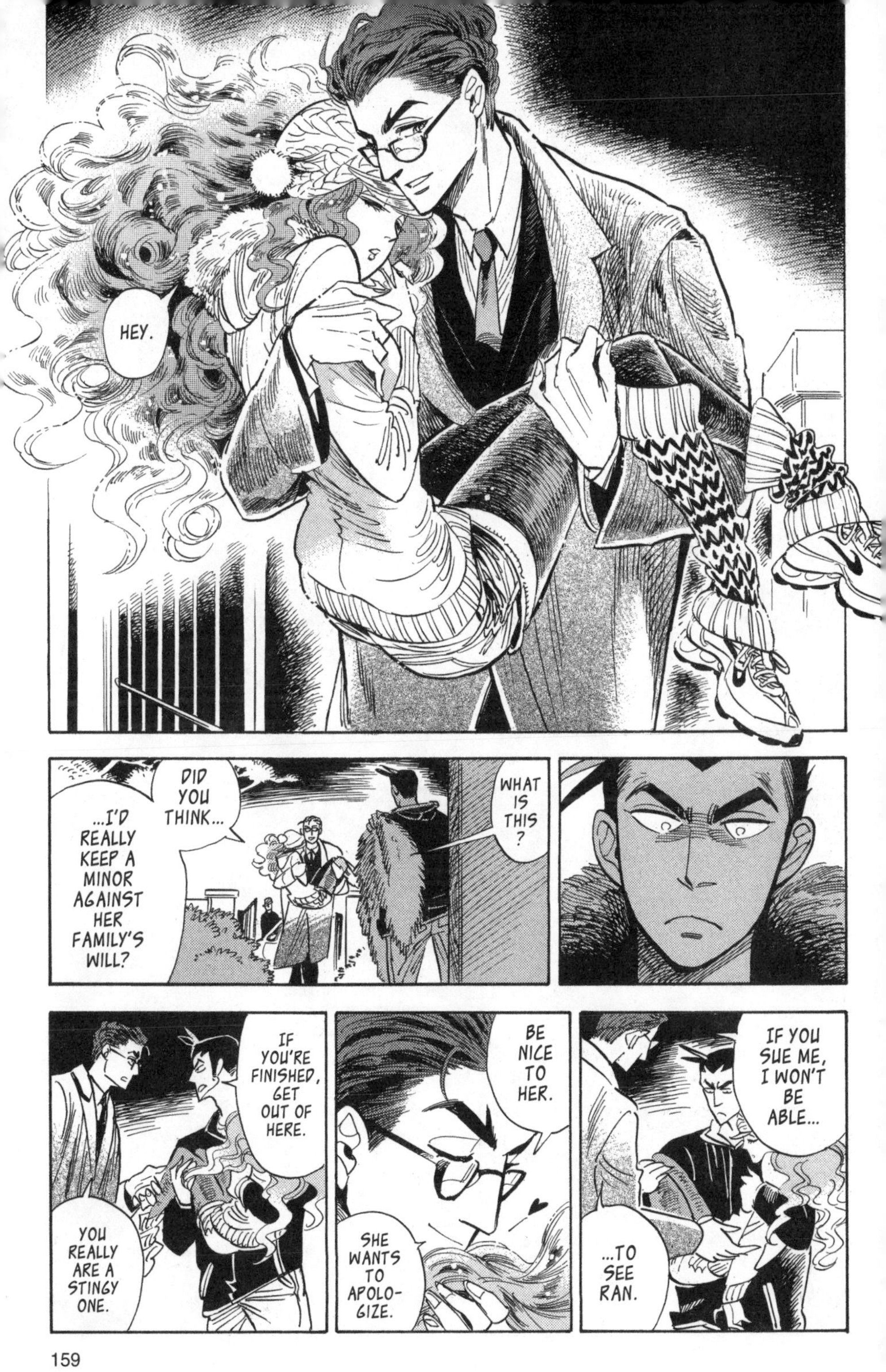
HEY.
WHAT IS THIS?
DID YOU THINK...
...I'D REALLY KEEP A MINOR AGAINST HER FAMILY'S WILL?
IF YOU SUE ME, I WON'T BE ABLE...
...TO SEE RAN.
BE NICE TO HER.
SHE WANTS TO APOLOGIZE.
IF YOU'RE FINISHED, GET OUT OF HERE.
YOU REALLY ARE A STINGY ONE.

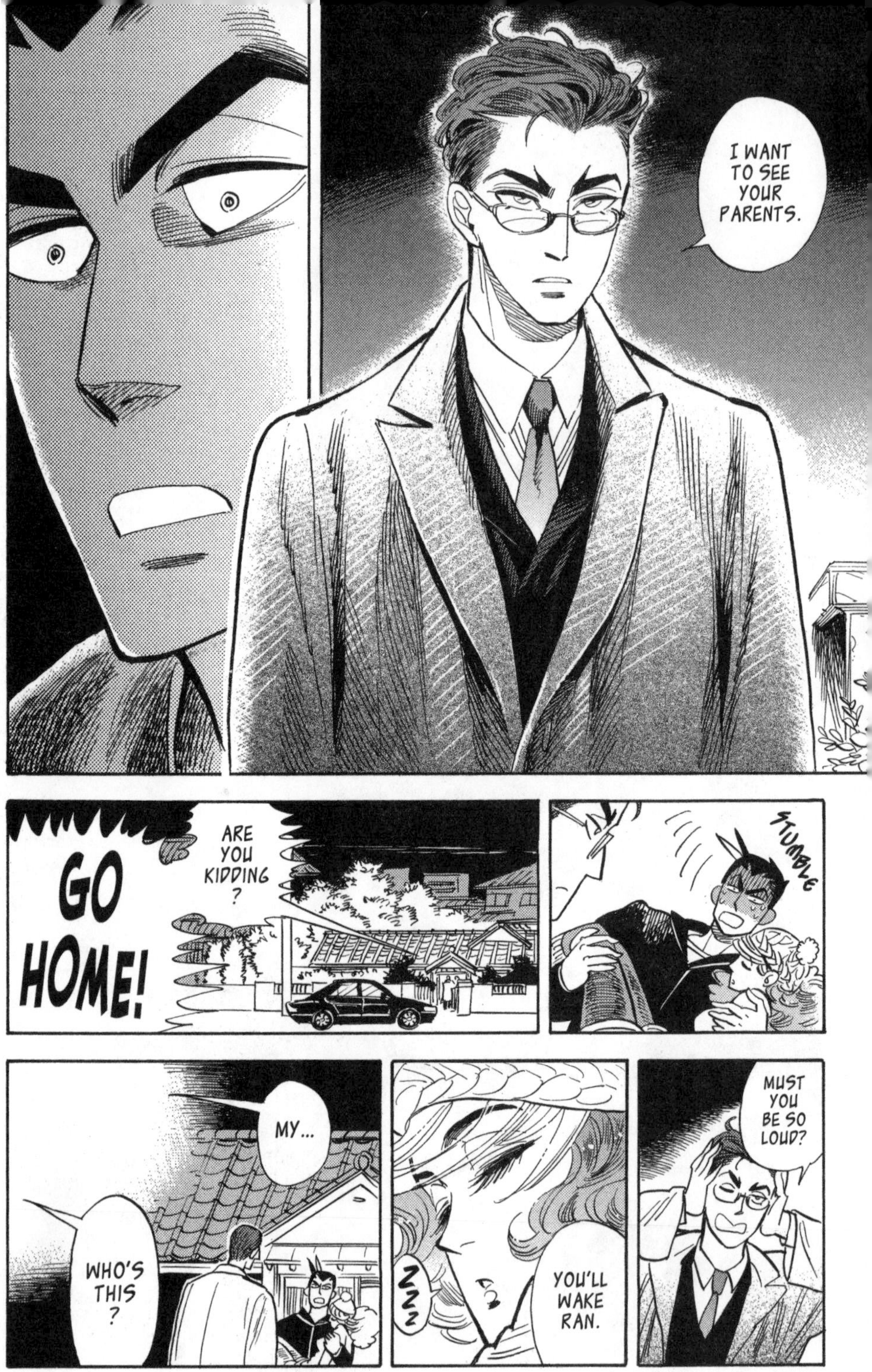
I WANT TO SEE YOUR PARENTS.
STUMBLE
ARE YOU KIDDING?
GO HOME!
MUST YOU BE SO LOUD?
YOU'LL WAKE RAN.
ZZZ
MY...
WHO'S THIS?

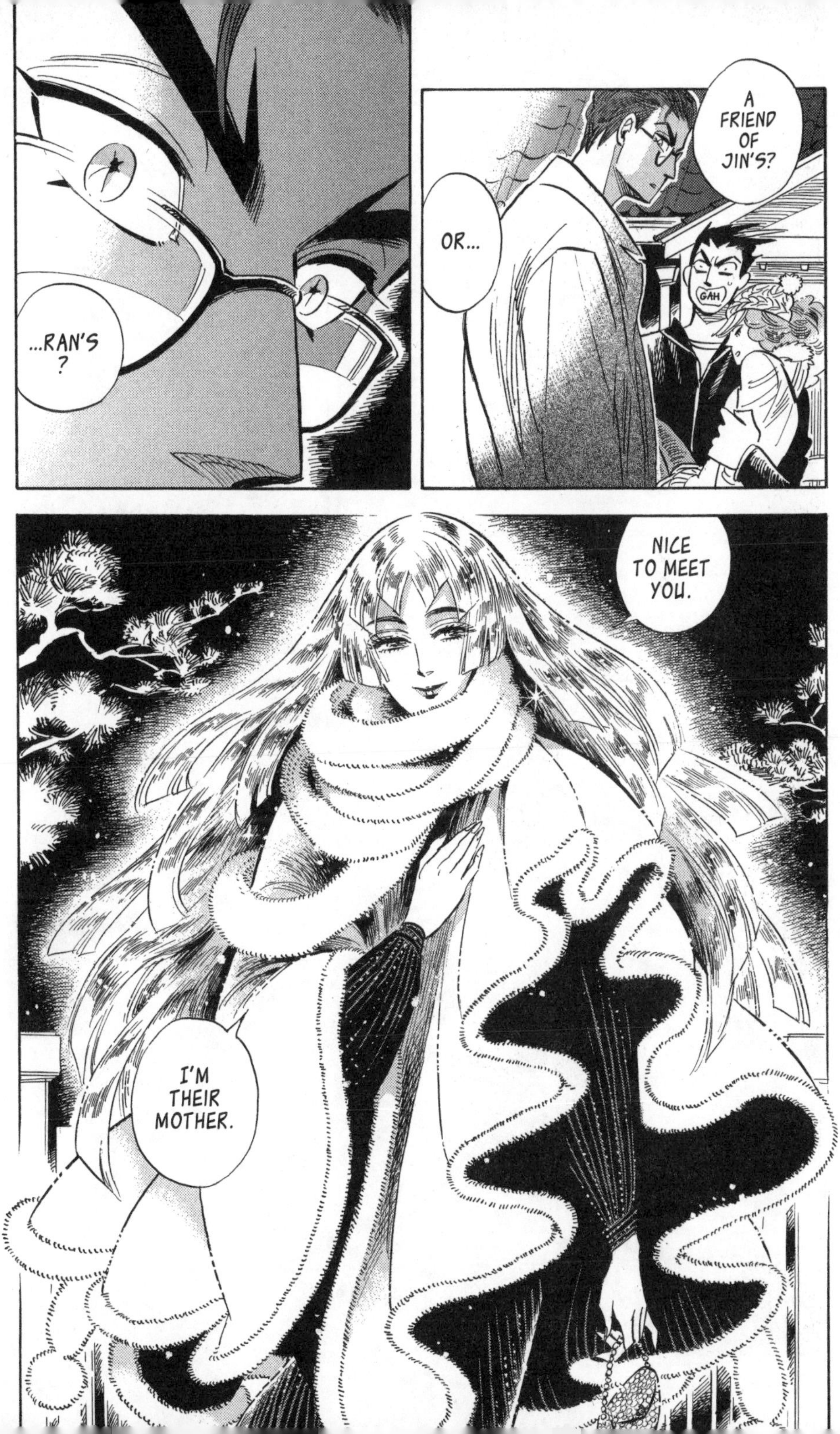
A FRIEND OF JIN'S?
OR...
GAH
...RAN'S ?
NICE TO MEET YOU.
I'M THEIR MOTHER.

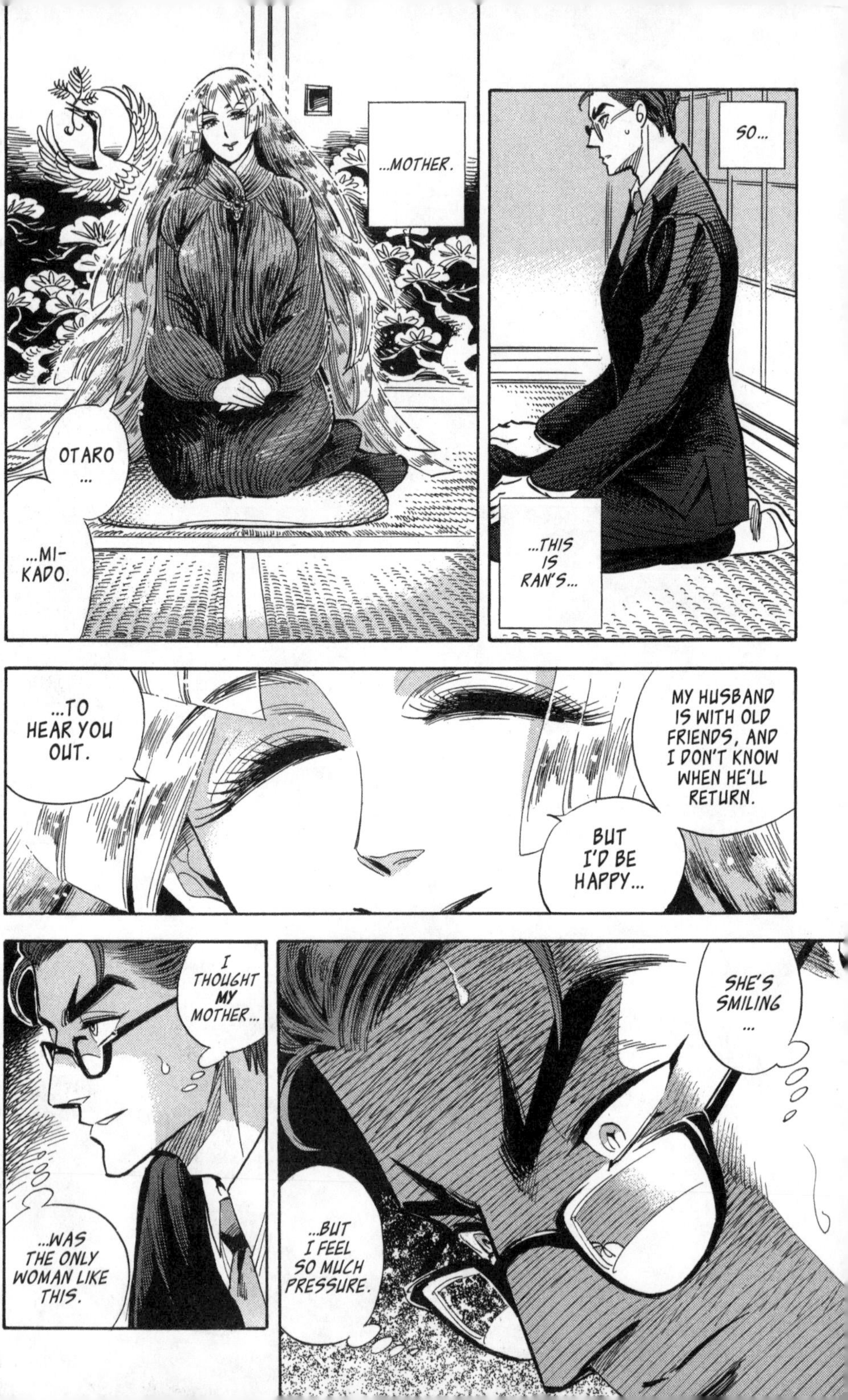
SO...
...THIS IS RAN'S...
...MOTHER.
OTARO...
...MI-KADO.
MY HUSBAND IS WITH OLD FRIENDS, AND I DON'T KNOW WHEN HE'LL RETURN.
BUT I'D BE HAPPY...
...TO HEAR YOU OUT.
SHE'S SMILING...
...BUT I FEEL SO MUCH PRESSURE.
I THOUGHT MY MOTHER...
...WAS THE ONLY WOMAN LIKE THIS.

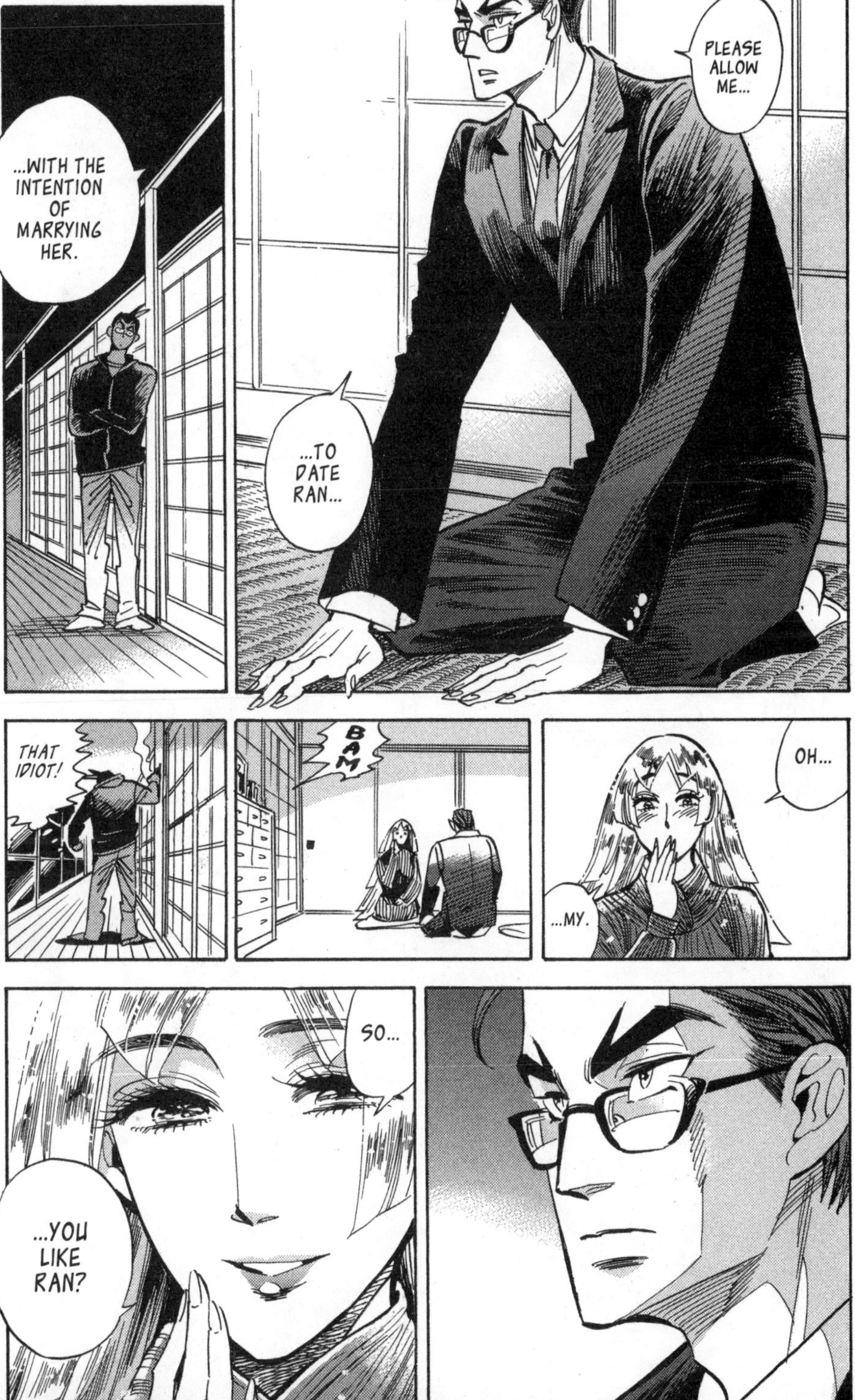
PLEASE ALLOW ME...
...TO DATE RAN...
...WITH THE INTENTION OF MARRYING HER.
OH...
...MY.
BAM
THAT IDIOT!
SO...
...YOU LIKE RAN?

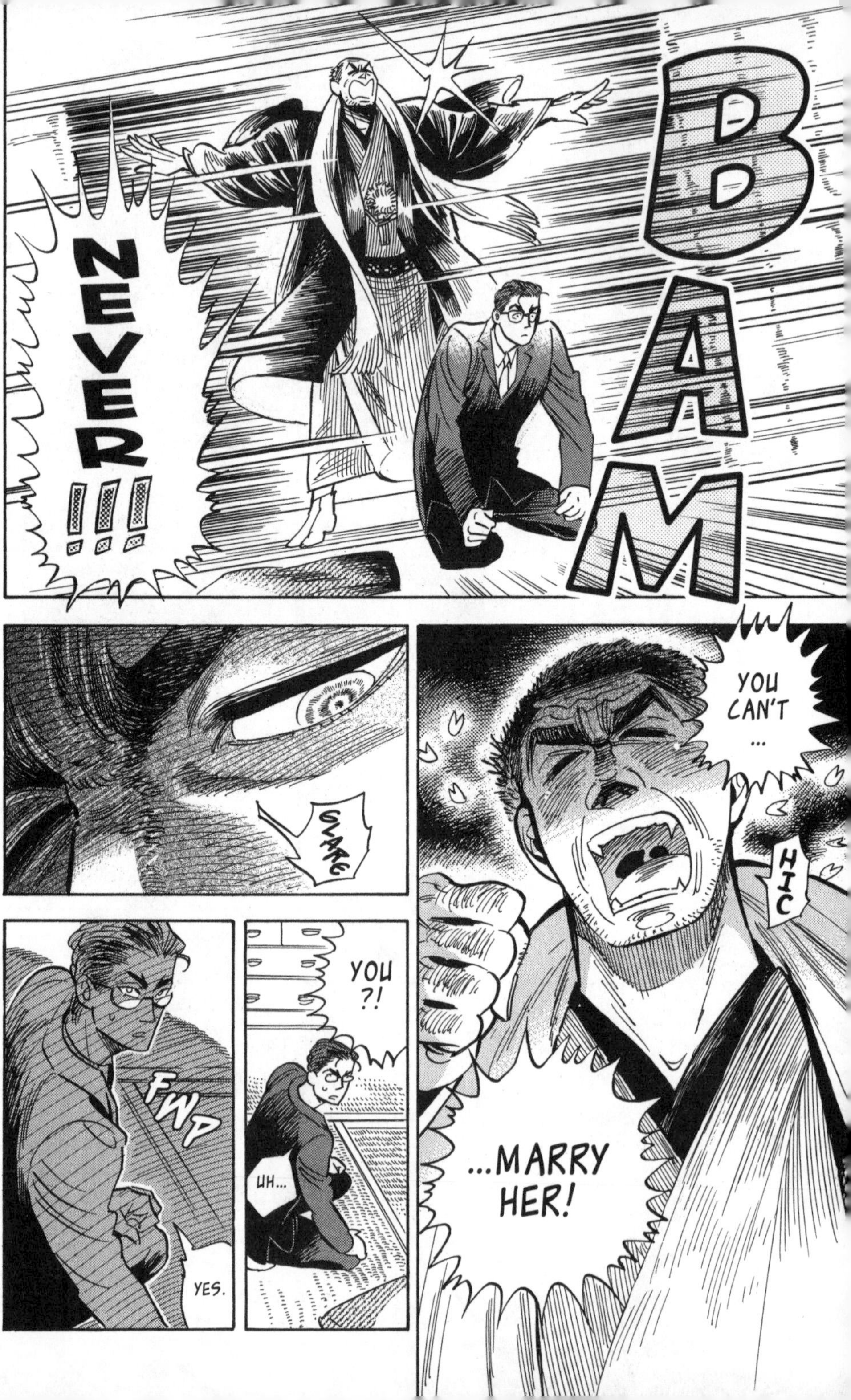
BAM
NEVER!!!
YOU CAN'T ...
HIC
...MARRY HER!
GLARE
YOU ?!
UH...
FWP
YES.

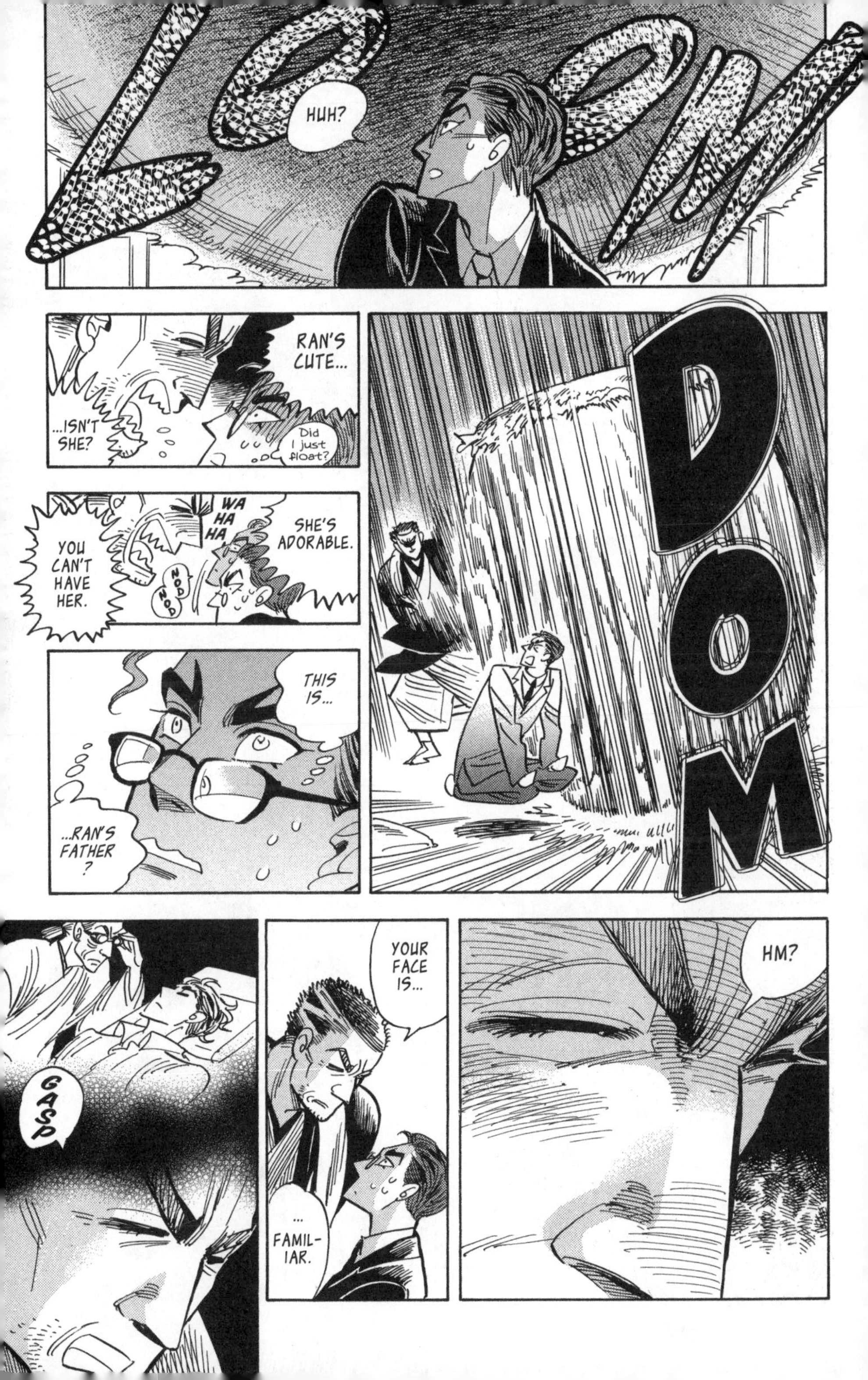
LOOM
HUH?
DOM
RAN'S CUTE...
Did I just float?
...ISN'T SHE?
SHE'S ADORABLE.
WA HA HA
NOD NOD
YOU CAN'T HAVE HER.
THIS IS...
...RAN'S FATHER?
HM?
YOUR FACE IS...
...FAMILIAR.
GASP

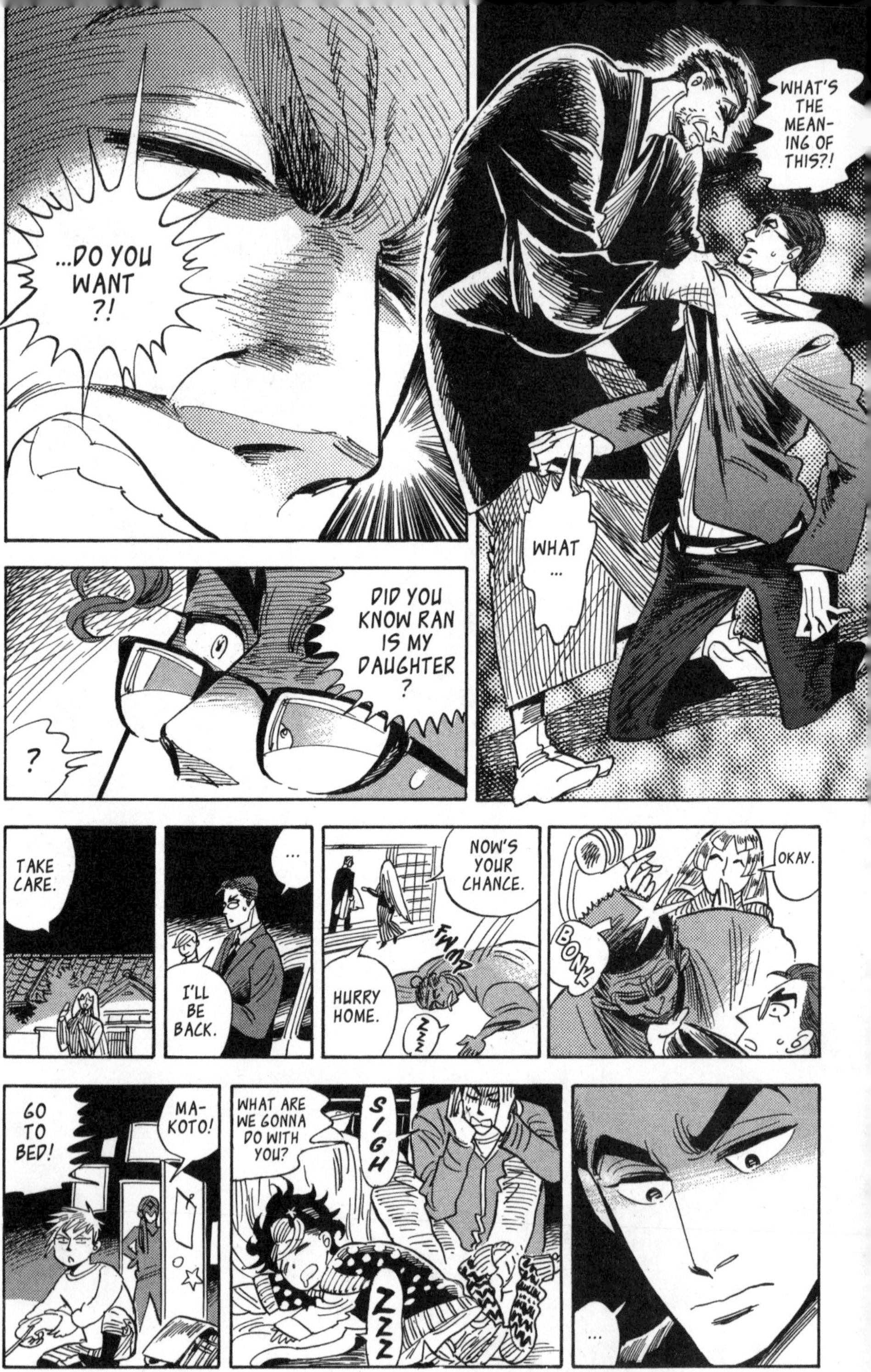
WHAT'S THE MEAN-ING OF THIS?!
WHAT ...
...DO YOU WANT ?!
DID YOU KNOW RAN IS MY DAUGHTER ?
?
OKAY.
BONK
NOW'S YOUR CHANCE.
FWMP
HURRY HOME.
ZZZ
...
I'LL BE BACK.
TAKE CARE.
...
SIGH
WHAT ARE WE GONNA DO WITH YOU?
ZZZ
MA-KOTO!
GO TO BED!

Chapter 17 / The End

Chapter 18

The Girl I Like Is Dating That Guy

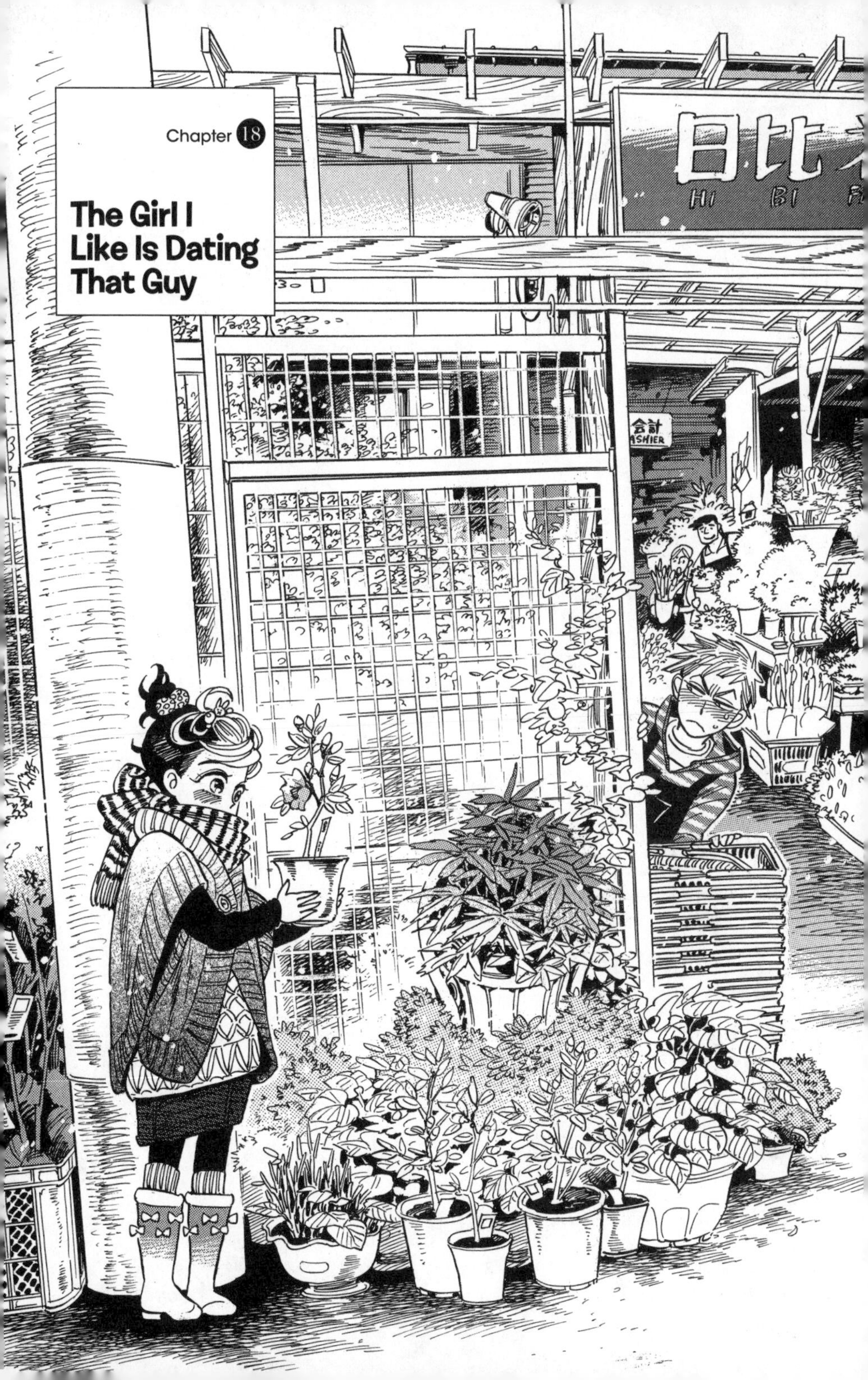

日比
HI BI
会計
ASHIER

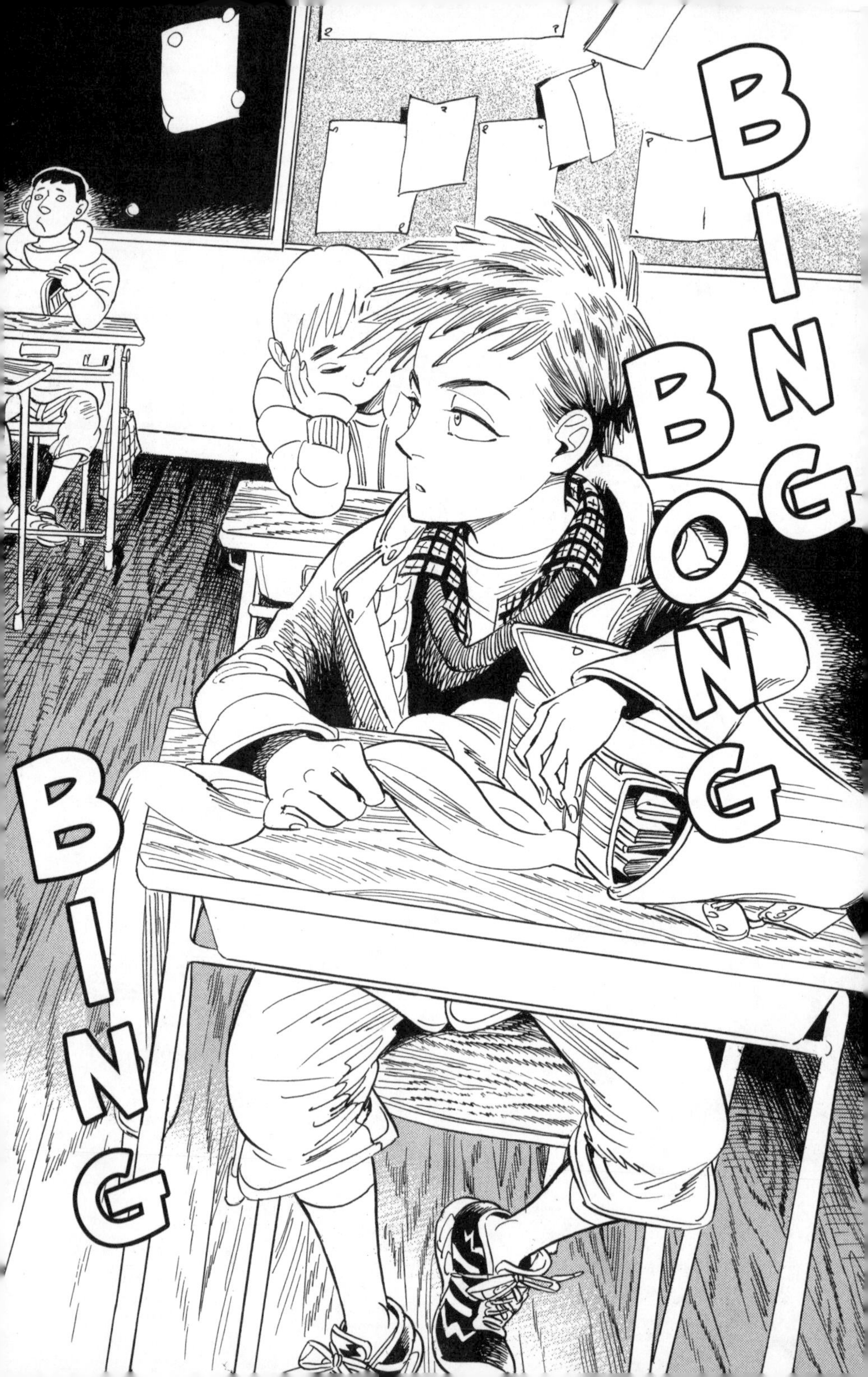
BING
BONG
BING

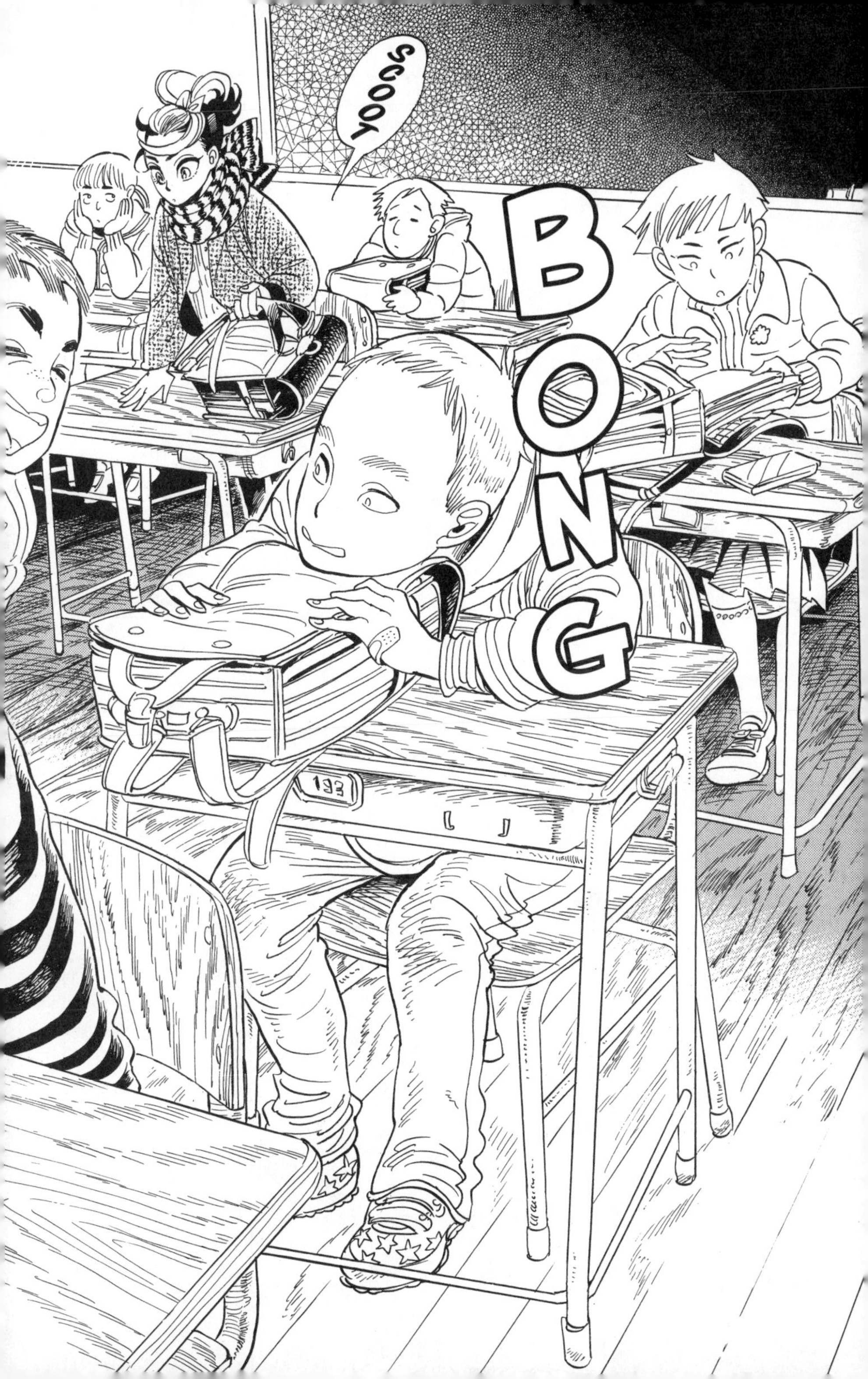
SCOOT
BONG

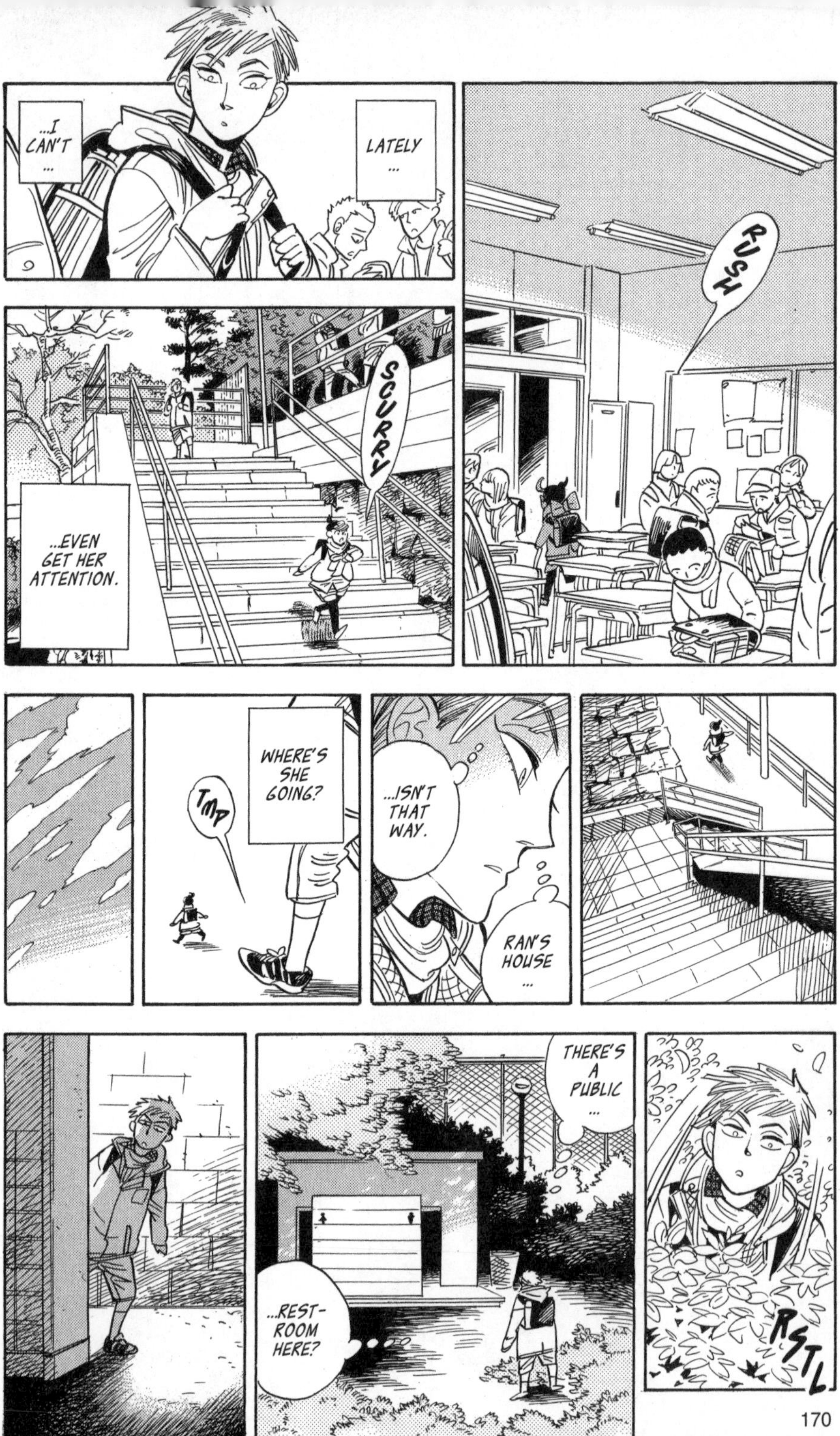
RUSH
LATELY ...
...I CAN'T ...
SCURRY
...EVEN GET HER ATTENTION.
RAN'S HOUSE ...
...ISN'T THAT WAY.
WHERE'S SHE GOING?
TMP
RSTL
THERE'S A PUBLIC ...
...REST-ROOM HERE?

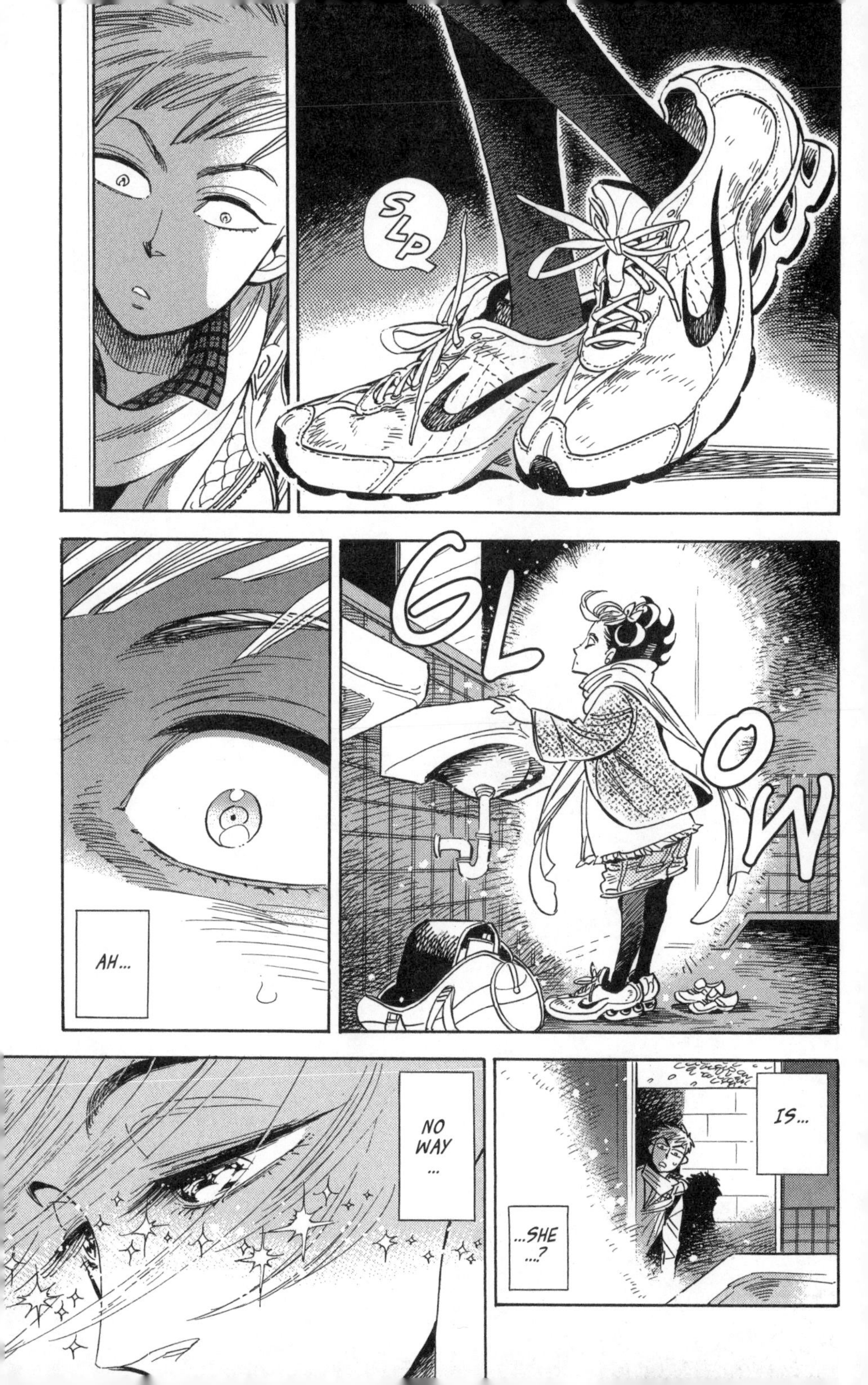
SLP
GLOW
AH...
IS...
...SHE ....?
NO WAY ...

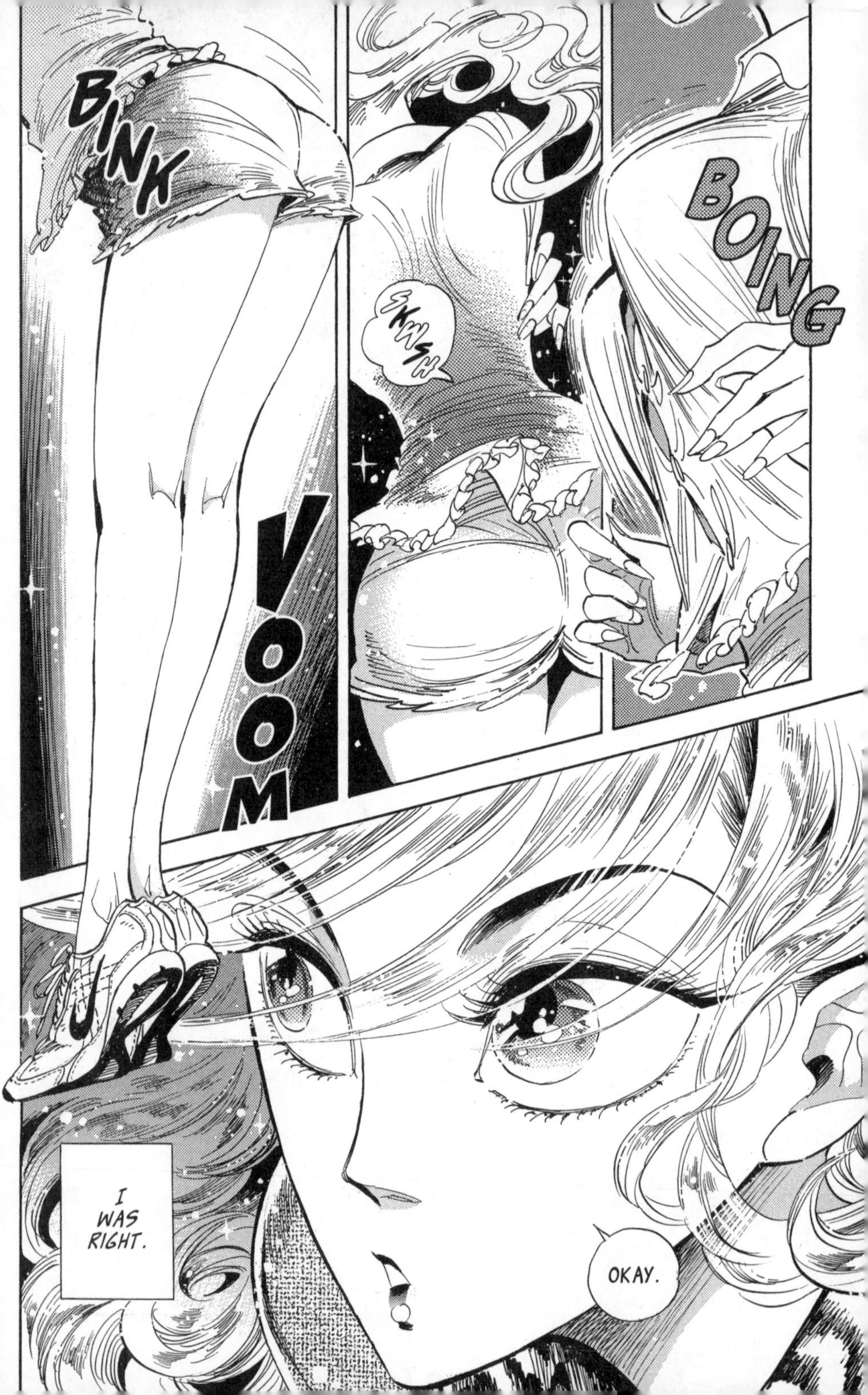
BOING
SKWSH
BINK
VOOM
OKAY.
I WAS RIGHT.

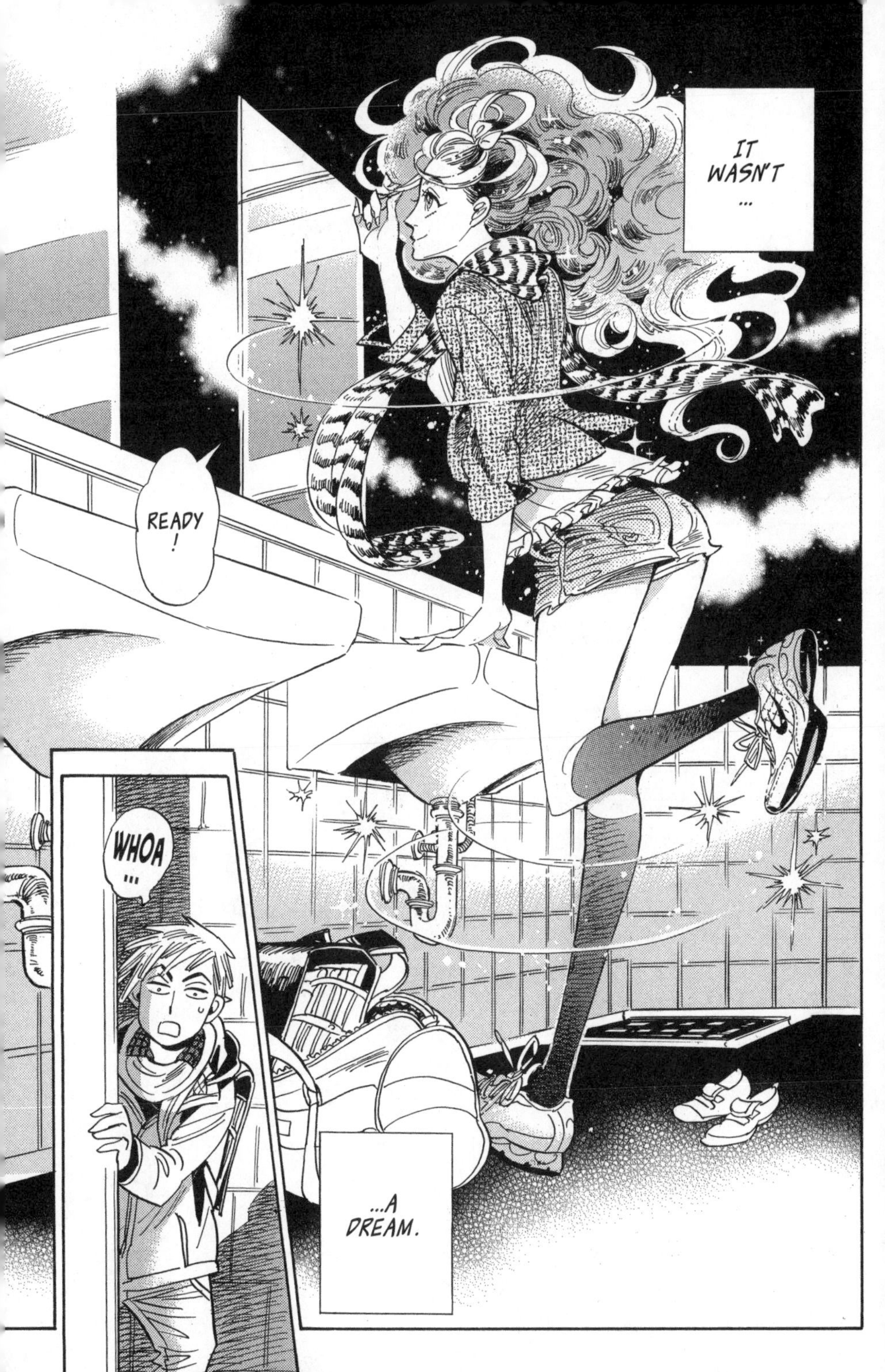
IT WASN'T ...
READY!
...A DREAM.
WHOA ...

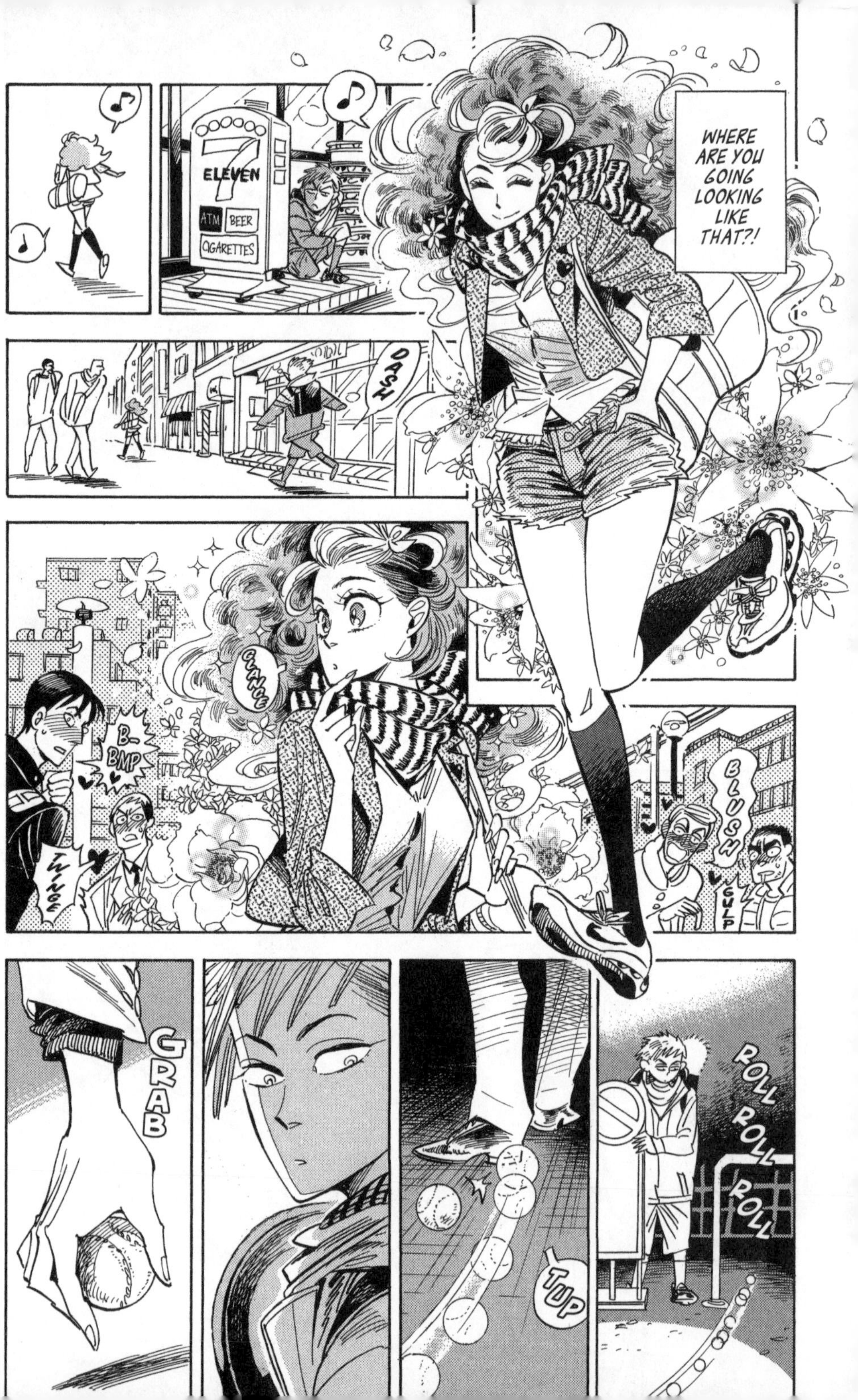
WHERE ARE YOU GOING LOOKING LIKE THAT?!
♪
7 ELEVEN
ATM
BEER
CIGARETTES
♪
♪
DASH
BLUSH
GULP
GLANCE
B-BMP
TWINGE
ROLL ROLL ROLL ROLL
TUP
GRAB

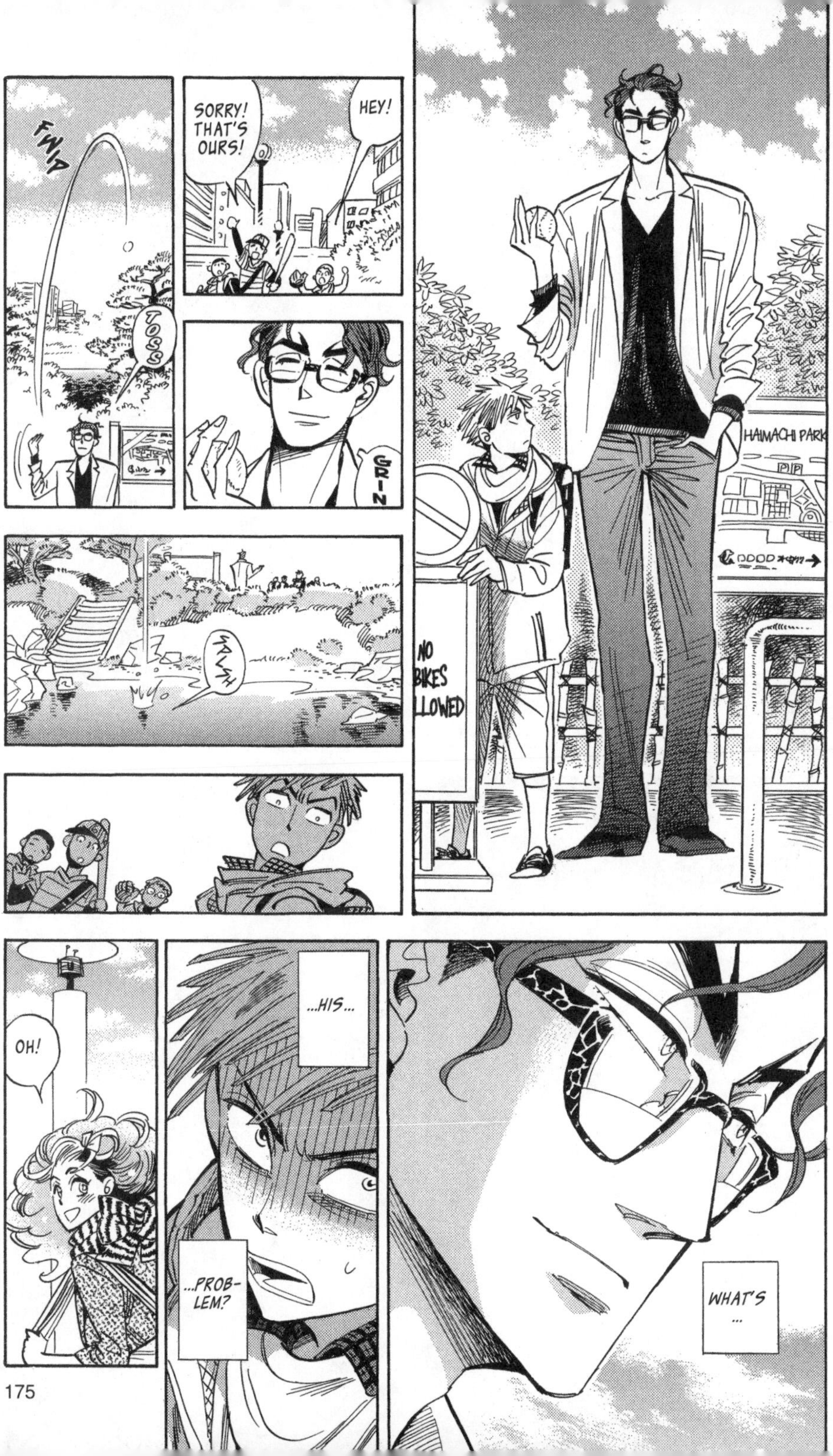
HAIMACHI PARK
NO
BIKES
LLOWED
HEY!
SORRY! THAT'S OURS!
GRIN
FWIP
TOSS
SPLSH
WHAT'S ...
...HIS...
...PROB-LEM?
OH!

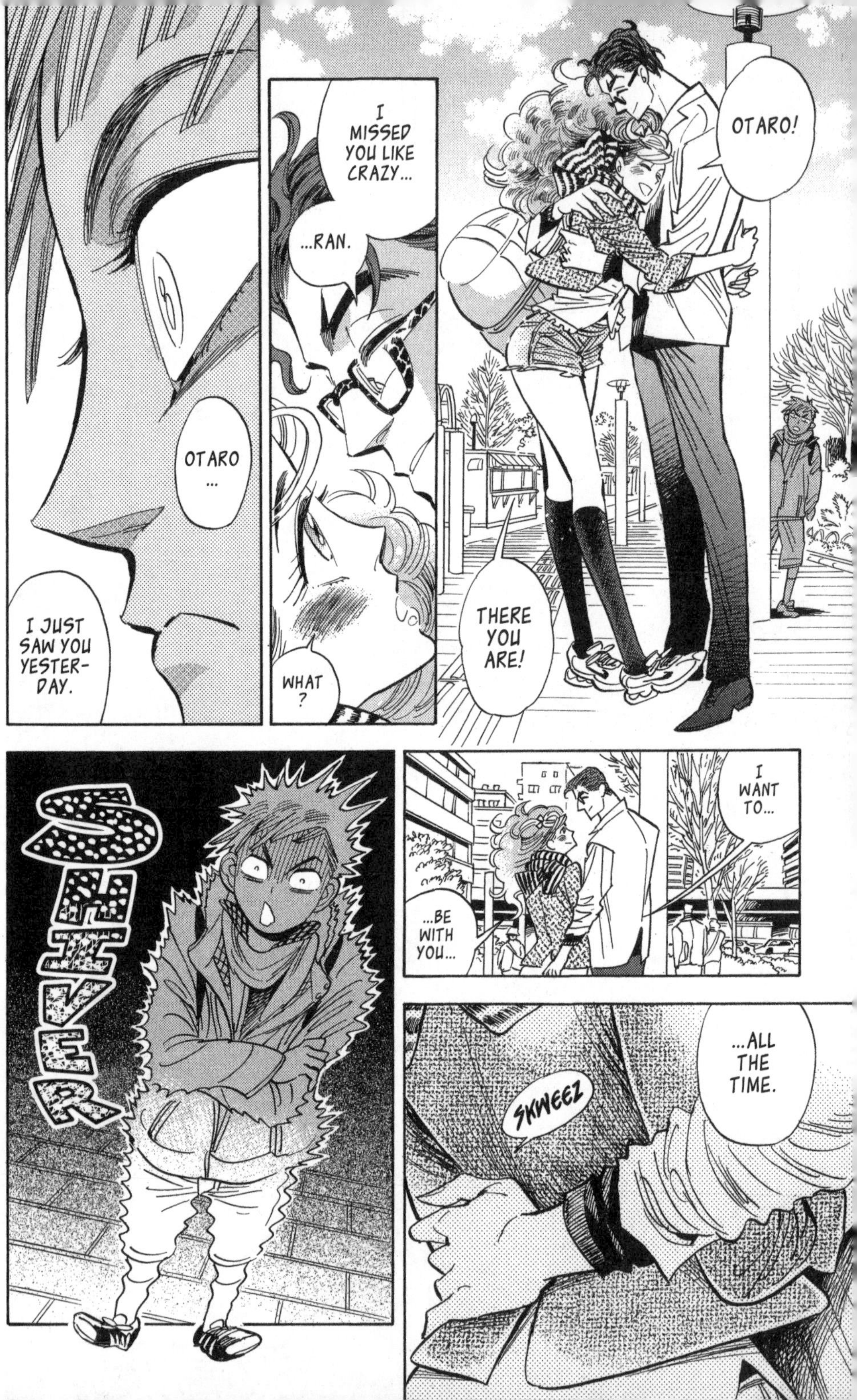
OTARO!
THERE YOU ARE!
I MISSED YOU LIKE CRAZY...
...RAN.
WHAT?
OTARO...
I JUST SAW YOU YESTER-DAY.
I WANT TO...
...BE WITH YOU...
...ALL THE TIME.
SKWEEZ
SHIVER

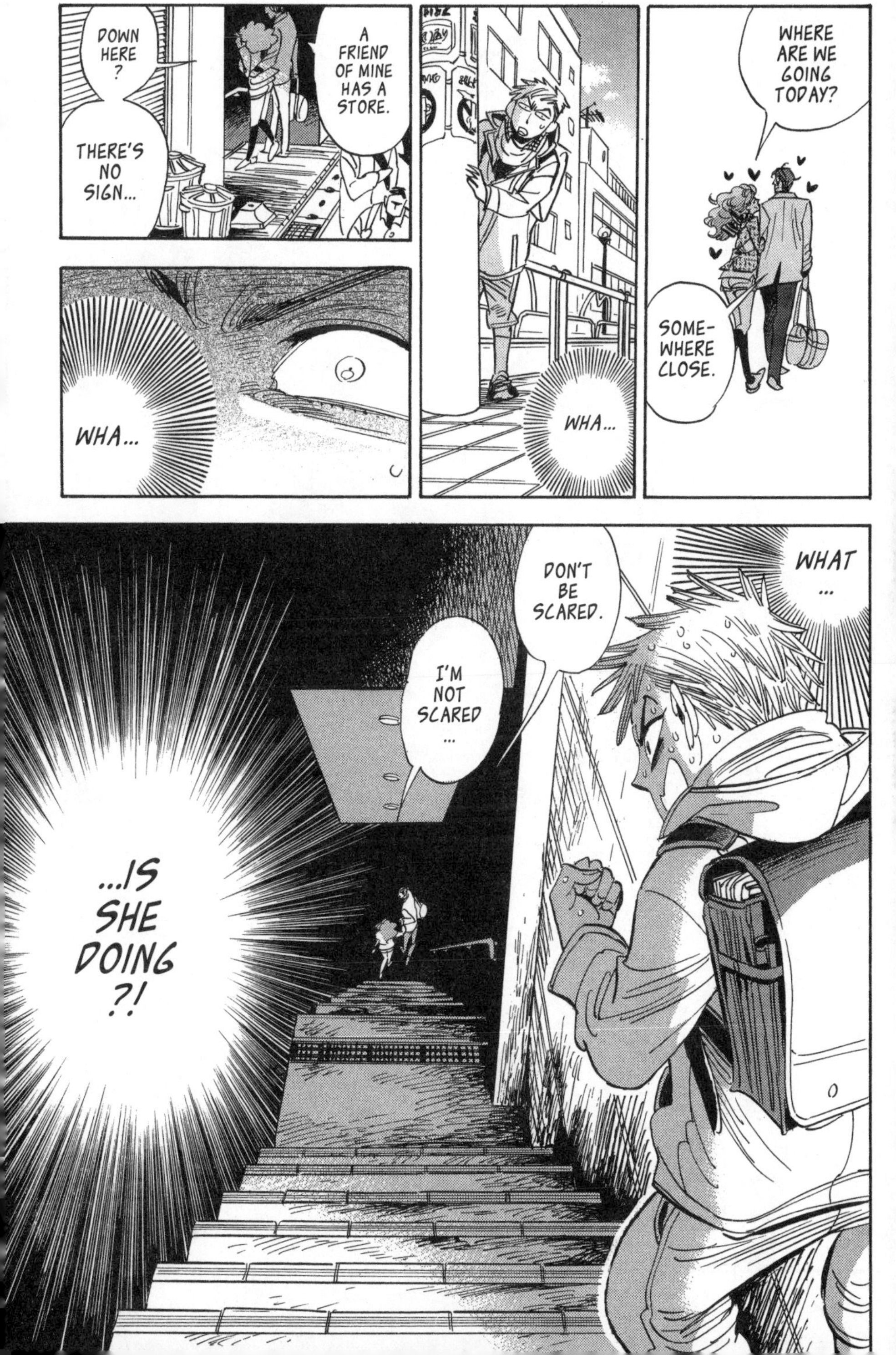
WHERE ARE WE GOING TODAY?
SOME-WHERE CLOSE.
WHA...
A FRIEND OF MINE HAS A STORE.
DOWN HERE?
THERE'S NO SIGN...
WHA...
WHAT...
DON'T BE SCARED.
I'M NOT SCARED...
...IS SHE DOING?!

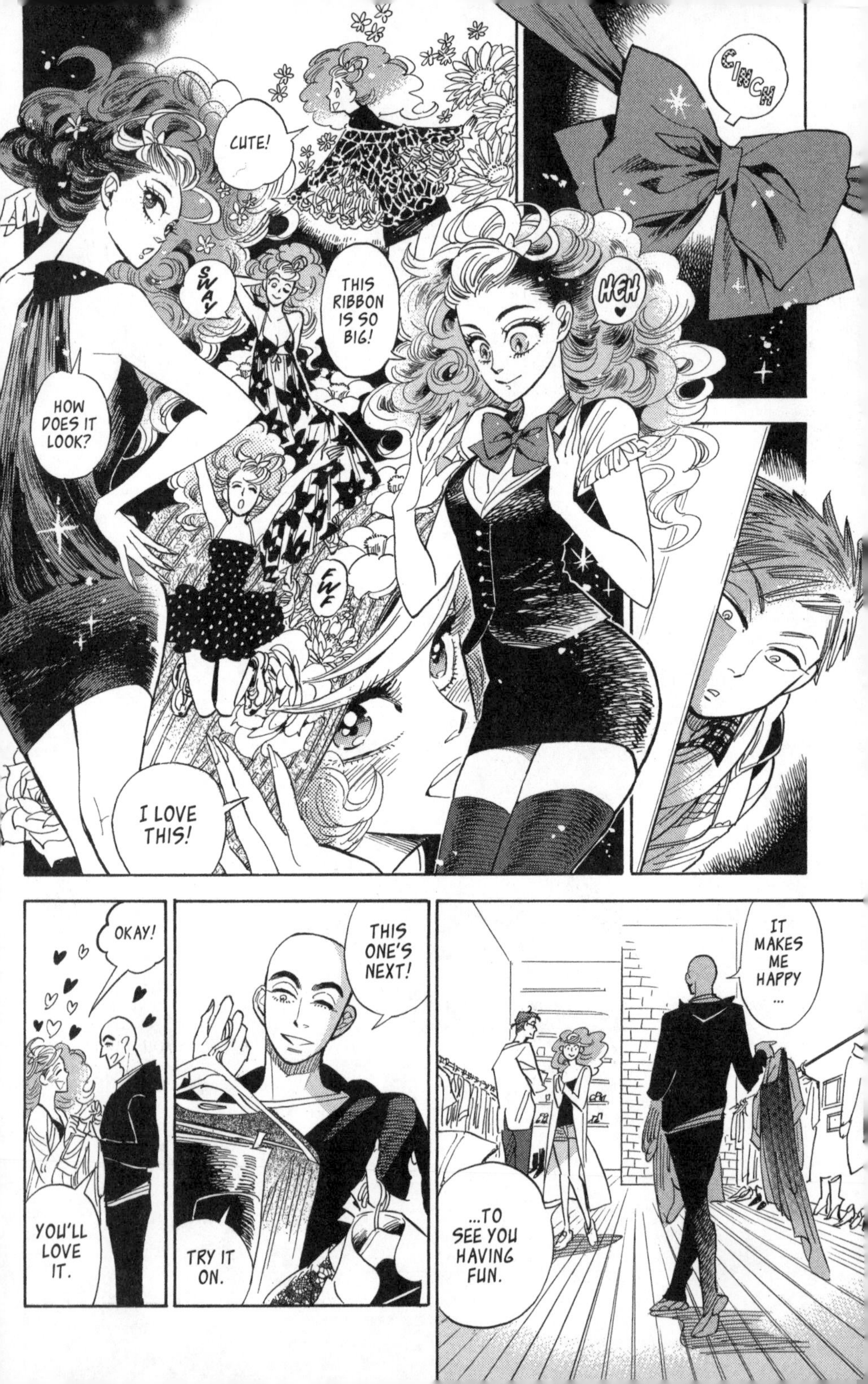
CINCH
HEH
CUTE!
THIS RIBBON IS SO BIG!
SWAY
HOW DOES IT LOOK?
FWF
I LOVE THIS!
IT MAKES ME HAPPY ...
...TO SEE YOU HAVING FUN.
THIS ONE'S NEXT!
TRY IT ON.
OKAY!
YOU'LL LOVE IT.

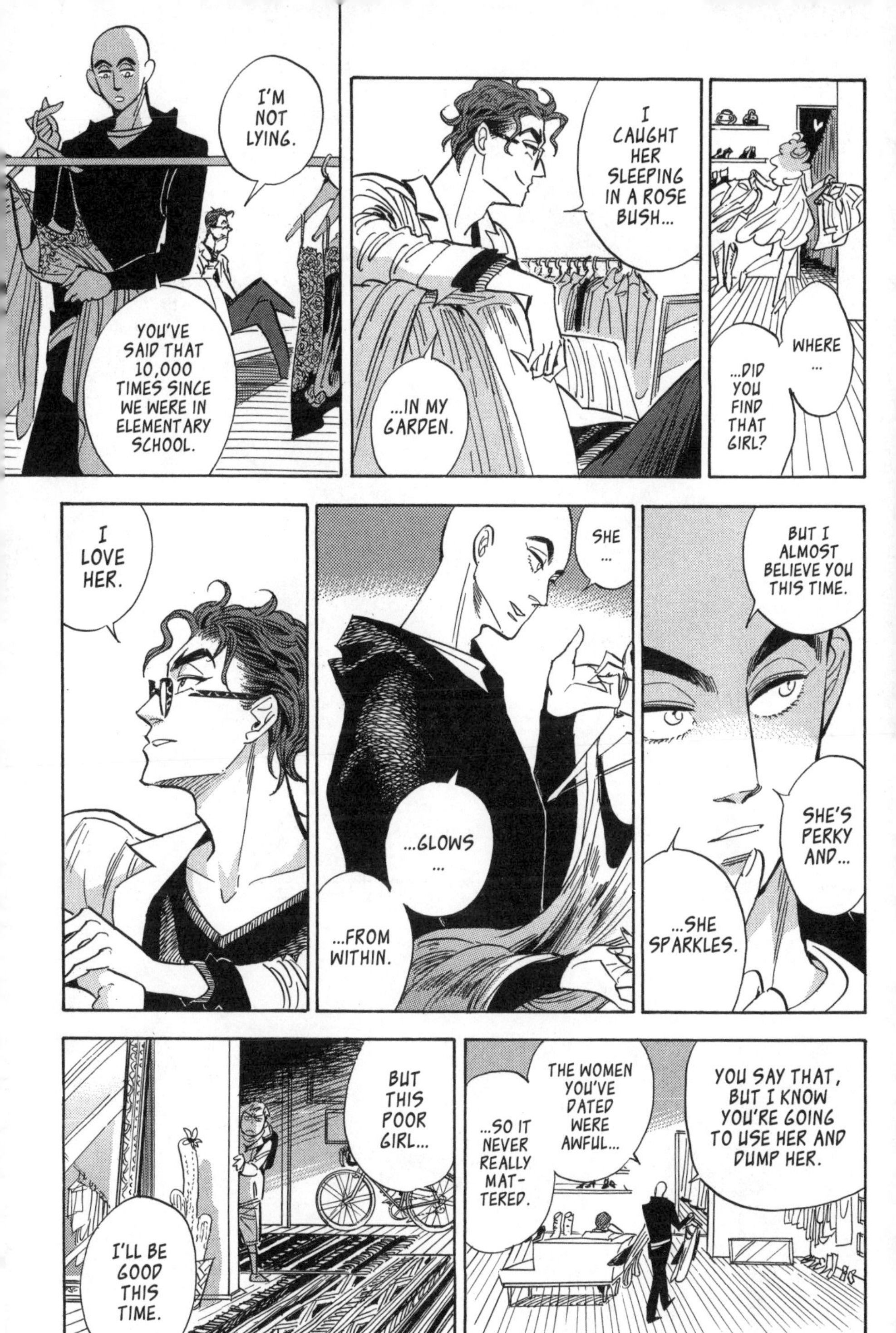
WHERE ...
...DID YOU FIND THAT GIRL?
I CAUGHT HER SLEEPING IN A ROSE BUSH...
...IN MY GARDEN.
I'M NOT LYING.
YOU'VE SAID THAT 10,000 TIMES SINCE WE WERE IN ELEMENTARY SCHOOL.
BUT I ALMOST BELIEVE YOU THIS TIME.
SHE'S PERKY AND...
...SHE SPARKLES.
SHE ...
...GLOWS ...
...FROM WITHIN.
I LOVE HER.
YOU SAY THAT, BUT I KNOW YOU'RE GOING TO USE HER AND DUMP HER.
THE WOMEN YOU'VE DATED WERE AWFUL...
...SO IT NEVER REALLY MAT-TERED.
BUT THIS POOR GIRL...
I'LL BE GOOD THIS TIME.

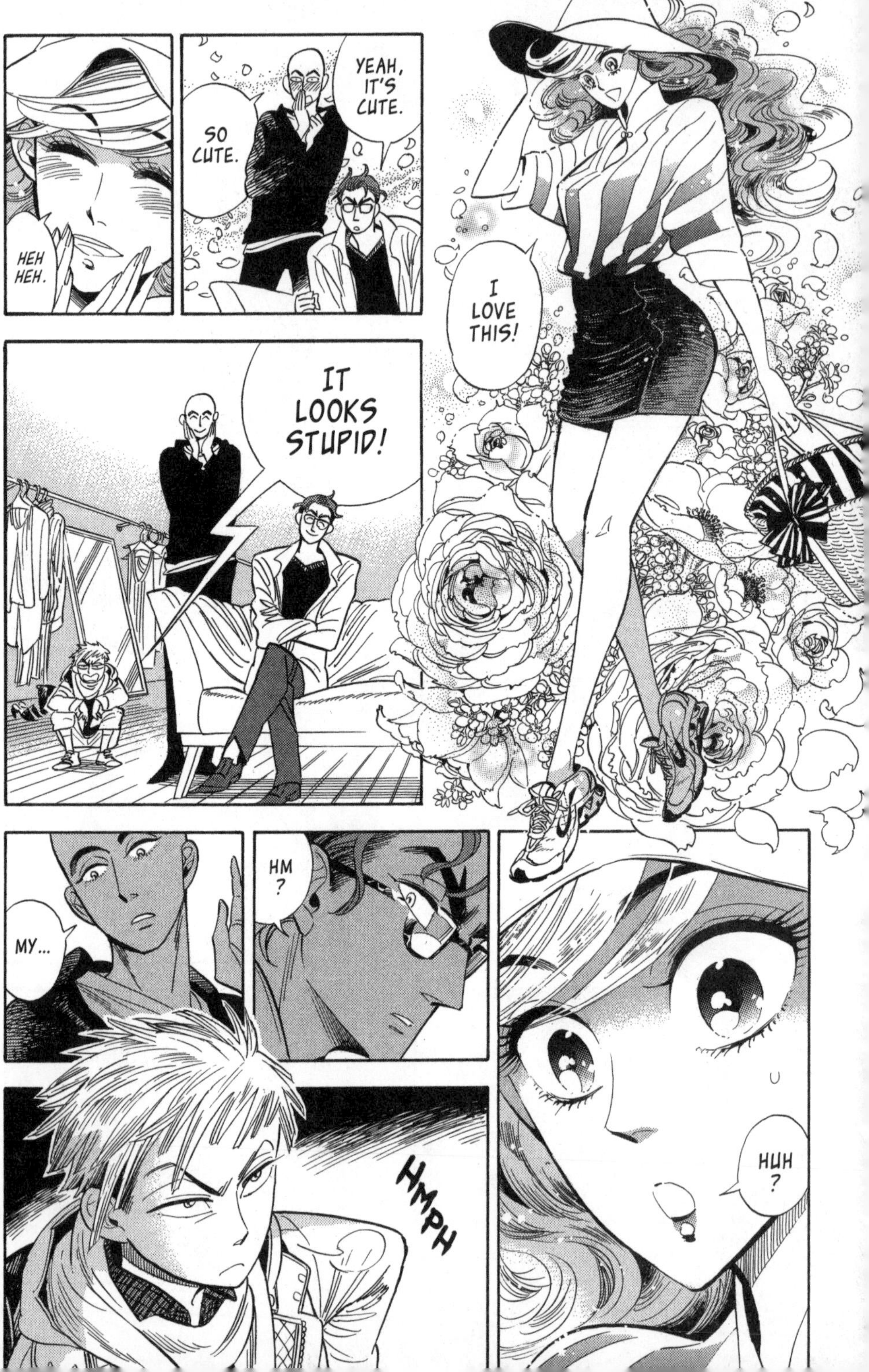
I LOVE THIS!
YEAH, IT'S CUTE.
SO CUTE.
HEH HEH.
IT LOOKS STUPID!
HUH?
HM?
MY...
HMPH

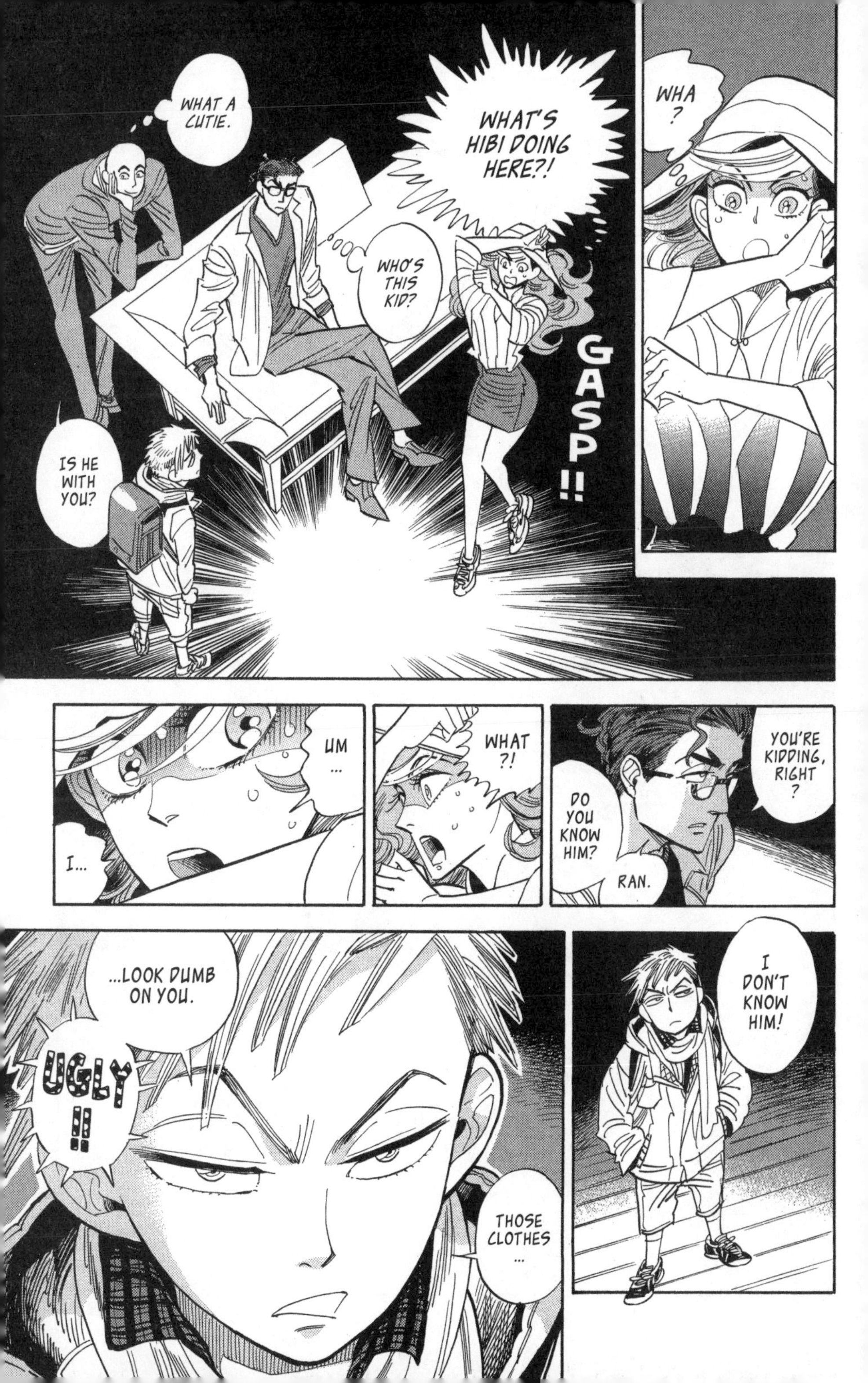
WHA ?
WHAT'S HIBI DOING HERE?!
WHAT A CUTIE.
WHO'S THIS KID?
GASP !!
IS HE WITH YOU?
YOU'RE KIDDING, RIGHT ?
DO YOU KNOW HIM?
RAN.
WHAT ?!
UM ...
I...
I DON'T KNOW HIM!
THOSE CLOTHES ...
...LOOK DUMB ON YOU.
UGLY !!

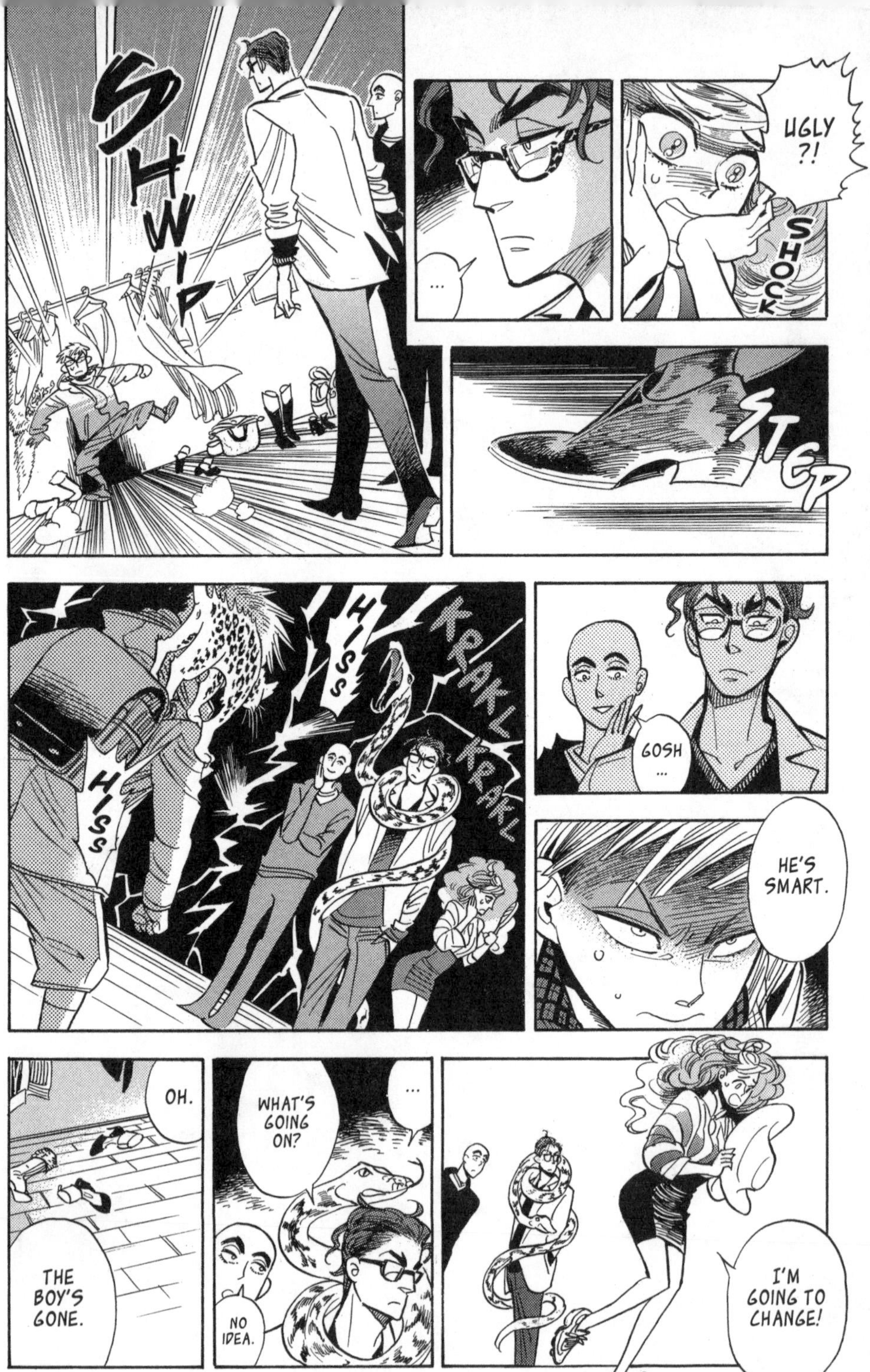
UGLY ?!
SHOCK
...
STEP
SHWIP
GOSH ...
HE'S SMART.
KRAKL KRAKL
HISS
HISS
I'M GOING TO CHANGE!
...
WHAT'S GOING ON?
NO IDEA.
OH.
THE BOY'S GONE.

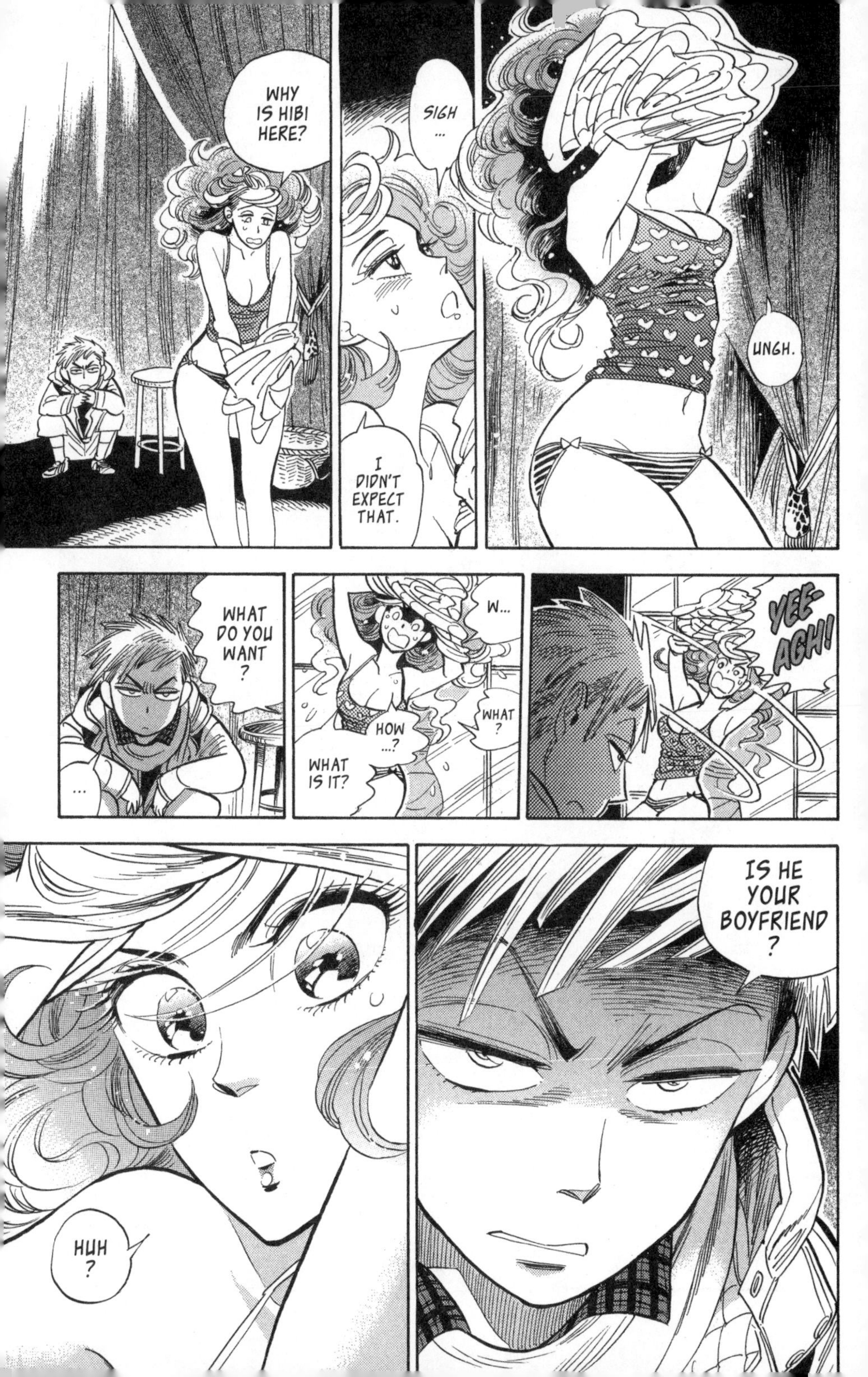
UNGH.
SIGH ...
I DIDN'T EXPECT THAT.
WHY IS HIBI HERE?
YEE-AGH!
W...
WHAT?
HOW ...?
WHAT IS IT?
WHAT DO YOU WANT?
...
IS HE YOUR BOYFRIEND?
HUH?

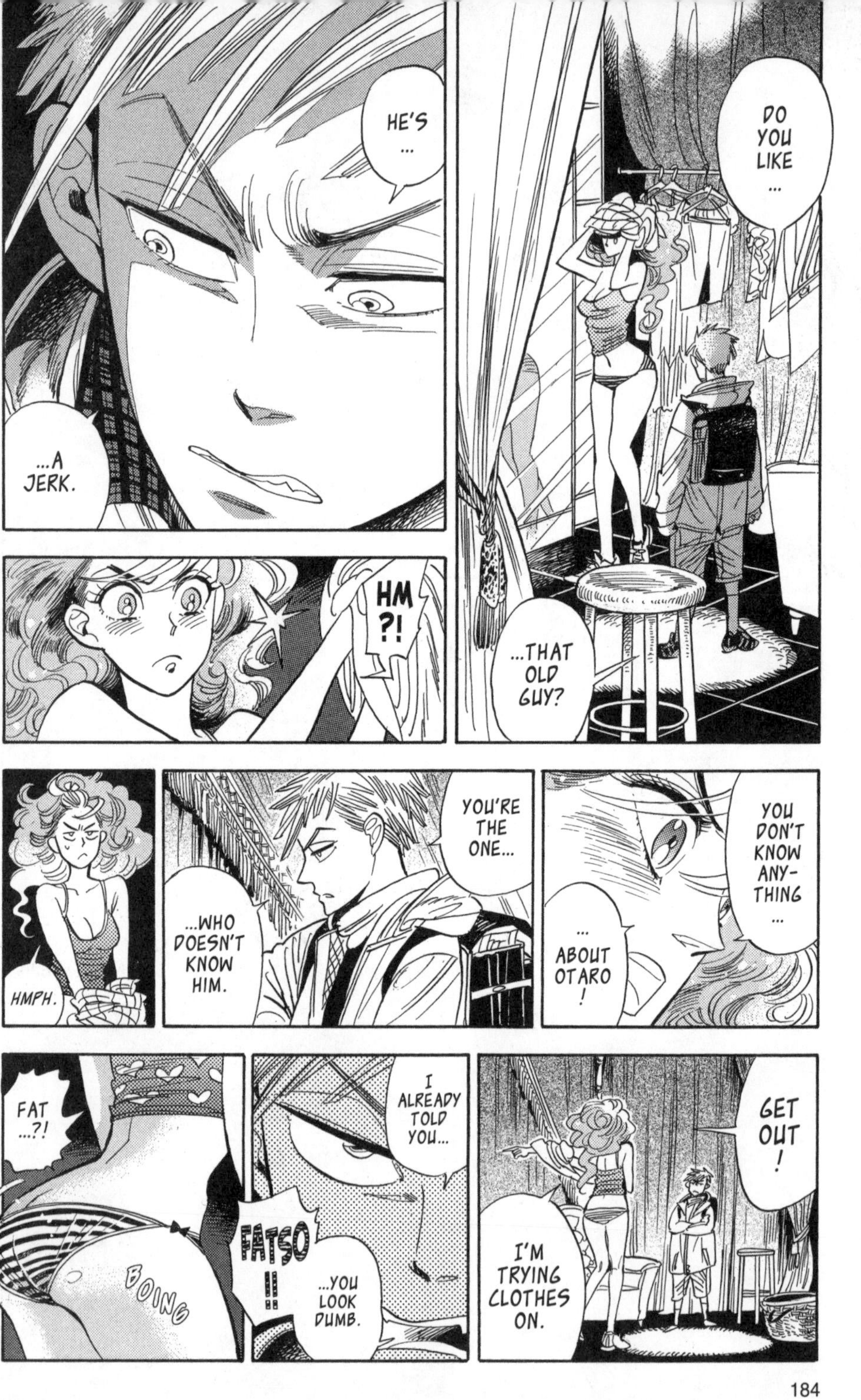
DO YOU LIKE ...
...THAT OLD GUY?
HE'S ...
...A JERK.
HM ?!
YOU DON'T KNOW ANYTHING ...
... ABOUT OTARO !
YOU'RE THE ONE...
...WHO DOESN'T KNOW HIM.
HMPH.
GET OUT !
I'M TRYING CLOTHES ON.
I ALREADY TOLD YOU...
...YOU LOOK DUMB.
FATSO !!
FAT ...?!
BOING

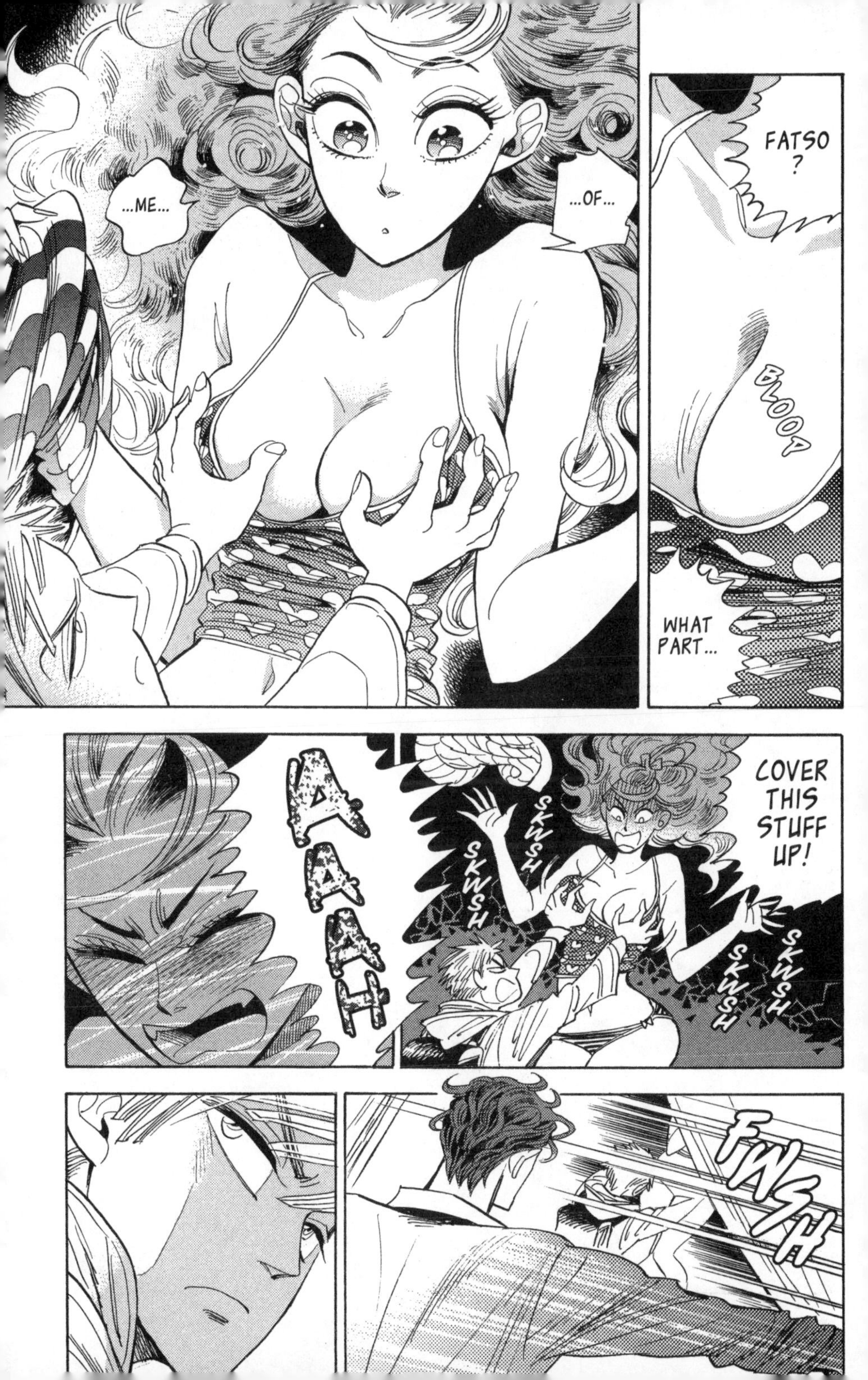
FATSO?
BLOOP
WHAT PART...
...OF...
...ME...
COVER THIS STUFF UP!
SKWSH
SKWSH
SKWSH
SKWSH
AAAH
FWSH

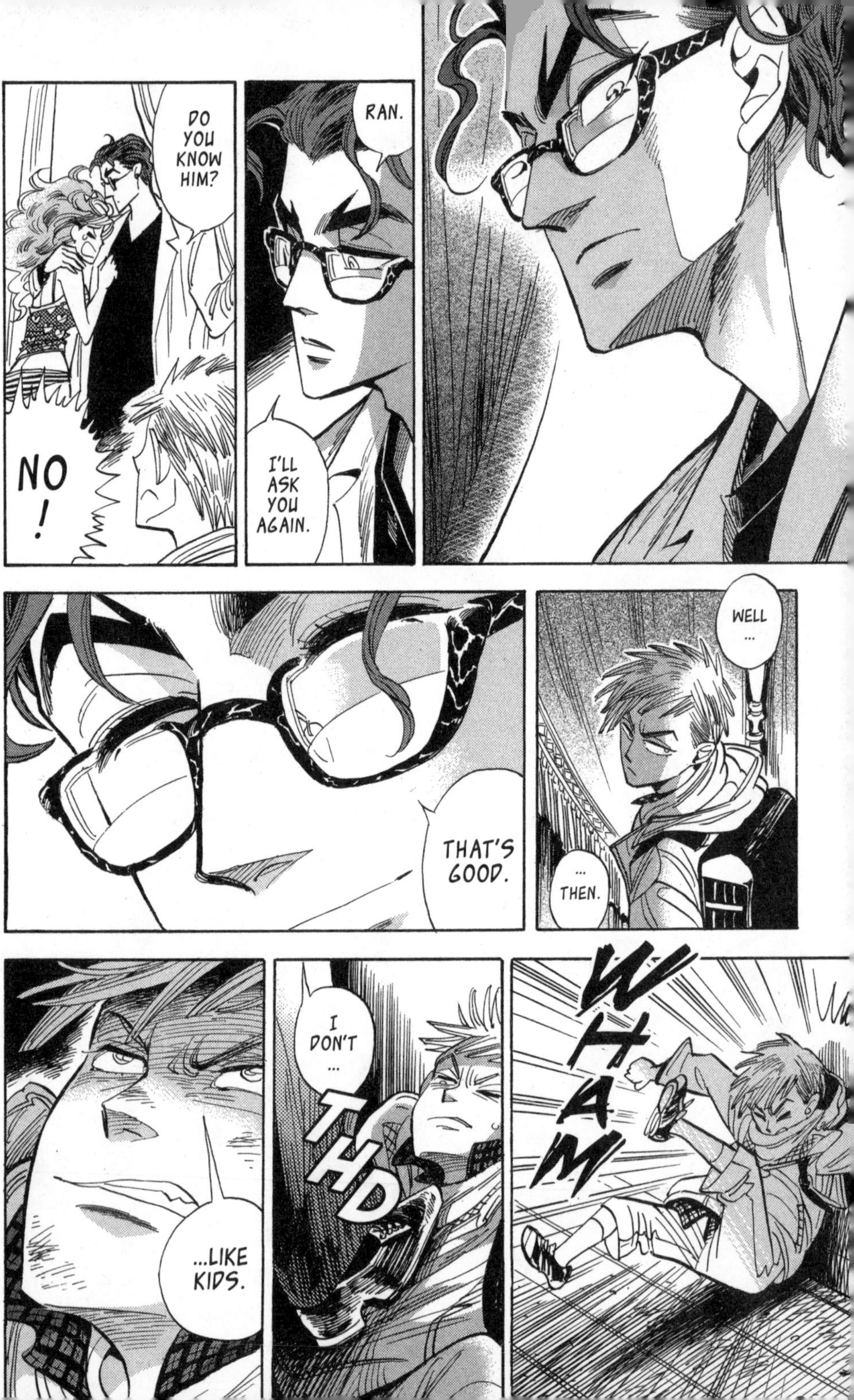
RAN.
I'LL ASK YOU AGAIN.
DO YOU KNOW HIM?
NO!
WELL ...
... THEN.
THAT'S GOOD.
WHAM
I DON'T ...
THD
...LIKE KIDS.

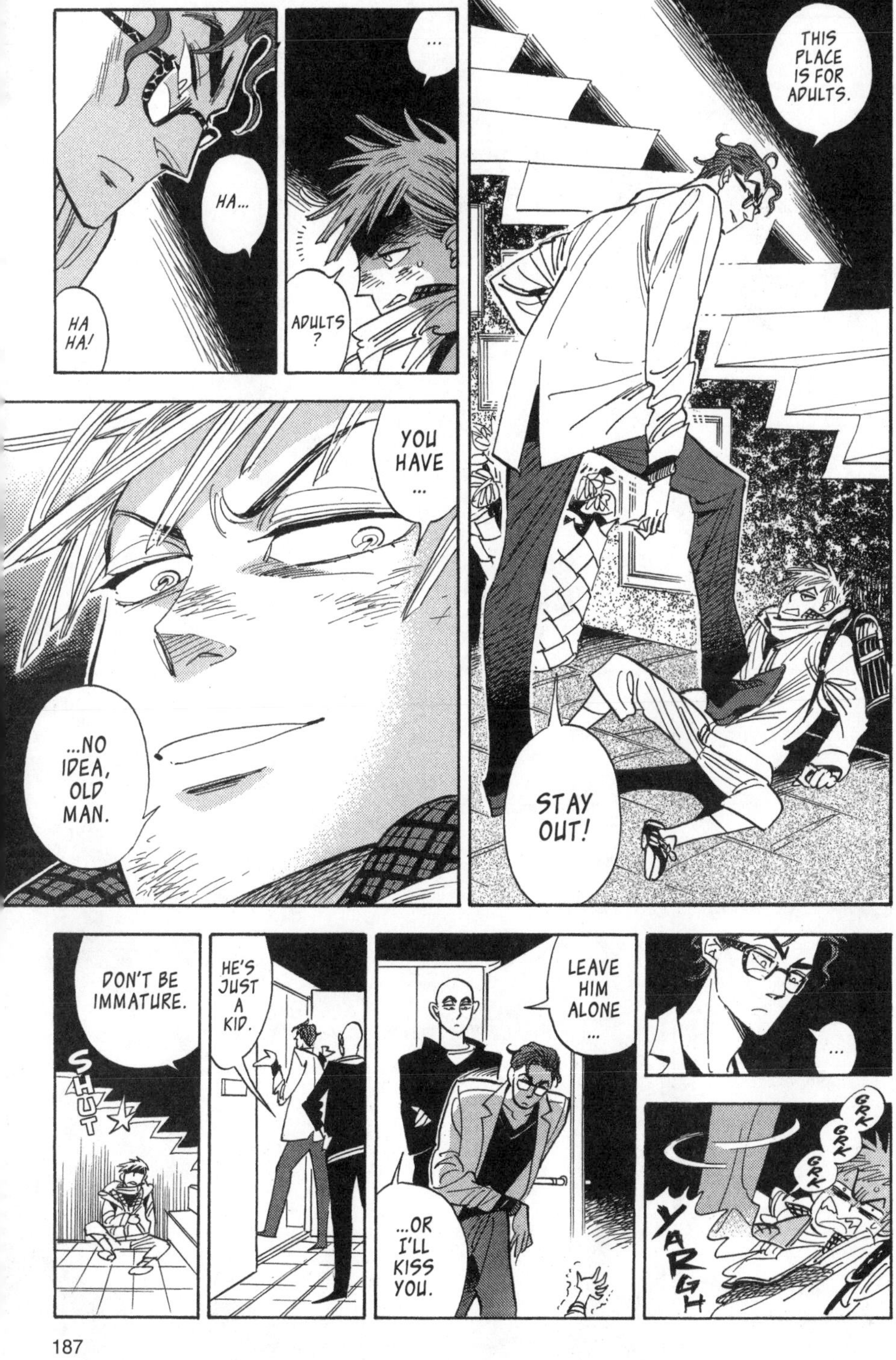
THIS PLACE IS FOR ADULTS.
STAY OUT!
...
ADULTS?
HA...
HA HA!
YOU HAVE...
...NO IDEA, OLD MAN.
...
GRK GRK GRK
YARGH
LEAVE HIM ALONE...
...OR I'LL KISS YOU.
HE'S JUST A KID.
DON'T BE IMMATURE.
SHUT

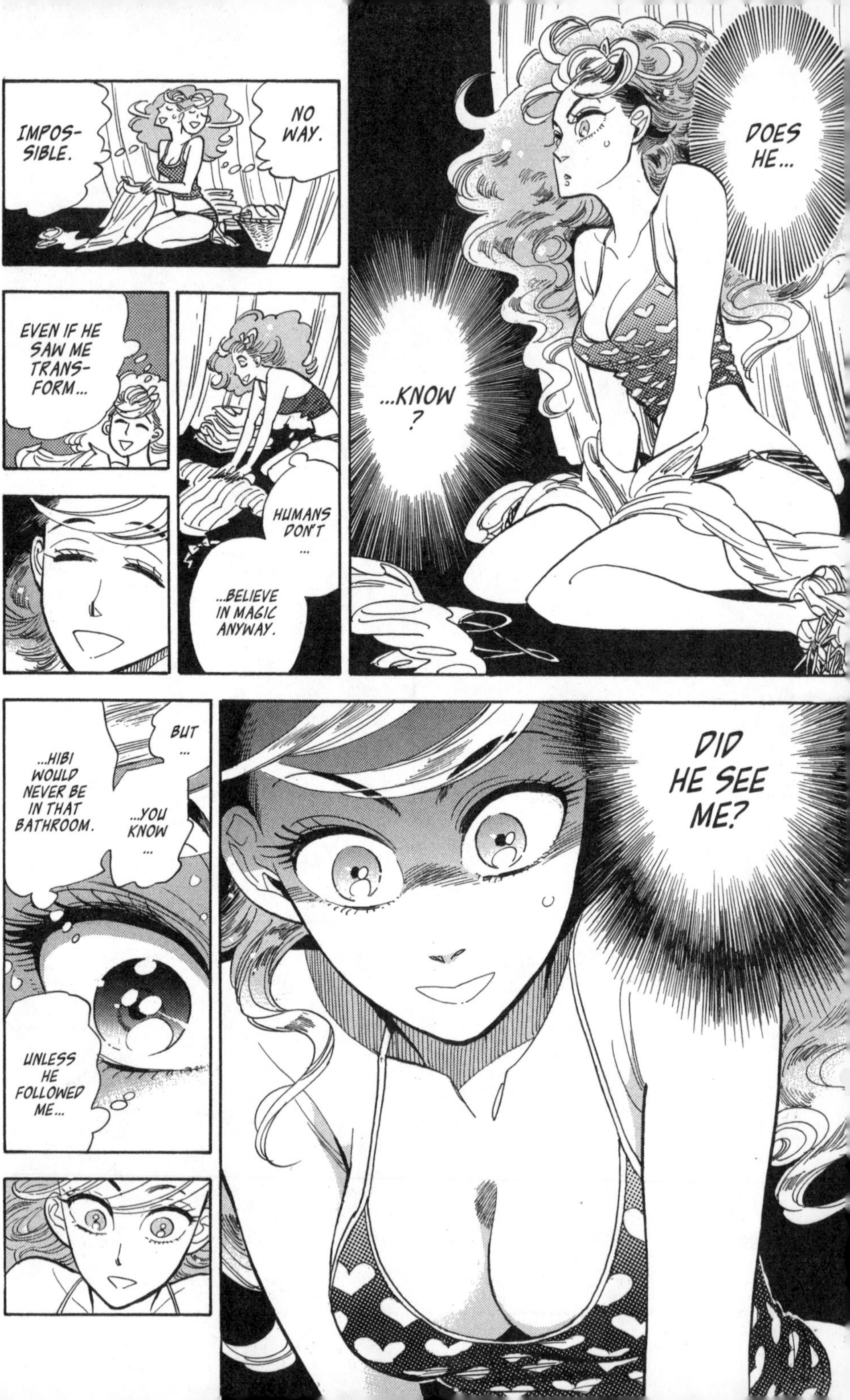
DOES HE...
...KNOW?
NO WAY.
IMPOS-SIBLE.
HUMANS DON'T ...
...BELIEVE IN MAGIC ANYWAY.
EVEN IF HE SAW ME TRANS-FORM...
DID HE SEE ME?
BUT ...
...YOU KNOW ...
...HIBI WOULD NEVER BE IN THAT BATHROOM.
UNLESS HE FOLLOWED ME...

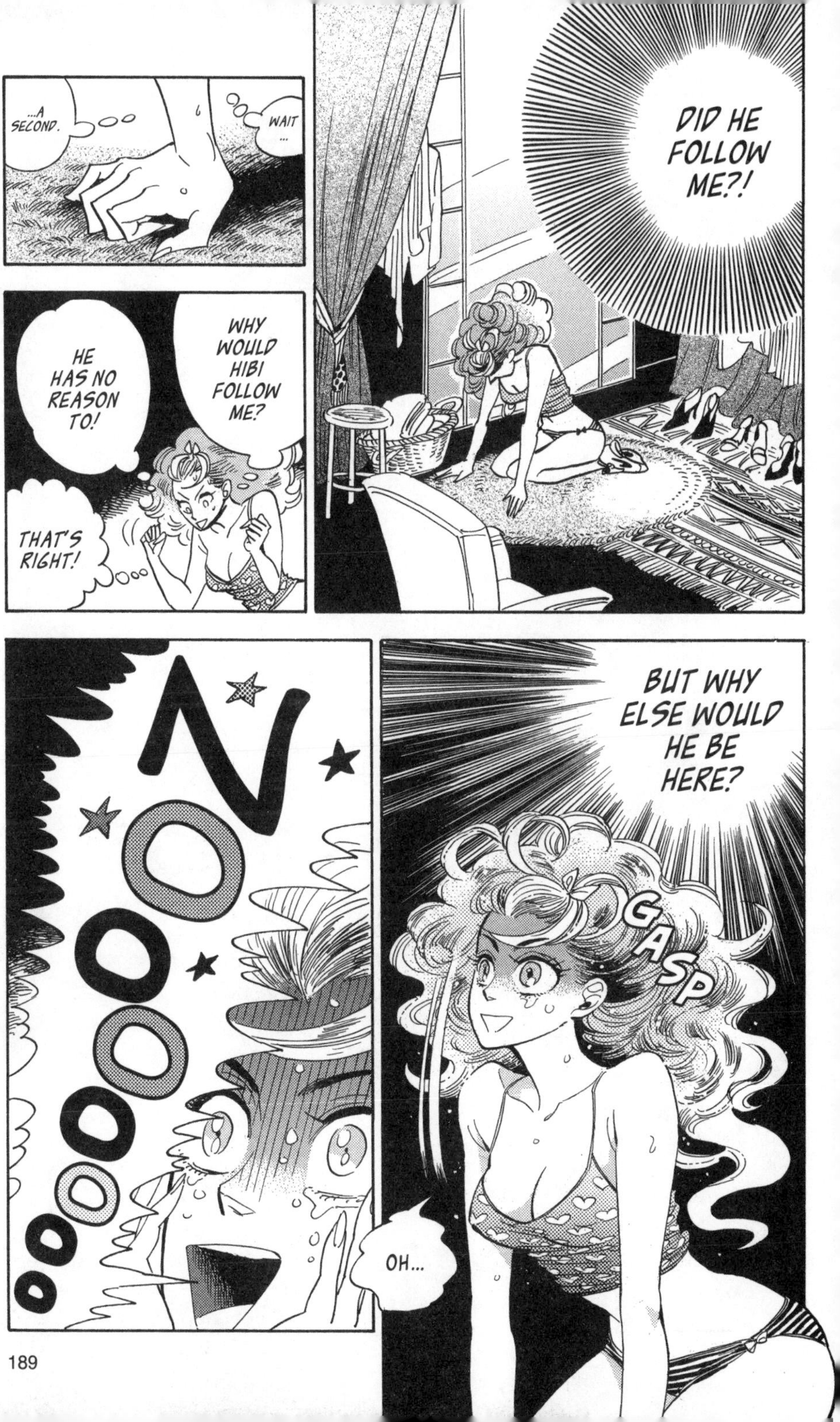
DID HE FOLLOW ME?!
WAIT ...
...A SECOND.
WHY WOULD HIBI FOLLOW ME?
HE HAS NO REASON TO!
THAT'S RIGHT!
BUT WHY ELSE WOULD HE BE HERE?
GASP
OH...
NOOOOOOO

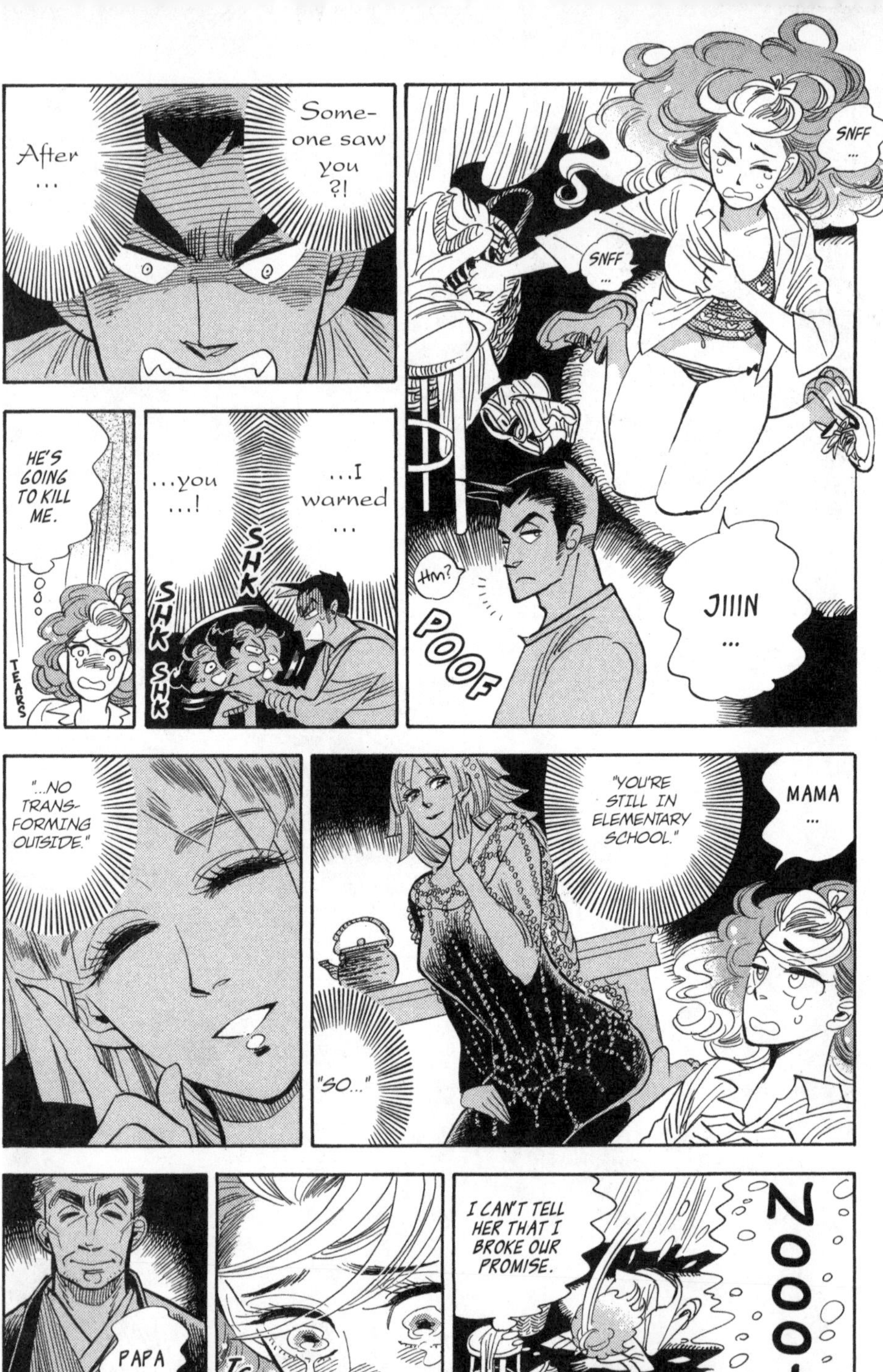

SNFF ...
SNFF ...
JIIIN ...
Hm?
POOF
Some-one saw you ?!
After ...
...I warned ...
...you ...!
SHK SHK SHK
HE'S GOING TO KILL ME.
TEARS
MAMA ...
"YOU'RE STILL IN ELEMENTARY SCHOOL."
"SO..."
"...NO TRANS-FORMING OUTSIDE."
NOOO!
I CAN'T TELL HER THAT I BROKE OUR PROMISE.
TEARS
PAPA ...

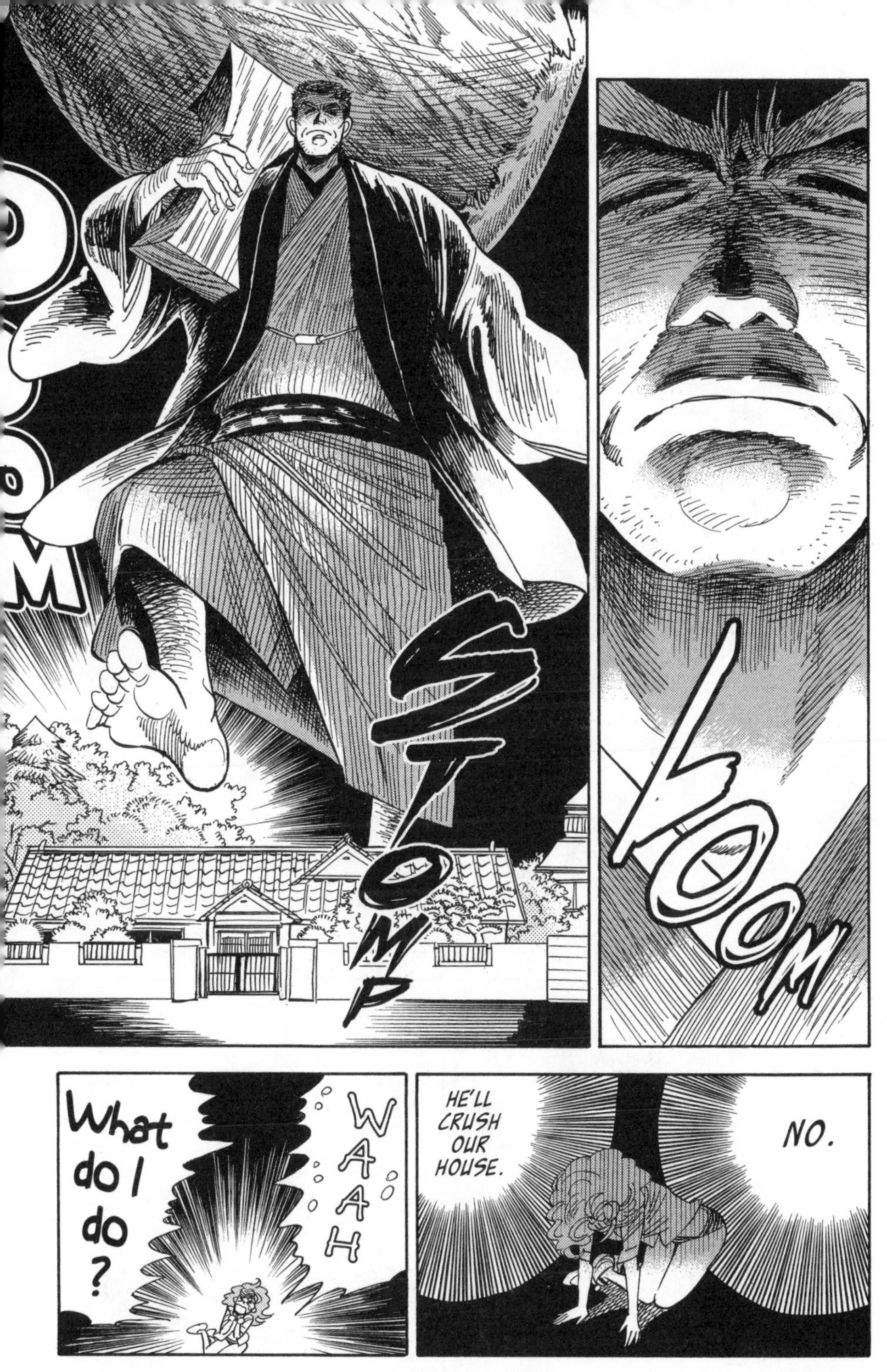
VOOOM
DOOM
STOMP
HE'LL CRUSH OUR HOUSE.
NO.
WAAH
What do I do?

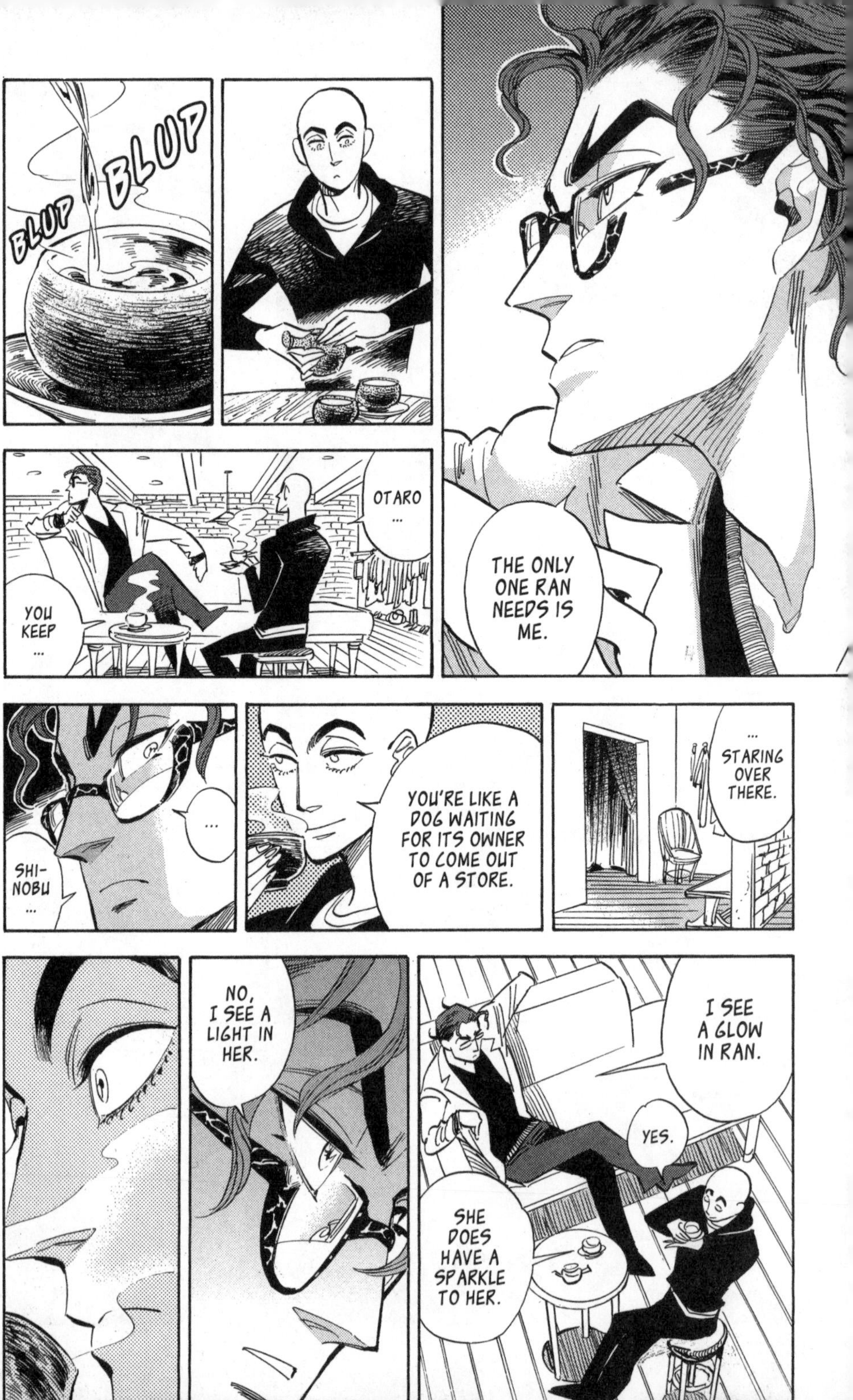
THE ONLY ONE RAN NEEDS IS ME.
BLUP BLUP
OTARO ...
YOU KEEP ...
... STARING OVER THERE.
YOU'RE LIKE A DOG WAITING FOR ITS OWNER TO COME OUT OF A STORE.
...
SHI-NOBU ...
I SEE A GLOW IN RAN.
YES.
SHE DOES HAVE A SPARKLE TO HER.
NO, I SEE A LIGHT IN HER.

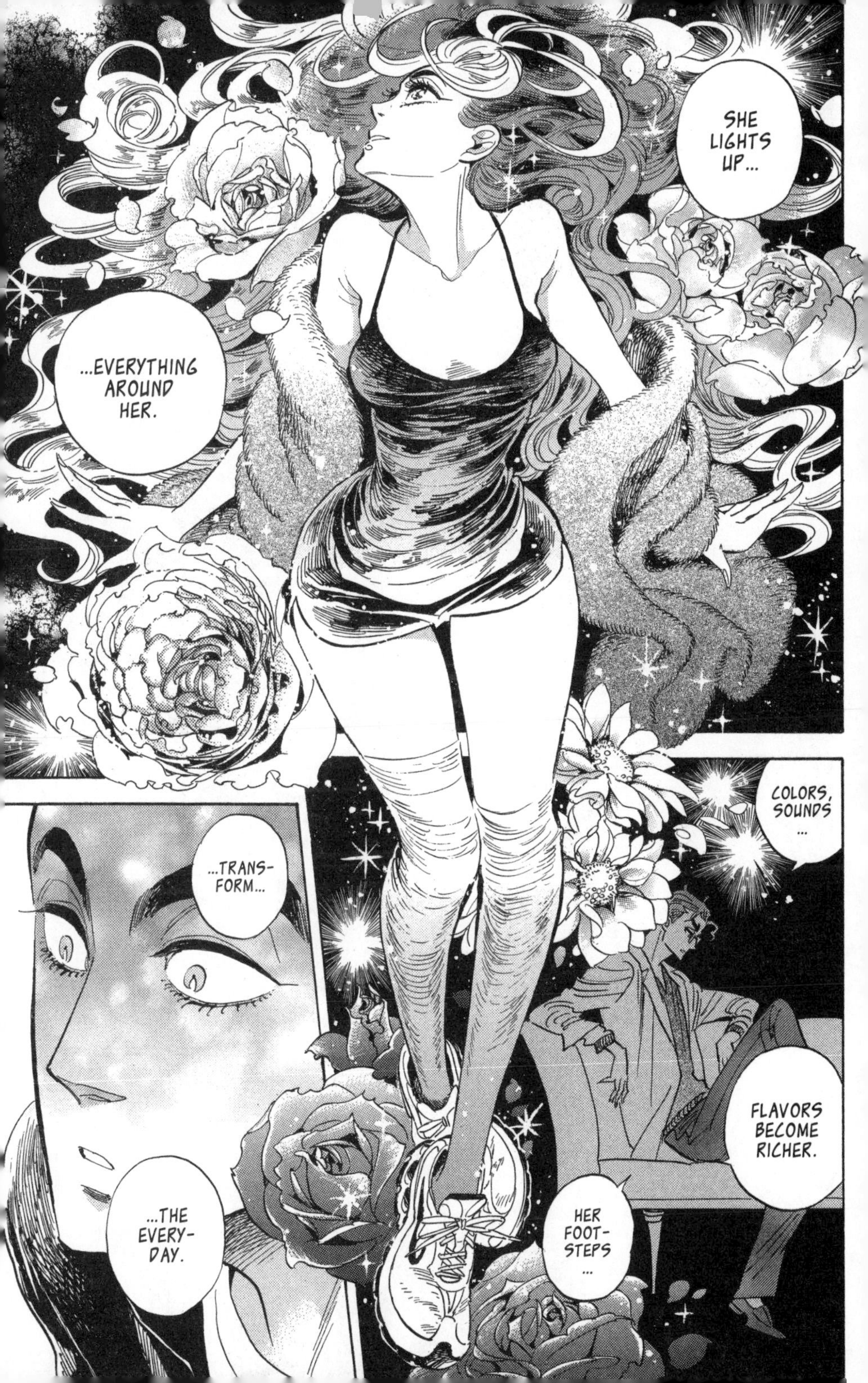
SHE LIGHTS UP...
...EVERYTHING AROUND HER.
COLORS, SOUNDS ...
FLAVORS BECOME RICHER.
HER FOOT-STEPS ...
...TRANS-FORM...
...THE EVERY-DAY.

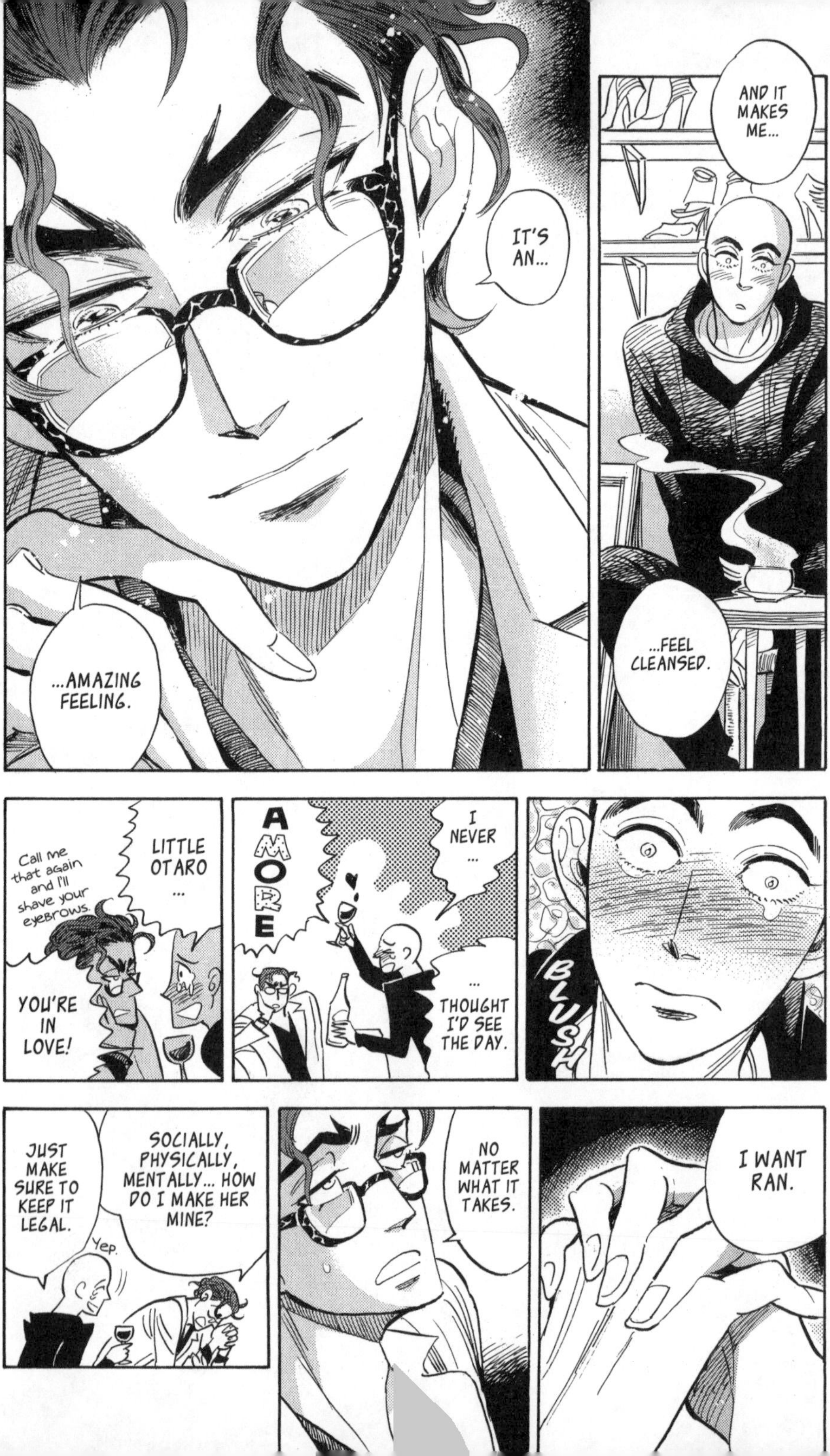
AND IT MAKES ME...
...FEEL CLEANSED.
IT'S AN...
...AMAZING FEELING.
BLUSH
I NEVER ...
... THOUGHT I'D SEE THE DAY.
AMORE
LITTLE OTARO ...
YOU'RE IN LOVE!
Call me that again and I'll shave your eyebrows.
I WANT RAN.
NO MATTER WHAT IT TAKES.
SOCIALLY, PHYSICALLY, MENTALLY... HOW DO I MAKE HER MINE?
JUST MAKE SURE TO KEEP IT LEGAL.
Yep.

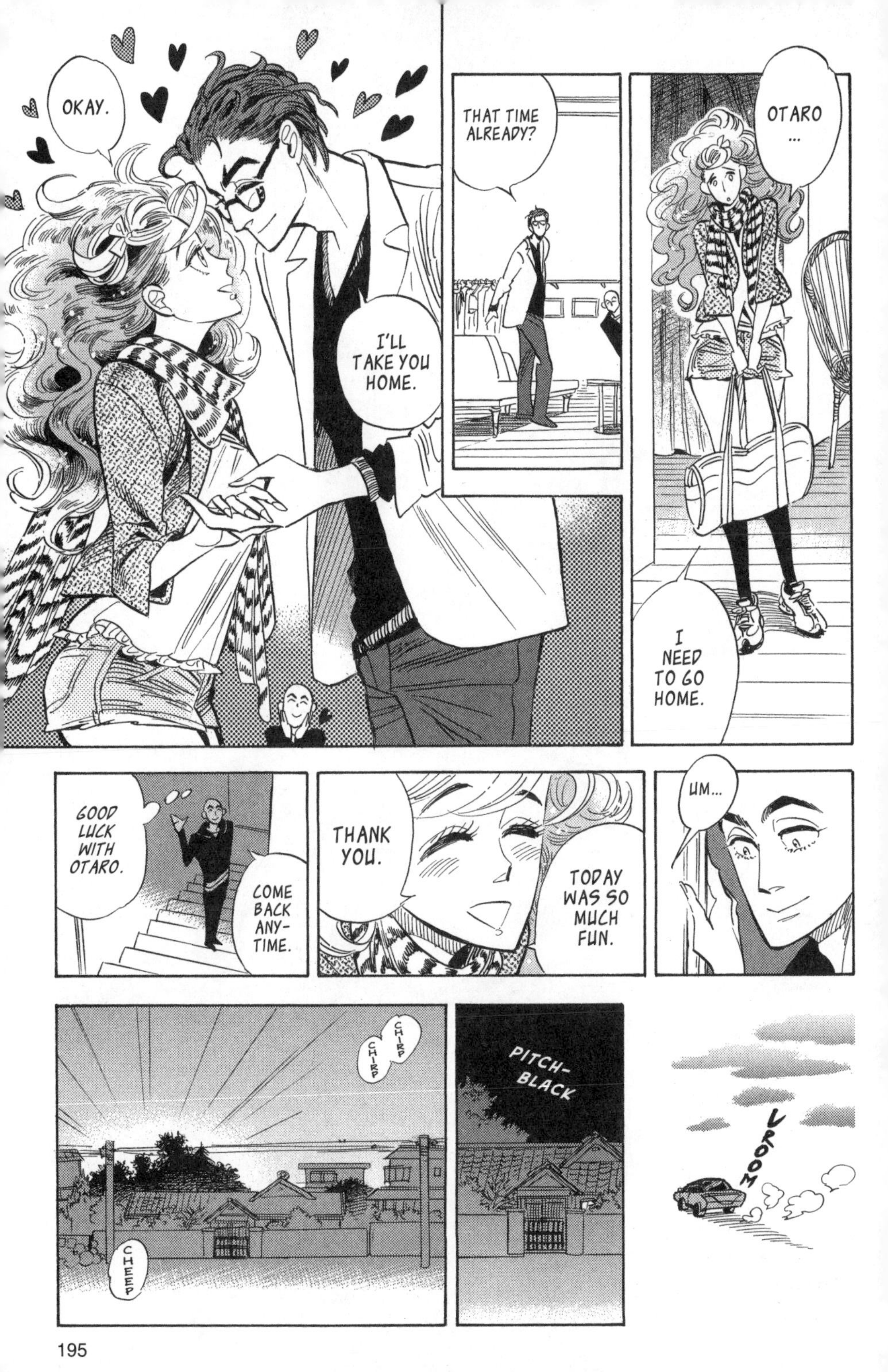
OTARO ...
I NEED TO GO HOME.
THAT TIME ALREADY?
I'LL TAKE YOU HOME.
OKAY.
UM...
THANK YOU.
TODAY WAS SO MUCH FUN.
COME BACK ANY-TIME.
GOOD LUCK WITH OTARO.
VROOM
PITCH-BLACK
CHIRP
CHIRP
CHEEP

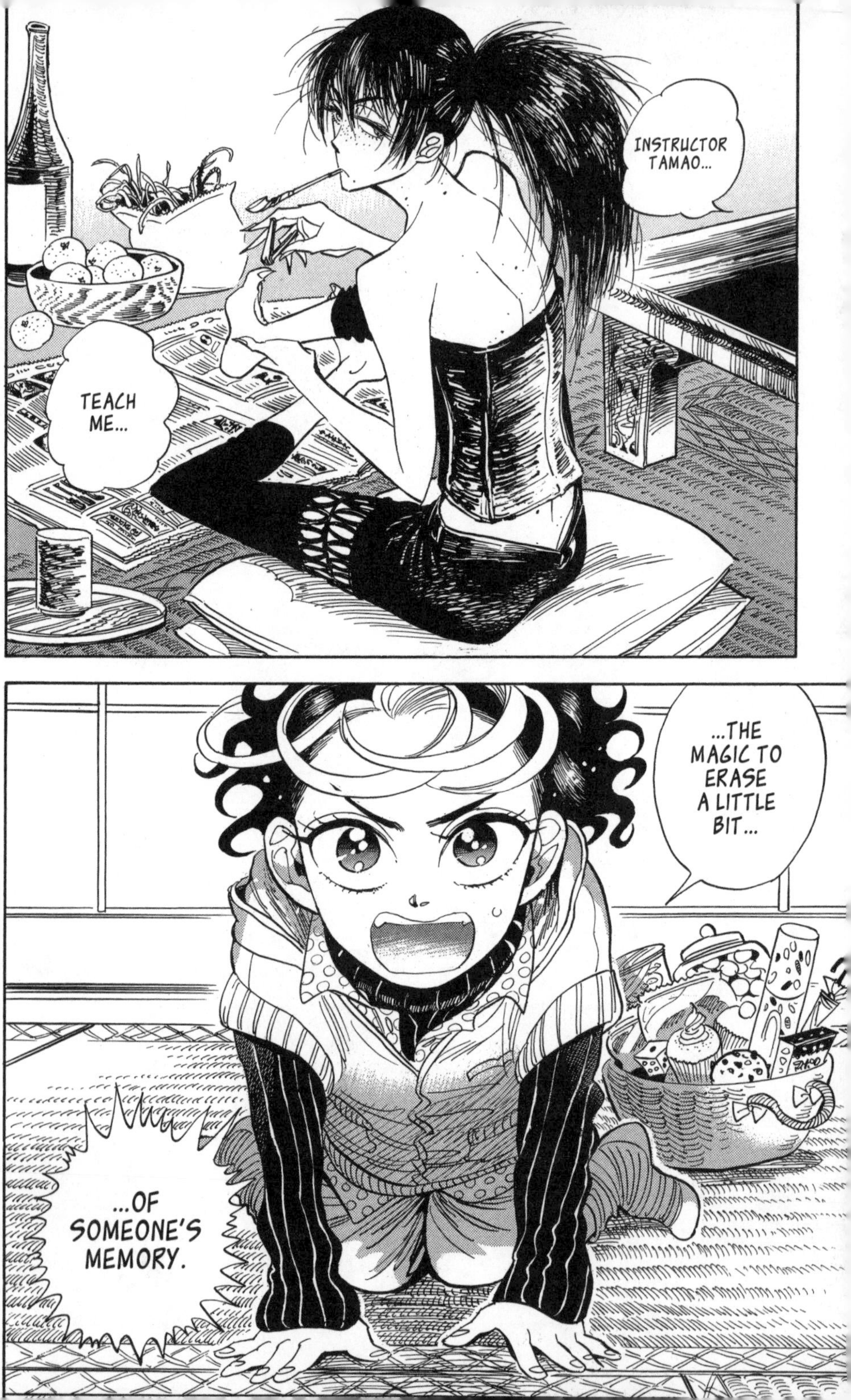
INSTRUCTOR TAMAO...
TEACH ME...
...THE MAGIC TO ERASE A LITTLE BIT...
...OF SOMEONE'S MEMORY.

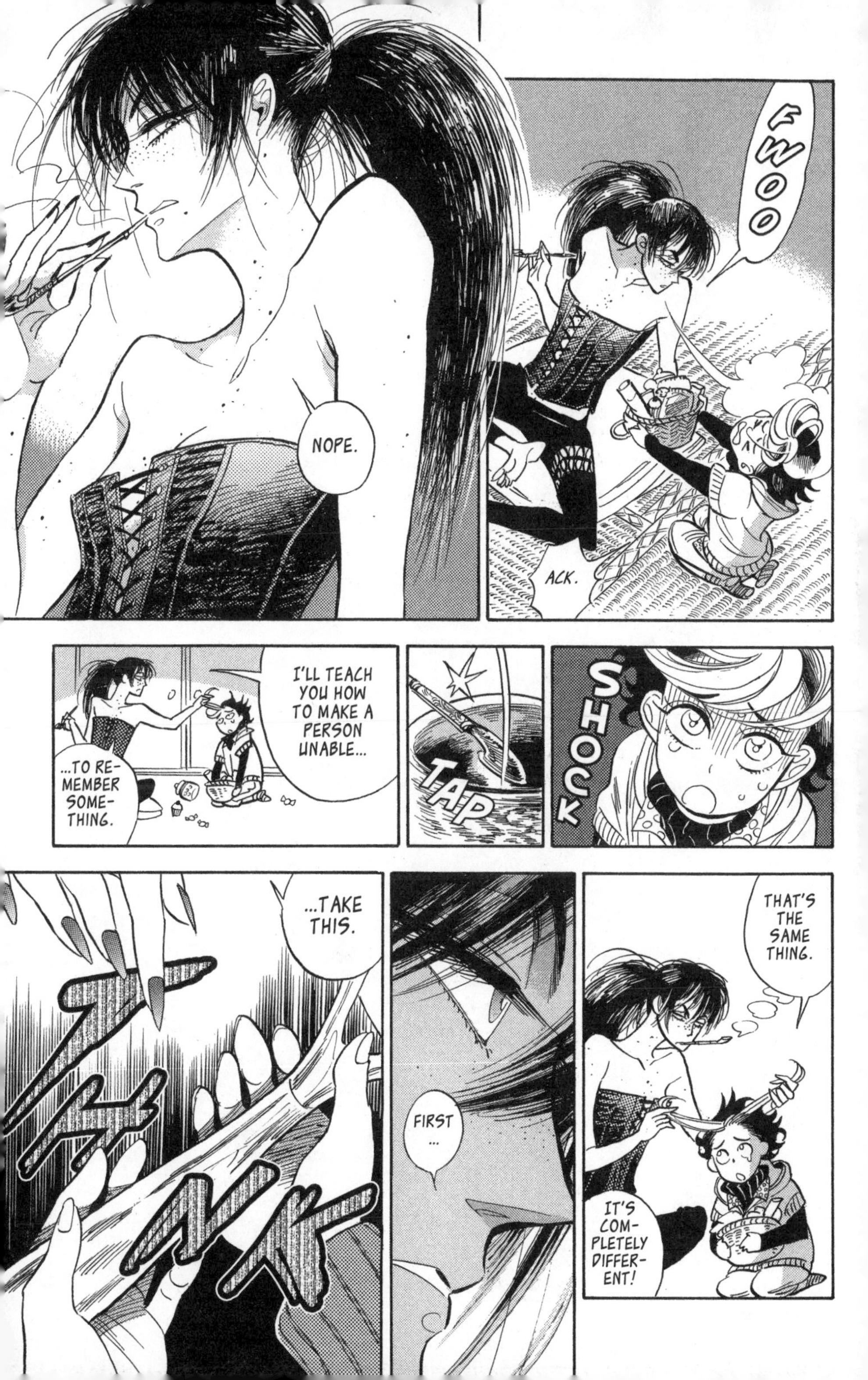
FWOOO
ACK.
NOPE.
SHOCK
TAP
I'LL TEACH YOU HOW TO MAKE A PERSON UNABLE...
...TO RE-MEMBER SOME-THING.
THAT'S THE SAME THING.
IT'S COM-PLETELY DIFFER-ENT!
FIRST ...
...TAKE THIS.

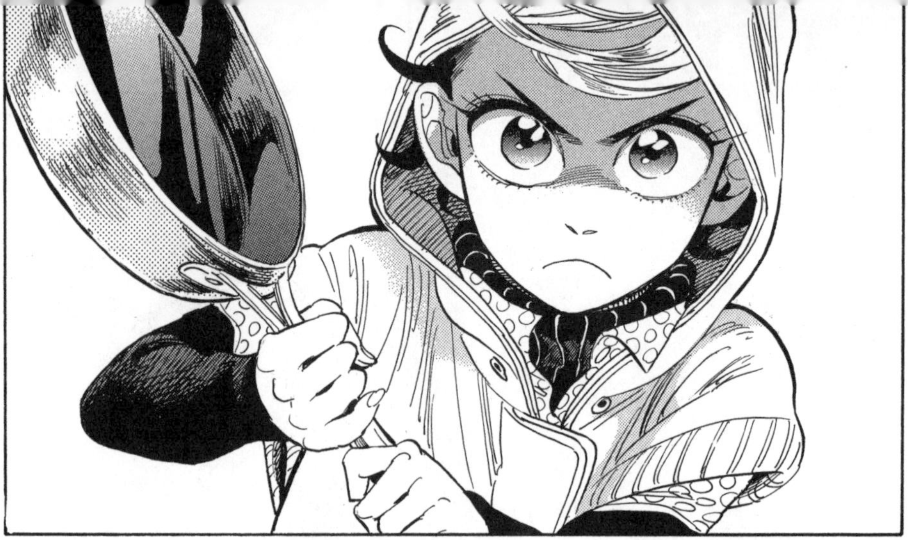

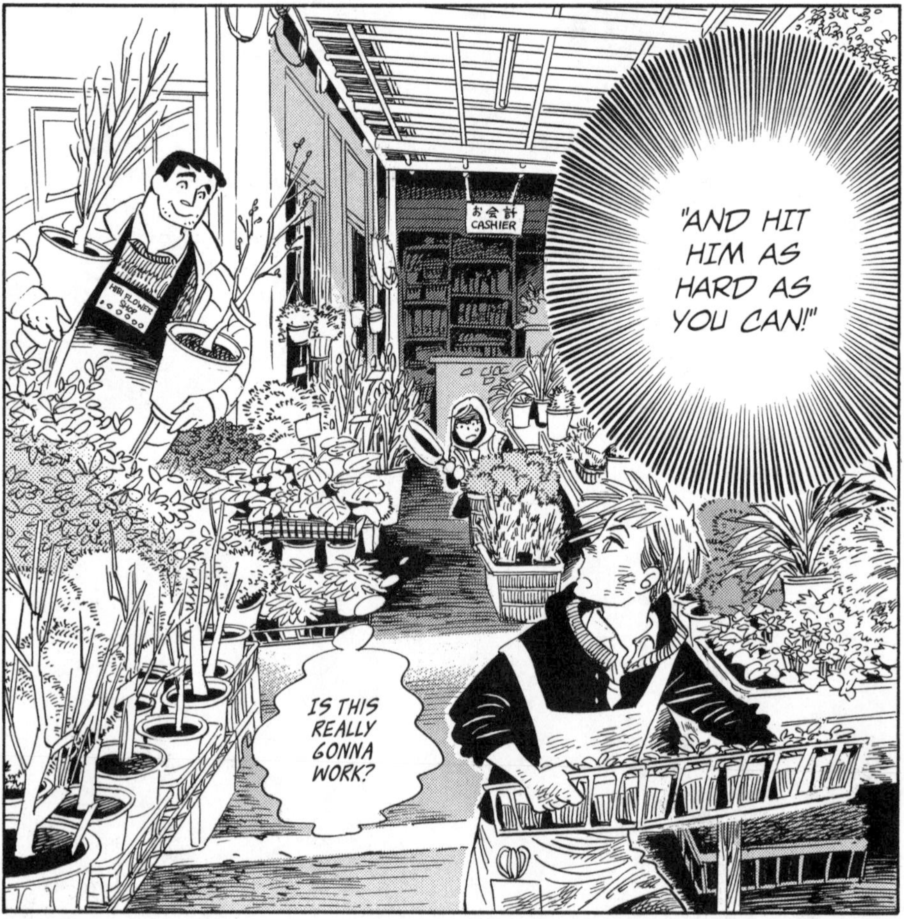
HIRI FLOWER SHOP
お会計
CASHIER
"AND HIT HIM AS HARD AS YOU CAN!"
IS THIS REALLY GONNA WORK?

Chapter 18 / The End

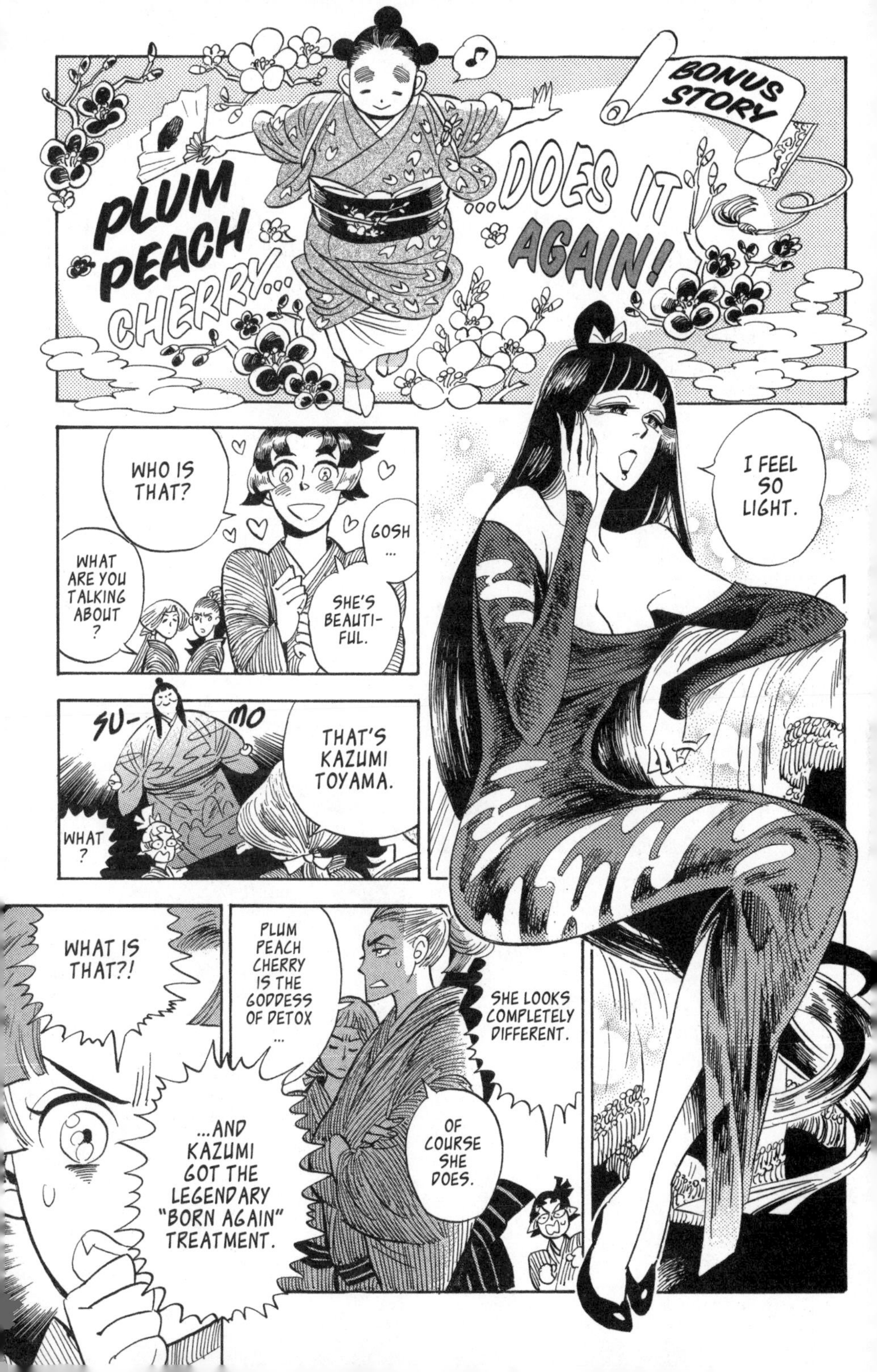
BONUS STORY
PLUM PEACH CHERRY...
...DOES IT AGAIN!
I FEEL SO LIGHT.
WHO IS THAT?
GOSH...
SHE'S BEAUTI-FUL.
WHAT ARE YOU TALKING ABOUT?
SU-MO
THAT'S KAZUMI TOYAMA.
WHAT?
SHE LOOKS COMPLETELY DIFFERENT.
OF COURSE SHE DOES.
PLUM PEACH CHERRY IS THE GODDESS OF DETOX...
...AND KAZUMI GOT THE LEGENDARY "BORN AGAIN" TREATMENT.
WHAT IS THAT?!

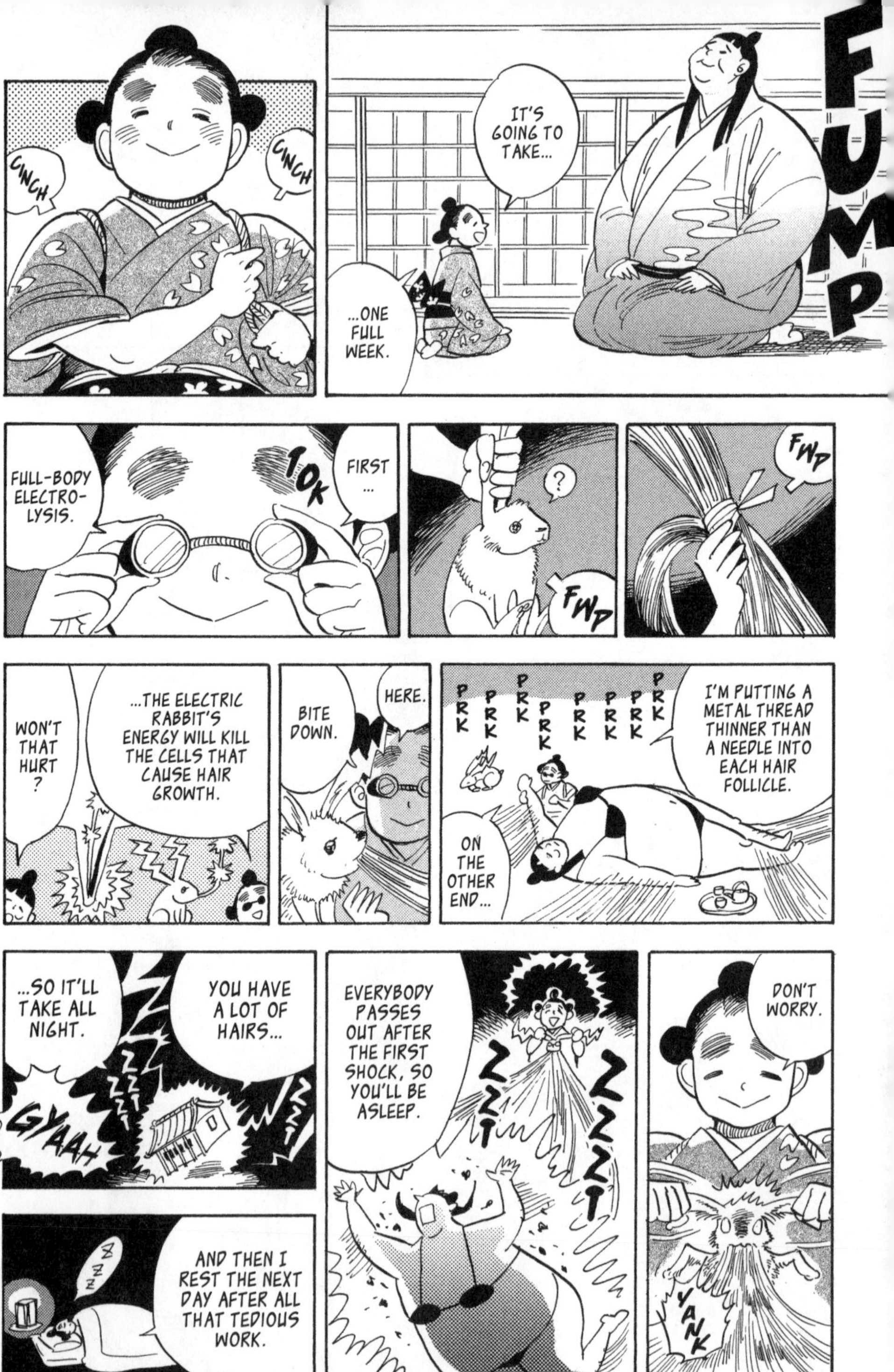
FUMP
IT'S GOING TO TAKE...
...ONE FULL WEEK.
CINCH
CINCH
FWP
?
FWP
FIRST...
TOK
FULL-BODY ELECTROLYSIS.
I'M PUTTING A METAL THREAD THINNER THAN A NEEDLE INTO EACH HAIR FOLLICLE.
PRK PRK PRK PRK PRK PRK PRK PRK
ON THE OTHER END...
HERE.
BITE DOWN.
...THE ELECTRIC RABBIT'S ENERGY WILL KILL THE CELLS THAT CAUSE HAIR GROWTH.
WON'T THAT HURT?
DON'T WORRY.
YANK
EVERYBODY PASSES OUT AFTER THE FIRST SHOCK, SO YOU'LL BE ASLEEP.
ZZZT
ZZZT
YOU HAVE A LOT OF HAIRS...
...SO IT'LL TAKE ALL NIGHT.
ZZZT
ZZZT
GYAAH
ZZZ
AND THEN I REST THE NEXT DAY AFTER ALL THAT TEDIOUS WORK.

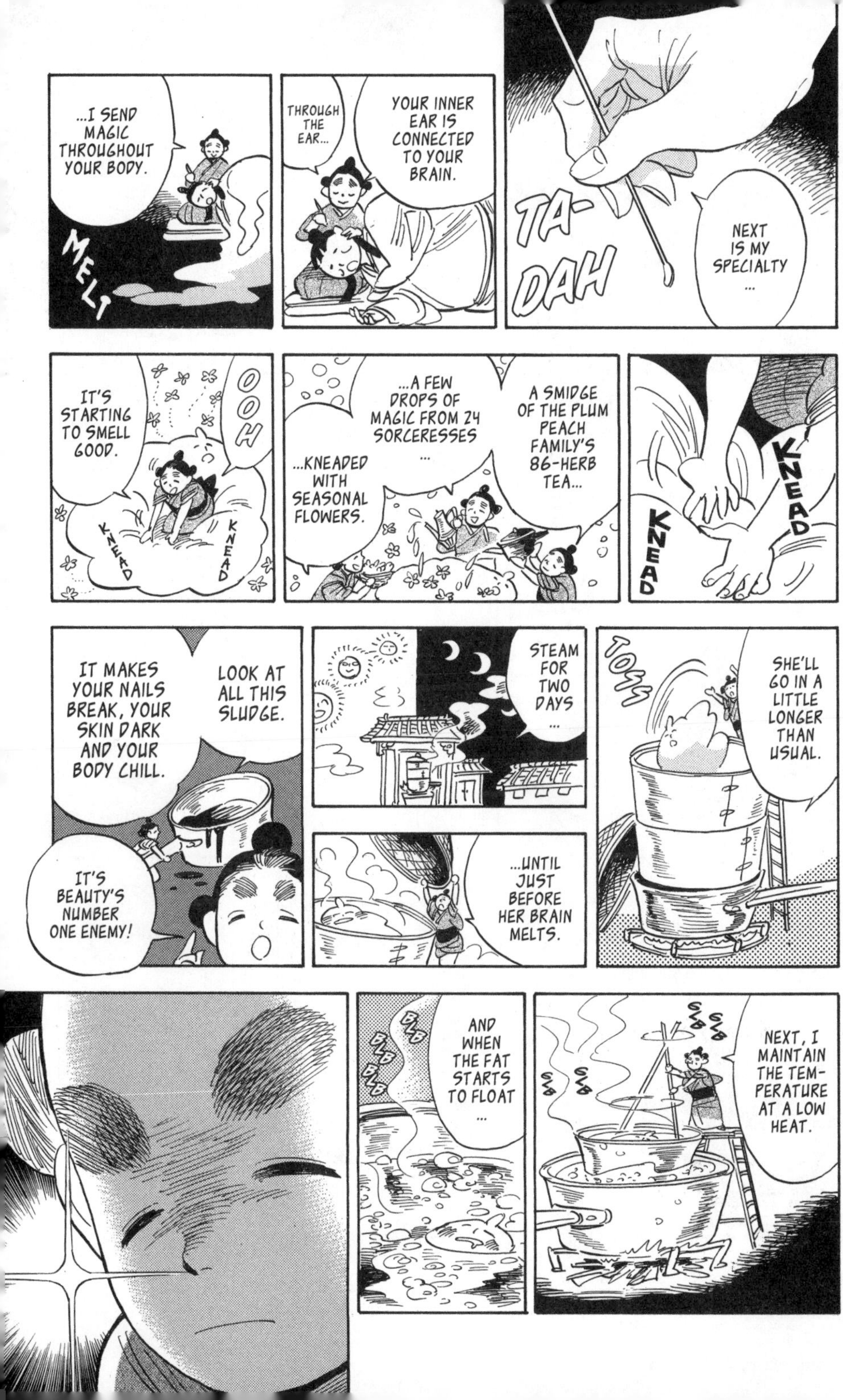
NEXT IS MY SPECIALTY...
TA-DAH
YOUR INNER EAR IS CONNECTED TO YOUR BRAIN.
THROUGH THE EAR...
...I SEND MAGIC THROUGHOUT YOUR BODY.
MELT
KNEAD
KNEAD
A SMIDGE OF THE PLUM PEACH FAMILY'S 86-HERB TEA...
...A FEW DROPS OF MAGIC FROM 24 SORCERESSES...
...KNEADED WITH SEASONAL FLOWERS.
OOOH
IT'S STARTING TO SMELL GOOD.
KNEAD
KNEAD
TOSS
SHE'LL GO IN A LITTLE LONGER THAN USUAL.
STEAM FOR TWO DAYS...
...UNTIL JUST BEFORE HER BRAIN MELTS.
LOOK AT ALL THIS SLUDGE.
IT MAKES YOUR NAILS BREAK, YOUR SKIN DARK AND YOUR BODY CHILL.
IT'S BEAUTY'S NUMBER ONE ENEMY!
NEXT, I MAINTAIN THE TEMPERATURE AT A LOW HEAT.
AND WHEN THE FAT STARTS TO FLOAT...
BLB
BLB
BLB

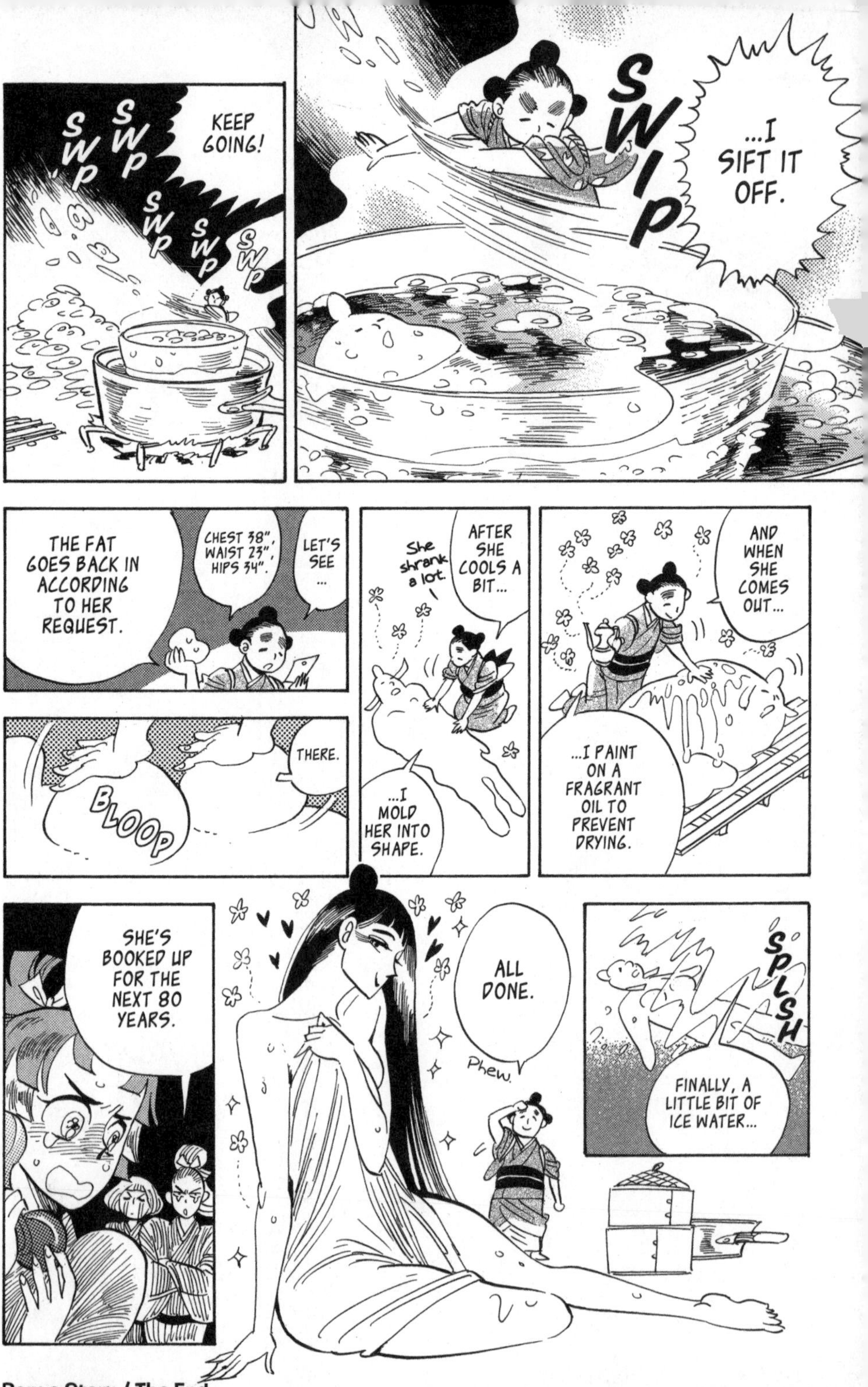
SWIP
...I SIFT IT OFF.
KEEP GOING!
SWP SWP SWP SWP SWP
AND WHEN SHE COMES OUT...
...I PAINT ON A FRAGRANT OIL TO PREVENT DRYING.
AFTER SHE COOLS A BIT...
She shrank a lot.
...I MOLD HER INTO SHAPE.
LET'S SEE ...
CHEST 38", WAIST 23", HIPS 34".
THE FAT GOES BACK IN ACCORDING TO HER REQUEST.
THERE.
BLOOP
SPLSH
FINALLY, A LITTLE BIT OF ICE WATER...
ALL DONE.
Phew.
SHE'S BOOKED UP FOR THE NEXT 80 YEARS.

Bonus Story / The End

Ran and
the Gray World

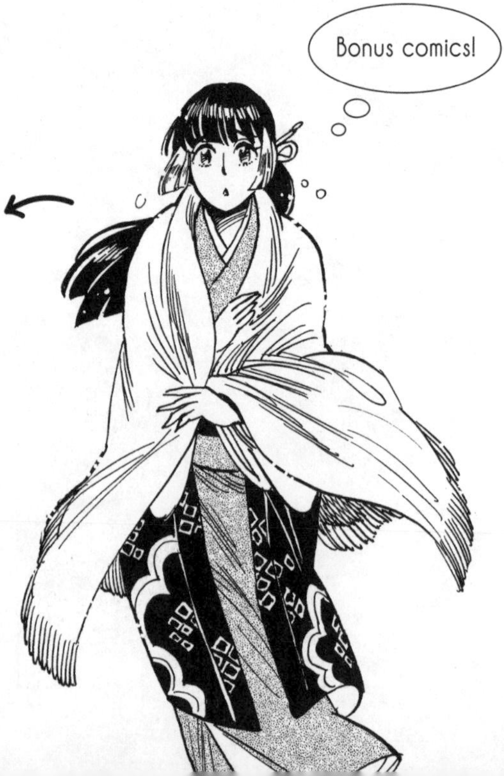
Bonus comics!

RTTL
RTTL

RTTL

HUH
?

NO
ONE'S
HOME
?

...

TMP
TMP

RSTL
RSTL

RSTL

RSTL

WELL,
GUESS
I HAVE
TO...

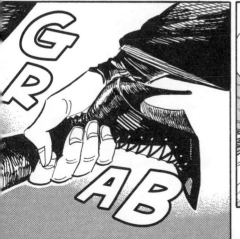

GR
AB

NICE.

AND
RATHER
CARE-
LESS.

ZWAK

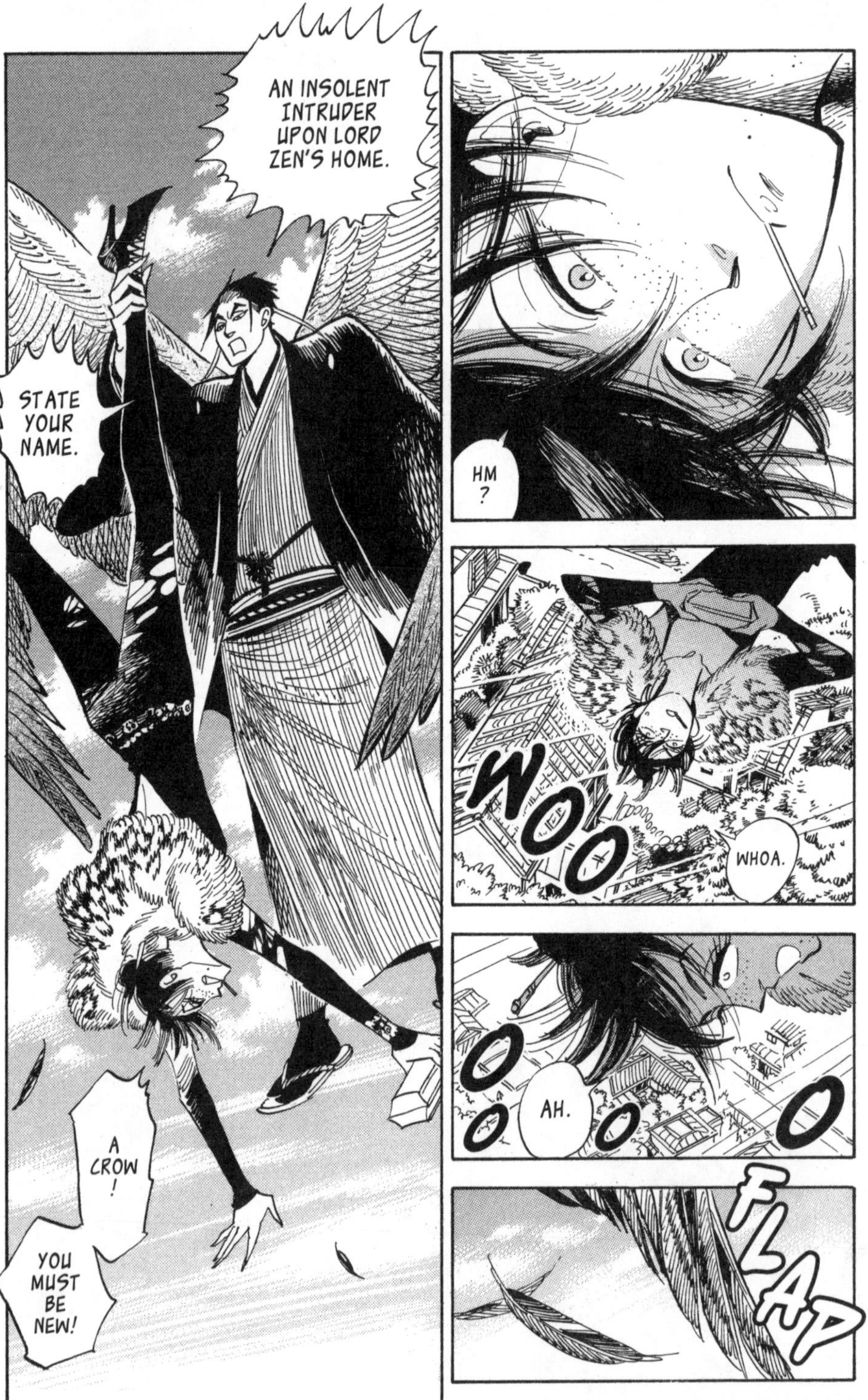
HM?
WOOO
WHOA.
OOOO
AH.
FLAP
AN INSOLENT INTRUDER UPON LORD ZEN'S HOME.
STATE YOUR NAME.
A CROW!
YOU MUST BE NEW!

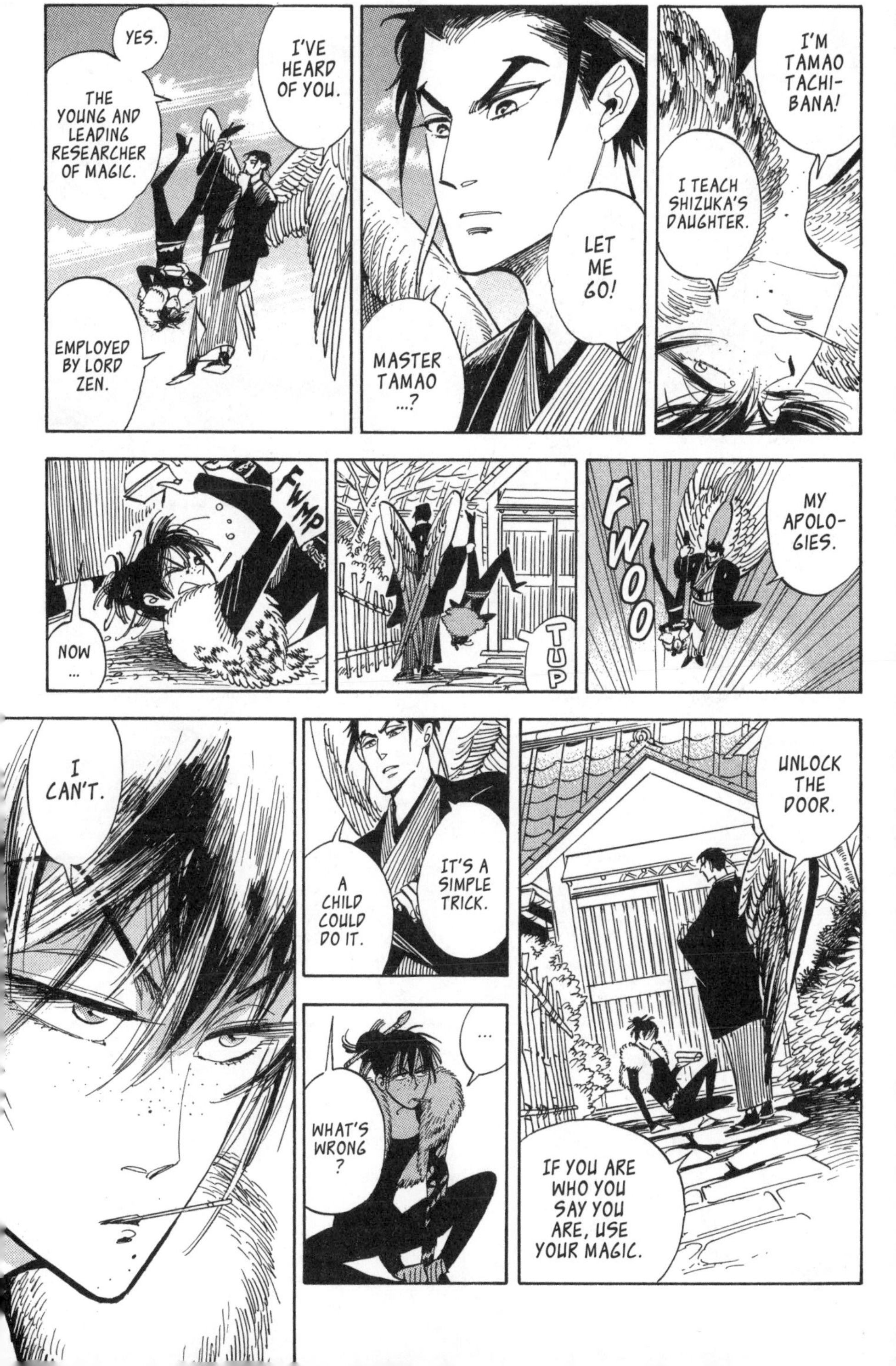
I'M TAMAO TACHIBANA!
I TEACH SHIZUKA'S DAUGHTER.
LET ME GO!
MASTER TAMAO ...?
I'VE HEARD OF YOU.
YES.
THE YOUNG AND LEADING RESEARCHER OF MAGIC.
EMPLOYED BY LORD ZEN.
FWOO
MY APOLOGIES.
TUP
FWMP
NOW ...
UNLOCK THE DOOR.
IF YOU ARE WHO YOU SAY YOU ARE, USE YOUR MAGIC.
IT'S A SIMPLE TRICK.
A CHILD COULD DO IT.
...
WHAT'S WRONG ?
I CAN'T.

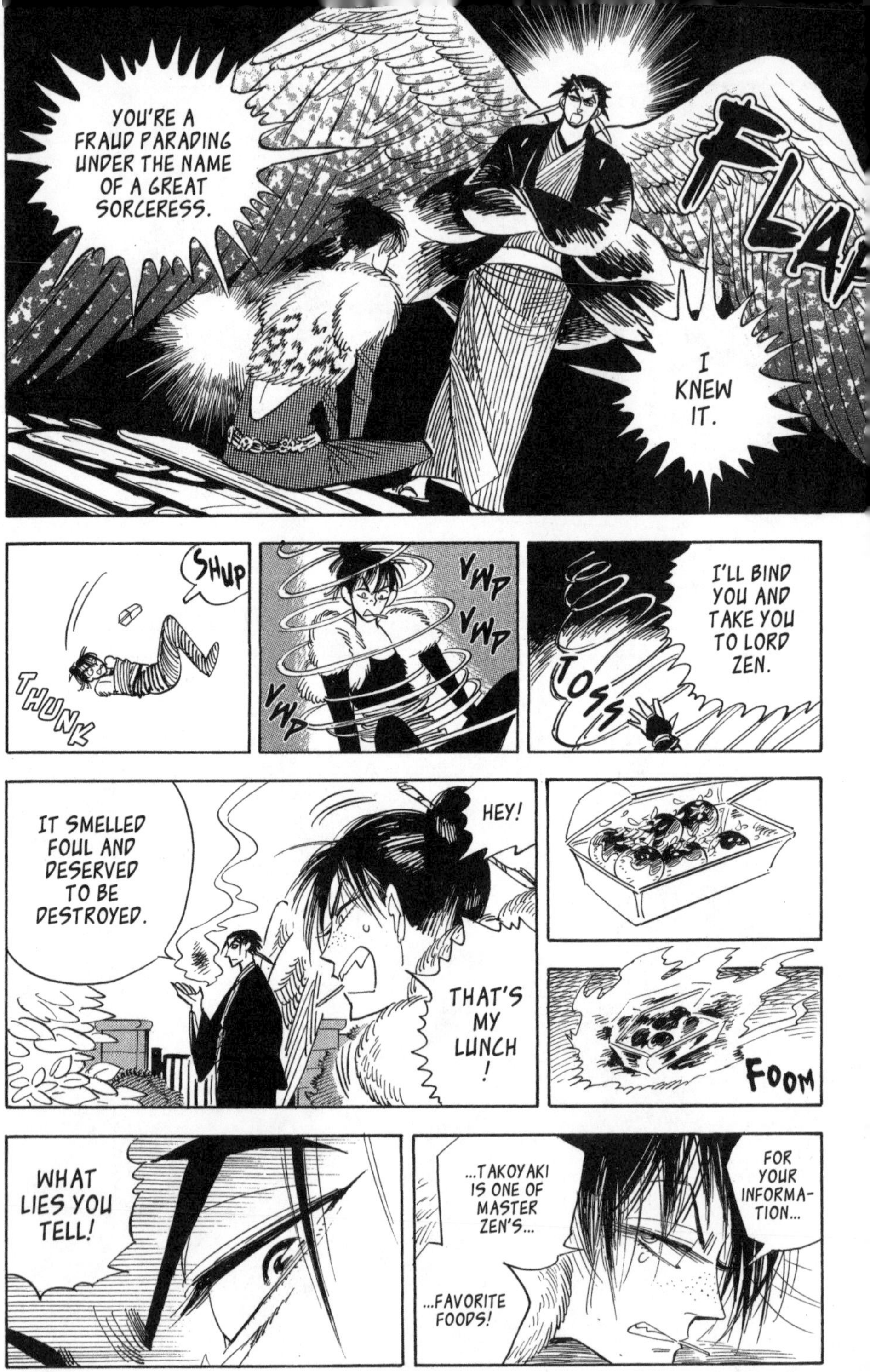
FLA
I KNEW IT.
YOU'RE A FRAUD PARADING UNDER THE NAME OF A GREAT SORCERESS.
I'LL BIND YOU AND TAKE YOU TO LORD ZEN.
TOSS
VWP
VWP
VWP
SHUP
THUNK
FOOM
HEY!
THAT'S MY LUNCH!
IT SMELLED FOUL AND DESERVED TO BE DESTROYED.
FOR YOUR INFORMATION...
...TAKOYAKI IS ONE OF MASTER ZEN'S...
...FAVORITE FOODS!
WHAT LIES YOU TELL!

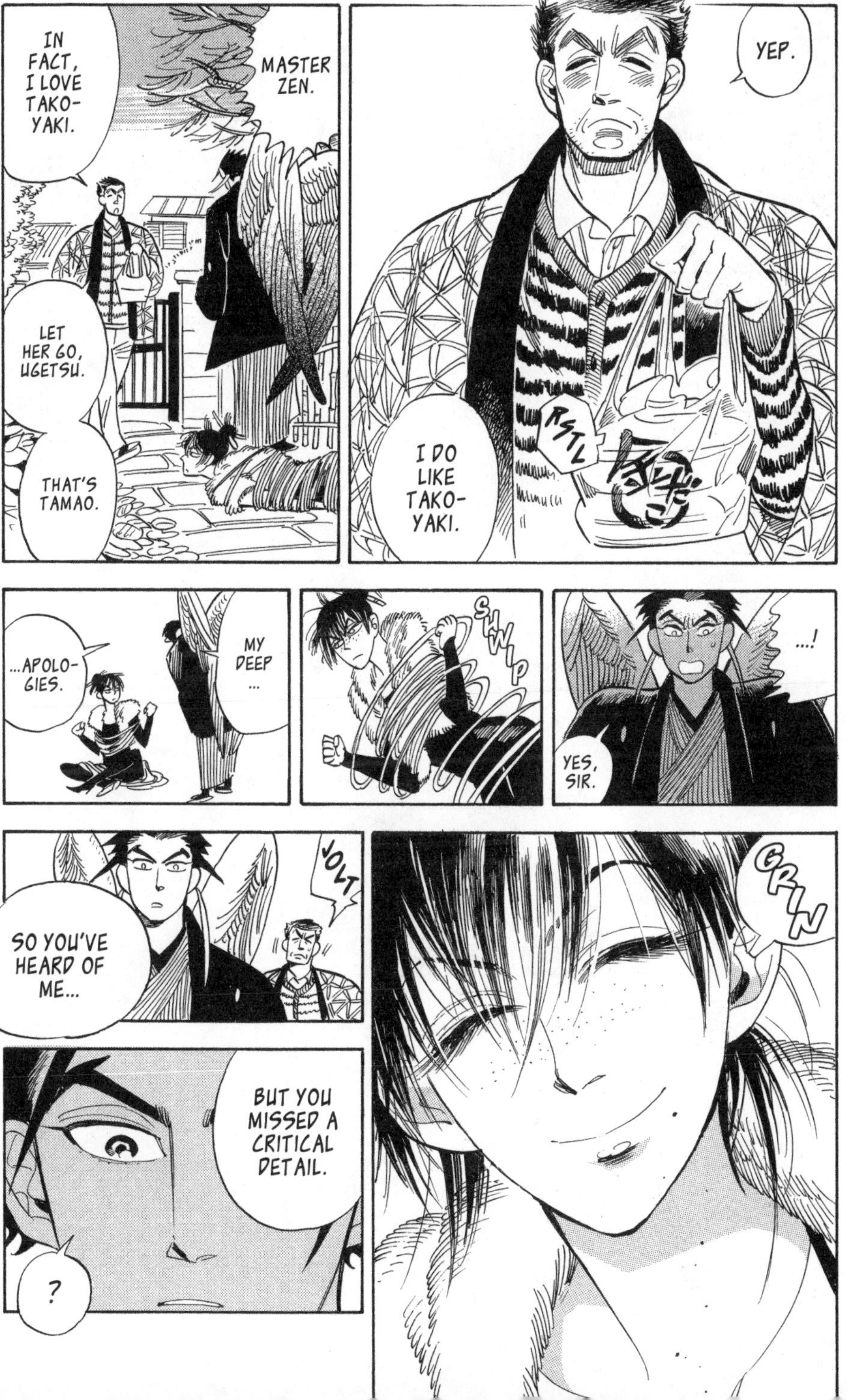
YEP.
RSTL
I DO LIKE TAKO-YAKI.
MASTER ZEN.
IN FACT, I LOVE TAKO-YAKI.
LET HER GO, UGETSU.
THAT'S TAMAO.
...!
YES, SIR.
SHWIP
MY DEEP ...
...APOLOGIES.
GRIN
JOLT
SO YOU'VE HEARD OF ME...
BUT YOU MISSED A CRITICAL DETAIL.
?

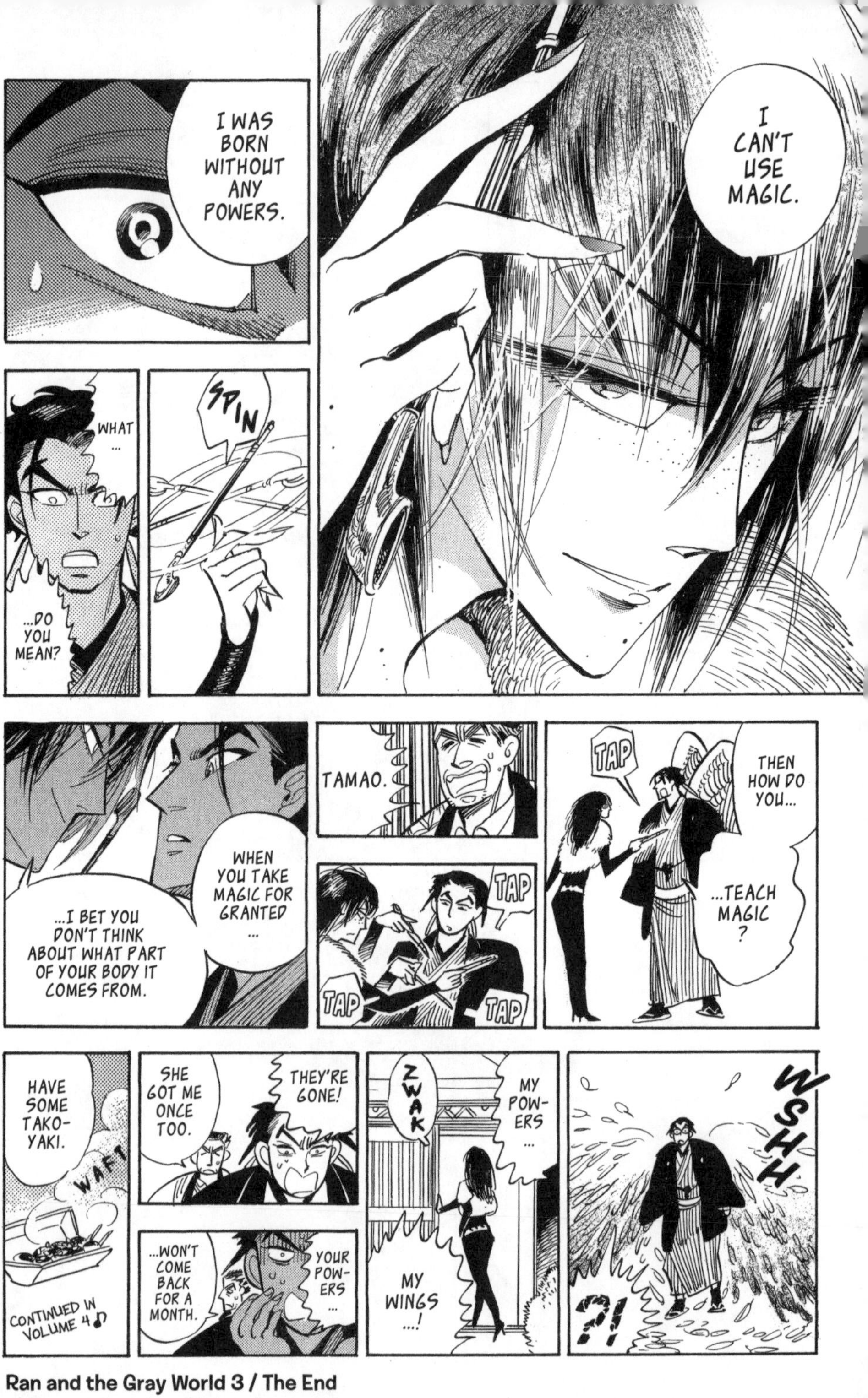
I CAN'T USE MAGIC.
I WAS BORN WITHOUT ANY POWERS.
SPIN
WHAT ...
...DO YOU MEAN?
TAP
THEN HOW DO YOU...
...TEACH MAGIC?
TAMAO.
TAP
TAP
TAP
WHEN YOU TAKE MAGIC FOR GRANTED ...
...I BET YOU DON'T THINK ABOUT WHAT PART OF YOUR BODY IT COMES FROM.
WSHH
?!
ZWAK
MY POW-ERS ...
MY WINGS ....!
THEY'RE GONE!
SHE GOT ME ONCE TOO.
YOUR POW-ERS ...
...WON'T COME BACK FOR A MONTH.
HAVE SOME TAKO-YAKI.
WAFT
CONTINUED IN VOLUME 4♪

Ran and the Gray World 3 / The End

Aki Irie was born in Kagawa Prefecture, Japan. She
began her professional career as a manga artist in
2002 with the short story "Fuku-chan Tabi Mata Tabi"
(Fuku-chan on the Road Again), which was published in
the monthly manga magazine *Papu*. *Ran and the Gray
World*, her first full-length series, is also the first
of her works to be released in English.

RAN AND THE GRAY WORLD
VOL. 3
VIZ Signature Edition

Story & Art by
AKI IRIE

English Translation & Adaptation / Emi Louie-Nishikawa
Touch-Up Art & Lettering / Joanna Estep
Design / Yukiko Whitley
Editor / Amy Yu

RAN TO HAIIRO NO SEKAI Vol. 3
©2011 Aki Irie
All rights reserved.
First published in Japan in 2011 by KADOKAWA CORPORATION ENTERBRAIN
English translation rights arranged with KADOKAWA CORPORATION ENTERBRAIN

Printed in Canada

Published by VIZ Media, LLC
P.O. Box 77010
San Francisco, CA 94107

10 9 8 7 6 5 4 3 2 1
First printing, May 2019

viz.com   vizsignature.com